ABOUT TIME:

Exploring the Gay Past

By Martin Bauml Duberman

ABOUT TIME:

Exploring the Gay Past

by

Martin Bauml Duberman

A SeaHorse Book
Gay Presses of New York
New York City
1986

Some of the articles here have appeared either as here or in slightly
altered form in the following publications:

*New York Times, Christopher Street, New York Native, Radical
History Review, The New Republic, Signs, Skeptic, New Times.*

First Edition

LIBRARY OF CONGRESS CATALOGING IN PUBLICATION DATA

Duberman, Martin Bauml
  ABOUT TIME: Exploring the Gay Past   86- 045959

      I. Title
ISBN: 0-914017--12-8
ISBN: 0-914017--13-6

A SeaHorse Book
Gay Presses of New York
P.O. Box 294, Village Station, N.Y., N.Y. 10014

To my aunt,

THERESA BAUML

and

To the memory of my mother,

JOSEPHINE BAUML DUBERMAN

CONTENTS

PART TWO: ESSAYS

PART THREE: CODA

ACKNOWLEDGEMENTS

I want to acknowledge my debt to Felice Picano for pressing me to rethink the shape of this book after I'd pronounced myself satisfied; to Gary Glickman for his help in preparing the final manuscript for press; to my friend and agent, Frances Goldin, who has, as always, been a mainstay; and to my friends Michael S. Kimmel and George Chauncey Jr. who along with providing moral support, took on the onerous job of checking galley proofs.

ABOUT TIME:

Exploring the Gay Past

INTRODUCTION

In 1969, when the modern gay liberation movement came into being after a riot at the Stonewall bar in Greenwich Village, there was virtually no public record of homosexuality in the American past. Sexuality itself had been treated as such a shameful part of our history—diaries bowdlerized, relationships concealed, photographs and letters burned—that any straying from mainstream mores, any permutation at all, had, through time, been ignored, denied, hidden, and, ultimately forgotten. Until recently the official image of the typical American was hysterically suburban: Anglo-Saxon, mono-gamous, heterosexual parents pair-bonded with two children and two cars—an image as narrow and propagandist as the smiling workers of China saluting from the ricefields.

Such was the general mood of widespread ignorance, even through the 1970's, that all scholarship on sexuality was suspect—curtailed or suspended by archival custodians, by foundations which allocate research funding and by academic institutions which control student degrees and faculty promotions. As a result, any new information has added significantly to our almost nonexistent knowledge of intimate life. Some major steps have been taken over the past ten years, a new scholarship about the lives of gay people and the nature of homosexuality has begun to emerge—as exemplified in the contributions of Allan Berube, John Boswell, George Chauncey Jr., John D'Emilio, Lillian Faderman, Estelle Freedman, Jonathan Katz, Joan Nestle, Judith Schwartz, and Martha Vicinus.

Even so, and despite a decade and a half of genuine liberalization in moral values, the paucity of available information is still striking. To help rectify this situation, I undertook for two years (1981-1983) to write a column for the *New York Native,* a gay, bi-monthly publication. Entitled "About Time", the column consisted of docu-ments relevant to the history of sexuality in general, and gay sexuality in particular, which I had uncovered during my research trips to various manuscript libraries* and which I hoped might help disabuse readers of the Puritan, official version of the American sexual past that we had all ingested with our pablum. I introduced each document with a headnote of varying length containing whatever

*The American Antiquarian Society, the American Philosophical Society, The Countway Medical Library, The Kinsey Institute, The Library of Congress, The Lilly Library, The Massachusetts Historical Society, The Pennsylvania Historical Society, The National Anthropological Files of the Smithsonian Institute, The New York Academy of Medicine.

background information and historical context I was able to provide. Although it was only a year old in 1981, the *Native* had already begun to claim a readership well beyond New York City, embracing a national audience.

During the ten years preceding "About Time", I had acquired a variegated reputation—as historian and biographer teaching at Princeton and then at The City University of New York; and as an openly gay journalist, playwright, and critic. Straddling these two worlds, I indeed had a lot in my historian's files that was meant for my activist signature. It was a new honor to be signing both with the same pen.

About a year after I stopped writing the column, Felice Picano asked me if I was interested in collecting the documents for the Seahorse Press; their historical importance, he thought, warranted presenting them in book form. I liked the idea, even while concerned that such a collection might be skimpy—especially after, in the name of coherence, he and I decided to drop those columns which had dealt with heterosexuality.

It was then that I got the idea to fatten the package with a second part to the book: essays and articles I'd published during roughly the same few years in a variety of periodicals other than the *New York Native,* which had focused on the same general themes of gay sexuality and had approximated the same format used in the *Native* column (though reversing the amount of space allotted to personal reflection versus documentary material). These pieces—"Part Two: Essays" in this volume—describe events, theoretical disputes and organizational beginnings in which I myself had been a participant or close observer: the founding of the Gay Academic Union, the Leonard Matlovich trial, the Anita Bryant hysteria, the emergent new literature on homosexuality. Part One, then, is a sample of my research findings in the new discipline of gay history. Part Two is a sample of the opinions and values I developed in the new gay liberation movement. An emergent scholarship combines in this volume with an emergent politics.

In addition, I decided to include in the book two essays that also fit the overall format but which, for reasons of length, I had never before submitted for publication: "Walt Whitman" and "Sex Variant Women." I have placed a third essay, "Writhing Bedfellows"—also based on a major research find and recounting as well some of the hurdles of archival research into sexual history—first in sequence, a sort of second introduction, since its format combines the two chief modes employed in this volume, "documents" and "essays".

I think the addition of the second half of the book does help, and without undue artifice, to expand its substance and justify its publication—since for "gay studies", an area of inquiry in its infancy, any filling in of the blanks can prove useful, however incomplete and tentative in nature. One particularly gaping blank that remains is representation of the lives of lesbian women. I owe them a double apology—first, for the lack of space (itself a reflection—so I like to think—of the lack of scholarly findings), and second, for designating them at all in a volume essentially devoted to male experience. I hope at least some lesbian women won't mind being joined together with gay men one more time (for limited purposes, and with separate identities maintained) in a common enterprise holding out hope of mutual benefit.

Part One of this book reflects its journalistic origins as a *Native* column. The campy tone of some of the headnotes was not designed to suit the tastes of scholarship—and gave me some pause about memorializing in the permanent format of a book. But I decided that the tone was an intrinsic part of the historical record—reflecting as it did the playful, fragmentary nature of the *Native* column. Both parts of the book ultimately reflect the particular time frame in which the pieces were conceived; the primitive state of the scholarship and insight they represent is, I believe itself worth preserving.

Accordingly I've tried to resist cleaning up and weighing down the pieces with too many subsequent meditations and amplifications. Now and then I've restored some of the material originally excised for lack of space, cut some of the less illuminating redundancies, and rearranged some of the more glaring typos and grammatical transformations which crept into the pieces in the form in which they had been originally published. They are reprinted here not in the order in which they appeared, but rather in chronological sequence.

In general, however, I've stayed clear of the sort of excessive rearranging and cleaning-up which can so easily disfigure the original tone and scope. To fabricate unwarranted intricacy for the available historical data, or to pretend to undue breadth, clarity and consistency in my personal ruminations seemed a disservice to the actual state of an incipient scholarship and a fledgling political movement. Better, I reasoned, to represent honestly a given moment in time than to blur through grandiose revision and overestimated claims that which in fact has until recently been little understood.

Like the documents from the *Native* column, the essays in Part Two are products of the same first decade of homosexual liberation. They stand alone, I hope, as speculative pieces, but may also be read as personal documents. As historian and social critic, I had entree to the privileged pages of the *The New York Times;* as a radical/gay activist, I could address the readers of the *Native* and *Christopher Street.* An openly gay writer with traditional credentials, my position was perhaps unique—an outsider's perspective with an insider's access to power.

Thus the disparity of tones in the pieces. The bantering, irreverent voice of, say, "Intimacy Without Orgasm," (or a headnote beginning "We gay men") could not comfortably introduce a *New York Times* feature, nor particularly resonate for its readers. Nor, oppositely, would my *Times* article, "The Literature of Homosexuality", with its formality and distance, quite suit the readers of the *Native.* Moreover, all these pieces were written before the onslaught of the AIDS epidemic, which has made their sometimes playful tone seem gruesomely inapt when compared to current realities, to the appalling threat physically and psychologically which hangs (especially) over the gay male community. The disjunction between past tone and present reality could prove offensive to many, but again, to efface the originals would dishonestly remove them from their own historical context.

The isolated fragments in this volume are far from a comprehensive reflection of the collective experience known as gay liberation, nor anything approaching a narrative account of the gay past preceding liberation. Rather, they reflect the limited passage of one gay man in this critical, transitional generation—half a lifetime before, half a lifetime after a revolutionary change in consciousness. Not to pretend otherwise, and in order to preserve the integrity of the nature of the essays as documents, I have left as much as I dared undoctored, unhomogenized, still speaking to their original audiences.

M.B.D.
June 10, 1986

PART ONE:

Documents

"WRITHING BEDFELLOWS": TWO YOUNG MEN FROM ANTEBELLUM SOUTH CAROLINA'S RULING ELITE SHARE "EXTRAVAGANT DELIGHT"

The two manuscript letters that form this article's centerpiece have been concealed from public view for 150 years. No portion of them has been previously published, nor even obliquely paraphrased. Yet as will be seen at a glance, the content of the letters is startling, and opens up immensely suggestive new avenues for historical interpretation. The importance of the letters requires that they be "introduced" on several levels.

To start with the simplest, we need to identify who wrote the letters ("Jeff") and who received them ("Jim"). In 1826, when the letters were written, Jeff and Jim were inconsequential young men— yet both destined for distinguished careers, Jim (James H. Hammond) eventually achieving national renown. Jeff (Thomas Jefferson With- ers) was also to cut a considerable, if lesser swath—as journalist, lawyer, "nullifier," and Judge of the South Carolina Court of Appeals.

In 1826, twenty-two year old Jeff Withers was studying law at South Carolina College—discontentedly. "An useful man," he wrote Jim Hammond, "must, at last, be self-educated." In Jeff's view, it was "behind the state of society" to concentrate on the "dead languages" of Greek and Latin; it was time "murdered", preparing a student poorly for "the duties of life." By 1826 Jeff Withers had reached some basic decisions about his future. Henceforce, he wrote Jim, he would "sacrifice" his previous "Northern mania" and devote himself to what he now realized was his "appropriate sphere of action"—the South- ern states. Though in general he did not have "strenuous opinions upon political matters," he did feel strongly about the intensifying controversy between "strict" and "broad" constructionists—over the kind and amount of power the Constitution had given to the federal government. Withers stood with the strict constructionists. South Carolina Senator William Smith, probably the country's fiercest defender in the early 1820s of the sovereign and "inviolable" rights of the individual states against the threatening encroachments of national power, had become his hero.[1]

To activate his newfound convictions, Jeff Withers in 1828 became editor of the Columbia Telescope, *an organ of the powerful nullification movement that had arisen in South Carolina to protest and defy the recent federal tariff. For several years thereafter he gave full energies to the struggle, delaying the completion of his law studies until 1833 (the same year he married Elizabeth Boykin, whose niece, Mary Boykin Chestnut, later won enduring fame for her Civil War journals, published as* Diary from Dixie). *Elected a common-law judge soon after, Withers later moved up to the state Court of Appeals, where he served until his death in 1866. His moment of greatest public prominence came in 1861, when he was chosen to be one of fifty delegates sent by the seven seceded states of the lower South to meet in Montgomery, Alabama, there to draw up a provisional government for the pending new "Confederacy."[2] Except for a few additional details, little more is known about Withers' public career.*

Still less is known about his private life. He seems to have been generally viewed as an "irritable" man, quick-tempered and sarcastic, though we have the testimony of at least one close friend that Withers was "a very kind-hearted gentleman and most indulgent and affectionate in all relations of life."[3] It's tempting—given the contents of the letters printed below—to read innuendos into that description; but since such phraseology was then commonplace, the temptation is better resisted.

We know a great deal more about "Jim" (James H. Hammond). Hammond became one of the antebellum South's "great men," his career ranging from politics to agricultural reform to pro-slavery polemics. At various times he was governor, congressman and senator from South Carolina, a leading exponent of southern economic diversification, and a highly influential "moralist" whose theories in defense of slavery became cornerstones of the South's "Pro-Slavery Argument." Hammond's name may not be well known today, but in the antebellum period he was likened in importance to John C. Calhoun—and considered his likely heir.[4]

For the limited purpose of elucidating two letters from 1826, a detailed description of Hammond's subsequent public career would be gratuitous—especially since it has been ably recounted many times.[5] Still, certain aspects of Hammond's public life, plus what little is known of his private life, are indeed vital to our attempt at interpreting young Jim's erotic activities, as described in the 1826 letters—and for tracing continuities in Hammond's behavior and temperament over time.

We need to begin by getting acquainted with young Jim himself— the lusty roisterer revealed for the first time in these hitherto unpublished letters from 1826.

THE DOCUMENTS

The following letter was written by Withers to Hammond, May 15, 1826, Columbia, South Carolina.[6]

Dear Jim:

I got your Letter this morning about 8 o'clock, from the hands of the Bearer ... I was sick as the Devil, when the Gentleman entered the Room, and have been so during most of the day. About 1 o'clock I swallowed a huge mass of Epsom Salts—and it will not be hard to imagine that I have been at dirty work since. I feel partially relieved—enough to write a hasty dull letter.

I feel some inclination to learn whether you yet sleep in your Shirt-tail, and whether you yet have the extravagant delight of poking and punching a writhing Bedfellow with your long fleshen pole—the exquisite touches of which I have often had the honor of feeling? Let me say unto thee that unless thou changest former habits in this particular, thou wilt be represented by every future Chum as a nuisance. And, I pronounce it, with good reason too. Sir, you roughen the downy Slumbers of your Bedfellow—by such hostile—furious lunges as you are in the habit of making at him—when he is least prepared for defence against the crushing force of a Battering Ram. Without reformation my imagination depicts some awful results for which you will be held accountable—and therefore it is, that I earnestly recommend it. Indeed it is encouraging an assault and battery propensity, which needs correction—& uncorrected threatens devastation, horror & bloodshed, etc. ...

The remaining two pages of the letter deal with unrelated matters of no special interest. But the way the letter signs off, does:

With great respect I am the old
Stud,
Jeff.

Withers' second letter to Hammond is dated Sept. 24, 1826:

My dear Friend,

... Your excellent Letter of 13 June arrived ... a few weeks since[7] ... Here, where anything like a systematic course of thought, or of reading, is quite out of the question—such system leaves no vacant, idle moments of painful vacuity, which invites a whole Kennel of treacherous passions to prey upon one's vitals ... the renovation of spirit which follows the appearance of a *friend's* Letter—the diagram of his soul—is like a grateful shower from the cooling fountains of Heaven to reanimate drooping Nature. Whilst your letters are Transcripts of real—existing feeling, and are on that account peculiarly welcome—they at the same time betray too much *honesty* of purpose not to strike an harmonious chord in my mind. I have only to regret that, honesty of intention and even assiduity in excition [?] are far from being the uniform agents of our destiney [sic] here— However it must, at best, be only an a priori argument for us to settle the condemnation of the world, before we come in actual contact with it. This task is peculiarly appropriate to the acrimony of old age—and perhaps we had as well defer it, under the hope that we may reach a point, when 'twill be all that we can do—

I fancy, Jim, that your *elongated protruberance*—your fleshen pole—your [two Latin words; indecipherable]—has captured complete mastery over you—and I really believe, that you are charging over the pine barrens of your locality, braying, like an ass, at every she-male you can discover. I am afraid that you are thus prostituting the "image of God" and suggest that if you thus blasphemously essay to put on the form of a Jack—in this stead of that noble image—you will share the fate of Nebuchadnazzer of old, I should lament to hear of you feeding upon the dross of the pasture and alarming the country with your vociferations. The day of miracles may not be past, and the flaming excess of your lustful appetite may drag down the vengeance of supernal power.—And you'll "be dam-d if you don't marry"?—and felt a disposition to set down and gravely detail me the reasons of early marriage. But two favourable ones strike me now—the first is, that Time may grasp love so furiously as totally[?] to disfigure his Phiz. The second is, that, like George McDuffie,[8] he may have the hap-hazzard of a broken backbone befal him, which will relieve him from the performance of affectual family-duty—& throw over the brow of his wife, should he chance to get one, a most foreboding gloom—As to the first, you will find many a modest good girl subject to the same inconvenience—and as to the second, it will only superinduce such domestic whirlwinds, as will call into frequent exercise rhetorical displays of impassioned Eloquence, accompanied by appropriate and perfect specimens of those gestures which Nature and feeling suggest. To get children, it is true, fulfills a department of social & natural duty—but to let them starve, or subject them to the alarming hazard of it, violates another of a most important character. This is the dilemma to which I reduce you—choose this day which you will do.

COMMENTARY:

The portrait of young Hammond that emerges from these 1826 letters is in startling contrast with the standard view of the adult Hammond. Nineteen-year-old Jim's "flaming excess" and "lustful appetite," bears no resemblance to James H. Hammond of the history books—conservative moralist, staid traditionalist pillar of the traditional Old South. In an effort to reconcile this gross disparity in Hammond's image, some additional biographical details are needed.

By birth, Hammond was a "commoner"—his father a native New Englander who had gone south to teach school, his mother a native South Carolinian of undistinguished ancestry. Through his own talent and drive (Hammond graduated near the top of his college class) and then through what is called a "fortunate" marriage, Hammond entered the ranks of the Southern planter aristocracy. His wedding to the Charleston heiress, Catherine Fitzsimmons, was critically important: overnight Hammond became owner of Silver Bluff, a 10,000-acre plantation on the Savannah River worked by 220 slaves—instantly one of the ruling elite.[9]

He used his opportunities well. Always the apt pupil, Hammond quickly acquired the cultivated externals—manners, rituals and social preoccupations—of the master class. Just as quickly, he internalized its values. By the mid-1830s, Hammond had already won high regard as a "brilliant" advocate of "states' rights," a zealous defender of slavery, and a "superb" manager of his landed estates. (He had also acquired a reputation for willingness to use the lash and to send his slaves to cut fodder in malaria-infested swamps.)[10] A number of Hammond's contemporaries thought his temperament more enigmatic than his social values, often describing him as mercurial and impetuous, And as well, aloof, vain, willful and proud, though such traits, for that region, class, and time, were not necessarily epithets.

But that Hammond the adult was sometimes considered "impetuous" does suggest that the tumultuous young Jim of 1826 had never been wholly superceded in later life by the Statesman and Seer. We have few details about the nature of his adult "impetuousness", but of those we do, none suggest it ever took the form it had in his youth—of "furious lunges" at male bed partners, lusty "charges over the pine barrens" to seek out "she-males." If those youthful penchants and impulses did continue to exert some hold over him in adulthood (given how pronounced they'd been in his youth, it's hard to believe they totally disappeared), if homoerotic images did maintain some subterranean sway on his fantasies, there's no scintilla of evidence he acted them out.

But if there is no direct evidence from Hammond's later years of the homoerotic zest he'd shown as a young man, there is considerable evidence to suggest that Hammond's lusty appetite in general— however much its loci may have shifted—continued to be strong throughout his life, his public image notwithstanding. As an adult, Hammond had the reputation for stern rectitude, and was at pains to reinforce it. For example, he haughtily denounced as "grossly and atrociously exaggerated" the abolitionists' charge that racial mixing was common on southern plantations; the actual incidence of miscegenation,, he insisted, was "infinitely small" in contrast to the "illicit sexual intercourse" known to be widespread among the factory populations of England and the North. As a plantation owner, he sternly enforced puritanical sexual mores among his slaves. He allowed the slaves on his plantation to marry but not to divorce unless a slave couple could manage to convince him that "sufficient cause" existed; even then he subjected both members of the couple to a hundred lashes and forbid both the right to remarry for three years.[11]

Hammond's entrenched reputation as the guardian and exemplar of traditional morality got a sudden, nasty jolt in 1846. In that year, George McDuffie resigned his seat in the U.S. Senate, and the state legislature seemed on the verge of choosing Hammond to succeed him. Hammond's brother-in-law, Wade Hampton, thwarted that result. He warned Hammond that he would publicly reveal an incident that took place three years earlier unless Hammond immediatley removed his name from contention for the Senate seat. The nature of that incident was finally revealed tweny years ago, when the historian Clement Eaton discovered and published excerpts from Hammond's secret diary. The diary revealed that Hammond had seduced Wade Hampton's teenage daughters.[12]

Hardly a peccadillo, one might think. Yet Hammond himself apparently viewed it as no more than that. He agreed to withdraw his candidacy for the Senate; rumors of the sexual scandal had already circulated and Hammond could hardly afford to let Hampton confirm them. Hammond also gave up his family mansion in Columbia and retired to manage his estates—a retirement which lasted fourteen years. But he did none of this in a spirit marked by contrition or chagrin. The dominant tone he adopted (in diary entries and in letters to friends) was aggrieved petulance—*he* was the wounded party! Merely for "a little dalliance with the other sex," for an incident marked by "impulse, not design," he wrote, he had been forced into political retirement, whereas numerous other public figures, past and present, had indulged "amorous & conjugal infidelity" without incurring censure or retribution of any kind.[13]

Hammond's unapologetic tone, astonishing in itself, reveals much about his actual (as opposed to his rhetorical) sexual morality. The casual view he took of "dalliance" suggests that he had far more personal experience with it than we can currently document (indeed, aside from the 1846 run-in with Hampton we have no documentation). But his attitude towards "dalliance" is the least of it. His truculent defense of seducing teenage girls—relatives through marriage, no less—as an event of neither great import nor cause for remorse, makes it hard to imagine what if any erotic expression he considered beyond the pale.

The "two" Hammonds— the youthful sexual adventurer of 1826 and the staid eminence of 1846 —no longer seem unrelated. Hammond's range of sexual tastes as an older man may have narrowed (*may*; that impression could be due to the paucity of extant evidence), but his sex drive apparently remained strong, impulsive, self-justifying, defiant of the convention mores of the day. The external circumstances of Hammond's life changed radically from youth to middle age, but his inner life apparently underwent less of a sea change.

As both a young and a middle-aged man, his lust—whether aroused by male college friends or by teenage female relatives—continued strong, arrogantly assertive, ungoverned. Hammond never seems to have struggled very hard to control it. Certainly not as a young man. Nothing in the 1826 letters suggests that Jim Hammond expended much energy, or saw any reason to restrain his impulses and curtail his pleasures. He may have made more of an effort as an older man, if only to maintain his staid public image and safeguard his privileges. Even that is conjecture; conjecture based, moreover, on our assumptions about what constitutes "logical" behavior for a man of Hammond's position. Judging from his actual behavior in the 1840s, and his indignant reaction to discovery and threatened exposure, our logic and values don't seem to coincide at all closely with Hammond's own.

Which deepens the enigma. How might we understand this uncategorizable man? Looked at from the angle of 1826, Hammond seems (by my mores) admirably playful, exploratory and free-wheeling, uninhibited and attractively unapologetic. Looked at from the angle of 1846, he seems merely repulsive: grossly insensitive and irresponsible, perhaps pathologically willful. But possibly the change in perspective is at bottom a function of a shift in *our* angle of vision (and the moral assumptions which underlie it), not in Hammond himself; the shift in context between the 1826 and 1846 episodes encouraging us to adopt radically different judgments of what were in fact unwavering traits in his personality.

The discomforting fact is that we "understand" very little—whether about Hammond the man, or the alien social climate which made possible the 1826 Withers letters. Having exhausted the scanty historical data available for trying to construct a plausible context in which to read the erotic meaning of those letters, we can only fall back on conjecture. Like the tone, say, of Withers' letters— consistently ironic and playful, it strongly suggests that his sexual encounters with Hammond carried no emotional overtones of a "romantic" involvement between the two men. Not that we can be sure. Irony, as we know, is a common device for concealing emotion. Besides, an occasional phrase in the letter—such as Withers' reference to the "exquisite touch" of Hammond's "long fleshen pole"—could be read as more than "playful." Unfortunately, no other correspondence from the period of remotely comparable content exists to which we might turn in an attempt to draw parallels, clarify attitudes, consolidate or amplify tentative "conclusions" which now derive wholly from skimpy internal evidence within the two letters themselves.

Given our impoverished results in trying to pin down what the two letters mean, it may be foolish to move beyond the Withers/Hammond relationship itself and try posing broader questions still: "foolish," because to do so invites additional futility and frustration. Yet broader questions are implicit in the material—they seem to suggest themselves—and posing them may alone be of value, though answers prove elusive.

The critical question, historically, is whether the erotic experiences described in the two letters should be regarded as "anomalous" or "representative." Was Withers and Hammond's behavior unique, or does it reveal and illustrate a wider pattern of male-male relationships—till now unsuspected and undocumented, yet in some sense "typical" of their time, region, race, and class? The question, on its face, is an enigma wrapped in a mystery. At best, we can approach, not resolve it. Let the reader be forewarned: What follows is hypothesis nearly pure, to be taken with generous grains of salt.

The best clues are provided by the internal evidence of the letters themselves, and especially their tone. It has a consistent ring: off-handed, flip. Jeff's bantering call to repentence is transparently mocking, his "warnings of retribution" uniformly irreverent—"campy," in the modern vernacular. The letters are *so* devoid of any serious moral entreaty or fervor, of any genuine attempt to inspire shame or reformation, as to take on negative significance. The values and vocabulary of evangelical piety had not yet, in the 1820s, come to permeate American consciousness and discourse. Even when those values carried most influence—roughly 1830-1870—they seem to have held sway in the South to a lesser extent than elsewhere in the country.[14]

So the geographical locale and time period in which Jeff and Jim grew up may be important factors in explaining their free-wheeling attitudes. The American South of the latter part of the eighteenth and early part of the nineteenth centuries was (for privileged, young, white males) one of those rare "liberal interregnums" in our history when the body could be treated as a natural source of pleasure and "wanton" sexuality viewed as the natural prerogative—the exemplification even—of Manliness.

In this sense, Jeff and Jim's relaxed attitude toward sex in general, far from being anomalous, may have been close to mainstream mores. Whether that also holds for their high-spirited, unselfconscious attitude about same-gender sexuality is more problematic. At the least, Jeff's light-hearted comedic descriptions of male bedfellows "poking and punching" each other with their "fleshen poles" seems so devoid of furtiveness or shame, it is possible to believe that male-male sexual contact was nowhere nearly stigmatized to the degree long assumed. Withers and Hammond, after all, were ambitious aspirants to positions of leadership and power. Could Hammond have indulged so freely (and Withers described so casually) behavior widely deemed disgraceful and abhorrent, outside the range of "permissible" experience? If homoeroticism had been utterly taboo, wouldn't one expect Withers' tone to betray some evidence of guilt and unease? Instead, it is breezy and nonchalant, raising the fair possibility that sexual contact between males (of a certain class, region, time, and place), if not commonplace, wasn't wholly proscribed either. Should that surmise be even marginally correct, our standard view of the history of male homosexuality in this country as an unrelieved tale of concealment and woe needs revision.[15]

The surmise, of course, is shaky, lacking any corroborating evidence, any additional documentation from the period recounting attitudes and experiences comparable to those of Jeff and Jim. That much is undeniable, but perhaps not in itself sufficient proof that same-gender sexuality never (or rarely) happened. Other corroborating records may still survive, and are only waiting to be retrieved. After all, to date we've accumulated only a tiny collection of historical materials that record the existence of *heterosexual* behavior in the past. Yet no one claims that that miniscule amount of evidence is an accurate measure of the actual amount of heterosexual activity which took place.

Just so with Jeff and Jim. What now appears unique and anomalous behavior may one day come to be seen as unexceptional—casually tolerated, if not actively encouraged or institutionalized. This will only happen if the new generation of scholars continues to press for access to previously suppressed materials and if the new generation of archivists continues to cultivate its sympathy toward such scholarship, declassifying "sensitive" data at an accelerated pace. I myself believe that additional source material, possibly a great deal of it, relating to the history of homosexuality has survived and awaits recovery from well-guarded vaults. I base this belief on my own research experiences over the past decade. The two Withers/Hammond letters presented here are a case in point. Until they turned up, few if any scholars (myself included) would have credited the notion that "carefree" male-male sex ever took place in this country (let alone in the 1820s)—or that off-handed, unemphatic descriptions of it could ever be found.

In that vein, it may be worth providing some additional details about how the Withers/Hammond letters were discovered. The tale might encourage other scholars to persevere in the search for long-suppressed material; might suggest tactics for extracting it; might alert them to some of the obstacles and ploys custodial guardians will use to deflect the search—and suggest how these can be neutralized or counteracted.

RECOVERING THE WITHERS/HAMMOND LETTERS

In offering this cautionary tale, the chief purpose is not to establish the villainy of archivists. As a group, they are no more the enemy of innovative scholarship nor the defenders of traditional morality than are historians as a group—most of whom scornfully dismiss the study of sexual ideology and behavior as a non-subject. During my research travels to manuscript libraries, several individual archivists have been enormously supportive: people like Stephen T. Riley of the Massachusetts Historical Society, Sandra Taylor of the Lilly Library in Indiana, and Richard J. Wolfe of the Countway Library of Medicine in Boston. Such people (I could name others) acted from the conviction that research into the "history of intimacy" was overdue and held great potential importance for better understanding our national experience and character.

Their attitude is still a minority one within the archival profession as a whole (in the historical profession, too). Many of those who stand guard over the nation's major manuscript collections see their function as protective and preservative—of traditional moral values in general and of a given family's "good name" in particular. They tend to equate—as is true everywhere in academia (and perhaps to a greater degree than in the population at large)—the libidinous with the salacious, and to be profoundly distrustful of both. Given this discomfort, some archivists invent obstacles to put in the researcher's path or claim to be hamstrung (and, in truth, even sympathetic curators sometimes *are*) by certain access restrictions which the donor of a given manuscript collection originally appended to the deed of gift.

The six-month tangle I had over the Withers/Hammond letters illustrates all this. The trail began (confining myself to the main outlines) with Catherine Clinton, a doctoral student in history at Princeton. She first brought the letters to my attention, and although she has modestly asked that her efforts not be detailed, I did at least want to acknowledge her pivotal role.[16] Once having seen the letters and realized their importance, I started in motion the standard procedures for acquiring permission to publish manuscript materials. On March 6, 1979, I sent a formal request to that effect to the South Carolina Library (henceforth, SCL), where the original letters are housed.

That move, according to one of the several legal experts I later consulted, was my first, and worst, mistake. By formally requesting permission, I was (to quote the expert) being "super-dutiful" and, in the process, making life infinitely more difficult for *all* parties concerned. Technically, I had done the "correct" thing—I had gone through proper channels, adhered to the terms most manuscript libraries require regarding permission to publish manuscript material. But in real life, my chiding expert added, what is technically correct can prove functionally awkward. In practice, it seems (and after twenty years of archival research, this came as a surprise to me), some scholars publish manuscript material without making any formal request to do so. And libraries, it seems, prefer it that way. A formal request, after all, requires a formal reply. The given library is pressured to make a clear-cut decision, one that can place it (sometimes unwillingly and unfairly) in a no-win situation: should the library grant permission, it risks the wrath of a donor or family descendant, charges of dereliction, possible loss of future acquisitions; should the library deny permission, it risks accusations of censorship from an outraged scholar. Let others take note: though archivists will not or cannot say openly, they may well prefer to be handed a *fait accompli,* and will feel silently grateful to researchers who adopt what might be called the Macbeth ploy: "do what ye need to do, but tell me not of it till after 'tis done" (roughly paraphrased).

Lacking such wisdom at the time, I instead sent off a formal letter requesting permission to publish. This left SCL with two choices: to act on my request (which, given the contents of the 1826 letters, almost certainly assured a negative response), or to do nothing. They opted for the latter, letting my letter go unanswered. If SCL had thereby meant to signal me to proceed (quietly) without insisting on their formal acquiescence, I misread the signal. Instead of quietly retreating, I noisily persisted. On April 15 I sent them a second letter, a near duplicate of the first. That, too, went unacknowledged. I got angry (blame it on the Zodiac: Leos can't stand being ignored). In early June, after thirteen weeks without a response, I sent—no, shot off by certified mail—a third letter, this one longer and decidedly more testy than its predecessors. SCL's obdurate silence, I wrote, could only be interpreted as "silence giving consent" or as a subtly calculated attempt at censorship. Should I opt for the first interpretation(my letter went on), I would simply publish the letters without further ado—and on the assumption I had tacit approval. Should I instead opt for the second interpretation—their disaproval—I would then feel an obligation to other scholars to report the incident to the prestigious Joint Committee of Historians and Archivists, a group empowered to deal with matters of censorship. While deciding between the two courses of action, my letter concluded, "I would be glad to receive any information which might have a bearing on my pending decision." (Leos get snotty when pushed.)

Within the week, I got a reply—proving once more, I suppose, that threats may not bring out the best in people, but they do bring out something. The reply came from SCL's Director (Dr. Archer, I'll call him). He began by expressing regret that I had "found it necessary to write such a sharp letter"—although he acknowledged that the delayed response to my previous letters might have contributed to my ill temper. Nonetheless, he went on, I could surely understand that he had had to put my letters aside while "awaiting a convenient opportunity" to seek advice "on the status of the restrictions" attached to the Hammond Papers. Such an opportunity had finally presented itself; he was now able to report that the original donor of the Hammond Papers had "asked" (the choice of word, subsequently pointed out by several of my consultants, is significant, implying as it does a request from the donor, not a binding stipulation) that none of the manuscripts be used in a way that might "result in embarrassment to descendants." The donor was dead, but Dr. Archer considered the "restriction" to be "still in force." He was also of the view that the two Withers letters were unquestionably "embarrassing." Therefore, he had decided to deny my request to publish them.

In a curious concluding paragraph, Archer suggested he might reconsider my request if I could provide "full assurances" that the letters would be published in such a way as to disguise their provenance and prevent their identification with Hammond or Withers; that I would agree, in short, to strip the letters of all historical context—a context integral to their meaning and importance—and treat them as floating objects unanchored in time or space. That suggestion struck me as comparable to insisting a Haydn string quartet be performed solely with tambourines and vibraharp. I declined the suggestion.

I embarked instead on a double course: drafting a reply to Dr. Archer and starting up a round of consultations with various scholars, friends, and legal experts about what to include in my reply. My advisors diverged on this or that particular, but concurred on the main one: legally and morally, I was justified in proceeding straightaway to publication. In support of that conclusion they cited several arguments but put special stress on the legal doctrine of "fair usage": an author's right to quote (without permission) an appropriate amount of copyrighted material. The body of law defining what does or does not constitute a "fair" amount of unauthorized quotation has shifted over time, but in recent years (most significantly in *Nizer v. Rosenberg*) the courts have leaned consistently toward a permissive view.

One of the experts I consulted in copyright law felt "absolutely confident" that I was entitled to publish the two Withers letters *in full*, if I wished—though I ultimately decided to use only the erotic portions as relevant to my purpose. In that expert's opinion, SCL "had already fatally weakened its copyright claim to the Hammond Papers, however unintentionally". The library's long-standing practice of allowing scholars access to the papers (instead of sealing them off) was tantamount to admitting that the original deed of gift had not been encumbered by any substantive, detailed restrictions—and that aside from some vague admonitory advice, the donor had apparently left final discretionary power to the library itself. The fact that SCL had, in addition, catalogued the two Withers letters and provided photocopies of them on request had further weakened their position in the view of the copyright lawyers—indeed, had made my legal right to publish "unassailable." All this I dutifully incorporated in the ongoing draft of my letter to Dr. Archer. In the upshot, I never sent it. My Council of Experts finally persuaded me that I had nothing further to gain and might needlessly stir quiet waters. As one consultant put it, "If you formally notify SCL of your intention to publish, the library might feel obligated to bring suit, though they'd much prefer not to, given their shaky legal case and the additional publicity any litigation would give to the contents of the letters. Do yourself and them a favor: Say and write nothing further; simply proceed to publication."

Which is what I did. Not, I should add, without misgivings. I felt a direct challenge to SCL, though it would likely have involved time-consuming, expensive litigation, might have yielded an important precedent useful to future scholars. I also regretted that Dr. Archer had never gotten the chance to read my unmailed final letter, especially the part in which I had asked him to spell out his specific reasons for deciding that publication of the Withers manuscripts would prove an "embarrassment." "For two men like Hammond and Withers," I had written Archer (hot tongue in hard cheek), "who have gone down in history as among the country's staunchest defenders of human slavery, I should think their reputations could only be enhanced by the playful, raucous—the humanizing —revelations contained in the two letters." Yes, I was being patently disingenuous; and yes, it was unlikely I could force from Dr. Archer an explicit avowal of homophobia. Still, it would have done my soul good to try (it's doing it some good just quoting the unsent letter here).

Certain ethical considerations implicit in my decision to publish the Withers letters without authorization leave me the most uncomfortable: that familiar array of moral conundrums (in however diminutive a form) long associated with acts of "civil disobedience." To explain why I proceeded nonetheless, I have to step back a bit and approach the matter indirectly through some general observations.

There is a long-standing and long-sanctified notion that academia consists of a "community of scholars"—in the ideal sense of a disinterested collectivity of truth seekers. This is an exalted, but to me, illusory conceit. In practice, as I see it, the notion has served as a useful device for codifying professional behavior and a convenient rationale for denying credentials to those who might challenge the academy's entrenched values —women, gays, ethnic minorities. The conceit of a community of scholars, in short, has characteristically been a blind for parochialism and discrimination.

Yet the *ideal* of such a community remains attractive (as does the related notion that a genuinely unharnessed scholarship could provide needed data for challenging the status quo and nurturing alternative visions of the good society). In my view, a scholar's prime allegiance and responsibility should be to the ideal itself, not to those academic guilds which claim to represent it (even as they enforce standards for membership and employ definitions of "legitimate" inquiry that straightjacket and subvert it). Most of the scholarship emanating from universities functions primarily, if "unintentionally," to rationalize existing arrangements of power; and the academic guilds, in excluding or ostracizing mavericks, play an important role in perpetuating such arrangements. What may seem obvious on an abstract level becomes less so when reduced to a personal one; then the whole question of "responsibility" becomes much stickier. As someone who chose to join the academic community and to remain in it (with attendant profit, such as a secure salary), it could be argued that I, and others like me, are obligated either to abide by academe's conventions or—if convinced we cannot—to resign. In response to that argument, I'd say that a scholar owes *primary* allegiance to what academe might be—to its promise, not its practice—and would add the specific observation that academe's own official standards about what constitutes "acceptable" professorial behavior and proper scholarly inquiry are muddled and slippery. To give one example, there is no agreement among university-affiliated historians about what constitutes "correct" (or even preferred) research procedures, modes of analysis or styles of presentation: Cliometricians battle impressionists, generalists disparage specialists, literary stylists war with statistical analysts.

Adding to the confusion is academe's contradictory record in its treatment of dissenters. It is not a record of monolithic repression. Many principled and innovative academicians have indeed suffered grievously for their political, personal, and professional nonconformity (as well as for belonging to a particular sex, class, and race). But it is also true that academe has sometimes honored its eccentrics and insurgents, if often belatedly; the political radical, William Appleman Williams was elected President of the Organization of American Historians. While the academy is assuredly not the free-swinging arena of open inquiry its champions claim, neither is it as tightly sealed against novelty or as unvaryingly hostile to fractious upstarts, as its detractors insist.

Academe's ambiguous traditions help persuade many intellectuals who by temperament, conviction, or lifestyle are "deviant"—i.e. outside mainstream orthodoxy—to establish and maintain university affiliations. Some of these intellectuals would claim ("lull themselves into believing," left-wing skeptics might say) that academe is one of the few arenas in which innovative inquiry remains possible, and that the "long march through the institutions" at present seems the only promising tactic available for creating substantive social change. But others among the group of "deviant" intellectuals do worry that by retaining their ties to academic disciplines and educational institutions which function essentially as "conservators"—preservers and transmitters of conventional knowledge and norms—that they are putting their own values at risk. The danger of cooptation is always present; unorthodoxy and personal integrity can be gradually, sometimes undiscernibly, sapped. The best one can do to guard against that prospect is to try to stay vigilant—in touch with the different drummer within, resistant to the efforts to muffle it. But vows of vigilance, as we know, are more easily made than kept.

Anyway, that's about as close as I can come to delineating (and probably idealizing) the relationship I've tried to maintain within the academic world, and also to conveying, however circuitous the route, some of the ingredients that went into my inner debate about publishing the Withers/Hammond letters. By finally deciding to publish them against the wishes of their official custodian, my own personal discomfort played a considerable role—discomfort at the prospect of yielding to the prevailing (and to my mind dangerously narrow) view of what is acceptable historical inquiry and, by implication, "permissible" norms of behavior. I also concluded, on more general grounds, that the public *does* have the "right to know"—and in regard to the Withers letters specifically, the gay public has a desperate *need* to know.

That last consideration proved decisive. I felt it was essential to challenge the tradition of suppressing information which might prove useful to gay people in better understanding the historical dimensions of our experience, the shifting strategies we've adopted over time to cope with oppression, and the varied styles we've developed to express our special sensibilities. If the "lawless" tactics I've resorted to seem extreme to some, well, so is our need; more orthodox tactics (like polite letters of inquiry), have done little to meet it. The heterosexist world has long held a monopoly on defining legal and ethical propriety, has long imposed its definitions on the rest of us, using them as weapons for keeping us in line by denying us access to knowledge of our own antecedents. Let heterosexism take the blame then if, having finally despaired of gaining that knowledge by humble petition through proper channels, we now turn, by default and in anger at the continuing impasse, to "improper" tactics. It seems better to stand accused of impropriety than to go on accepting someone else's right to control access to *our* heritage.

Power has created that "right" in the past. In the future, other claims to right must be pressed—like the right of a people to a knowledge of its own history (to *memory*)—an indispensable prerequisite for establishing collective identity and for enjoying the solace of knowing that we too have "come through", are bearers of a diverse, rich, unique heritage. To press those claims, it may be necessary to defy entrenched conventions and to risk the attendant consequences, professsional and legal, of doing so. Not the sort of thing one welcomes. But the alternative is still less palatable: to continue to accept and abide by anachronistic definitions of what constitutes "sensitive material" and "acceptable" areas of historical inquiry. To go that route is to collaborate in sustaining "things as they are"—to be complicitous, in sum, in our own oppression.

Journal of Homosexuality
Fall/Winter, 1980-81

NOTES

1. Thomas J. Withers to James H. Hammond, September 24, 1826, Hammond Papers, South Caroliniana Library, Columbia, S.C. The preceding quotations and paraphrases are from portions of his two letters not printed in this article.

2. Most of what is known about Withers can be found in two studies: William H. Freehling, *Prelude to Civil War: The Nullification Controversy in South Carolina, 1816-1836* (New York: Harper & Row, 1965); and Charles Robert Lee, Jr., *The Confederate Constitutions* (Chapel Hill: The University of North Carolina Press, 1963).

3. Lee, *op. cit.*, pp. 28, 71, 75, 135.

4. See, for example, Clement Eaton, *The Mind of the Old South* (Louisiana State University Press: 1964), p. 21.

5. For those interested, the following studies (along with those by Freehling and Eaton, already cited) are the most authoritative. For Hammond's political career: Charles S. Sydnor, *The Development of Southern Sectionalism* (Louisiana State University Press: 1948); Allan Nevins, *The Ordeal of the Union* and *The Emergence of Lincoln* (Scribners: 1947; 1950); Avery Craven, *The Growth of Southern Nationalism* (Louisiana State University Press: 1953); Holman Hamilton, *Prologue to Conflict* (University Press of Kentucky: 1964); and Steven A. Channing, *Crisis of Fear* (Simon & Schuster: 1970). For Hammond's economic views: David Bertelson, *The Lazy South* (Oxford: 1967); Robert S. Starobin, *Industrial Slavery in the Old South* (Oxford: 1970); Richard C. Wade, *Slavery in the Cities* (Oxford: 1964); R. R. Russel, *Economic Aspects of Southern Sectionalism* (University of Illinois Press: 1924); and Eugene Genovese, *The Political Economy of Slavery* (Pantheon: 1965).

For Hammond's theories on slavery (and his treatment of his own slaves): William S. Jenkins, *Pro-Slavery Thought in the Old South* (University of North Carolina Press: 1935); William Stanton, *The Leopard's Spots* (University of Chicago Press: 1960); Eugene Genovese, *The World the Slaveowners Made* and *Roll, Jordan, Roll* (Pantheon: 1969; 1974); Kenneth Stampp, *The Peculiar Institution* (Knopf: 1956); William Taylor, *Cavalier and Yankee* (Braziller: 1957); John Hope Franklin, *The Militant South* (Beacon: 1956); and Herbert G. Gutman, *The Black Family in Slavery and Freedom* (Pantheon: 1976).

6. For reasons explained in the article, I've excerpted and published here only the erotic portions of the two letters. The remaining material is at any rate of little historical interest, dealing as it does with various mundane matters—news of friends, complaints about the Boredom of Life, youthful pontifications on public events.

7. If Hammond's letter is extant, its whereabouts is unknown.

8. A leading figure in politics in the antebellum period.

9. Freehling contains the best description of South Carolina in this period and the life-style of its ruling elite (see *op. cit.*, especially pp. 11-24). Eaton is most helpful for biographical detail on Hammond himself. I've relied heavily on both books for the factual material in this section.

10. For additional details on Hammond's severity as a slaveowner, see Gutman, *op. cit.*, pp. 221-2; Freehling, *op. cit.*, pp. 68-71; and Genovese, *Roll*, p. 455, 561. For more on Hammond's skills as a planter, see Nevins, *Ordeal*, pp. 482-3.

11. Wade, *op. cit.*, p. 122; Gutman, *op. cit.*, pp. 62, 572.

12. Eaton's account (*op. cit.*, pp. 30 ff.), or perhaps the secret diary itself, is blurred on the central question of whether (and in what manner) Hammond's seduction "succeeded"—though the weight of the blurred evidence suggests it did.

13. Eaton, *op. cit.*, pp. 31-32.

14. The importance of regional variations in sexual mores is marginally confirmed in the linkage Walt Whitman made (in a letter to John Addington Symonds, Aug. 19, 1890): *My life, young manhood, mid-age,* times South [italics mine], *etc., have been jolly bodily. . .".* See also (for a later period) the references to the South in "Therapy and Bisexuality" p. 249.

15. Orlando Paterson (in his review of Bertram Wyatt Brown, *Southern Honor: Ethics and Behavior in the Old South,* in *Reviews In American History,* March 1984), makes this provocative comment: "There is not a single reference to homosexuality in the work. I draw attention to this not out of intellectual fashion, but simply because anyone acquainted with the comparative ethnohistory of honorific cultures will be immediately struck by it. Homosexuality is pronounced in such systems, both ancient and modern. Southern domestic life most closely resembles that of the Mediterranean in precisely those areas which are most highly conducive to homosexuality. Does the author's silence imply its absence in the prounounced male bonding of the Old South?"

16. This seems the appropriate point to thank several other people whose advice or expertise proved of critical importance: Jesse Lemisch, Joan Warnow, Jonathan Weiss, Eric Foner, Martin Garbus, and Ann Morgan Campbell. To prevent any one of them being held accountable for actions and decisions for which I alone am ultimately responsible, I deliberately refrain from specifying which individual gave what advice or recommended which line of strategy.

c. 1820

THE FEMALE HUSBAND

We have considerable historical documentation about women who dressed, worked, and lived their lives—and often passed—as men. We have considerably less evidence about their sexual and affectional histories. The document excerpted below goes some way towards broadening our knowledge in that area, though not as much as we might like. It is one the earliest records of "passing women", and among the richest in detail.

The selections below are taken from a rare forty page pamphlet, published in London about 1820 (the frontispiece has no date), entitled The Female Husband: The History of An Extraordinary Individual named James Allen, whose Sex Remained Undiscovered, although Married To A Woman, upwards of Twenty-one Years. *I found the pamphlet in the Countway Medical Library at Harvard, bound into a volume of other rare items under the collective title "The Collyer Pamphlets".*

No author is credited on the title page of The Female Husband. *But judging from internal evidence it was almost certainly written by a woman; in one place the context in which "our own sex" is mentioned is unmistakably meant to refer to the female sex. Explaining her motives for writing James Allen's story, the author cites the need to "correct the manifold misrepresentations" making the rounds in the "gossiping world," and also the wish to "gratify public curiosity as far as possibly can be done by a plain, correct and authentic narrative." Whether the author's stated motives were her strongest is dubious; the pamphlet clearly has a strong didactic purpose.*

James is frequently denounced for "his" perfidy, Abigail tirelessly defended for her loyalty, purity and innocence. Interestingly, most of the denunciations of James are for his being a typically deceiving man: "he" is made to stand as an exemplar of the immoral deceptions practiced by all men. Conversely, the author expresses scant sympathy or understanding of James' wish to "pass", or any acknowledgment that there is anything to understand—beyond recognizing God and Nature's inscrutable anomalies.

We will probably never know to what extent the narrative is authentic; the author cites no sources for her information beyond several hints that much of it came directly from Abigail Allen herself.

Possibly Abigail herself was the author, though given her limited education (at least as described in the pamphlet) and the elegant fluency of the writing, that possibility seems remote. At any rate, the narrative is engrossing, and I regret that limited space prevents me from excerpting larger portions.

In several places I've had to add a phrase or two to bridge the narrative gap, and to summarize information from those sections of the pamphlet not excerpted. Occasionally I've added a few words of comment to call attention to an off-hand remark in the text that seems to have wider significance than the author consciously intended. Both the bridging phrases and the occasional commentary have been bracketed. Otherwise the text is reproduced as it was printed, the vocabulary and grammar of the early 19th century, peculiar to our ears, left intact. I've not excerpted any part of the pamphlet's first ten pages, which describe James and Abigail's courtship; they are abstract, flowery, devoid of revealing detail. It is important to note, however, that the author does state early on, and thereafter frequently reiterates, her firm opinion that the couple had no sexual contact before their marriage in 1807, and that Abigail was utterly "deluded" as to her husband's gender.

We pick up the narrative on the first night of the couple's married life, spent at a "public house"—an inn—in Gray's Inn Lane, London:
. . . .

. . . .Shortly after they had retired to bed, James complained of being very unwell, alleging that he had taken something in the course of the day which had disagreed with him: he arose frequently during the night, and groaned and sighed much; so that his wife had not the most remote idea but that his illness was positively real. On the following night he still remained indisposed; the third day and night found him no better; and to this cause, and no other Mrs. A. now solemnly avers she imputed the total absence of any advances towards her. But, as a very singular coincidence, the bride was also suddenly and particularly indisposed on the evening of her marriage, which indisposition lasted the whole of the time she remained in London; so that instead of feeling any regret at her husband's supposed illness, she was secretly glad of that or any other cause that could relieve her from the embarrassment that must otherwise have ensued. The reader will therefore perceive that in the outset of this ill-starred union there was a most extraordinary coincidence of circumstances in favour of the wicked and unpardonable part which James Allen was at this time too successfully acting. On the morning of the 17th of December, Mrs. Allen after exchanging vows of eternal love with her new lord and master, left town for her situation at Margate, where she was to remain, as had been previously agreed upon, till he had obtained some furniture, &c. to enable them to begin life in a respectable and comfortable manner. Soon after his wife's departure, James hired himself as a groom to a gentleman of fortune, named Lonsdale, then residing at the Maze, Blackheath, where his clean personal appearance, obliging disposition, and extraordinary skill in horses, procured him the confidence and respect of his employer.

[*A month later, by mail, James informed Abigail of his intention to take a job aboard a ship bound for the East Indies.*]

Abigail received [*this news*] in a state of mind bordering on distraction.

[*Some six months later James wrote Abigail*] ... to give immediate warning to her employer, soliciting her forgiveness for past neglect, and begging of her to come to London at the expiration of her month, when she would find a home comfortably prepared for her, and hoping that all past uneasiness which he had occasioned her would be amply compensated by his future affection and attention to her interests ....

It was on the 12th of August, 1808, when Mrs. Allen came from Margate to London to join her fate, "for better or worse," with her future partner. She found him—but how?—not the smart and dapper groom she expected to have seen, but degenerated into a labourer to a noted cow-keeper of that day, named Ford, in the neighbourhood of Bermondsey ... James was not considered a strong young man; but what was wanting in this respect was sufficiently made up in activity and a devotion to the will of his employer, and the duties of his situation. He had contrived to furnish some apartments ... in a tolerably decent manner, in the house of a tradesman ... To this domicile Abigail accompanied him with a heart filled with affection ... But alas, soon was she miserably awakened to the deception practised upon her unsuspecting confidence: she arose from her bed on the following morning as unsullied a virgin as on the hour she first laid down on it. The remarkable aversion to coming in contact with her which he evinced during the night, but too far convinced her she had made an unhappy choice. The manifest embarrassment of her husband on the following day, his half smothered sighs, his face which betokened sorrow rather than cheerfulness, produced in her mind a compassion for him, which subdued all feelings of resentment for the injury which he too manifestly had inflicted upon her. Night after night but confirmed the revolting truth that she was condemned to the unnatural state of wedded widowhood . . . .ashamed even to her own father to confess her situation, much less expose her husband's conduct to a slandering world, she passed over her misfortunes in sorrowing silence, and never, till a very late period of his life as she now solemnly states, did she ever utter a syllable of reproach to the author of her sufferings, and then only in answer to a charge which he brought against her fidelity to him.

James's voice, like his features, were strictly feminine; added to which, the total absence of those distinguishing marks of manhood, the whiskers and beard, excited in the minds of the workmen a suspicion that he laboured under some defect of nature, and, in short, that he was of that rare and peculiar class of human beings who have no positive claim to either sex. This suspicion was not a little increased by the aversion he ever shewed to join either in their cups, their rude sports, or in that empty and lewd conversation so generally prevalent among the lower class of workmen—this modesty being a trait peculiar to his character through life . . . .

But . . . a terrible alteration was manifest in the temper of James; he betrayed an unusual nervousness, and he became suddenly inaccessible, and generally soured in his manners. It was at this time that his wife first perceived the symptoms of a change in his treatment of her—from the most friendly, confiding, and affectionate terms, he was altered to an ill-natured and suspicious being . . . .

James Allen was an habitual smoker of tobacco when at his own fire-side, and while at labour he chewed it. These habits conferred on his features a coarse and anti-feminine tinge . . . Another trait in James's character was the aversion which he frequently expressed of seeing females carry loads; he would, upon seeing women on such occasions, express himself in angry terms upon the unnatural imposition, and frequently take the burden upon himself.

His wife affirms most seriously, that if by accident she approached him when he was to all appearance asleep, he was immediately aroused, and placed himself in an attitude of security; and she deemed herself fortunate if she escaped his marked anger. Again: many inquiries are made how it was she did not show the very natural resentment of her sex and insist upon a fair explanation of his situation . . . .—to which we answer, his superior size and strength was at all times sufficient to keep her in awe; and upon her shewing anything like a spirit of insubordination, he became violent, and did not hesitate to strike her, particularly towards the close of his life. Another effectual bar to the possibility of accident, circumstances ever favouring his disposition, to "make assurance doubly sure," was the manner in which he was swathed with belts of flannel, drawers, under-waistcoats, &c., under the specious pretence, that flannel was essential to secure him from the effects of cold, being, as his wife well knew, in the constant habit of going up to his waist in water, by night and day. But the circumstance which was doubtless James Allen's best security in that respect was the settled opinion which his wife arrived at upon the subject of his supposed infirmities; and, as she solemnly declares, never having, at any period of her life, for a moment supposed that he was positively and perfectly of her own sex. So that our readers will perceive, that, in the outset of their association, shame and a sense of delicacy, not altogether without a feeling of commiseration, barred her utterance; the friendly and affectionate manner in which he demeaned himself towards her for a series of years, his solicitude to provide for her, by working late and early, and his general kindness, as evinced in a thousand ways, won upon her gratitude, and to such an extent, that she made a vow to heaven, that come what might, she would never disclose her situation to the last hour of her life; and this she affirms she never would have done, had not the melancholy accident which hurried him out of the world disclosed the secret for her ...

[*And so the relationship continued—for more than twenty years. Then one day—*] ... James, as a temporary act of kindness to the regular sawyer, descended into the sawpit to assist in severing a log of fir ... it rolled off the supports, and fell into the pit;—there was no escaping; he was struck on the head ... he uttered a faint cry, feebly raising his hand, but it was his last struggle .... The fatal news was quickly carried to his wife, who left her home in the most frantic manner ... being actuated, as she says, by a desire to prevent any public exposure of his person, believing, as she did then, and all through life, the deceased to have been an "Hermaphrodite," and feeling an anxiety to prevent the scandal inevitable upon such a discovery.

The body was consigned to the dead-room, where it was stripped by the female friends of Mrs. Allen, and at this juncture was the astounding discovery of the sex of this extraordinary person first made. They, (the females above alluded to) hastened to Mrs. Allen, and informed her of the strange circumstance; and she now in the most solemn manner that a human being can assert a truth avers, and will willingly make oath, at any time, that she was, till this period, in entire ignorance of the fact of James Allen being actually a woman.

The first view of the body excited very general admiration as to the symmetrical proportions of the entire subject. As fine a formed woman was presented to their eyes as ever was looked upon. The skin, having been swathed with bandages and other thick coverings, was of the purest white, intersected with veins of fine blue. The arms, legs, hips, & c. exhibiting the truest female proportions. As a striking contrast to the general beauty of the person, was remarked, the colour of the face and roughness of the hands, occasioned by the deceased's anti-feminine habits. The breasts, which were moderately full, were forced, by the compression of the bandages, under the armpits . . . .

[*A postmortem on the body was then done*] As the chief object of this examination was to observe whether there existed any impediment to the functions of nature; the most minute attention was paid to the organs of generation, which was found to be entire and perfect, with the exception of the absence of certain symbols of purity [an intact hymen?], on which some of the gentlemen present declared their perfect conviction that she had been ill-treated at an early period of life. The funeral took place in the cemetry of St. John's . . . and was conducted with the greatest decency, but for the brutal and inhuman attacks upon the widow, by a set of ignorant beings of the very lowest class, who chose to form their own uncharitable opinions [lesbianism?] of the affair and act accordingly; the presence of the proper officers, however, kept them in awe; and Mrs. Allen escaped, but not without having menaces of the most daring nature thrown out by the rabble who followed her back . . . .

The deceased . . . belonged to a benefit society; it was that noble institution, "The Associated Brethren," and it is in justice due to its members and officers to state, they they never objected to pay the funeral allowance, as was falsely reported; on the contrary, Mrs. Allen was immediately paid the full sum . . . .

Of the culpability of James Allen's conduct in the outset of his married career there cannot be two opinions. The secret motives of the heart which induced so unnatural a resolve is now laid open before the tribunal of his Creator; but since it was the errors, of a human being, and perhaps a deeply injured one, subject to all the frailties of humanity, as fellow-mortals, we are bound to balance the merits against the faults; and throw the pall of charity over her remains and "No farther seek her merits to disclose, Or draw her frailties from their dread abode."

THE END

[*There follows this postscript*]

...Mrs. Allen is said to have discontinued the name of Allen, and taken her maiden name...[*This was false*] She retains that of Allen. It [*a newspaper article*] also asserts roundly, that the deceased had given birth to a child, now living, and upwards of twenty years of age. We have the evidence of Dr. Paul, the eminent surgeon, who has assured us most positively, that not the slightest proof existed upon the post mortem examination of the body, to induce a belief that the deceased had ever borne one ...

1878

THE PERILS OF MASTURBATION

Certain subjects being timeless, we take as our text for today's lesson Dr. N. Emmons Paine's 1878 essay, "Masturbators,and What Shall Be Done With Them." Dr. Paine was an attending physician (not a patient) at the New York State Homoeopathic Insane Asylum. His essay first appeared in The Transactions of the Homoeopathic Medical Society of the State of New York, *a publication that—for those with a lurid cast of mind—can be read in its entirety in the archives of the New York Academy of Medicine.*

Gigglers be forewarned: Dr. Paine was no freakish crank: views such as his were commonplace among physicians in Victorian America and, in modified form, still have residual influence.Think, if you will, of today's priests or athletic coaches admonishing their flocks to practice continence, drawing direct equations between "spilling one's seed" and, respectively, wanton sin or loss of"vitality." Think, too, if you can—the exercise will probably come easiest to those over 40—or those unbidden spasms of guilt that tend to accompany any prolonged bouts of "self-pleasuring."

MASTURBATORS, AND WHAT SHALL BE DONE WITH THEM
by Dr. N. Emmons Paine

There are two classes of masturbators. The first class claims all those who do or have practiced this vice, provided they have will power enough to exercise a general self-restraint. (They are liable to pass on this aberration to their children.) The great ... majority will marry and in that probability lies the danger to the coming generation. On them should be directed all efforts toward reformation and repurification.

The second class includes those who are or have become unable to exercise self-restraint. This inability may be an inheritance of excessive passion or weakness of the will, or it may be due to a morbidly excited condition consequent upon long indulgence. In this class the individual may yet adhere to his vocation; or steady work and study may have become impossible; or dementia may have already grasped its victim.

They are mostly young men who later, will be claimed by religious melancholia or some other form of insanity, or suicide, unless the advance in this wrong direction be checked.

It is only by early instruction of the young that this great evil can or will be stamped out, by preventing its inception. Now, after the practice has been commenced, the wrong doer must still be advised of his guilt and warned of his danger. Bed fellows are often of great service in strengthening good resolutions during the night—the most dangerous time ... [If this and other methods fail] they fall under our second class, and enter the wards of an asylum.

It cannot, by any means, be stated that, in every case of insanity in which masturbation co-exists, that insanity has been caused by it. In some, this incessant drain upon the nervous system has undermined the mental structure, and it has reeled and collapsed in utter dementia. In other cases, there has been an unusual excitement of certain functions and organs ... patients may not appear to be very insane, and many would question the propriety of their removal to an asylum, but their disease is obstinate and intractable, and the physician's patience and skill are tried beyond belief. Just as soon as any symptoms of mental aberration appear, in addition to a strong suspicion of masturbation, the family physician should send his patient to an asylum. (If the patient lacks the will power, he may need mechanical restraints.) Drugs cannot be relied on to purify the imagination or to subdue this terrible, all compelling desire; and they are ... next to useless.

The latest form of restraint is a protector. This garment is made of canvas, reaching from the lower part of the sternum down to just above the knee, and fitting the form quite closely. An opening behind extends downward to the sacrum. At the proper place a hole, three-and-one-half inches in diameter, is cut in the canvas to allow the penis and scrotum to pass through into a tin receiver. This apparatus allows the use of the hands, but prevents their reaching the dangerous parts. The brass loops behind do not permit the patients to lie comfortably on the back, and thus it acts as a preventive and cure at the same time.

If necessary, it could be used at times in private practice. If mechanical restraints ... prove impotent to check the downward rush, one more and last resource remains, and that is castration. If the patient is already far advanced in dementia, even castration would be useless, as the brain change would be too serious to allow a return to a healthy mental condition. [Castration is necessary in others who are not as demented] who may marry and ... multiplying in the children the sins of their parents, swelling the already overstocked ranks of poverty, prostitution and vice. It is not claimed that castration would remedy all the evil, but it certainly would suppress one of the common sources of crime.

It is opposed by hopeless parents who cannot realize the debased condition of their offspring ... or the advantages of a removal of the disturbing element ... a law should be made requiring the Super-intendent of the State Insane Asylum to operate in those cases in which the result would be beneficial. Such a law would accomplish more good than any medicine or any form of mechanical restraint and certainly more than in allowing these cases to glide along into incurable dementia.

1880

UNCENSORING THE MOUNTAIN CHANT

History and anthropology have established traditions of primly evading or smugly distorting the study of sexual behavior; nowhere more so than in their accounts of American Indian culture. I give one such example in the article on page 000, where I introduce new documentation on Hopi transvestism. Here is a second example, this time regarding Navajo sexuality.

In 1887, the respected ethnographer, Dr. Washington Mathews, published his pamphlet, The Mountain Chant, *which summed up his research on that celebrated Navajo ritual. The text contains the curt remark that "Parts of the 'Mountain Chant' have not been allowed to appear in this essay", strongly suggesting censorship—and pique. Apparently Dr. Mathews did not take kindly to having the integrity of his findings tampered with.*

Nor did he let the situation go uncorrected for long. In 1892, five years after the appearance of the first pamphlet, Dr. Mathews circulated a three-page transcript (printed below in its entirety) containing the previously suppressed material. I discovered the transcript while doing research in the National Anthropological Files of the Smithsonian Institute in Washington, D.C. An anonymous Smithsonian archivist had attached a "puzzled" note to the transcript warning that no corroboration had turned up for Mathews' glancing reference to having extracted the three pages from a second pamphlet on "The Mountain Chant." The Smithsonian noted that it had been unable to locate a single reference anywhere to such a pamphlet, not even in Elsbeth E. Freudenthal's comprehensive "Catalogue of the Washington Mathews Collection at the Museum of Navajo Ceremonial Art, Santa Fe, New Mexico, July 1951." The three-page typescript, the Smithsonian concluded, "had been prepared from [an] unidentified original."

Strange goings-on, for the world of scholarly politesse. *Hints of falsified formats (that non-existent "second pamphlet"), illicit stratagems and curious contentions—hints so bare as to preclude additional speculation. But not fantasies. My own favorite—herewith irresponsibly offered—is of an embittered and stubborn Dr. Mathews, finally deciding after brooding for five years on the suppression of his research, to defy the censors and to release the interdicted material himself in the form of a three-page transcript masquerading as an extract from a longer "pamphlet."*

A fantasy. But it is factual to claim that the suppressed portions of
the Mountain Chant printed below provide suggestive new perspectives on Navajo sexuality in particular and, more generally—as if
further confirmation were needed—on the history of suppression
illustrative of the sex-negative bias long dominant in the social
sciences. That bias, reflective of the mainstream culture's values, still
holds sway—still keeps a prim veil drawn over the exploration and
discussion of materials relating to sexual behavior, ritual, and
ideology. It does this to the impoverishment of us all, regardless of
our sexual orientation.

The Suppressed Part of
"The Mountain Chant"

I. After paragraph 130, p. 433, of "The Mountain Chant
[Mathews' original pamphlet]," read the following:

While the dancers are circling around the fire in the dance of
Nahikai, if one is found in a stooping or kneeling attitude before the
fire, trying to burn the down on his wand, another may come up
behind him, mount him, and imitate, without actual pederasty, the
pederastic motions of an erotic dog. While thus engaged a third
dancer may mount the second and a fourth may mount the third and
enact a like play, just as a number of dogs are often seen engaged.

Sometimes one or more of the actors wear a large imitation penis,
made of rags or inflated sheep-gut; such may enact the part of dogs,
feign to masturbate or to manipulate the part to produce erection.

Sometimes, when the down has been burned from the wand and
before it has been restored, they treat the wand as if it were a penis;
hold it erect or semi-erect between the thighs, rub it and manipulate it.
This is done mostly by the last remaining dancers, who effect to have
difficulty in restoring the down to the ends of their wands.

Their motions are of such a nature that many white spectators of
this play have conjectured that the dance of Nahikai is symbolic of the
sexual act; that the down on the wand represents the desire which is
destroyed in the flame of gratification, and, with trouble, restored;
and this seems not an unreasonable conjecture.

II. After paragraph 145, p. 441, of "The Mountain Chant," read
the following:

That portion of the drama which succeeds the finding of the

hoshkawn or yucca, I have seen enacted with varying detail and dialogue, but with the essential parts always similar. To preserve the unity, I will describe it as seen on the night of November 5th, 1882.

Dramatis Personae. The old hunter and the man dressed as a woman, who will be referred to as He and She.

He: Come, my wife, I have found something good. This is what I have looked for. Are you not glad I have found it?

She: Yes, I am very glad, my sweet.

He: It tastes like you. (He gives her a piece to eat.)

She:—It is sweet, but not as sweet as you.

(After this compliment he draws close to her and begins to dally, not over decently. One act is to put his hand under her clothes, withdraw it, and smell it. At length he puts his hand in at the neck of her dress as if to feel her bosom and draws forth a handkerchief hidden there. He becomes furious.)

He (Squealing in feeble wrath): Where did you get this?

She: My aunt lost it at the spring and, when I went for water, I found it there.

He: I don't believe you! You have been cohabiting with someone else. This is your pay.

She: No, truly, my aunt lost it.

He: (Still in a jealous fury, lights a cigarette and tries to smoke, presently throws cigarette peevishly away): I will go away and never see you again.

She: Don't leave! Don't leave! You are a fool!

He: Yes, I know it; but I will be one no longer. Now I go away. (He moves off.)

She (Pouts a moment, then takes a pinch of dust in her fingers, blows it toward him and says): Thus do I blow away my regard for you. I will follow you no more.

(With head averted, and sitting, she watches him furtively till he shuffles off out of sight, among the crowd of spectators; then she runs after him and soon reappears dragging him back.)

He: You were not strong enough to blow me away, I am so sweet. (Again they sit side by side and indulge in dalliance and loud kisses.)

He: I don't like you to cohabit with others while I am away hunting. I find you food and sweet things to eat, but you are bad.

She: Do not leave me. I will never touch another man again. (They eat together of the yucca fruit.)

He: How sweet this fruit is! Let us see which is the sweeter, this or coition. (Each puts a piece in the mouth and they proceed with the most complete realism of action, but without exposure, to imitate the sexual act. When through, he tumbles off with a groan as if completely exhausted.)

She (Spitting the fruit from her mouth): The hoshkawn is sweet, but not half so sweet as what we have been doing. (She rises, takes a handful of dust from the ground, and acts as if scattering it on the vulva. They put the fruit into the basket and depart.)

The spectators of this scene are persons of both sexes—married and unmarried—of all ages; a most promiscuous audience.

The act of dusting the vulva I have heard of as done by Indian women of other tribes in the arid region after the act of coition al fresco.

The dialogue given above was obtained for me by Mr. A. M. Stephen of Keam's Canyon, Arizona, who witnessed with me the night ceremonies of November 5th, 1882, and next day, learned the words of the play from the man who enacted the part of the woman. I have since heard other versions of the dialogue, but none superior to this.

W. M.
[Washington Mathews]

1881

WATER SPORTS

Captain John C. Bourke, a member of the Third Cavalry under the leadership of General Sheridan, was stationed in the southwestern territories in 1881-2. Having an interest in ethnology, he used his spare time to gather materials relating to "the manners and usages of the Indians" in the region, particularly the Pueblos. Many years later, in 1920, Bourke privately published a seven-page pamphlet about "one of the most curious rites" of the Indians he had studied; its title was "The Urine Dance of the Zuni Indians of New Mexico." Sternly printed at the top of the pamphlet were the words "NOT FOR GENERAL PERUSAL." Bourke saw himself as a scholar (he became a Fellow of the American Association for the Advancement of Science, and a member of the Anthropological Society of Washington, D.C.) and intended his pamphlet for distribution only among other scholars. Perhaps for that reason, the pamphlet is exceedingly rare.

Fascinated with his newfound subject, Bourke spent much of the 1880s extending and broadening his investigations. The result was a second, much longer (fifty-six pages) pamphlet of more wide-ranging scope, entitled "Human Ordure and Human Urine in Rites of a Religious or Semi-Religious Character among Various Nations" (1888). It too is rare (I discovered it in the Smithsonian), in the double sense of "uncommon" and "choice."

The materials below are excerpted entirely from Bourke's first pamphlet, "The Urine Dance." The opening section contains an insouciant description of the Feast of Fools, a rite widespread in Continental Europe for some 1,500 years, not ending in France until the Revolution: "the principal actors (taking possession of the church during high mass) had their faces daubed and painted ... were dressed as clowns or as women ... ate upon the altar itself sausages and blood-puddings. The word blood-pudding, in French is boudin — *but* boudin *also meant excrement ... after leaving the church [they] took their stand in dung-carts and threw* ordure *upon the bystanders ... some of these actors appeared perfectly naked." Both fans ("absolutely original") and foes ("absolutely disgusting") of Pasolini's* Salo *might wish to alter their evaluations.*

The second pamphlet, not reprinted here, contains an irresistible discussion of "Chinook Olives"—acorns soaked for five months in human urine. The dish is considered a supreme delicacy by certain peoples, but palates being variable, different groups prefer to ingest their urine in different forms: the Mokis of Arizona mix it into bread; the Indians of Bogota serve it, combined with palm scrapings, as salt; and so on.

The Urine Dance of the Zuni Indians of New Mexico

On the evening of November 17, 1881, during my stay in the village of Zuni, New Mexico, the *Nehue-Cue,* one of the secret orders of the Zunis, sent word to Mr. F. Cushing (whose guest I was) that they would do us the unusual honor of coming to our house to give us one of their characteristic dances, which, Cushing said, was unprecedented.

The squaws of the Governor's family put the long "living room" to rights, sweeping the floor and sprinkling it with water to lay the dust. Soon after dark, the dancers entered; they were twelve in number, two being boys. The center men were naked with the exception of black breech-clouts of archaic style. The hair was worn naturally with a bunch of wild turkey feathers tied in front, and one of corn-husks over each ear. White bands were painted across the face at eyes and mouth. Each wore a collar or neckcloth of black woolen stuff. Broad white bands, one inch wide, were painted around the body at the navel, around the arms, the legs at mid-thighs and knees. Tortoise-shell rattles hung from the right knee. Blue woolen footless leggins were worn with low-cut moccasins, and in the right hand each waved a wand made of an ear of corn, trimmed with the plumage of the wild turkey and macaw. The others were arrayed in old cast-off American army clothing and all wore white cotton night-caps, with corn-husks twisted into the hair at top of head and ears. Several wore, in addition to the tortoise-shell rattles, strings of brass sleigh-bells at knees. One was more grotesquely attired than the rest in a long India-rubber gossamer "over all" and a pair of goggles, painted white, over his eyes. His general "get-up" was a spirited take-off upon a Mexican priest. Another was a very good counterfeit of a young woman.

To the accompaniment of an oblong drum, and of the rattles and bells spoken of, they shuffled into the long room, crammed with spectators of both sexes, and of all sizes and ages. Their song was apparently a ludicrous reference to everything and everybody in sight, Cushing, Mendeleff, and myself receiving special attention, to the uncontrolled merriment of the red-skinned listeners. I had taken my station at one side of the room, seated upon the banquette, and having in front of me a rude bench or table upon which was a small coal-oil lamp. I suppose that in the halo diffused by the feeble light and in my "stained-glass attitude" I must have borne some resemblance to the pictures of saints hanging upon the walls of old Mexican churches; to such a fancied resemblance I at least attribute the performance which followed.

The dancers suddenly wheeled into line, threw themselves on their knees before my table, and with extravagant beatings of breast began an outlandish but faithful mockery of a Mexican Catholic congregation at vespers. One bawled out a parody upon the Pater Noster, another mumbled long in the manner of an old man reciting the rosary, while the fellow with the India-rubber coat jumped up and began a passionate exhortation or sermon, which for mimetic fidelity was inimitable. This kept the audience laughing with sore sides for some moments, until at a signal from the leader the dancers suddenly countermarched out of the room, in single file, as they had entered.

An interlude followed of ten minutes, during which the dusty floor was sprinkled by men who spat water forcibly from their mouths. The *Nehue-Cue* re-entered; this time two of their number were stark naked. Their singing was very peculiar and sounded like a chorus of chimney sweeps, and their dance became a stiff-legged jump, with heels kept twelve inches apart. After they had ambled around the room two or three times, Cushing announced in the Zuni language that a "feast" was ready for them, at which they loudly roared their approbation and advanced to strike hands with the munificent "Americanos," addressing us in a funny gibberish of broken Spanish, English, and Zuni. They then squatted upon the ground and consumed with zest large "ollas" full of tea, and dishes of hard tack and sugar. As they were about finishing this a squaw entered, carrying an "olla" of urine, of which the filthy brutes drank heartily.

I refused to believe the evidence of my senses, and asked Cushing if that were really human urine. "Why, certainly," replied he, "and here comes more of it." This time, it was a large tin pailfull, not less than two gallons. I was standing by the squaw as she offered this strange and abominable refreshment. She made a motion with her hand to indicate to me that it was urine, and one of the old men repeated the Spanish word *mear* (to urinate), while my sense of smell demonstrated the truth of their statements.

The dancers swallowed great draughts, smacked their lips, and, amid the roaring merriment of the spectators, remarked that it was very, very good. The clowns were now upon their mettle, each trying to surpass his neighbors in feats of nastiness. One swallowed a fragment of corn-husk, saying he thought it very good and better than bread; his vis-a-vis attempted to chew and gulp down a piece of filthy rag. Another expressed regret that the dance had not been held out of doors, in one of the plazas; there they could show what they could do. There they always made it a point of honor to eat the excrement of men and dogs.

For my own part I felt satisfied with the omission, particularly as the room, stuffed with one hundred Zunis, had become so foul and filthy as to be almost unbearable. The dance, as good luck would have it, did not last many minutes, and we soon had a chance to run into the refreshing night air.

To this outline description of a disgusting rite I have little to add. The Zunis, in explanation, stated that the *Nehue-Cue* were a Medicine Order which held these dances from time to time to inure the stomach of members to any kind of food, no matter how revolting. This statement may seem plausible enough when we understand that religion and medicine among primitive races are almost always one and the same thing, or at least, so closely intertwined that it is a matter of difficulty to decide where one begins and the other ends.

Religion in its dramatic ceremonial preserves is, to some extent, the history of the particular race in which it dwells. Among nations of high development, miracles, moralities, and passion plays have taught, down to our own day, in object lessons, the sacred history in which the spectators believed. Some analogous purpose may have been held in view by the first organizers of the urine dance. In their early history, the Zunis and the other Pueblos suffered from constant warfare with savage antagonists and with each other. From the position of their villages, long sieges must of necessity have been sustained, in which sieges, famines and disease, no doubt, were the allies counted upon by the investing forces. We may have in this abominable dance a tradition of the extremity to which the Zunis of the long ago were reduced at some unknown period.

INTIMACY WITHOUT ORGASM

We gay men often congratulate ourselves on the quality of our friendships. We talk about how supportive we are of each other (unlike straight males), how we're there in time of need ("substitute family," etc.). We also talk about our physical openness, how we're able—again in contrast to uptight straight men—to express our affection through touching, kissing, hugging. There may well be some basis for this self-congratulation, but it isn't firm enough to justify the chauvinistic smugness that often accompanies it. That gay friends treat each other better and are physically more affectionate than their straight counterparts has hardened into dogma. Scrutiny of that dogma is overdue.

One way to begin is to look at male friendship from a historical perspective—a suggestion, I realize, that is likely to produce instant yawns, history being for most Americans a subject devoid of charm, excitement and relevance. But bear with me. I hope to change your minds—with a little help from a remarkable unpublished diary that I recently discovered. The diary's most significant entries (for our purposes) date from the 1880s, and they provide some startling standards against which to measure our own presumed "enlightened" attitudes and behavior. To help set the stage, a few words about the context in which the diary was written, and about the man who wrote it: The diary, kept for some 50 years (1870s-1920s) by a minor writer named F.S. Ryman, is of enormous size, length, and potential historical importance. It consists of some forty folio volumes (each one roughly three times the size of a typical hardcover book today) and was in private hands until the early 1970s when it was acquired by the Massachusetts Historical Society (M.H.S.), one of the country's great archives for unpublished historical manuscripts.

That the Ryman diary ended up at M.H.S. was for me a piece of good luck. I'd spent many years working there on two of my early books (biographies of Charles Francis Adams and James Russell Lowell) and thus knew the staff well. It was lucky for me, too, that when I reappeared at M.H.S. in 1977, Stephen T. Riley was still its director. Riley is an uncommonly open man, and when I told him I was in search of previously unknown source materials on the history of sexuality, he gave me free run of the stacks, allowing me to peer into all those fiercely labelled boxes ("RESTRICTED! NO AC-

CESS!") ordinarily closed to researchers.

To call this "good luck" is an understatement—as anyone will confirm who has tried to do research in sexual history. Riley not only allowed me to browse freely, but went out of his way to bring to my attention certain special and uncatalogued items I might otherwise have missed—such as the Ryman diary. I remember the mischievous twinkle in his eyes when he pointed down the shelf toward the formidable set of bound volumes. "Those ought to have some material of interest for you."

Ah, New England understatement! The early (1880-1895) Ryman diaries turned out to be filled with detailed accounts of the erotic adventures and fantasies of their lusty young author. These accounts are almost all rigorously—roisterously—heterosexual. On the face of it that would seem to make them of limited interest to gay readers, but, as I hope to demonstrate, the opposite is true.

Apart from the evidence in the diaries of his rich libidinous life, we know surprisingly little about this man, F.S. Ryman. For all their enormous length, the diaries record almost nothing of the ordinary details of Ryman's life. (Sex, for him, was not ordinary.) Though I've read through the entire diary, I'm still able to provide only a skeleton biography:

Ryman was born in 1858 in Pennsylvania. His father was a farmer; of his mother we know nothing. Ryman did have considerable schooling, including some college education (though he never graduated). His ambition was to be a writer, but grandiose claims far outpaced perfc ·mance. He did have a few poems published in small town papers while still in his twenties; thereafter he published and produced little. Nor does Ryman ever seem to have worked steadily at any other job; apparently he had a small inheritance and occasionally pursued "business ventures", all of which failed. From 1882 to 1884 he lived in Cortland, New York, then in Catskill-on-Hudson, finally settling in Boston, where, in his thirties, he married.

Ryman's early diaries (especially those from the 1880s) are the more historically important ones. They reveal an earthy, lively, sensuous young man of "advanced opinions" (and particularly advanced on the rights of women). Part of what makes Ryman's early diaries significant is the frequency with which they record his erotic adventures; this, and the casual tone he uses in describing them, imply that such adventures were nothing out of the ordinary—hardly the standard image we have of small town prudery in late nineteenth-century America. The Ryman diaries are bound to become a prime

new document fueling the debate already raging among historians of
the Victorian period about the country's libidinous habits. That
debate, in brief, centers on whether the "prescriptive" literature of the
period—official marriage manuals and the like—reflects the actual
behavior of the citizenry or merely the official code of morality.
Ryman's early diaries are important for still other reasons. Amidst a
tidal wave of entries about heterosexual exploits, they contain a few
descriptions of same-gender love and lust—few, but immensely
suggestive. In both tone and content these entries throw into question
conventional wisdom on a number of important topics: how "gay"
men were regarded by "straight" friends; the extent to which gay men
tried to conceal their orientation; whether straight men were ever
themselves conscious of physical attraction to members of their own
gender, and how they viewed that attraction. But perhaps many will
find most fascinating of all those excerpts which relate to another
subject entirely: the quality and expression of male/male hetero-
sexual friendships. The diary entries describing Ryman and his friend
Rob may shatter the glib assumption that we gays live in "superior"
times—and in superior ways.

I have kept Ryman's punctuation and grammar intact.

Nov 15 1885
Catskill-on-the-Hudson:
Jim Asher & O.L.F——[last name—Fuller—has been blacked
out] called on me today. F. [Fuller] gave me Hell for being so fierce
for the women & then he went on to express his own disgust for all
things pertaining to sexual intercourse & he also talked vilely about
passionate women.

... all praise & preach what their own passions demand. F. is as
consistent as anyone. He told me in so many words one day that he is
a "C—-sucker" & that he loves & enjoys that d--d custom so revolting
to every right minded person & yet he thought I suppose that he was
beautifully consistent to-day in giving me the devil for my amours. Of
course he only knows of my loves in a general way but he seems to
never tire of slurring me as a "Byron", a "Don Juan" etc.

No truly passionate person says aught against passion & how
tired it does make one to hear the d--d passionless fools talk against
the only thing that ever did or could form the basis of a great &
powerful character. F-- was horrified at me almost when I told him

that I would be willing to sign my soul over to the devil at the end of five years to burn as long as he liked if in the interim I could have any & all women that I desired to enjoy as much as I liked. Passion is the only pleasure of life worth naming.

3 May, 1886

While walking down to Lewiston I saw one of the prettiest boys I ever saw in my life. It is next to never that beauty in my own sex attracts me but he was beautiful. He was about 13 I should say tall & trim for a boy of that age. He was very ragged. He & his little brother & sister I guess they were in the woods along the top of the bluff about 2 or 3 miles below Suspension Bridge. I think he had no shirt on but he held his head & shoulders so gracefully & he was so polite that I was truly charmed with him. The children all seemed rather afraid of me when they first saw me as I had a stick in my hand & looked rough & dirty I suppose from tramping. They started off rather as if they were going to run but I called to them that I would not hurt them & then my pet as I will call him stopped & acted rather ashamed till I came up with them & asked them about the distance to Lewiston, Youngstown, etc. etc. I would like to see that boy when he is about 19. I'll bet he will be a veritable Apollo in form & face. I cannot tell why I was so attracted by him. He & Fred Squires are about the only male beings now living whose beauty I ever gave a second thought & I think the Apollo Belvedere is the only statue of a male figure that ever impressed me in the least & that did thrill me through & through ... It is said I believe that there is something feminine not effeminate about the face of every great man nearly. I think I would say face and features.

Aug, 1886

Rob [Robert M. Luke] came over to stay with me last night. I have slept with him many a night at the American Hotel [where Rob was a clerk] but last night was his first night with me. Though a man & his wife moved into the next room yesterday for a short time Rob & I had a good time talking to-gether concerning our lives loves etc. I confess I like the oriental custom of men embracing & kissing each other if they are indeed dear friends. When we went to bed Rob put his arms around me & lay his head down by my right shoulder in the most loving way & then I put my arms around his neck & thus clasped in each others arms we talked for a long time till we were ready to go to sleep & then we separated as I cannot sleep good with anyone near me. This a.m. Rob got up to go at 5 o'clock & as he was starting he came to the bed & threw his arms around my neck & we kissed each other good bye though I expect to see him again to-day. Now in all this I am certain there was no sexual sentiment on the part of either of us. We both have our mistresses whom we see with reasonable regularity & I am certain that the thought of the least demonstration of unmanly & abnormal passion would have been as revolting to him as it is & ever has been to me, & yet I do love him & I loved to hug & kiss him because of the goodness & genius I find in his mind. Christ kissed & embraced those whom he loved I believe & why shall I fear to do the same?[1]

Sept 30, 1886
Rob Luke is one G-d d——d good fellow I think. I truly love him. He gave me his picture to-night & as I left him he took my right hand in his & quick as thought put it up to his lips & kissed it before I knew it hardly. I am truly proud to be so loved by any one & especially by one whom I can love & respect in return as I certainly do him.

Oct 7th 1886
Rob is Twenty two to-day ... Rob came up to the room with me & sat awhile. I read Byrons Dream aloud to him. I was sorry he could not stay all night but he could not so I had to part with him.

Nov 2, 1886
Last night about midnight Rob Luke came over to the house. I was in bed asleep but he called & I got up & went down & let him in. He threw his arms around my neck & kissed me as soon as I opened the door. By God I do love Rob no use of talking. He bunked with me & says he is doing well in Rochester. I am so glad. He is grand.

Nov. 1886
I am going to introduce Fred Squires & Rob Luke to each other by letter. How dear they both are to me. I truly love them not as ideals or instructors for I am much older than either of them [Ryman was 28; the "boy" Rob, 22] but as true noble boys worthy of the love of the best men & women.

(1891)
... received from Rob's wife (Edith) a letter stating that he was buried one week ago today [May 4] in Cold Spring Cemetery at Lockport N.Y. He was indeed very dear to me & I miss him very much but I hope & can believe that he has only added one more link

to the infinite Chain of Life & that grief is indeed uncalled for & inappropriate...

It should be said, first of all, that we have so little evidence about the history of intimacy that we can't presume anything about how representative or unique the two men's behavior was for their time, place, age, and class. Still, it takes no scholar to recognize that the excerpts from Ryman's diary raise unexpected, disquieting questions.

When was the last time any of us, like Ryman one hundred years ago, slept cuddled in the arms of a close friend—a friend, not a lover, not a trick? When was the last time we fantasized about doing so? How many of us have ever done so, or ever fantasized about it? If, like me, your answers to the above questions are "never," "never," and "rarely," my guess is you're mainstream male, gay or straight— though I'd also guess more gays than straights take for granted certain limited expressions of physical affection—touching, kissing, hugging—with their friends (with bare acquaintances, in kissy-poo Manhattan).

But lying passionately clasped all night in a close friend's arms, replete with open declarations of love, an exchange of pictures, the impulsive kissing of hands? No, that's behavior we associate with lovers, either the long-term live-in variety or one-night infatuations. The lines we draw between "friendly" and "erotic" gestures may be as blurred as they are artificial. A peck on the lips, a hug at the door, occasional handholding while walking—these are considered "suitable"—appropriate—expressions of friendship, at least within the confines of a gay subculture. But change those gestures slightly, accentuate or prolong them (a passionate kiss), and the ambience shifts from affection to lust, from generalized warmth to erotic arousal. For us, that is. Evidently not for Ryman and Rob. It would seem that comparable gestures can decisively shift their symbolic meaning in the course of one hundred years, can "signify" quite different emotions during different eras.

How "prudish," then, were the Victorians? How "liberated" are we? On the basis of the Ryman diary—and keeping in mind the danger of overgeneralizing from a single source—we are now able at least to say that some 19th-century men were (contrary to the traditional view) remarkably full and unselfconscious in physically expressing affection for each other. By contrast, today many gay men seem able to give freely of their loins to strangers, but are far more chary than Ryman and Rob of giving freely of their affection to friends. Perhaps what's been involved is a tradeoff, not (as some glib liberationists would have it) an advance. It's possible we're "freer" than ever before sexually with members of our own gender—but more emotionally constricted. A still gloomier assessment would go further: we have lost the capacity for intimacy, physical or emotional. If so, "sexual liberation" may be a gruesome misnomer. What profiteth a man if he be able to shoot off 1,000 orgasms but be unable to embrace a beloved friend passionately?

I don't say I'm persuaded by this analysis. I do say its cogency begins to grow on me. I'm still not one to see sexual promiscuity and emotional commitment as necessarily at odds, but there seems a disquieting lack of evidence that they're mutually reinforcing. As lust roars round the land, the capacity (even the wish) for intimacy seems progressively to wither. No causal connection has been shown, but I could do with a little reassurance that the correlation is merely coincidental. Many of us feel deeply the loss of the kind of intimate male friendships we once took for granted, wonder what our own complicity may have been in their demise, and wince at the scorn with which many seem to regard such "sentimental attachments." It isn't only the Rymans and Robs of yesteryear they're laughing at. It's the Al Lowensteins, too.

Recently one of Lowenstein's friends tried to describe[2] in print how Al would talk about his need to be physically close to other men, to hold them—"it was something he liked to do with men he cared about." I was moved at the description, and I assumed most people would be. Not at all. I've since heard many gay men dismiss Lowenstein's words as "pure closetry" (those with a psychiatric vocabulary have labelled his feelings "displacement"). I knew Al as a casual acquaintance for more than thirty years. He may well have been sexually active with some men. With others, he may "merely" have wanted to cuddle for the night (Ryman and Rob would have understood). In the latter mood he wasn't necessarily "denying" sexual desire. On different occasions he may simply have wanted different things—which is true of most of us when we allow it to be. No "denial" or "displacement" need be involved, other than the denial that we are fixed essences, forever locked into a single impulse.

The real deniers may be those among us—preeminently the sexual athletes—who have forgotten, or perhaps never knew, the pleasure and comfort to be had from non-genital physical closeness. Their numbers seem to be growing, men who equate "feeling" with getting hard—and getting it on. I myself am exceedingly fond of doing both. Yet like those "quaint Victorians" Ryman and Rob, my most satisfying memories are of lying close to someone I care about.

The New York Native, 1982

Notes

1. For heterosexual women in the 19th century, friendships of great emotional and physical (not to be confused with genital) intensity of the kind between Ryman and Rob described above have been well documented. For those interested, here's a short bibliography: Carroll Smith-Rosenberg, "The Female World of Love and Ritual: Relations Between Women in 19th Century America," *Signs* Vol. 1,no.1, Autumn 1975; Nancy Sahli, "Smashing: Women's Relationships Before the Fall," *Chrysalis* 8:17-27; Martin Bauml Duberman, "'I Am Not Contented': Female Masochism and Lesbianism in Early 20th-Century New England," *Women: Sex and Sexuality* (Stimpson and Person, eds, Univ. of Chicago: 1980); Mary Wells, *Miss Marks and Miss Wooley* (Houghton Mifflin: 1978), Doris Faber, *The Life of Lorena Hickock, E.R.'s Friend* (William Morrow: 1980) Carl N. Degler, *At Odds: Women and the Family In America,* Oxford: 1980; Lillian Faderman, *Surpassing the Love of Men* (Morrow: 1981), and *Scotch Verdict* (Morrow,1983); and (for contra "platonic view"), Judith C. Brown, "Lesbian Sexuality in Renaissance Italy: The Case of Sister Benedetta Carini", *Signs,* "The Lesbian Issue", vol. 9, no. 4, Summer 1984; also Kenneth Plummer, ed., *The Making of the Modern Homosexual* (Hutchinson: 1981); Alice Echols, "The Demise of Female Intimacy in the Twentieth Century", *Michigan Occasional Papers in Women's Studies,* no. 6, (Fall: 1978).

However, the Ryman-Rob relationship is the only evidence that has yet come to light (so far as I know) of comparable passion between heterosexual men of the period.

2. Larry Bush in *The New York Native,* July 13-26, 1982.

MY GAY LIFE

Most of the initial year and a half of writing this column on the history of sexuality was fun—and easy. As each deadline approached, I'd reach across the desk and pluck another manuscript from one of the piles of unpublished historical documents I had accumulated over a decade of sporadic research in archival libraries, append introductory remarks—and mail off the whole to The New York Native. *Painless and pleasant. The day—and my come-uppance—came when I reached out my hand to the piles of documents and—it closed on air. Those seemingly bottomless piles had, after a mere year's pillage, shrivelled. Why hadn't I noticed sooner? How had I managed to ignore the basic truism every historian learns at his/her mentor's knee: In the U.S.A. evidence of the past is swiftly swept away—eviscerated.*

What to do? One obvious answer was to stop writing the column. But I quickly dismissed that option: the alternative? If I was to continue to publish fresh materials I had only one—unappealing—recourse. I'd have to search out the materials I'd gathered during my earliest *research expeditions, and which I'd long since pushed out of sight, buried in the inner recesses of file cabinets and cartons. To burrow into such musty nooks would entail* real *work, difficult and time-consuming. A piteous prospect, with the likely upshot being that after a dozen years of breathing the fresh air of Liberation, I'd end my days where I'd already spent too many of them: sealed away in some suffocating closet.*

I bit the bullet. Donning full scholar drag—galoshes, gas mask, old chinos—I bravely plunged into a hallway closet, trying to keep a light heart by shouting bracing slogans like "we need to recover our gay heritage!", "in memory lies identity!"—etc. To slight avail. Part of the trouble was faulty equipment. It had been foolish to buy the gas mask at New York Jock). Plus the cruel disappointment of not instantly unearthing historical items of major importance. Six hours into my first dig I'd come up with little more than a snapshot of ex-Mayor Wagner sitting on top of—oh, never mind!

It was a bitter pill. Somewhere I'd harbored the illusion that an assault on those mouldy cartons filled with the fruits of my earliest research expeditions would quickly yield a succession of priceless treasures. Alas, no. I came away with armfuls of detritus instead. What had ever possessed me, I mused, to photocopy and drag home so much irredeemable trivia? The best explanation I could manage was that like all Pre-Historic Hunters I'd grabbed at anything available to help fill the empty cave.

After my third closet foray, self-pity mounting, depression deepening, all came right. I suddenly hit upon some 50 or so typed manuscript pages of what seemed to be a lengthy and unpublished gay male memoir that covered much of this century. Spirits soared, self-congratulation resurfaced. The dig would after all prove worth the trouble; important booty did await me in all those unsifted cartons. But troubling questions soon supplanted initial euphoria. Why had I photocopied only fifty pages of what—judging from internal evidence—was a manuscript roughly six times that length? Why those fifty non-consecutive pages? Why no title page, no record of the author's name, no note on the manuscript's provenance— where, when and how I had located it? Despite several careful re-readings, I remained mystified. I still drew a blank—had no recollection about the memoir, no recall of where I first ran across it.[1]

The only plausible (if embarrassing) explanation I came up with was simple negligence. My first research trips, some dozen years ago, were heady times: I uncovered more material more rapidly than I'd dreamed possible. Too exhilarated at the time to make the needed effort to sort and catalogue the manuscripts in properly scholarly fashion, anxious to get back on the research trail, I simply let them accumulate, persuaded their provenance would stay fresh in my mind until I could get around to filing and labeling. A soothing rationale at the time, but as the present condition of this memoir makes evident, a mistaken one. The truth is that exuberance eventuated in sloppy scholarship.

Lucky for me, remorse and apology aren't attitudes much in vogue these days. Besides, some portion of a significant early gay memoir has been salvaged. Though the excerpts are undeniably scattered and slight, I think taken together the autobiographical fragments are rewarding. The prose is sophisticated, the tone surprisingly "contemporary", the insights often rich, the glimpses provided into an earlier epoch of gay male life both rare and tantalizing.

MY GAY LIFE
1909-1960s

To clarify this aspect of my life I want to preface my story with a few remarks characterizing in general terms my sexual inclination, or as some would say, deviation. How I turned out to be a homosexual I am at a loss to explain. Some say a domineering mother or a spineless father, or again the reverse, turn a boy into a homosexual. But nobody knows for certain. At any rate, no such case seems to apply to me. I have never been ashamed of this leaning of mine, never felt guilt or self-disdain about it, although it has been a fact which seldom in my life I felt encouraged to admit and mostly found advisable to hide. Nor have I ever wished to change it, even had this been possible. For I always considered homosexuality a natural though variant form of human sex behavior and not a deviant one—deviance having usually the connotation of sickness and execration.

Not once in my life have I known a woman physically. This is a source of regret to me, for I felt eager to sample life in all its aspects and am, of course, aware that the union of man and woman is one of the basic experiences of life. But my aversion to and ignorance of heterosexual contact have kept me from seeking that experience. My aversion to physical relations with women? Again I cannot find a reason. Women have shown me love and I have returned it in a platonic way; some even offered to have sex with me and I was hard put to refuse without offending them. How different my easily aroused sensuality where men are concerned!

Few recollections remain of my early school days [the author was born in Germany, in 1903], but I recall the awakening of feelings of sexual pleasure. When I was six or seven years old, my mother and I visited some relatives in nearby Halle. There was a handsome young cousin, about ten years older than I, who wore shorts. After we had indulged in *Kaffe und Kuchen* [coffee and cake], he showed me some of his books and we sat close together. Our bare legs touched for a long time, and this made me feel excited and affectionate. I would have sat with him all day. At the same age, I sometimes played with myself under my small wooden desk at school, which gave me pleasurable sensations. These are my earliest recollections of erotic pleasure . . . . Even in those early days, [I held the opinion] that sex was a natural human function, with which I did not associate any feelings of guilt.

I believe I did not fully comprehend at that time how dangerously my particular inclination put me in conflict with the accepted mores of society. Youthful sex, I held, knew no barriers, although the furtiveness which accompanied some of my contacts should have given me clear warnings. If it did, I chose to ignore them.

At the age of thirteen or fourteen I met an older man [B.N.] who became both patron and friend .... While skiing with classmates on a snowy slope in the Leipzig woods, I noticed being watched by a distinguished-looking elderly gentleman in a sable-collared fur coat. After a while he accosted me, commented on my "nice, straight legs," and asked if I would be willing to teach him skiing. I saw no harm in it and said yes. Thereupon he invited me for the following Sunday to his residence at a fashionable address. My parents had no objection, so I went to call upon him. A butler opened the door and I entered an elegant villa, filled with oriental art treasures, for [B.N.] had been Imperial German consul at [a Far Eastern country], where he had assembled an outstanding collection of woodcuts, screens, porcelain and armor .... .

America, 1935-1958

... I stood on the threshold of a new and happy phase of my life. Leaving New York I went to [a town in New England to teach at a] coeducational school there .... .Despite my preference for the boys and emotional involvement with them I had no sexual relations with any of them, realizing the disastrous consequences such action might have. Still, with some of the more mature ones I philosophized about the erotic element in education—"pedagogic eros" was the term I had adopted from the German educator Gustav Wyneken. I talked about the affection that follows naturally when an older man sees his teaching bear fruit in the younger, or the mutuality of giving and taking in such a relationship, where both are stimulated to greater creativeness and enrich each other in equal measure. There was no scheming or ulterior motive in these talks. I sincerely believed what I said and believe it to this day. I am happy to say that some of the boys understood and returned my feelings through subtle demonstrations. Handsome [H.L.] was one of them. One summer he came with me to a mountain climbing school I ran in the Rockies of Colorado. When we stood on our first summit, he embraced me and said: "I shall never forget that you have opened this mountain world and other worlds to me." I felt wonderfully justified and rewarded.

During the years I taught in New England I often visited New York and Boston. Sex, which was totally banned at school, was permitted to assert itself in the cities. To satisfy my urges I spent active—and sleepless—nights in the YMCAs and Turkish baths.

Occasionally I met a soldier or sailor—uniforms having a strong attraction for me—on Times Square or Scollay Square [Boston] and took him to my room. These brief encounters were usually disappointing. I prefer physical contact to be accompanied by a measure of warmth and affection. This may be too much to expect under such circumstances, but I know that it is possible. I have often found a combination of sex and affection, even in "quickies", with Europeans, but rarely with Americans.

One year I arrived in New York on the eve of my birthday. [L.S.] met me at the station, then we dined luxuriously. Afterwards he led me to his apartment where I was to spend the night. As we reached his house he bade me wait a few minutes and went upstairs. I assumed that he wanted to light candles, but when I joined him in the room, my eyes were lit up by another sight. Naked in a corner of the room stood a charming young sailor, a friend of [L.S's] with a red ribbon tied around a protruding part of his body. This was my birthday present, and I enjoyed it thoroughly in the following hours. In the war years, unlimited opportunities existed for servicemen in search of sex and extra pocket money. [L.] had heard of a unique establishment, open to males only, and took me there one night. We went to a large basement apartment in Brooklyn and, upon identification, were received with great cordiality by George, the owner and host. His living room was warm and cozy. Young servicemen were sitting on sofas and easy chairs, relaxed and friendly. Coffee and snacks were being served, light banter went back and forth. We felt as if we had entered a happy family circle, George being Dad and Mom combined. He knew the boys' problems, helped where he could, supplied shelter, food and money, and was loved with the casual affection that children show their parents. He confided to us newcomers that this was a bad night, as all the boys had to report for duty; and soon they left, kissing George goodbye. When they had gone, he asked us not to be disappointed and named a "good" night for us to return, a night when several big ships were due in harbor. He then proceeded in a business like fashion to inquire about our tastes in servicemen. "What color of eyes and hair do you prefer?" he asked. "Do you like them tall, medium or your own size?" All the details were jotted down in George's notebook. "Is there any nationality you like best?", and then he described how nationalities differ in anatomical as well as temperamental qualities. Even the branch of service was left to our choice, for George commanded an unlimited supply. When we were fully "booked" and promised unfailing delivery of the stipulated goods, we took our leave.

On the designated night we found the living room and adjoining bedrooms bustling with activity. A large friendly crowd of servicemen was present. Some were drinking coffee while waiting for a vacant bed. The waiting list was long and occupancy of a bedroom was limited to thirty minutes. I had "ordered" a tall marine, dark and blue-eyed; and indeed there he was, shy, friendly, and willing. When I asked him how old he was, he said with a grin: "old enough to know better." But during our half hour I gained the impression that he would never know better.

George's establishment breathed a spirit of family friendliness; it was a super-USO. I am afraid, though, that the official USO did not approve of it. When I arrived on another night, I found a crowd in the street and a policeman guarding the door to the premises. Upon inquiry, I was told that a "house of vice" had been raided and its proprietor carted off to prison. The closeness of my own escape made me shudder. Of kindly George, whom I was never to see again, I thought with sympathy and sadness.

[*This gay brothel is almost certainly the one Gustav Beekman (known to habitues as "George") ran near the Brooklyn Navy Yard and to which Senator Walsh of Massachusetts was linked in a 1942 scandal that had national repercussions. (See Tripp,* Homosexual Matrix, *pp. 224-227, and Lawrence R. Murphy, "The House on Pacific Street: Homosexuality, Intrigue and Politics During World War II",* the Journal of Homosexuality, *Vol. 12, No. 1).*]

After these ventures I would return to [New England] to the life of an enthusiastic and successful teacher, a trusted counselor of students, a lover of nature and outdoor activities. One door was closed behind me, another opened in front. There was no communication between the two compartments, except in my mind. Nor was there any strain of adjustment in changing from one world to the other. In both spheres I was myself, behaved naturally, and made no effort at playing a role. Still, the separation between the two spheres was tight. People I met in one were absent from the other. Very few of my friends shared both aspects of my life. The attitudes I held, the standards I observed, even the tone of conversation changed effortlessly from one to the other. There was no overlap, and—to the best of my recollection—I never made a slip that revealed the other side.

My proclivity to separate spheres of feelings and experiences also extended to personal relationships. Some of my closest friends spoke of the "barriers" they encountered in me and of the "sense of exclusion" I conveyed to them. This saddened me and I tried to remove these obstacles to fuller communion. But hiding had become part of my nature, and almost instinctively I often kept my innermost soul apart from others.

*

[*During the early Forties, the author moved to Philadelphia, became involved for a time with the American Friends Service Committee and half-heartedly proposed marriage to a woman friend he liked—a proposal she turned down, which at the time caused the author "no suffering" and which he later recognized had been a favor to them both ("In retrospect, the naivete ... of my move toward matrimony ... seems pathetic ... an attempt bound to fail"). During the same period, he frequented "a number of the notorious steam-baths in Philadelphia ... acquired a boy friend in Trenton and even found a congenial soul, or rather body, among the Quaker work campers."*

Subsequently as World War II was drawing to a close the author became a member of the armed forces, and later, during the occupation held "the privileged position as an officer" posted in Germany.]

The life of an occupation officer had many compensations as well as temptations. Not the least among the latter was the ease with which sex was obtainable. For a Hershey bar or a pair of stockings a G.I. could find a girl to share his bed as often as he wanted. Boys were equally eager to please those who preferred them.

The number of homosexual encounters I had while stationed in Europe was legion. In war-darkened London, while the V-2 bombs were still falling, many servicemen of various nationalities on leave from the Continent found it pleasant and convenient to satisfy their sexual urges with comrades-in-arms. Soldiers and Sailors Clubs, washrooms in the underground and hotel lobbies were places where one glance would bring you a friend for the night. The same I found true six years later in Tokyo when on leave from the Korean War.

Still, the number of eager sex partners in postwar Germany was greater by an order of magnitude. Quite often the problem was not so much to find partners as to ward off undesirable ones. If sailors are reputed to have a girl in every port, I resembled them insofar as I had boy friends in most of the cities I visited on official errands. When I served in Stuttgart I discovered that, by strange coincidence, most of the other heads of departments were also "gay". We lived in a large villa, where our young German chauffeurs or boy friends were welcome day and night. That this rather obvious arrangement remained undisturbed during my three years in Stuttgart seems almost incredible considering the attitude of the military toward homosexuality. From headquarters in Stuttgart we ventured into other parts of Europe, sometimes on business, sometimes on leave. In Paris, Brussels, Vienna and Rome we had friends and introduced them generously to one another.

Before long, however, the promiscuity of the early occupation days gave way to exclusive relationships with one person. This was encouraged by the charming tendency of the German boys to seek not only physical contact but also a sentimental tie with the American friend. No doubt, their expectance of material benefits also played a part.

[B.W.] my closest American friend of Stuttgart days and many years to follow, set the style for building close relationships with young men that went far beyond sex and often lasted for years. I myself found "Wolf" [*a 19 year old Berliner who had fled that city when the Russians approached—the author and Wolf were together for several years*].

[*We skip to 1950 and the author's tour of duty in the Far East*]

On one of my visits to Tokyo I was strolling on the famous Ginza. Strangers constantly accosted me offering to serve as guides to erotic adventure. One of the suggestions I was unable to resist. My guide and I hopped a taxi and were soon deposited in an ill-lit alley of the northern suburbs. I entered a flimsy building where I was welcomed by a garishly dressed madame, whose deep voice gave the lie to her female appearance. "She" graciously asked me to sit down and sip a cup of tea with her. When my impatience began to show, she smiled and consented to introduce her boys. They were a varied lot, ranging from rather sinister looking "butch" types to willowy girlish figures. I made a selection from the middle range, and the boy and I retired to a small cubicle. One has heard of the exacting and sophisticated training which Japanese geisha girls undergo. The boy who stayed with me must have had similar training. His language was flowing and beautiful. He looked at me long with warm intensity, and the kiss he gave me after a slow smile continued the words which his eyes had spoken. We lay together, not in frenzy but quietly absorbed in one another. His fingers and lips knew the places of my body—as perhaps only another male can know—where his touches could bestow the greatest bliss. I felt as though he wanted to show me love of passion, and for the brief spell of our being together could but love him for his gentleness. Never before or since have I derived such rapture from sex. On a later visit to Tokyo I looked for him again. But he was gone.

[*The final years—1958-1972—covered in the manuscript are sampled below in three snippets.*]

I. 1956: First summer vacation on the West Coast a friend from occupation days in Germany who had become a clinical psychologist in San Francisco, joined me on a trip to the Canadian Rockies. I met a young man, a grade school teacher ["S"], who after some pleasant conversation was eager to accompany me to my hotel and spend the night with me. ["S"] told me that he had accepted a teaching position [and in] the fall planned to move to my neighborhood. Of course, we would then see each other. And so we did.

I was then forty-seven years old. Middle age had arrived. Youthfulness, so highly prized by homosexuals, was slipping by. Often I looked enviously at passing cars in which two seemingly happy young men were riding together. The idea possessed me that I wanted to have a young man by my side too . . . ["S"] initially fulfilled that wish. We spent much time together on weekend trips, at concerts, in bed. He [reacted] to me with affection. Perhaps he was pleased by an [older man's] interest in him, perhaps the comfortable circumstances I offered—good meals and travel in a flashy sports car—[held] the greater appeal. His mind was pleasure-bent, he liked me—no doubt—[but] I clung to him almost desperately, though I was fully aware of how radically we differed in tastes and interests. My feverish possessiveness could not fail but cool him off. He began to seek other contacts. Not knowing where he spent the night would drive me into unbearable spells of jealousy. My life once more was darkened and near a breakdown.

After months of agitation, a curious chain of events opened the road to recovery. In the steamroom of the YMCA I met an attractive negro. We became good friends and he introduced me to [F.H.] a highly cultured physician of German ancestry. I saw much of [F.H.] afterwards and we shared intimate thoughts. He tried his best to pull me out of the bit of misery in which I wallowed because of [S] but nothing seemed to help. As a last resource [F.H.] introduced me to [B]. [A woman who in 1956 was already a noted sexologist of pioneering (positive) views about same gender love and lust.] This was the turning point. In many talks at [her home] I began to look at my life from a changed perspective and [began] to reaffirm the values by which I must live. [She] taught me to get angry at my own humiliation and to insist on the rights of mutual consideration and truthfulness to which friends are entitled. She understood that it was imperative for my recovery that I no longer [cater to] [S's] ways and standards and thus betray the values that had supported my own life.

II. 1960: Eager as I have been on my travels to sample mountains and historic sites, I have also not been blind to the charms of man. My erotic encounters—most of them of the "quickie" type—are far too numerous to list. But I will recount a few outlandish ones.

An American acquaintance had given me the address of a London pension that catered to special tastes. When I got there, I was first puzzled and then tickled to learn that the price of a room was either 3 pounds, solo, or 4 pounds, incl. bedfellow. Expressing my willingness to pay the higher rate, I was shown a list of availables. My chosen fellow arrived at the appointed hour and proved good company. Next morning over breakfast, I learned to my surprise that he was happily married and had a little boy. "We are short of money," he said, "so my wife is glad to have me occasionally bring in a little extra by staying out for night work."

Of still briefer duration was the encounter with an attractive young guard in the Egyptian Museum in Cairo. I had noticed that he followed me from room to room as if suspecting me of scheming to steal Tutankhamen's treasure. When I entered a back room with him close on my heels, he suddenly gave me a big wink and beckoned me to a dim-lit recess. There he took me by the hand and led me behind a big sarcophagus containing the crumbling mummy of a pharao [sic.]. Sure of my consent, he then went wordlessly to work. When we had parted, he murmured to me in heavily accented English: "There must be international understanding through touch of bodies."

III. 1970-1972: Summation. My own sexual partnerships were certainly not of a durable character. This used to worry me. But over the years my views on this point have changed. Why should I make durability the test of anything enjoyable coming my way? Insistence on duration is only too apt to throw a shadow on an experience that can be happy for the moment. I learned to be content with the *Nunc et Hic* and to take it unshadowed into my memory.

In homosexual relations youthfulness is generally at an inordinate premium. As I grew older, the availability of sex partners sharply diminished. Hand in hand with this went a reduced interest on my part in sexual acts with a mate, although my practice of self-satisfaction continued with the old frequency and enjoyment. Instead of having physical contact, I found myself satisfied by watching men, talking with them, experiencing comradely warmth, the felt touch of a hand, or some other expression of tenderness. The glow I can derive from that kind of relation has proven more intense and lasting than the momentary excitement of sex. I share the sentiment of the aging marquise de Noailles who said: "*Quant a moi, je n'ai plus envie de faire l'amour, je veux faire l'amitie*". [For me, now, it's friends I want to make, not love]. This may sound like a logical prescription for a man of age and nature. Yet, it has not always been easy to follow for my sexual urge has by no means withered away...

Notes
1. Gregory Sprague has since written to tell me that the original manuscript is housed in the Kinsey Institue, Bloomington, Indiana, where he too found and read it.

1911

THE THERAPY OF C.M. OTIS

Most of the great manuscript libraries scattered around the country are woefully understaffed. Some of their richest collections are uncatalogued, still in crates. Many archivists lament this condition as much as scholars. But not all archivists. Some—by temperament and training—prefer acquisition to information. A few are downright hoarders, guarding their treasures like ferocious stone lions fronting on some fabled monarch's tomb. When archivists of this breed receive an inquiry from someone lacking "proper credentials," they dismiss it with hauteur. Should a "genuine" scholar—one with the "correct" number and kind of degrees, publications, and academic appointments—knock at the door, their reaction shifts to fright. An invader, a potential enemy, has appeared—someone who might disseminate (and thus dilute the unique value of) the archive's "holdings" (revealing term!).

If I exaggerate, it's not by much, as I think Jonathan Katz, for one, will attest. An independent scholar unaffiliated with any academic institution, Katz often met with overt hostility—when polite evasion failed—as he gathered material for his anthology, *Gay American History*. Anyone looking for historical documents on sexual behavior, including the heterosexual variety, must be prepared for a substantial amount of resistance; even with traditional credentials, I've run up against a fair share of it in my own research travels around the country. But whereas all of us attempting to do research in this field face the double obstacle of puritanism and homophobia, Katz had to parry sheer academic snobbery as well.

Difficult though it is to locate and gain access to unpublished sources on sexual behavior in the past, all is not gloom. There's a brighter side, typified by my experience at Harvard's Countway Library of Medicine, in Boston. Its chief archivist, Richard J. Wolfe, is a man of enormous good and energy. Scarcely had I set foot in the Countway when Wolfe began filling the table in front of me with carton after carton of documentary material—much of it recently acquired and never before researched. Lost between euphoria and incipient numbness at the days of digging which I realized lay ahead, I apprehensively mentioned that Barbara Sicherman, the feminist scholar, had suggested I also have a look, while at The Countway, at

L. Eugene Emerson's papers. Wolfe's eyes lit up and off he raced. He was back within minutes. "Marvelous tip!" he said, dumping eleven more cartons in front of me. "Emerson was one of the first psychotherapists in Boston, worked at the Psychopathic Hospital in Boston, should be lots of stuff in there for you, nobody's ever really gone through it . . ."

It was only many days later that I got around to exploring the Emerson papers. Sicherman's tip had indeed been marvelous. Among other items in the collection, were hundreds of pages of handwritten notes Dr. Emerson had taken down while listening to his patients talk. For the pre-World War I period, this type of documentation, nearly stenographic, is exceedingly rare. And—as it proved—exceedingly difficult to decipher. I battled for weeks with the photocopies of Emerson's notes that I carted away with me. I'm not sure even now how accurately I've decoded all of his elliptical, abbreviated scrawl. Clearly Emerson had written at top speed, trying to get down verbatim what each patient was telling him. His attempt to be comprehensive accounts for the special value of the material.

But also its special limitations. Emerson had scant time (and perhaps inclination) to record his own reactions to what he was hearing. His notes contain only a few parenthetical remarks, the barest hints, of what at the time he himself had thought, felt—and prescribed. I found myself yearning to know more about how the 38-year-old New England therapist—during those tumultuous early days of the Freudian movement—had responded to the personal intimacies being revealed to him. Its a curiosity that will never be satisfied. But at least we do have his jottings about the case histories. Many are fragmentary, lacking the detail necessary to satisfyingly reconstruct personalities and events. (One exception is extraordinary: 150 pages of notes, plus correspondence, about a "masochist" woman Emerson treated over a period of several years*.) One reason for the brevity of most of the case histories is that therapists at the turn of the century typically didn't see their patients for the long stretches of time that have since become commonplace. Even those few whom Dr. Emerson (in his words) "intensively studied and analyzed" were discharged after several months. And not, it should be added, with glib claims of "cure." In a summary Emerson wrote up on December 9, 1912, he conscientiously recorded that of the sixteen patients that year with whom he had attempted "psychoanalytic treatment for therapeutic purposes," seven had been "without much success."

*See "I Am Not Contented", pp. 68.

"Case No. 15" of the preceding year (1911) would surely have fallen into the "without much success" category. The "case" was a 33-year-old man named C.M. Otis, a patient at the Psychopathic Hospital with whom Emerson held a total of six therapy sessions between April and August. He took thirty-three pages of notes on Otis—one of the fuller histories extant.

The initial session took place on April 26, 1911. Here are the very first words Emerson jotted down on his note pad (which doesn't necessarily mean, of course, the first words Otis spoke):

Reading a farm paper, about horse breeding, saw a picture of stallion, & had an erection—Abt. [About] 13 [years old].

"Mmm," I thought, gliding into a slow canter in my chair, "at last—a male Catherine the Great." I was wrong; but it took several more pages before C. M. Otis came into better focus. Switching into the third person—as Emerson's notes often do—they continue:

Remembers before he came to Michigan ... had a girl ... Never touched her—just adored her from afar...

Mother died when he was 10.

Played very intimately with brother.

Can't remember that he was especially loving towards his mother.

Never has had sexual intercourse.

First time masturbated abt. 17—Saw[?] a boy, they were lying on the ground[?], he took his penis out & showed how it was done—When he masturbated it gave him a very agreeable sensation ... has masturbated off & on ever since. Stopped when he was abt. 30 and joined the Church (Congregationalist)— 2 ½ yrs—When he was traveling in the south [as a salesman] for D. M. Ferry he got discouraged, location was so bad, roads so bad, was late & company called him down for being so slow ... Then he began to masturbate again ... Saturday night would report the week's work—supper time till 12—Would feel ... tension inside & a dread of starting the work, & before starting this report would masturbate...

inscribed a single word in the middle of the page (as if entitling an essay)—I hadn't yet gotten the message, but Dr. Emerson had. The single word?: Boys.

The notes then shift back into the first person:

The first experience that I had, didn't know anything abt. it then, had a class of boys [Otis was teaching Sunday School], it was when I joined the church ... There was a boy ... I used to like to have him come & go out walking... After I quit my work in the bank, this boy & my brother, wanted to go camping, so I arranged it. This chap & I slept together. Then this thing happened. I don't know why or how it happened. I used to sleep with my arm around him, & I awoke one night & instead of finding my hand where it ought to be, it was down on his private parts. He awoke ... I took him aside & said I wouldn't want to do anything to you that [would harm you?]. Had him come out to see me at the farm but never touched him again.

The next paragraph in Emerson's notes is all but illegible. Still, the few words I've been able to decipher do give some sense of Otis's subsequent experiences: "Has slept with other boys, in the south—touched two ... erections frequently ... those two boys also had erections ... "

Otis next began to talk about his brother. The two, he said, had often read poetry together—"Oliver Wendell Holmes, etc., we had our window open, it was cold, so we cuddled together." Otis hastened to add that "my brother never learned anything from me." It had simply been a matter of finding it cold when they got up—"so we'd hop back into bed and cuddle up close together naked."

Otis next touched in brief (at least Emerson's notes are brief) on several subjects—that he had once met "a nice young fellow" while traveling to Battle Creek one day "who came to sit beside me—he was musical & we talked abt. music"; that he feared the "men patients in the Psychopathic Hospital know," and was apprehensive that they would persecute him; that his mother had been an invalid for two years ("She was one of the most nervous persons ... "); that in 1905 he had attended a dental college for a year, but "when it came to examinations, I couldn't satisfy my professors." Emerson's notes on the session conclude with Otis's painful statement that he: "dreads to see a boy with his hands in his pockets, hates to see pictures of boys in papers, in fact I wish the boys would get off the earth (laughs), or else I would".

In the following session, (April 27, 1911), Otis talked about his hopes, when younger, of becoming a market gardener. His family, he told Emerson, had "jumped up & down & said it was impractical ... just because I couldn't plough ... they were dead against me." Having no money of his own, Otis put aside his dream of becoming a farmer and in the intervening years shuttled among a variety of unsatisfying jobs: ferry boat operator, bank clerk, salesman, gas-meter reader. He was worried, he told Emerson, about how his family would react to his hospitalization, formulating his concern in a revealing analogy: "Suppose nothing is done for me here ... Suppose I'd committed a crime & had been sent to a state institution, they would have looked for some change when I came out—-Well, they will look for some change now."

From there, Otis began speculating about what had caused his "peculiar trouble." It "had been brought on," he thought, "by masturbation," and also by the reading he'd done. In 1895, at age 17, he had followed the newspaper accounts of Oscar [Emerson spelled it "Oskar"] Wilde's trial: "reading that case of Oskar Wilde, didn't help my case a bit." He felt he had been further harmed by consulting "medical dictionaries abt. the habit I had, how it came abt."—that material had apparently been suggested to him by a "medical doctor at the asylum" in Pontiac, Michigan, with whom Otis had once talked. "All this homosexuality," Otis told Emerson at one point— momentarily shifting the blame off masturbation—"took its start in [my] study of abnormal psychology." He may have meant—I'm guessing here—that the readings had simultaneously stimulated his desires while convincing him "he could not change them." What seems certain is that they enhanced his sense of persecution: while reading one day in the public library in Battle Creek, "I heard the telephone ring & after the librarian answered it, she couldn't keep her eyes off [me]—a degenerate abroad! ... the police called her up."

Otis came back to the theme of persecution often during the remaining sessions. At one point he blamed his "notoriety" on having mistakenly confided in a dentist for whom he briefly worked; Otis was "positive" he had been overheard—"& now it is all over there, that I am what I am." At another point, Otis blamed the boy he had touched while on the camping trip: "he talked abt. it—& they watched to see if I was all right—He wouldn't talk abt. it would he? I think he would, & I think he did." Otis's fear of discovery and harassment sometimes became acute. During the fifth session (May 11, 1911), he told Emerson that there was an organized effort—"like the nightriders—to do him harm." He was "afraid to leave & go to work ... feels safe in the hospital." At another session, he confessed that he'd thought about suicide a good deal—about how some people blew their brains out, others took chloroform.

Emerson was not the first doctor Otis had seen. Earlier he had consulted two of the most prominent medical figures of the day—Dr. John Duncan Quackenbos of Columbia University and Dr. Isador Coriat, twice (1924, 1937) elected to the presidency of the American

Psychoanalytic Association. Coriat remained all his life a highly respected orthodox Freudian, but Quackenbos (destined by his name?) was more on the fringes of respectability. Nathan G. Hale, Jr., in his valuable book *Freud and the Americans*, recounts Quackenbos's widely publicized use of hypnosis in "curing" everything from "neurasthenic insanity" to "erotomania" to tea and coffee drinking. Hale describes the "nattily dressed, gorgeously moustached" doctor hypnotizing his patients "with a red carnelian [a variety of quartz] or a diamond mounted on the end of a gold pencil." Jonathan Katz, in *Gay American History,* has republished an 1899 paper by Quackenbos entitled "Hypnotic Suggestion in the Treatment of Sexual Perversions and Moral Anaesthesia," in which the doctor records his successful treatment (in two visits) of "a gentleman of twenty-five." The "line of suggestion" Dr. Q. used was simplicity itself: he told the man to resist his "abnormal feeling" and acquire "a natural desire for the opposite sex properly directed and controlled." For good measure, Quackenbos depicted—doubtless flashing that red carnelian—the "moral, mental, and financial ruin" consequent upon "indulging the unnatural lust." The patient, Dr. Quackenbos reported, at oncr responded with "exaltation of the will power and an acquired ability to resist."

Otis's consultation with Dr. Q. took a quite different turn. When he tried to tell the doctor about his fears of "being watched" then Quackenbos "pooh-poohed the idea"—later, Dr. Coriat did "the same"—and quickly showed Otis to the door. Otis told Emerson that he thought Quackenbos had preconceived notions of how a neurasthenic ought to behave. Perhaps he had told Quackenbos at the time, thus leading to his rapid dismissal. More likely, that came about because he did not "weep with mortification" as had the "gentleman of twenty-five"; nor did he have that gentleman's financial resources: the anonymous earlier patient had held "a position of trust in the office of one of our great life-insurance companies". Whatever the reason, Otis "never had the chance to talk this thing out" with Quackenbos. He expressed gratitude to Dr. Emerson for at least listening to him—for the "thing" had "got [him] down."

The future concerned him especially. Otis had no job. He had no confidence that he could "change." From age 16 onward, he admitted, "I can say that I seem to have noticed certain attractive younger boys much as others will have noticed girls". He continued to dream of suicide, continued to fear exposure and persecution, and wondered if his "symptoms" might signify some "serious mental trouble like paralysis or softening of the brain." He could conjure up only a plaintive vision of what lay ahead: "... if I can get my position [job], if I have the physical vigor to do the work, & I can get it, & everything else falls into line, I can work out my own salvation, I think, I don't know." Plaintive—yet not without a touch of dignity and self-esteem.

After five sessions spanning little more than two weeks (April 26-May 11, 1911), Dr. Emerson apparently terminated Otis' "therapy." The last line he wrote in his notes at the close of the final (May 11) session seems on its face stern and bleak: Otis "shows no adequate emotional reaction to my suggestions." When I first read that last line it surprised me. Up to that point I'd gotten the impression that Emerson felt considerable compassion for Otis—though I could identify it only through negative evidence: nothing in Emerson's notes had suggested the self-congratulatory posturing of a Dr. Quackenbos, or the rigid conformity of a Dr. Coriat. Perhaps, I thought, Emerson's final outburst of pessimism had erupted from a sense of helplessness in the face of misery. Abruptness—particularly in New Englanders—sometimes substitutes for concern.

Some confirmation for that interpretation can be found in two pages of notes Emerson appended three months later. On August 4, he made this entry, which I reproduce nearly in its entirety:

When I came home this afternoon, a little after 4, I found Otis waiting for me at the corner. He came back to the house with me & we sat a while in the piazza. The reason he came to me was because I had not condemned him & he wanted some advice—I gave him some & think he will take it. He said I had helped him a good deal.

I told him of Leonardo da Vinci ...

He has been on a farm helping the man who has charge of the baths. [?] at Hospital.

We'll never know for sure what "advice" Emerson offered. But the fact that he mentioned Leonardo suggests some effort on his part to provide comfort and support—at the least, an effort to be non-judgmental. Otis evidently thought so, too, since he had made the special trip to Emerson's house to thank him for "not condemning [me]"—though the oppressed cannot always distinguish between condescension and acceptance.

Thus stands our knowledge of "Case No. 15." It is all we are ever likely to know of C. M. Otis—his fears and hopes, his experiences, his subsequent fate. The little we do know is the result of the chance preservation of a few dozen pages of a physician's notes. Only through that accident are we able to give a name and the bare outline of a personal history to one of millions of our anonymous predecessors who have suffered through time because of their attraction to the "wrong" sex.

Christopher Street, 1977

1912

"I AM NOT CONTENTED": FEMALE MASOCHISM AND LESBIANISM IN EARLY TWENTIETH-CENTURY NEW ENGLAND

Like the "Otis Therapy" documents (see pp. 60-67) the following material has also been excerpted from the L. Eugene Emerson Papers at the Countway Library of Medicine in Boston. This considerably larger packet divides naturally into two parts. First, the handwritten, penciled notes Dr. Emerson jotted down in 1912-13 during his therapy sessions with Honora Downey, a twenty-three year old patient at the Psychopathic Hospital in Boston where Emerson was a staff member. The second consists of excerpts from Downey's letters to Emerson after she had been discharged. Emerson's notes focus on Downey's masochism; Downey's own letters are of most interest for their information on lesbianism among working-class women.

Beyond the scant biographical details contained in the documents themselves, we know nothing of Honora Downey's life. Of Dr. Emerson we know little more than his dates (1873-1939) and the fact that he was among the earliest followers of Freud in America. By contrast, the literature on the main subjects of these documents— female masochism and lesbianism—is in the former case vast (and currently in theoretical disarray) and in the latter case recent (and to date still slight). Given the controversial and/or scarce nature of the literature, it is not possible to generalize confidently about the "significance" of Honora Downey's history. It may take a generation or more of scholarship before there can be informed debate about how "representative" Downey's attitudes and experiences were, before we can place them in any assured context. For now, only the most tentative estimates are possible. I have tried to offer some preliminary interpretations in footnote queries and commentary.

Part I: Emerson's Notes
[August 12, 1912; (Mass.) Psychopathic Hospital]
A relative began masturbating her when she was abt.[about] 8. He threatened to tell her fa.[ther] abt. some childish error if she wouldn't let him do as he pleased & she was afraid of her fa. He used to tie the boys in bed thrash them & she was afraid of that. This relative tried to have connection w. [with] her when she was abt. 12 but was not successful.

A Dr. in Lynn told her she should have connections [sexual intercourse] that it would cure her desire to cut herself.

The reason she cut herself first was to scare a cousin who was trying to have connection with her. He was afraid of blood. She wanted connection last night & that was why she cut herself ...

Mother never washes; father seldom.

Hates her family.

All but youngest brother asked for "connections" ...

Stuck a German silver wire in her hand so the surgeons would have to cut her open ...

The man she went with at dr.'s advice 3rd night wanted her to take it in her mouth so she got up, dressed, & refused to have anything more to do w. him ...

[August 13, 1912]

Has cut herself 28 or 30 times.

Arthur [brother?] called her a "whore" when she told him abt. herself & she went upstairs, drank a glass of bro's [brother's] whiskey, took his razor & cut a "W" on her right leg ...

Believes in neither god, devil, heaven, nor hell ...

Cuts herself slowly to bring out the pain.

Fa. tied her bro. to a post in the cellar and whipped him.

Mother whipped her with horsewhip. Shows mark on cheek.

Family would think it a disgrace if they knew she was in Psy. Hos. Wants to hug and kiss somebody, doesn't know whom ...

"I don't think anyone could despise anyone as much as I despise myself." She almost cried.

[August 15, 1912]

Father loved her much till 5 when other girls began to come. Sec. [second] time she cut herself abt. 3 wks. after 1st. Bad feeling in head. She had had a bad headache & bad feeling 3 days when cousin attempted assault. While she cut to scare him she noticed her headache stopped & thought of it as a cure. Never felt that life was worth living till yesterday.

Always had these bad feelings in her head. During the worst periods would sit morose & sullen & no one dared to speak to her.

Hates being fat. Fat girls never flow regularly.

Stuck pen-knife in her Vagina once, to make herself flow.

Thought bleeding would reduce fat.

Girls in shop used to say fat girls will go it forty diff. [different] ways. Hated it ...

Mother wouldn't let her wear corsets—became so fat, girls said she was "up"[pregnant]. Sometimes would plan to cut, & sometimes impulsively do it ...

Never wanted to kill herself; but sometimes didn't care. Once, "didn't care" so much she almost cut an artery, but the feeling passed before she had cut deep enough ...

Yesterday was the first time she thought life endurable, the first day she was willing to live.

Never flowed regularly, always wanted to.

Father used to beat the boys till they couldn't stand up. Then one of her brothers told the Police & showed his bruises. The Police came & told Fa. if he did it again he would be arrested. He took him upstairs & beat him worse than he had ever done before and said if he told he'd give him a still worse one.

She used to hide her head in the pillow to keep from hearing her brothers scream.

Fa. used to kick her, but he never whipped her as he did her bros.

She used to hug and kiss the boarders who used to bring her candy etc. Says she knows she will never cut herself again...

[August 20, 1912]

... Said she had made up her mind this afternoon never to have relations w. a man again ..

It was a common belief among the girls where she worked that if a girl did not flow regularly she would either have consumption or go insane. When she began to cut herself she thought she was insane.

When the story was abt. the shop that she was pregnant, the girls asked her best friend if it were true. She said it was. Luckily, she never lost a day at work, that year. If she had, they would say she had gotten rid of a baby ...

This relative began, after a while, to masturbate her sister. This she could not stand & she told him if he didn't stop she would tell her father. From this she discovered he wasn't going to tell on her & so she never went with him anymore.

She has a strong feeling against her mother continuing marital relations with her father.

[August 21, 1912]

Not feeling so well today. Has the queer feeling.

Has a slight discharge, whitish, evil smelling, & staining her clothes. This has previously always preceded cutting ...

Denied there was anything on her mind but finally I got her to close her eyes. She said she always saw babies when she closed her eyes ...

She told me her Uncle was the man who masturbated her.

[August 22, 1912]

Had a good afternoon. No dreams. All right this morning. In probing for the specific reason as to why she cut herself last—it brought back the bad feeling she had & in the mood wh. [which] persisted she told the following.

Abt. 3—in highchair at table—wasn't feeling very well & didn't want oatmeal—pushed it away. God-mother pushed it back & hit her over the hand. Caused blood.

When she was abt. 20 bro.[ther] came to her room, made suggestive movements with his fingers. Offered her some money—threw it in his face. "Say you needn't mention this."

Fa. had habit of coming into her room. Broke in the door. Uncle 15. Bro. pushed her down the stairs onto boards with nails ...

Blacksmith bro. punched her in side ...

Time she cut her vagina 3 a.m. Half asleep ...

Didn't go to doctors because girls said they would handle her and have intercourse w. her ...

[August 26, 1912]

Dr. Briggs [a previous physician she'd consulted] stroked her arms & breast, an hour or so. First time she ever remembers being sexually excited ...

Feels terrible—especially at the loss of respect for Dr. Briggs whom she regards as having experimented on her.

"Let sleeping dogs lie."

She thought this all out from my having said stroking arms was a kind of masturbation.

[August 27, 1912]

Dr. Briggs got a "hard-on." Took her hand & put it on his penis, wanted her to "jet" him. Did not have connection, at this time at any rate, though she has done something she has promised not to tell of.

After she left Dr. B. that night was offered $20. to spend the night w. a man.

What Dr. B. did was repulsive to her, but if she had thought he really wanted it she would have done anything to please him.

She felt he had forgotten himself for a moment.

With his defection she felt there were no good men in the world ...

Has felt like cutting herself all day, but won't.

It is to drive away a big pain by a little one. She feels so badly over what Dr. Briggs did she wants to take her mind off it.

A doctor in Lynn masturbated her over an hour without its producing the slightest effect. He caressed her breasts & manipulated her genitals & said he never saw such a girl ...

[August 29, 1912]

The sec.[ond] time Dr. Briggs saw pt. [patient] he examined her heart & lungs. Then he masturbated her breasts & genitals over an hour. It had no effect on her but did on him ...

[August 30, 1912]

... Hated fa. Hurt self. Tried to cut him once—cut self. He said she was out on a pick up. Told mo.[ther] better keep girls in or they'd be coming home w. a big belly.

Beat mother & dragged her around by the hair ...

[September 2, 1912]

Looks very stern and decided.

Saturday decided never to have children.

Intends to work, study psychology, write, & do social service. Gives herself 10 years to become the equal of Dr. Briggs. Regards the wrong he did her greater than that of her father ...

One of the reasons she gave for not bringing children into the world was her heredity. With her family she felt she had no right to bring children into the world.

[September 10, 1912]

Dreamed she killed her Uncle & was being tried for murder.

Dreamed she had a baby ...

[September 12, 1912]
She is going to Miss Hitchcock, Welcome House, tomorrow.

[September 13, 1912]
    At Welcome House—1 hour & made good so far—Miss Hitchcock likes her—Said yesterday she was sorry, in a way, to leave hospital.

[November 11, 1912]
    Wanted to go w. a man last week but wouldn't till she had seen me. Now isn't. Has decided to stay at Welcome House for the present...

[November 25, 1912]
Lying awake nights thinking how she could assist girls in the wickednesses.
    Never had such temptations till lived in Welcome House ...

[December 23, 1912]
    Sitting in window ledge. Thought of going out & then thought of my saying she hurt herself as a sort of club over people, etc. It frightened her.
    Sister Alice probably pregnant: mother asked her to get something to bring on a miscarriage.

[January 20, 1913]
    Sister is pregnant.
    Much disturbed because she told Miss Hitchcock abt. Dr. Briggs.

[January 27, 1913]
    Took sister for operation. Won't come back to see me.

[March 28, 1913]
    Remembers once when Uncle had stopped she wanted him

terribly at night, to hurt her. He often used to hurt her horribly when he masturbated her. Sometimes when she had terrible headaches, Uncle could stop them by knocking his two fists against her head ...

[March 16, 1914]
Met her at Pub. Library ... Had to tell truth to me ... things that were not true were that she had ever had intercourse, or done the things she wrote in her diary. They were stories she had heard at the factory & had told Dr. Briggs thought she must tell me to be consistent.

[December 1, 1914]
Said she hadn't been feeling very well. Sexual conflicts. Said it was her difficulty in controling [sic] her sexual cravings. Had been going out w. a man & felt she might give in if she went tonight so came suddenly to Boston & wasn't going to get back till too late ...
Planning on Waltham Training Sch. for Nurses.
Looked remarkably well.

[December 6, 1914]
Still doing well.
Discussed sister. Gives up trying to control.
Feels a little bad when colleagues question abt. cuts on arm, but is able to put 'em off, & knows she must bear it, so forgets.
[July 29, 1916; last entry made by Emerson in his notes]
Has seen that she has excited herself sexually by her own attitudes & thoughts—(Narcissism) ... [1]
Sees her own bisexual nature & tendencies [see the letters in Part II, which follows]. Speaks of a "sexual attraction" quite distinct from looks. Thinks she herself looks best in a sheet-like toga, but as she can't sleep so makes herself beautiful night-gowns.

Part II: Downey's Letters[2]
[Downey to Emerson, July 25, 1917]
I am writing to you about this crush business I am getting mixed up in.
A crush means that one girl arouses a desire in another girl for sex satisfaction(3). This is —I don't know just how to make it plain—she acts like a man would if he wanted to seduce a girl. The girls in the

majority of cases do not understand what has happened, or how it has happened that they are crazy over this girl who has played the part of a man. For a time the crushes are practically nuts, they spend every cent they can get on their crush— at first they buy her candy and flowers. They idealize their crush so much, that they do not dare offer her things more useful, but the crush soon intimates to them what she would rather have and gets it, and when her gifts are to her liking seems to be about the time she gets her solid work in on the girls, that is about the time they begin to spend all their time together, even sleeping together if they can manage it. Of course the crushes outgrow this phase and cool off, but it leaves them hardened—and they are not quite such nice girls, as they were before they were hurt.

I was shocked when I realized just what a crush was—I could not see any difference between a prostitute and a crush—they both work in the same manner (practically) for what they can get—

For a few days I said nothing, then I went for the nurse who is the worst at the business. First I mentally dissected her from the crown of her head to the soles of her feet—There was nothing extraordinary about her & I was puzzled as to why the girls should fall for her so easily—I watched her and analysed everything she did every oppurtunity [sic] I got.

I no longer wonder why Faculty disapproves of this crush business. This nurse in particular who gets a crush on two or three girls in every new class that comes in—always the girls who have plenty of money—I went for hot and heavy—I intimated to her what I thought about them. She immediately intimated that there was nothing wrong in them that she and her girls simply liked each other pretty well—I spoke very plainly telling her that I knew just what a crush was & what I was talking about—She insinuated that it was none of my business, but I have made it my business & for quite a while now I have bombarded her with sarcasm, & contemptuous remarks—always in public—remarks to which she could make no answer but to laugh and try to pass it off. Then to shut me up she conceived the idea of making me have a crush on her—At first I felt puzzled as to why I was trying to think her nicer than I thought her— then one day when I had made an especially cutting remark I saw something flash in her eyes—You may laugh—but I knew that she was falling for me in earnest and I knew why and also the secret of her success with her crushes—It is simply that she excites them sexually, consciously, but she would do it unconciously [sic] anyway unless she controlled it for she would not be able to help it—and unconsciously I exerted the same influence over her—now I do it consciously for I want to make her look rediculous [sic] and I can do it—that is why I am afraid—I am afraid that I may carry it too far—but I despise her so that nothing that can happen to her seems bad enough to suit me— She cannot help haveing [sic] that sex influence but she can help prostituting— really can not explain all I am afraid of when I think it over—It is all disgusting and I feel disgusted with myself that is all I know. I must be doing wrong although it does seem as if the end I have in view will justify the means (4).

This my fourth week housekeeping. I like it very much—but at times it is almost impossible to realize that it is I who have control of everything that the hospital & nurses need—

[April 22, 1913]

I have come to realize that great as you are you are only a man after all, and therefore incapable of understanding some things.

[November 6, 1915; Waltham Hospital]

P.S. In fact I am in such a mixup with my thoughts of the past & present that at times I am very unhappy—at others scornful & skeptical of everything good ... Perhaps you will understand the mental condition I am in at present. I hardly do myself. I only know that I am struggling to rise over obstructions that threaten to submerge me. I am very glad that I am here and that they placed me in the men's ward. I like the work very much, much better than I had any right to expect I would, and what is best I have very little time to think about anything but my work excepting when I am in bed, then my bones are so still & sore that I could not go wandering around even if I were at liberty to do so; which I am not. I would not be able to write this letter today at all only that I happen to have what is called "morning time" off, and there are no other nurses to bother me by coming into my room to talk. Perhaps you will understand—I do not know but I hope you will, and please don't praise me very much until I tell you I deserve it, and when I think I deserve it you will probably think I won't, which will be true—

[n.d.; Cutler House, Waltham]

After telephoning to you last night I felt much more contented except for that feeling of having left something untold that I wanted to tell you. ... I called up someone in Boston. I told him I was lonesome. He understood, and said he would meet me in Newton, so I went to Boston by way of Newton. He suggested several things to do for amusement, but I was tired and said so. I said I would rather talk, so we went to his rooms. I knew when I got there that I had come with a definite purpose, yet I stayed. I used whatever sex influence I had. I deliberately tried to arouse a sexual desire in him, by willing him to want me, and by using what sex influence I had. He yielded to it. I knew he would before I went there only I hadn't been conscious of knowing it or of just what I had come for. He wanted to touch me, but I would not let him because of a certain bodily exclusiveness I have acquired somehow. I willed him to continue and break down my resistance and he did. He was rough and brutal yet I liked it. If he had hurt me much more than he did I would have liked it. Then I realized suddenly that he was about as hot as I had started out to make him and I thought it was time to stop—so I tried to stop him but couldn't and before I knew what was happening I was quite as hot as he and was wanting him to be as passionate as he could. I loved him because he was so strong. The more he hurt me better I liked it. My arms are bruised, but I love the bruises and the strength that caused them. I relaxed unconsciously, quite willing to give in—suddenly understanding what was the cause of all my restlessness—although of course I had always known it subconciously—I must have—I decided I would take what I wanted so badly and that every time the restlessness attacked me I would come to Boston to him and have him give me what I wanted and what I felt I needed. He was murmuring to me of his desires—What he said doesn't matter—it vaguely displeases me, yet it was what I wanted to hear—He was sure of me because he could see that I was quite as passionate as he if not more so. I at least loved his strength if not him—but I did like him—so I forgot what he was saying. It seemed to me as if I were on fire I was so hot—and I wished him to hurry. My whole body was one leaping pulse and I was in such agony, yet the pain was exquisite. I was mad with desire and could have begged him to give it to me. When he did try to do so all the heat left me, I became as cold as ice & felt absolutely stony. Then I was compelled to fight to get away from him. When he saw I meant it he let me go, but he argued, coaxed & threatened—I don't know what did happen—but when he touched me to do that, such a feeling of repulsion swept me that it wiped out all passion and left me cold. If he had gone any further I would have killed him when he finished and thought me complacent. He could have gone further if he had dared—for I would not have made an outcry and he was much stronger than I, but if he had I would have killed him just as surely as I am writing to tell you about it, and I am sure to tell you everything eventually. He accused me of everything I had done and I admitted the justness of his accusations, but yet could not tell him why I would not be a good sport and go all the way. Why couldn't I Dr. Emerson?

And why should I have gone to him last night when I had not thought of it even before I telephoned to you?

After coming back here it seemed as if I could not go to sleep for hours. When I finally did I dreamt such awful dreams. One was that I saw a man I knew coming right through the door of my room, and on his face was such an expression of leering triumph I shrunk from him, but he came straight on right to my bed. I was mad with anger and waited for him, waiting to spring. The next dream I remember was that there was a car in Central Sq. without a motorman and Margaret Wright was going to run it. I saw her in the vestibule of the car and was horrified to think of her even trying to run the car, for she was not strong and has had to wear a brace for spinal trouble ever since she was a child. I said, no she could not, for she was not strong enough. If there was no one else I would run it. The interior of the Car held about nine people. I knew none of them nor could I see them distinctly. I started the car. It was an awful night and the rain pelted down like fury, and in places along the route the tracks were entirely obliterated by mud. I had to go so carefully, practically feel my way along. Sometimes it seemed as if I had lost the track and that we were way off our course but always we hit the track a little further on. Finally we arrived at the end of the route, and everyone got out. I also got out and took care of a patient all night. In the morning I drove the car back to Central Sq. with practically the same experience with the track. I drove the car every evening for six evenings in succession also took it back to Central Sq. six mornings in succession, always with the same trouble with the track and at night and in the morning it rained and rained and there was mud holes everywhere. Always there was that awful fear of losing the track, and of feeling my way through gallons of mud.

I am so tired today, exhausted mentally and physically, yet there is an haunting feeling of dissatisfaction and an incipient restlessness. I won't have to go through the experience of last night for at least another month will I? I cannot do a thing like that very often for I would soon use up the few men friends I have, for of course I can't expect a man to want to see me again who got fooled the way that one did last night.

I know now that I do not need overdoses of migraine when those fits of restlessness attack me. You will say control them. Impossible! You don't know at all what they are like. You may have some idea, but you don't know. I do—and I am so afraid of the next one.

I use [sic] to hope that the maternal feeling was stronger than the restlessness, and sometimes I thought it was. Lately I don't feel in the least like mothering anybody or thing. I don't even want a baby. Yet when I think I will never have one it makes me frantic and I try to forget it. Sometimes I succeed—⁵

[June 5, 1916; Waltham Hospital]
... I am in the Diptheria Ward and have two patients one a Graduate Nurse and the other a baby boy 22 months old he has been intubed and extubed nine times today was the ninth—the more I see of him the more I love him and the more I want a baby of my own— This morning I woke up with a positive feeling that I would never have any children of my own—You will laugh and think it nonsense, but I have a great deal of faith in my feelings and prophecies. I felt very badly and still do for as yet I have not seen a child whom I could think would be as good as one of my own would be—I am so sorry that I must wait until I am thirty-five before I can marry [see "May 9, 1917"], for it does seem such an awful long time to wait.

[July 19, 1916; Elmwood, Conn.]
So far I have been fairly contented here. I really have not done very much sightseeing ...
That which I told you seemed so simple to me, does not seem at all simple now—and I am sorry that it should be so, for if one must sin, it is so much easier to sin when you think you are really not sinning—I cannot think it simple to do as I want, after being here with Lulu for a week and also I remember everything you said to me the last time I saw you—I resented some of the things you said then, but I don't think I resent them now—I know that everything you said is quite true although I do not like to admit it.
Just the same knowing that you are right and that my doing what I wanted to do was not so simple as I thought—does not cure me of what I want so much.
I do wish so very much that I could have gone away as a war-nurse and if ever there is a chance of my going I will most certainly nab it on the first opportunity—I do want excitement and to feel that I am really living—I don't feel as if I were living now at all. . . . I do a little (a very little) housework, sew and read a great deal—I hate Dickens' works and yet I read them—I have gone out on a few after calls—It seems to be that all anyone here in Elmwood does is accumulate babies and that is all they talk about.
The only single man Lulu has introduced me to talked about nothing but his sister, her husband and her children. Very interesting? Not. He ended up by saying that every woman who was married

should have at least twelve children and more if possible, for the more children they had the less they were apt to get into mischief. I was so angry I could have slapped him good. He made me feel like a suffragette and I don't like to feel like a suffragette for I have no desire to be one. I was all the angrier for I recognized a tiny grain of truth in what he said. When he was leaving he asked me if I would go to the Hartford to the Theatre with him, but I slammed him good—Perhaps you don't know what slammed means—It means to snub some one hard and yet do it politely—What the dickens do people want twelve children for I wonder? I am sure I don't know, but it seems to be the ambition of Elmwood ...

Perhaps when it is time for me to leave here I will be all over those wretched feelings and I won't want to do what is not right. I do know that just now I am not quite as stubborn about wanting it as I was at first.

[July 13, 1916; Elmwood]

... Elmwood is full of Children and Babies. Everybody seems to have at least two of them and everybody talks about themselves and their babies—and a few think it queer that I should prefer Nursing as a profession, to get married & having babies—They amuse and interest me very much ...

I am trying hard to control my sexual feelings and during the daytime I succeed very well, but I cannot control my thoughts and feelings at night. I try hard during the day to become so tired by night that I will feel sleepy & I do not go to bed until 12 but even then I stay awake several hours. I seem bound to have these spells every once in awhile, but never before has it seemed so simply all right for me to do what I want to do and I feel thwarted because I do not do as I wish now—.

Lulu is so good and she thinks me so wonderful that I feel ashamed, for I know that she never has had feelings similar to mine. ... she would be horrified if she knew just how I think about some things.

I am keeping busy and I try to be interested in everything and everybody and I do try to help everybody whenever I can, but at night I am very conscious of myself—and what I want—

[July 28, 1916]

I do want to get to the top & be really cultured, but it does seem impossible for me to accomplish. ... I do think that all that sexual excitement has held me back and made me see things crooked—I do so want to be all that you & others think I can be ...

[May 8, 1917]

... I am asking you why you did not recognize me when you saw me last evening in Harvard Sq. ... Do I not look sufficiently dowdy or respectable, even yet? Do I look like a prostitute even if I am not actually one?

[May 9, 1917]

I don't want joy-rides, booze, smutty stories or to be pawed over by irresponsible men. I am afraid I gave you that impression I did Monday. I do want a husband like you or Dr. Fuller sometime when I am around thirty-five & at present I do want sexual intercourse with a certain person whom you would not approve of.

[August 15, 1917]

... I have become reconciled to the knowledge that I will do the same things over & over again, if I want to and feel that I must. So of course I don't deserve sympathy—Truly I am sorry that I have ended up so badly and that I could not have managed to stay at least fairly decent—I am not contented and find no pleasure in anything but the power of being able to do things.

Signs, 1980, vol.5, no.4.

Notes

1. Excerpt from letter, Downey to Emerson, July 24, 1916: "I feel that somehow I must manage to cure myself. ... but I hardly feel as if I wanted to take the cure—for it is too strenuous a one—I know now that I myself have been unconsciously exerting a sexual appeal to my sexual self—I wonder if that is plain enough for you to understand, it sounds rather complicated to me—and it is complicated—it took me a long time to comprehend[?] what kept my emotions on the go so much—"

2. These excerpts are from Downey's letters to Emerson after her discharge from the Psychopathic Hospital. The location of Emerson's side of the correspondence is not known, if it ever existed. In a postscript to one of her letters not excerpted here (May 25, 1917), Downey wrote, "I think that I want you to answer this for I do want to know just what to do. Perhaps you do not know, but at least you can advise me what to do." Though open to interpretation, that postscript suggests Emerson was not in the habit of replying to Downey's letters regularly and may not have done so at all.

3. For more on the phenomenon of the "crush," see Carroll Smith-Rosenberg's path-breaking essay, "The Female World of Love and Ritual: Relations between Women in Nineteenth-Century America," *Signs: Journal of Women in Culture and*

Society, vol. 1, no. 1 (Autumn 1975): 1-29; and Nancy Sahli's important article, "Smashing: Women's Relationships before the Fall," *Chrysalis* 8: 17-27. I have never been entirely convinced that all of the relationships Smith-Rosenberg describes in her essay were, as she insists, sensual without being sexual—that is, intensely emotional (and to some extent physical) but never genital. Some of the internal evidence Smith-Rosenberg herself presents does, I think, allow for a contrary view, just as certain shifts and ambiguities in her use of key words (e.g., "sensual" and "physical") suggest that more debate on her conclusions is needed. It should be noted that some of the material in Honora Downey's letters—such as her direct references to "sex satisfaction"—provide significant data for such a debate. Downey's description of "this crush business," moreover, is the first evidence I am aware of that the phenomenon was not confined to the middle and upper class women Smith-Rosenberg and Sahli studied. It remains to be seen whether this is a case of cultural "filtering down"; did "crushing" affect lower class women like Downey later in time that it did their upper-class sisters? Do her direct references to "sex satisfaction" reflect differences between the classes in actual experience or only a difference in the less squeamish language lower-class women used to describe what was essentially the same experience? Further valuable additional data for debating these issues can be found in Lillian Faderman, "Female Same-Sex Relationships in Novels by Longfellow, Holmes and James," *New England Quarterly* (September 1978) and her book, *Surpassing The Love of Men* (Morrow: 1981); William G. Shade, "'A Mental Passion': Female Sexuality in Victorian America," *International Journal of Women's Studies,* vol. 1, no. 1 (1978): 13-29; Carl N. Degler, "What Ought to Be and What Was: Women's Sexuality in the Nineteenth Century," *American Historical Review* (December 1974), pp. 1467-90; Catharine R. Stimpson, "The Mind, the Body, and Gertrude Stein," *Critical Inquiry* 3, no. 3 (Spring 1977): 489-506; and Blanche Wiesen Cook, "Female Support Networks and Political Activism: Lillian Wald, Crystal Eastman, Emma Goldman," *Chrysalis* 3:43-61.

4. Why Downey's self-disgust? Was it solely for publicly humiliating another person? Or also because she sensed that she was negating her own "bisexual nature," as discussed with Emerson on July 29, 1916? Even Downey's aparent confidence that the end justifies the means raises questions. Did she feel it "right" and necessary—a la Freud, via Dr. Emerson—to exercise control over "natural" bisexual feelings, and over all sexuality in the name of "civilization"? That Downey housed a double, warring sense of the naturalness of same-sex attraction in tandem with the need to restrain it, seems confirmed in a passage from a letter Downey wrote to Emerson the following month (August 14, 1917): "That girl I told you about 'Farrar' does contrive to make me think about her. I have grown to like having her come up to the stock-room after something or other. I do so like the aggressive tilt of her chin when she enters on an argument. (We had one today—I did not give her what she wanted—but after she went I did wish I could have done so)." Maybe Farrar only wanted a jar of jelly, but in my reading the overtones are sexual.

5. Downey is able—in some moods—to face her strength directly and defy Emerson, just as she faces her strength indirectly in the heroic self-images she creates in dreams: running the car and taking care of a patient all night. She even has the strength to declare that her "maternal instinct" fluctuates—and is sometimes no match for the instinct of lust. Given the values of her day, this was strength indeed.

confidence that the end justifies the means raises questions. Did she feel it "right" and necessary—a la Freud, via Dr. Emerson—to exercise control over "natural" bisexual feelings, and over all sexuality in the name of "civilization"? That Downey housed a double, warring sense of the naturalness of same-sex attraction in tandem with the need to restrain it, seems confirmed in a passage from a letter Downey wrote to Emerson the following month (August 14, 1917): "That girl I told you about 'Farrar' does contrive to make me think about her. I have grown to like having her come up to the stock-room after something or other. I do so like the aggressive tilt of her chin when she enters on an argument. (We had one today—I did not give her what she wanted—but after she went I did wish I could have done so)." Maybe Farrar only wanted a jar of jelly, but in my reading the overtones are sexual.

1913

WALT WHITMAN'S ANOMALY

"The Sale of this Book is restricted to Members of the Legal and Medical Professions." That somber warning appears on the title page, and again on the facing page, of a seventy page pamphlet, Walt Whitman's Anomaly, *which was published in a limited edition in 1913 under the imprint of George Allen & Company, London. It's author was a Dr. W.C. Rivers, its style unflaggingly elevated, its tone stuffy, formalistic, homophobic. But its theme—that Walt Whitman was a homosexual—was for its day daringly direct, even path-breaking.*

Yet the Anomaly *has rarely been mentioned in Whitman studies.[1] Among contemporary scholars, only Robert K. Martin, in* The Homosexual Tradition in American Poetry *(1979), and Jonathan Ned Katz, in* The Gay/Lesbian Almanac *(1983) cite Rivers' pamphlet (though without quoting from it), and neither of the two most heralded recent books on Whitman, Justin Kaplan's biography and Paul Zweig's critical study* [Walt Whitman: The Making of the Poet, 1984]*, make reference to the* Anomaly. *One eminent Whitman scholar, Edward F. Grier of the University of Kansas, did recall, in response to an inquiry from me, that he'd read Rivers "a long time ago," had thought his pamphlet "historically important" and "franker than anyone else for about sixty years" about Whitman's homosexuality.[2]*

Far more important than the disappearance of Rivers' ultimately tiresome, moralistic little book has been the encompassing lack of awareness among Whitman scholars that publication of the Anomaly *led to a significant exchange of letters three quarters of a century ago between Rivers and a number of influential Whitman experts and intimates—and that a complete typescript of that correspondence still exists in the vaults of the Countway Medical Library at Harvard.[3]*

I should add at once that no special grace or merit—neither prescience nor investigative brilliance—accounts for my discovery of the letters. A knowledgeable and sympathetic archivist unceremoniously dumped them into my unwitting hands. It was not at all obvious to me how best to utilize the good fortune. Two pitfalls in particular arose: my lack of special expertise for analyzing the letters to maximum advantage; and the difficulty in deciding which portions of a lengthy correspondence should be excerpted for publication. As

*This essay appears here for the first time.

a guard against incompetence, I've decided to keep "interpretation"
to a minimum, confining myself to factual annotation, and to retain
possession of a complete set of transcripts, for the future use of
Whitman scholars.

"PART I" of the materials below contain excerpts from Rivers'
pamphlet, the Anomaly. *"PART II" consists of selected portions*
from the correspondence which followed the Anomaly's *publication.*

PART I: Excerpts from the *Anomaly.*

"The present writer—a medical man [W.C. Rivers]—chanced
one day to take up Walt Whitman's *Leaves of Grass,* and to open it at
the *Calamus* poems. Almost immediately the strong similarity in
sentiment to that of confessions of homosexual subjects recorded in
text-books on the human sex-instinct became astonishingly evident
... from E. Carpenter[4] and perhaps others of that kidney [have come]
indications of conscious possession of the secret ... and also some
veiled defences from members of the poet's personal circle of friends
and compatriots ... Havelock Ellis[5] ... shows himself ... well aware
of Whitman's true nature, although only touching the subject in
passing[6]. ... But all the above references put together amount to very
little, and the searcher [Rivers] did not find much until he came to the
three valuable works by Eduard Bertz[7]. ... my remarks will as far as
possible be supplemental to [his]. ... For his case, well put as it is, can
yet be strengthened. As an example, take his argument on grounds of
heredity ... the thesis that men of genius, men abnormal in
favourable ways, are also abnormal in unfavourable ways, and ways
which, to speak quite objectively, promote individual and racial
decadence—although this thesis is not exactly demonstrated, it is
considered by most judges of the question to be extremely likely to be
true.

[*A lengthy analysis of Whitman's poetry follows, designed to*
prove he was an "invert"]

Walt Whitman's personal character is ... typical of the male
invert. If ever one had the woman's soul in the man's body, it was he.
In almost everything except outward form he was a woman.

As witness a series of traits common in a ... male homosexual. He
never smoked ... he cared nothing for sport ... In cooking he
delighted, not as a sportsman sometimes will, but for its own sake....
Then he can talk about clothes with a woman's knowledge. ... For
nursing he had a truly feminine devotion and aptitude. ... feminine
admiration and feminine pity for military suffering were undoubtedly
his deepest motive in acting thus. ... No true man could feel like that,

however full of compassion and patriotism. . . . Of a piece with all this is his naturally unnatural indifference to women—one might indeed almost say, other women. . . .

Whitman's letters to Peter Doyle are love letters pure and simple . . . one need only mention the rows of kisses marked upon the paper with crosses, the old question as to whose affection is the greater, and the quarrel followed by renewal of love 'more than before'. . . .

[*Rivers next proceeds to examine previous studies on Whitman and— to his own satisfaction —demolish their misguided denials of Whitman's "true sexual nature." From there, Rivers moves to his conclusions:*] If Walt Whitman was homosexual, then, to what variety of male inversion did he belong? Essentially the *passive* kind, as one might expect from his pronouncedly feminine nature . . . Whitman liked rough, virile youths . . . Feminine passivity partly explains what we get a hint of here, namely the often-expressed love for criminals, which is also due, however, to sympathy from consciousness of some degree of fellowship in guilt. . . .

This invariable passivity has a bearing on the question as to whether Whitman confined his feelings of affection for his own sex to the emotional sphere only, or whether they found physical vent. . . . For the most part, as in all the nursing episodes, it was emotional, spiritual, wholly altruistic: nevertheless it was 'well rooted in the physical and sexual also'[8], especially up to middle age. . . . Partly on account of the passivity noticed, there is no need to charge the poet with the grossest unnatural indulgence of an active kind[9] but that he experienced orgasm seems certain . . . probably masturbation. For Whitman mere contact would suffice[10]. What, then, was his private moral self-evaluation? Enough has been already quoted. . . . to show his thorough consciousness of abnormality; which he sometimes rejoices in self-reliantly, sometimes repents of; the mean of his oscillation being on the whole much nearer confident avowal than shame. . . . it must be admitted that Walt Whitman was homosexual. The conclusion is as sound as an anvil."

[*That such was not "admitted" is evident in the following excerpts from letters written to Rivers after the* Anomaly *appeared in print.*]

PART II: Selected Correspondence.[11]

A. *Bliss Perry to Rivers, Nov, 13, 1913.* [*Perry was the well-known literary critic and professor of literature at Harvard. Among many other critical studies, his* Walt Whitman *continues to have its admirers among them the contemporary Whitman scholar, Paul Zweig.*]

".... As far as I am aware, there has never been the slightest evidence that Whitman practised homo-sexuality. When I wrote my own book on him in 1906 [*Walt Whitman;* reprinted AMS Press, New York: 1969], I had been in very close relations with most of his surviving friends, and I talked very frankly about his physical life to such intimates as Burroughs, Gilder, Stedman, Johnston, Talcott Williams, and Horace Traubel[12]—to say nothing of Dr. Weir Mitchell, his physician during the Camden period, and I have never heard, in talk or print until this last year, any rumor of the charge of homo-sexuality. The nearest approach to it was in a conversation with the widow of Whitman's friend W.D. Connor, with whom W.W. lived for many months in Washington. She [Ellen O'Connor] told me that J.S. Symonds[13] (whose 'case' is doubtless familiar to you as a medical expert) was 'troubled' about certain passages in *Calamus.* ... Mrs. O'Connor (afterwards Mrs. Calder) was a close friend of mine, and talked about Walt with the greatest frankness. She herself, it was clear, did not share Symonds' early scruples about the meaning of certain portions of *Calamus.* I knew Peter Doyle, but only in the last years of his life. He was a big Irishman, with a sense of humor; very loyal to Walt's memory. All I can say is ... I have never heard the slightest hint of the charge [that Whitman was homosexual] mentioned ... If there are any 'facts', they have eluded the search of the men who knew Whitman best."

In the Anomaly *(p.26), Rivers had written, "Doyle was no more than an uneducated young Irishman, a soldier to begin with, but in the sixties a Washington tramcar conductor (the occupations are the customary ones—[i.e. for proving attractive to homosexuals] although it is not certain that he wore a conductor's uniform").*

Whitman met Doyle in the 1860's. Despite an age difference of almost 30 years, the two men became passionately attached, the precise nature of that attachment still a subject of debate. Paul Zweig and Justin Kaplan, authors of the two most heralded books on Whitman of recent years, continue—in subtler form than their predecessors (as befits the progress of the age) the long tradition among critics and biographers of fudging the central question of sexuality in the Doyle/Whitman relationship. Zweig does venture the "guess" that "at least some of Whitman's young men [were] also bed partners"—and hastens to add the additional guess that such experiences could not have been "happy" ones. Why? Because

Whitman was in "desperate conflict" about his sexuality and to ease it must have resorted to "the erotic strategy of 'indirection'". The recent crop of openly gay critics such as Robert K. Martin, Jonathan Katz, Joseph Cady and Arnie Kantrowitz ("The Good Gay Poet", The Advocate, *September 2, 1982) deplore the tepid conclusions drawn by Zweig and others as veiled homophobia, as a dilution and mockery of the meaning of Whitman's life and art. The paucity of concrete historical data (due in part to Whitman's own obfuscations) guarantees a continuing debate—to which the new material contained in this essay will, hopefully, add some further illumination.[14]*

Far more direct illumination appeared—and to my knowledge has been wholly ignored by Whitman scholars ever since—in a brief memoir Gavin Arthur published in the winter 1978 issue of Gay Sunshine. *It seems worth summarizing here.*

According to Allen Ginsberg, in a headnote (July 1, 1977) for the Gay Sunshine *piece, he had prodded Gavin Arthur to set down an account of his sexual encounter as a young man in the 1920's with Edward Carpenter, then about 80 and nearing the end of his life. Arthur had done so and in 1967 turned the memoir over to Ginsberg, who than waited until after Arthur's death in 1972 before making it available for publication. Before summarizing Arthur's memoir as it appeared in* Gay Sunshine, *some background information on the man may be useful. Gavin Arthur was the grandson of President Chester Arthur (christened Chester Alan Arthur III, he adopted the name Gavin as a young man). Born to privilege, educated in elite schools, Arthur early turned his back on that world, worked his way around the globe, became friendly with such pioneering spirits as Havelock Ellis and Gertrude Stein, eventually took up astrology as an avocation and settled in San Francisco.*

Arthur's memoir is an altogether astonishing piece of personal revelation. Should it prove truthful—which at the moment is impossible to say, given the absence of any corroborating evidence— the memoir would definitely set to rest the protracted debate over whether or not Whitman's "homoerotic" impulses were ever "acted out". If we can believe Arthur's account—and it does ring true, containing no obvious falsities of tone or fact—it becomes beyond cavil that Whitman did actually have sex (and enjoyably) with another man (more than one, and more than once).

As Gavin Arthur tells it, his informant in the matter was none other than Edward Carpenter. The two men met when mutual friends took the youthful Arthur on a visit to Carpenter's home in England during the 1920's. They ended up in bed together when Arthur asked

*Carpenter, some 60 years his senior, whether he and Walt Whitman
had ever had sex together. "Oh yes," Carpenter replied, "—once in a
while—he [Whitman] regarded it as the best way to get together with
another man. He thought that people should 'know' each other on the
physical and emotional plane as well as the mental." Arthur then
blurted out his next question:*

"How did he make love?"

*"I will show you," Carpenter said with a smile. He suggested they
go to bed. Arthur describes what followed: "It was a warm night and
we had just a light eiderdown over us. We were both naked and we lay
side by side on our backs holding hands. Then he was holding my
head in his two hands and making little growly noises, staring at me in
the moonlight. 'This is the laying on of hands' I thought reverently.
'Walt. Then him. Then me.' . . . . He snuggled up to me and kissed my
ear. His beard tickled my neck. He smelled like the leaves and ferns
and soil of autumn woods. . . . I remembered Walt's indignant denial
to Symonds' inquiry [see preceding Note, under "Symonds"]. . . . The
old man at my side was stroking my body with the most expert touch
. . . caressing the flesh with feather lightness.*

*"I just lay there in the moonlight that poured in at the window and
gave myself up to the loving old man's marvelous petting. Every now
and then he would bury his face in the hair of my chest, agitate a
nipple with the end of his tongue, or breathe in deeply from my
armpit. I had of course a throbbing erection but he ignored it for a
long time. Very gradually, however, he got nearer and nearer, first
with his hand, later with his tongue which was now flickering all over
me like summer lightning. I stroked whatever part of him came within
reach of my hand but I felt instinctively that this was a one-sided
affair . . . And then when he was tickling my fundament just below the
balls and I could not hold it longer, his mouth closed just over the
head of my penis and I could feel my young vitality flowing into his
old age. He did not suck me at all. It was really* karezza [a male-
continence technique dating to the 19th century. For more information on karezza see Hal D. Sears, The Sex Radicals, The Regents
Press of Kansas: 1977.] *which I knew he recommends in his book. I
had not learned the control necessary to* karezza, *and he did not want
to waste that life giving fluid. . . . He was in no sense a succubus . . . the
emphasis was on the caressing and loving. I fell asleep like a child safe
in father-mother arms, the arms of God. . . ."*

*Since Carpenter has always been known as a truth-teller, even
among his detractors, those unconvinced of the authenticity of the
above account would be well advised to focus their skepticism on*

Gavin Arthur's trustworthiness as a source. That skepticism can be neither dispelled or confirmed—short of the unlikely appearance of a third party witness to what appears to have been an irreduceably private event.

B. William Osler to Rivers, August 19, 1913. (Osler was the noted English physician.)

"It is most kind of you to send your booklet on W.W. whom I knew for 4 years, as a patient and friend. Of course the *Calamus* group of poems is hard to swallow. Bucke[15], with whom I was very intimate, and who was a very level-headed fellow—except on the question of W.W.!—always resented the suggestion....

I think we must acknowledge a male passion which is not base— i.e. physical. Just before the war I was consulted by a big burly undergraduate [at Oxford] who was in despair over the depth of his attachment to a fellow student. The subject was bored to death—and terribly annoyed—sonnets, flowers, etc.!"

C. Eduard Bertz[16] to Rivers, Potsdam, March 12, 1913.

"Your book on 'Walt Whitman's Anomaly' came to me as a most valuable aid, and I beg to express to you my sincere gratitude.... I have been persecuted by the Whitmanites with the utmost hatred, and the obstinate denial, in those circles, is still so strong, that a confirmation like yours, especially as you are an Englishman, moves me to great rejoicing.

I was told, two years ago, that my books on Whitman are well-known in England, among people who take an interest in the question of inversion. Also Mr. Edward Carpenter wrote to me, in 1906, that he thought my first paper ['Ein Charakterbild'] 'extremely good and complete'. At the same time he mentioned that Dr. Havelock Ellis 'thinks highly of it'. But there was no public acknowledgement, till now. ... In his book entitled 'The Intermediate Sex', which first appeared in German, Mr. Carpenter curiously charges me with begging the question, because I had said that Whitman's gospel, as it originated in his personally abnormal instincts, was without value to the normal. Of course Mr. Carpenter cannot be impartial, seeing that he entirely shares Whitman's fatal delusion....

As to the question whether Whitman's inverted feelings found physical vent, you are right in hinting that in 'Whitman-Mysterien' I meant to reply to it in the affirmative. Still, I had a strong suspicion only, at the time. But subsequently, in a lecture which I was requested to give at Berlin, in April, 1911, before a medical audience, I was able to refer to living witnesses. The person mentioned on p. 171 of 'Whitman-Mysterien', is the well-known American writer James Huneker, who has personally investigated the case, and elicited a mass of details about Whitman's homosexual intercourse, from working-men, etc., who, when young fellows, had been the objects of Whitman's appetite, or knew all about it.[17]

And last year I heard from Dr. [Magnus] Hirschfeld that the German-American poet [George Sylvester Viereck; some eight words are here inked out] has told him of a personal avowal he received from an American lawyer still living at Chicago. This lawyer, when a boy of fourteen(!!), has been made an object of *fellatio* by the great Walt Whitman. In that and in similar cases, then, the poet was active. That, of course, would be an indication against your diagnosis of Whitman's 'passivity',[18] for *fellatio* is active in appearance only. And indeed, I believe that Whitman was a fellator in an objective as well as in a subjective sense. The poem quoted by you ... viz. 'I mind how once we lay', is, as I feel convinced, a confession, slightly veiled only, of *passive fellatio.* [i.e. giving head?] (By-the-by,, this form of homosexual practice seems to be especially common in the United States—at least that thought struck me when I read Ellis's 'Sexual Inversion').

In conclusion, let me say that you have certainly strengthened the case. And to me it gave an especial satisfaction that you arrived at your results quite independently of previous investigations. But indeed, the truth is so evident that one hardly understands how any sane man can have the courage to deny it."

D. Bertz to Rivers, Potsdam, March 29, 1913.

"I was very glad that my letter gave you pleasure. I hope you will be able to pursue your investigations. By united effort, even the slightest doubt about Whitman's sexual practice should soon be removed. ... most of the American and French Whitmaniacs read no German. ... far more dangerous than [their] ... open attacks is their change of tactics, viz. the conspiracy of silence to which they have resorted...."

E. Bertz to Rivers, Potsdam, June 18, 1913.

"James Hunekers' letter[19] which you kindly transmitted for me, interested me much. Your conclusion that he does not care to say anything definite, is no doubt right. He evidently is afraid to have his name publicly mentioned in that connection, as people might surmise that Whitman's intimates would not have imparted their secret to any one of whom they had not good reason to believe that he belonged to their kind.

But, at the same time, he admits that he heard much, etc. That, to a certain degree, is a confirmation of what I was told about his knowledge.

Now let me repeat: [George Sylvester] Viereck and Prince-Stevenson [Xavier Mayne] are total strangers to each other, and never met, perhaps do not even know of each other's existence. But I heard the same story about Huneker from either of them, and both asserted that he had told them. So he *must* have told them, for it would be a miracle if both had invented the same story about the same man, especially as there was no reason for such invention.

By-the-by, Viereck's later story, that of the Chicago lawyer[20], was *not* derived from Huneker, but extracted by himself. That story he told Dr. Hirschfeld from whom I got it.

I quite expect that Viereck, if cross-questioned, will likewise deny. I know nothing of Huneker's personal character, but of Viereck I know that he is a vain poseur who will pronounce any untruth if it should suit his interest, a man without a particle of sincerity in his constitution.

There will always remain this difficulty: only partners in guilt can know anything definite about Whitman's sexual activity, and they will be afraid because they would accuse themselves.

Pity that Peter Doyle died a few years ago. He, I think, would have spoken out, if only a sensible person had interviewed him. Bucke and Traubel[21] were too silly for the purpose...."

F. Bertz to Rivers, Potsdam, February 18, 1914.

"It would certainly be important to find at last some courageous witness to Whitman's homsexual deeds. For the diagnosis of homosexualtiy, such deeds are of secondary importance only, it is true; the manner of feeling, as unveiled in Whitman's works, is primarily evidential. But there are many people ... who do not believe in any merely psychical demonstration."

G. Havelock Ellis to Rivers, London, May 14, 1913.

"As regards Whitman as *fellator*, I should not regard this as absolutely impossible, but I am extremely skeptical in regard to all reports concerning celebrated people. I have often found the most detailed scandals, when there was not even a grain of truth in them, and sometimes when the real truth was of quite an opposite nature."

H. Solomon Eagle (J.C. Squire) to Rivers, London, October 5, 1914.
"By-the-by, ... an American writer to whom I was talking about Whitman on Saturday swore solemnly—I had not heard it before—that in spite of all Walt's talk about glorious clean bodies glistening on the beach the old boy went for 20 years without taking a bath."

I. Bertz to Rivers, n.d.
" ... in my opinion you overestimate the danger of a possible emancipation of homosexuals. Look at France and Italy where there are no laws against inverted acts as such: in those countries there is no more homosexuality than in Germany, or in England either. Indeed, from all I hear, the frequency of homosexual acts is hardly influenced by legislation, only the secrecy is, but the latter effect is attained in France by stern laws against *public* violation of decency. There cannot be the slightest doubt, I believe, that society is morally justified in protecting its *youth* against being debauched, as well as in preventing any *public* breach of modesty. But is there any justice in criminally punishing private homosexual intercourse among *adults*? In two respects such interference is in contradiction with the spirit of modern legislation. For one thing, it violates the principle of individual liberty. ... And, on the other hand, justice demands that there be no punishment where there is no *guilt*. And there really is not if, as cannot be doubted, homosexuality is an *inborn*, or *constitutional*, or pathological anomaly. Not all, but the majority of homosexual acts are committed under an impulse which to a great degree excludes responsibility. ... Of course Carpenter and other enthusiasts will never succeed in convincing normal people of the *social* utility of inverts. Though homosexuals, as individuals, may often be socially useful, as a class they are certainly not desirable... "

NOTES
1. Rather than attempt to review the vast literature on Whitman, I refer those interested to the first chapter of Robert K. Martin's thorough and penetrating book, *The Homosexual Tradition in American Poetry* (Univ. of Texas: 1979), and also to Joseph Cady's particularly sensitive study, "Homosexuality and the Calamus Poems," *American Studies,* Fall 1978.

For just one gem of scholarly attitudes toward Whitman's homosexuality (and homosexuality *per se*), I include here a letter from Gay Wilson Allen, a Whitman biographer, responding to a review of mine (of a television program on Walt

Whitman) that appeared in *The New York Times*, Jan. 11, 1976:

"Martin Duberman complains that there are no "gays" in our textbooks: 'The standard works on even celebrated literary figures (Gay Wilson Allen's biography of Walt Whitman, for example, or Leon Edel's 'Henry James') demurely bypass the question of sexual preference, presuming no more than an occasional elevated 'infatuation'. But the presumption of *sex*—Never! No one in our history, it seems, has ever been to bed with anybody of the same gender....'

Evidently Professor Duberman has not read my biography of Whitman with much attention (or Edel's later volumes of "Henry James" either), for in numerous places I discuss Whitman's deep homoerotic emotions. But I did not detail all the men the poet "slept" with, or state that he slept with them to engage in sodomy. That he may have I nowhere denied, but no detective broke into the room to record the act, and for all I *actually* know he may have shared beds because the beds he could afford were scarce. I think a biographer should go as far as his facts permit, but not to state as positive truth what took place in the dark of night without more evidence than Whitman's ambiguous words "slept with"—even Duberman admits the ambiguity.

Perhaps in 1973 it is fatuous to insist on a difference between physical sexuality and fantasy, especially for those who think that to be called "gay" is an honor. In 1955, when I published the Whitman biography, the term was not publicly sought, yet if I were writing the book today I would not handle Whitman's sex pathology differently. And I would still try to avoid simplifying a complex subject, for Whitman was not consistently a textbook example of a homosexual—perhaps no one is. My only regret is that when I began publishing I could not foresee that forty years later my first name would become an acute embarrassment."

Gay Wilson Allen

2. Grier to Duberman, April 20, 1977. I'd like to acknowledge here my gratitude to Grier for his lively encouragement and for the magnanimous way he shared his formidable knowledge of Whitman source materials. For the full importance of his contribution to this article, see the details in the following footnote.

3. One exception was eventually turned up by Edward Grier. Becoming as enthused as I about the value of the newly recovered "Rivers Correspondence," and as mystified about why and where it had lain buried, he ultimately came across a three page "note" ("Toward Destroying a Myth" by a Frances Oakes) in the *Walt Whitman Newsletter* of September 1956 that made some reference to the "collected but unpublished" letters. Maddeningly, Oakes (both Grier and I were unable to uncover any identifying information) fails to provide any hint in her "note" about the whereabouts of the original correspondence (at least as of 1956). Nor in her note has she turned her apparent access to the letters to any advantage. Unable to muster minimal competence to support her flatout assertion that the "charge" of homosexuality against Whitman has to be false because the trait "would have contradicted the very essence of his poetic expression," Oakes cannot even accurately identify familiar names (John Addington Symonds is called "Arthur Symonds" and Peter Viereck is mistakenly substituted for his father, George Sylvester Viereck). As incompetent—indeed borderline illiterate—as Oakes' discussion is, it does serve to reveal that somewhere the original manuscripts of the Rivers Correspondence do exist (or at least did some thirty years ago). The transcripts owned by the Countway Library seem to be careful and complete, but we cannot be sure short of checking them against the originals. Hopefully, those will one day resurface.

4. Edward Carpenter(1844-1929) was, in brief, among the major precursors of the modern homophile movement and consciousness. As early as the 1870's he committed himself to radical politics (socialist and anarchist), denounced organized religion and openly celebrated his homosexuality. Among Carpenter's voluminous writings, *Towards Democracy, Iolus* (the first—1892—gay literary anthology) and his autobiography, *My Days and Dreams* (1916) probably constitute his major legacy. For more on Carpenter, see especially Sheila Rowbotham and Jeffrey Weeks, *Socialism and The New Life: The Personal and Sexual Politics of Edward Carpenter and Havelock Ellis* (Pluto Press: 1977).

5. Ellis was, of course, the great English sexologist. For more on Ellis, see Phyllis Grosskurth, *Havelock Ellis: A Biography,* (Knopf: 1980). For additional discussion of Ellis and Kinsey, see Paul Robinson, *The Modernization of Sex: Havelock Ellis, Alfred Kinsey, William Masters and Virginia Johnson,* (Harper and Row: 1976).

6. See references in the *Gay Sunshine* article discussed on pp. 88-90.

7. *Walt Whitman, Ein Charakterbild: Whitman Mysterien, Eine Abrechnung: Der Yankee Heiland.* Bertz was an early champion of Whitman's poetry in Germany. In the three works cited, he had early on asserted that Whitman was homosexual—and condemned him for it. For more on Bertz, see his letters to Rivers in this article (pp. 90-93) and Robert K. Martin, *op. cit.,* p. 7).

8. Rivers is here quoting from Jonathan Burroughs, *Walt Whitman as Poet and Person.* For more on Burroughs, see footnote 12.

9. That is, apparently, fucking—which Rivers seems to have viewed as more "degenerate" than sucking.

10. For some illuminating parallels in analysis here see Joseph Cady's "Homosexuality and the 'Calamus' Poems", *American Studies,* Fall 1978.

11. The Countway Library collection of transcripts contain some dozen additional letters from which I have not drawn excerpts: those written by B. Dobell, W.N. Guthrie (Rector of St. Mark's Church in New York) and Barrett Wendell (the literary critic)—as well as additional letters from Havelock Ellis, Eduard Bertz and William Osler (the English physician).

12. John Burroughs, the great naturalist, met Whitman in 1863 when the former was still young and unknown. His first published work, *Notes on Walt Whitman as Poet and Person* (1867) was an admiring study, and remains useful. Burroughs was out of Whitman's circle within a few years.

Richard Watson Gilder was an influential writer and critic in the decades preceding World War I, a member of the so-called "genteel" generation. Gilder edited the highly regarded literary journal *The Century.* Though he admired Whitman's poetry, he was at no time an intimate.

Edmund Clarence (E.C.) Stedman, stockbroker and author, was a member of Gilder's literary generation and shared his modulated enthusiasm for Whitman's poetry; his 1880 essay on Whitman in *Scribner's Magazine,* partisan yet cautious, had particular influence. Like Gilder, Stedman was barely acquainted with Whitman—in no sense personally close, as Bliss Perry says. In his book *The Homosexual Tradition in American Poetry* (University of Texas, 1979, pp. 106-109), Robert K. Martin has suggested that some of Richard Henry Stoddard's love poetry may have been addressed (in disguised form) to Stedman; there is no parallel in Stedman's own work.

The "Johnston" referred to in Perry's letter is apparently John Johnston, who, with J.W. Wallace, wrote *Visits to Walt Whitman* in 1890-1891(London, 1917). (See, too, the reference to Johnston in Havelock Ellis to Rivers, November 13, 1912, not excerpted here, which refers to a visit paid by an Englishman named Johnston). I have found no reference anywhere in the standard works on Whitman to a "Talcott Williams". Doubtless he and Johnston can be located elsewhere in the Whitman canon—Bliss Perry was not given to outright fabrication—but the inability to identify both men readily, does strongly argue against Perry's classification of them as Whitman's "intimates".

Only Horace Traubel, among those Perry refers to as intimates, seems entitled to that designation—and then only for the last fifteen years of Whitman's life, when the youthful Traubel was among a handful of devotees surrounding the poet. Intimacy, however, is no guarantee of understanding or even accuracy. The several volumes Traubel published on Whitman after the poet's death contain many distortions, including his account of Whitman's sexuality.

For more information on these figures, see Roger Austen, *Playing the Game: The Homosexual Novel in America* (Bobbs-Merrill: 1977).

13. John Addington Symonds, the English writer, corresponded with Whitman for some 20 years. Especially enthused over the "Calamus" section of *Leaves of Grass,* Symonds persisted in pressing Whitman for confirmation that "Calamus" centrally celebrated the joys of "Greek friendship". In his final letter to Symonds, Whitman heatedly rejected that interpretation as invalid, asserting, among other things, that he was the father of six illegitimate children (a claim for which no significant evidence exists). For additional details on the Symonds/Whitman relationship, see the previously cited books by Martin and Kaplan as well as Jonathan Katz, *Gay American History,* Crowell, 1976, pp. 341-351.

14. For more on Doyle, see Katz, *Gay American History,* pp. 499, 628, and the books already cited, by Robert K. Martin, Kaplan and Zweig.

15. Richard Maurice Bucke, physician, alienist, and superintendant of an insane asylum in Ontario during the last decades of the twentieth century, first met Whitman in 1873 and became one of the poet's most strenuous champions. One of Whitman's three literary executors, Bucke published several volumes of the poet's work after his death in 1892—but 'glossed over' the question of his homosexuality. (Michael Lynch, "Walt Whitman in Ontario", *The Body Politic,* October, 1980.)

16. For information on Bertz, see footnote 7.

17. Typed onto transcript: "Huneker denies all knowledge of this; it may be a trifle overstated but I believe Bertz rather than H." The "I" in this note on the typed transcript is apparently Rivers.

18. See p. 86.

19. The letter is not among those in the Countway collection.

20. See p. 91.

21. See footnote number 12 and 15.

1914-1921

DOCUMENTS IN HOPI INDIAN SEXUALITY

Any scholar researching the history of human sexuality will attest to the formidable obstacles involved: the sheer difficulty of discovering new manuscript material to add to the pathetically scant stockpile currently available and—should such material be found—the Byzantine intrigues which must be embarked upon in an effort to get permission from the "proper authorities" to publish. Understaffed as they are, every great manuscript library in this country is years behind in cataloguing its accessions—and material of "dubious morality" rarely gets catalogued at all. To cope with the double jeopardy of archival staffs ignorant of the contents of their own collections or deliberately bent on concealing them, scholars in pursuit of new sources on human sexuality would ideally be equipped with the personality of Sherlock Holmes: psychic skill in divining clues, fierce tenacity (concealed by elegant surface civility) in running them down. Holmes' easy access to the inspirational white powder would doubtless help, too.

Most of us, alas, must make do with less: with a large tolerance for tedious, needle-in-the haystack research through pounds of documents "likely" (family correspondence, say) to yield occasional nuggets; with occasional leads from generous fellow scholars; with the unpredictable surrender of an archivist to our pleas, our perseverance, our prematurely grey hair.

As I've intermittently trudged around the country searching for manuscript materials, I've run into my fair share of roadblocks— angry disclaimers, cool dissimulations. The story behind the discovery of the particular documents printed here is one of the cheerier tales. A friend of many years, Charles Blitzer of the Smithsonian Institute, volunteered to query the archivists who head the varied departments of that vast depository to see if any might have documents pertinent to my work. One of them—James R. Glenn of the National Anthropological Archives—did. He led me to some ethnographic material not previously accessible to scholars—preeminently a set of "depositions," or affidavits, taken down between 1914 and 1921 in New Mexico and Arizona which described aspects of Hopi culture—and he expertly guided me through them.

The documents I finally chose from that bulky collection of

97

affidavits at the Smithsonian to publish here (in excerpted form) seemed to stand out from the rest for richness and diversity of detail or for the importance of the subjects discussed. The affidavits contain considerable material describing attitudes and acts. But description is not meaning. We need a much fuller understanding than we currently have.of what the described behavior signifies—*to the Hopi themselves, but also, by extension, to all of us.*

My original article in Radical History Review *is lengthy and heavily documented. In this version I have omitted the bulk of it, which is specifically heterosexual.*

The Documents

Commissioner of Indian Affairs,
Washington

Dear Sir:

I am enclosing letters concerning practices of secret dances by the Pueblo Indians.

These dances are too loathsome and repugnant for me to describe.

. . . It may be possible that in some of the pueblos the dances are not so immoral and degrading as in the others, but in practially all cases they are detrimental to the advancement of the Indians and counteract the work of the schools. . .

These dances have have become known as "secret dances," from the fact that they were forbidden by the Spanish authorities . . . when they were too vulgar for the sensibilities of a Spanish explorer of the sixteenth centry, you can imagine how bad they were.

I have obtained statements. . .

They are vulgar and I am almost shamed to send them through the mails, but they are the exact truth. . .

> Very respectfully,
> (Sgd) P.T.
> LONERGAN,
> Superintendent.
> Albuquerque, New Mexico
> December 7, 1915

L.R. McDonald to Superintendent T. Lonergan

Mr. P.T. Lonergan,
Supt. Pueblo Agency,
Albuquerque, New Mexico.
May 11, 1915

Dear Sir:

In reply to your letter regarding a secret dance at Santo Domingo that I observed in company with Mr. Lambert, wish to say that it is quite impossible to describe the dance in polite language ... The men and the women too had less clothes on than any dancing Indians I have seen. Their chief object and amusement seemed to be in imitating animals in the act of sexual intercourse. A man would chase a woman like a rooster chases a hen. The woman would not struggle to escape the man, but entered into the spirit of the game with as much zeal as the man. She would squat like a hen or bend over like a cow or sheep. The man would bend over the woman and hold her tight in his arms exactly as a stallion, a ram or a dog would do in the act of sexual intercourse, going through all the motions with his body. Some women would be held a few seconds and some a few minutes. Some of the men wore masks...

"Bestiality"

At Sichomovi Village I saw a clown commit sexual intercourse with a female burro. At Sichomovi also I saw two katsinas [clowns] coming into the plaza on his all fours, representing a burro, and the other driving him, sometimes riding him as a burro. After awhile the driver katsina dramatized the act of sexual intercourse with the katsina burro—the driver katsina with the burro katsina. This was done merely to make the people laugh...

I have seen for twenty years the Indians of Jemez and Sia pueblos dancing—fucking animals—like burrows and cows and horses. I have seen the same thing in Jemez and Sia pueblos, Indian men and women also. This year I went to Sia, close to the church, the Indians did not see me, and I saw the Indians fucking like goats, burros and horses fucking—many men and women.
(Deposition of Macario Garcia,
San Isidro, Oct. 29, 1915)

...at one time carried the mail from Albuquerque to Jemez. Going through with a passenger we saw the Indians dancing a very immoral dance, jumping up on each other imitating dogs, goats or other beasts ... They permit girls and boys to dance in these dances naked.

> (Deposition of Blas Casaus,
> San Isidro, New Mexico,
> November 7, 1915)

"Cross-Dressing"

Deponent states that when he was present at ... said dance [at Moencopi, the Hopi village near Tuba, Arizona] one of the katsinas, or katsina clowns, was on the street going about among the spectators playing the role of a prostitute soliciting men and boys to accompany her for purposes of sexual intercourse; that said katsina would catch the eye of a bystander and signaled him to follow her (katsina dressed as to represent a female) by beckoning with the hand, and then went through signs indicating the act of sexual intercourse; that this was done repeatedly, in the presence of men, women and children.

> (Deposition of David M. Wynkoop,
> stockman on the Western Navajo Indian
> Reservation, Tuba Arizona;
> August 16, 1920)

One day I entered the dance plaza through a little side opening and sat down, quite unobserved, it seemed ... Two clowns ... dressed as women came into the court. Their skirts were very short, not over eleven inches long. The men clowns would go up to them and try to pull the skirts down a little. The clowns who stood behind the women would try to pull the skirts down in the back but while doing so the skirts would slip up in front, then the clowns who stood in front would stoop down and look up under the skirt as if looking at a woman's private organs. Then the other clowns would come around and have a look, then all would make believe that they were trying to pull the skirts down, then stoop and look under to see how much they could see. All this brought forth much laughter and many yells from the crowd.

> (Deponent identified only as "woman
> employee"—apparently white).

Flogging and Urination

...deponent learned that the Hopi Indians were to initiate some of the school children into the ceremony of the bean dance, and that the school children were excused to attend said initiation ... Deponent states that a part of said initiation or ceremony consisted of flogging or whipping said children with the long leaves of the yucca or spanish-dagger plant. That it is deponent's understanding or information that said children are instructed not to make any outcry, but stood stolidly and endured said flogging; although it was evident to deponent that the same was quite severe...

> (Deposition of Mary A. Wynkoop,
> employed as a temporary Teacher [1905-6]
> of the Moencopi Day-School on the
> Western Navajo Indian Reservation

...that in said ceremony said children were brought before said katsinas and their bare arms beaten with yucca leaves; that one of said children began to cry under the pain of such beating; that thereupon one of the older Indians, the father of Sam Numkinu, thereupon stepped forward and bared his arm and told the katsina to beat him, whereupon he was beaten so severely with the yucca leaves that the blood flowed from the wound resulting therefrom, yet without any outcry or sound of suffering on his part...

> (Deposition of J.B. Frey, Superintendent
> of missions in Arizona for the General
> Conference Mennonite Church)

...One part of the play was for the Devil to chase a clown and throw him to the ground—after the clown was thrown the Devil would sit astride of his neck for a while and sometimes make motions as if he were going to urinate down the man's throat. Miss McMullen, one of the teachers at Polacca said she actually saw a clown urinate down another clown's throat at one dance which she attended.

> (deponent identified as "woman
> employee"—apparently white).

Male Sex Organs

Deponent states that when he was about ten years of age he took part ... in [his] first dance ... the clowns raised the question as to which katsina was the best dancer, to determine which they isolated one at a time from the line, and threatened that if he made a mistake in dancing, his punishment should be that they would remove his G-string or loin-cloth and expose him in the nude; that it was prearranged that most of the katsinas should pass this test, until a certain one was reached who intentionally blundered in the dance, and was thus rudely disrobed of his loin-cloth, that is, his outer loin-cloth; because, underneath this he had fastened to himself a fabricated penis-image of unusual size; that when this became exposed the crowd roared with laughter, some remarking that the said image was like that of a burro; whereupon, by prearrangement as a part of the drama ... they chased him from the court or open street where the dance was taking place, thus feigning to be running the man out of town...

> (Otto Lomavitu)

Statement of Sarah E. Abbot, December 8, 1920

I will relate a few things that I saw take place in one of the dances ... In the "Pollylokong" or mechanical snake dance, the snakes come thru an opening in a large screen, a man pretended to wrestle with one of the snakes, the snake tore off the mans gee string and fondled his private, there were present, white ladies Hopi women and young girls and children, at another time the clown Kachineas that entertain the people, some were dressed as Hopi women, and a man put his hand under her dress and showed the people he found blood saying even the men menstrate...

> (Signed)
> SARAH E. ABBOTT.
> Field Matron.
> Hotevella, Arizona
> 12-8-20

Premarital and Extramarital Intercourse

Q. When the dances are given, is there any immorality or wrongdoing going on among the Indians?

A. Yes. About sundown when the Snake Dance is over, everybody gets supper, and after that the men and boys have things of value—corn, or water-melon, or other fruit, or cloth, or ribbon, or anything of value and the girls and women run after the men to take the things they have. The man will hold it high, and the girls and women will try to get it. The man or boy will let the girl get it that he wants. When she gets it, it is understood that they are to have sexual intercourse that night. They will go off in the dark together. This is the custom at all the Hopi dances—the Snake Dance, or a kachina dance, or the women's basket dance, or any Hopi dance, this is the custom, like a law. No one must say, "She is my wife," or "He is my husband..."

> (Deposition of Steve Quonestewa,
> Toreva, Arizona, April 14, 1921)

Commentary

The material in the Smithsonian affidavits raises a number of intriguing questions about Hopi life not satisfied by the internal evidence of the documents or by the general anthropolgical literature on Pueblo culture.

The documents contain ample evidence of endemic promiscuity . . . Can that evidence simply be dismissed as a product of the deponents' Christian (sex-negative) bias?[1] . . . How we choose to understand the Hopi attitude towards non-marital sex in turn affects our view of other aspects of Hopi culture—pre-eminently, the meaning of the "sexual acts" performed during and after ceremonial dances. The "official" explanation—that they are depictions of fertility designed to bring rain—is derided in several of the Smith- sonian affidavits as an excuse, a cloak for "sexual license." Which version should we believe, and on what basis do we decide to believe it? If we follow Quoyayeptiwa's view that the functional purpose of the dances changed radically through time, with earlier "meanings" grafted on to later ones to form an indissolvable whole, we probably neither can nor should "choose" between the two interpretations; any more than we should try to determine whether the bawdy antics of the clowns were primarily designed to amuse the crowd or to instruct it, to impart moral lessons. (The Smithsonian affidavits—hardly a "random sample"—are replete with instances of audience hilarity, all but devoid of instances of audience fear or shame.)

Trained to be wary of static models and alert to the variations over time in the meaning of behavior, historians tend to be leery of the need or wisdom of choosing decisively between polar views (between interpreting certain antics, say, as designed either *to amuse* or *to instruct. Historians also tend to distrust anthropology's emphasis on the overriding importance of the* symbolic *(the representational, figurative) dimension of human behavior. Some ascribe that distrust to the mundane temperament with which historians are said to be afflicted; others to their fascination with particularity, their attention to detail. Whatever the reason, historians are likely to find uncon- genial the anthropologists' stress on "dramatic simulation" in ex- plaining the sexual content of the dances, and will want to caution against overemphasizing the abstract at the expense of the concrete. A selective use of the data in the Smithsonian affidavits readily confirms the element of "simulation." But when* all *the evidence in the affidavits is taken into account, the importance of symbolism in accounting for the sexuality associated with the dances seems less overwhelming. The language many deponents use leaves little doubt that they meant to describe acts of lust ("I seen a squaw suck a bucks prick") not mere "representations of fertility."*

Any piece of behavior, of course, can be—some will want to say must be—simultaneously literal and figurative. My point is simply to warn against the danger of ignoring the obvious as we pursue the arcane. The danger is heightened by the value structure we in the West have inherited, the particular blinders and emphases it encourages. Our dualistic habit of thought almost reflexively predisposes us to believe that the presence of one quality ("amusement") negates the possible presence of its "opposite" ("instruction"). Our neo-Platonic penchant for abstracting experience provokes in us a zeal for classification that can nullify what is most special— enrichingly eccentric—in a given event or gesture. Our receding but still deeply engrained sex-negativism can lead us into performing the most ludicrous intellectual contortions in order to avoid the most obvious evidence of our senses.

The pervasive influence that values exert on even conscientious and highly trained social scientists may also be operative in the way we fail to read certain aspects of Pueblo culture. A considerable portion of the Smithsonian affidavits deals with cross-dressing, public urination (with seemingly erotic overtones), flogging children during initiation rites, and skits that center on display of the male penis (or exaggerated representations thereof). None of the anthropologists to whom I've shown the material—I should add, in fairness, that only a few have seen all of it—made any comment on the portion dealing with cross-dressing, et. al. They focused instead on the more familiar part of the subject matter and couched their remarks in the equally familiar terminology of "symbolic ritual" and "metaphorical" depictions of fertility, "mini-dramas" designed to enforce social mores. In short, they jumped on evidence confirming what they already "knew" and avoided material that might "offend" the Hopi, embarrass their own sense of propriety—or stretch standard categories of interpretation.[2]

Yet a stretch is just what we need—if we are to make more sense than we now can of certain little understood aspects of Pueblo culture, and of human sexuality in general. What meaning(s) did cross-dressing have for the Hopi? Did it take place only during ceremonial dances and was it essentially a male phenomenon? We do have some scant evidence of female cross-dressing,[3] but we understand neither its extent nor significance (what it reveals, for example, about the differing socio/religious roles played by males and females in Pueblo culture). What interrelationship—if any—existed between cross-dressing and bisexuality or homosexuality? Mischa Titiev has offered some opaque suggestions that link cross-dressing with "bisexualism" (undefined) and bisexualism with "fertility"—further confounding the confusion by seeming to equate male "transvestism" and "homosexuality."[4] As unsatisfying as his discussion is, Titiev must at least be credited with a willingness to explore the subject— and with the grace to acknowledge that "greater study" is needed. We as yet have no firm ground, for example, for knowing whether cross-dressing in Hopi culture carried any of the attributions associated elsewhere in aboriginal North America with that familiar and relatively well-studied figure—the berdache.

Other puzzles abound. Did flogging children occur only during initiatory rites, and what significance—religious or otherwise—was attached to the practice? Was the whipping as severe and the children as stoic as the affidavits suggest, or was some degree of play-acting involved—and if so by whom and for what purpose? Was there any analogous inflicting of pain between Hopi adults (biting and scratching during sex, for example)? Did the floggings carry sexual overtones, bear any of the emotional or symbolic weight (dominance/submission, etc.) which in our own culture we increasingly connect with "sado/masochism"?

It is difficult to formulate, let alone "answer," such questions. The more so for the Hopi, who to this day remain profoundly secretive about their behavior and profoundly suspicious of outsiders attempting to probe its mysteries (historically, outsiders have been associated—accurately—with misrepresenting Pueblo life even as they forcibly attempted to alter it). But if acquiring information is difficult, it is not impossible. As the documents printed here demonstrate, more information has been available than has been used. Or used fully. The taboos of our own culture have acted to dim (even obliterate) the curiosity of social scientists for exploring facets of Hopi life—the ritual flogging of children, say—we would consider "illegitimate" behavior in ourselves.

Such circumspection is familiar enough. In every field, not simply in the study of Native American cultures, our social scientists are famously fastidious. The professorial experts are staunch in affirming their respect for "non-conformist" behavior—but avoid confronting its outer range. Faced with behavior that lends itself least well to traditional categorization and to standard measures of judgement, social science has usually reaffirmed—rather than reexamined—the sufficiency of its categories and measurements. Faced with cultures *whose norms challenge the universality of our own values, social science has rhetorically declared for catholicity but refrained from probing implications that might subvert its presumed cultural hegemony.*

None of this, as I say, is news. What might be, is a growing tendency among younger social scientists to challenge the entrenched defensive postures of their disciplines; to explore more deeply the evidence and meaning of human diversity; to welcome it as a source of enrichment rather than shun it as a threat. I hope this new material on the Hopi will make a contribution to that emerging tendency in the social sciences.

Radical History Review, *Spring/Summer 1979*

1. "Brittle monogamy"is the specialists favored term when describing Hopi marriages. (Eg. see Fred Eggan, *Social Organizations of the Western Pueblos,* Univ. of Chicago: 1950; Shiuchi Nagata, *Modern Transformations of Moenkopi Pueblo,* Univ. of Ill: 1970; Mischa Titiev, *The Hopi Indians of Old Oraibi,* Univ. of Michigan: 1972). As might be imagined, that vague term allows for a multiplicity of interpretations.

2. Some anthropologists have argued that the avoidance of sexual, or sexually related behavior is endemic in the profession. At the 1975 meeting of the American Anthropological Association, a group of anthropologists interested in research on human sexuality expressed their disappointment that so little had been accomplished to date. (Thomas K. Fitzgerald, "A Critique of Anthropological Research on Homosexuality," *Journal of Homosexuality,* Vol. 2, Summer 1977.) Even when anthropologists have explored sexuality, description has tended to be brief and perfunctory, analysis wary and finicky.

3. Eg. Titiev, *op. cit.,* 99-100, 153, 214-215, 302, 310.

4. *Ibid.,* 99-100, 153, 214-214.

1915

THERAPY AND BISEXUALITY

The following document is based on excerpts from Dr. L. Eugene Emerson's notes about yet another of his patients, a man ("Mr. L.") who, judging from parenthetical information in the notes, was apparently connected with the Massachusetts Institute of Technology, possibly as a chemist. I should add that the extent and nature of Mr. L.'s "bisexuality" is itself more subject to debate than my unequivocal use of the term in the title might suggest. I have retained the original grammar, capitalization and punctuation, and have made some annotative remarks, in brackets, within the body of the text.

■ ■ ■

March 17, 1915:

Began to masturbate at 10—w. [with] twin & another boy. Sucked penis a year or two.

Masturbated all his life.

Married 13 yrs.—Boy 12 girl 2½.

C.I. [coitus interruptus] ever since marriage. Wife objects. No c. [coitus] for 4 or 5 months. She wants children. He not ...

In Washington a yr., after marriage, Masturbated badly. First noticed dizzy spells after ret. [return] from Washington.

Fond of obscene lit. When he sees girls in streets thinks sensually.

March 18, 1915:

Had diff. [difficulty] at first but finally remembered he wanted to tell me that he thought his character was degenerate. Has been tempted to a double life.

So passionate, pictures would cause erection at times.

Very sensitive to social demands.

Certain amt. of homosexuality.

March 19, 1915:

Dreamed he was having c .... In the first part of the dream he thinks his wife had a male organ & he was sucking it. It did not seem strange. Then her organs changed to female ones & just as he was about to enter, he woke...

Has been sexually excited by boys ...

Wife allows him to suck her nipples when she is in right mood & he can excite her quickest that way.

March 20, 1915:
Better. No dreams. Headache. Not dizzy today or yesterday.
Coitus reservatus & c.i. last night.
Transition from Homo to hetero sex abt. [about] 13. Sister & girl—Boy took clothes off & showed organ—girls interested but refused to show theirs. Pt. [patient] too shy to show his. Later this girl handle his. Excited. With boy once & saw plump girl. Boy said he'd like to get hold of her. He got excited.

In bed. w. [with] sister once abt. 12 or so. Felt up [?] her to see if what [?] organ felt like [?].

Young boy in class. Pt. [patient] used to enjoy imagining him having relations w. a girl.

March 22, 1915:
... dreamed he saw a lot of women in bathing. They had on men's trunks. Then he dreamed his wife was under the ice in a stream drowning. He got her out & was glad to find she was alive, because she opened her eyes.

Thought Sat. afternoon that perhaps his dizzyness was due to c.i. of night before. (Conflict w. his desire for more c.).

Father always punished him—whipped—Mother, never; she would console.

Fa. told boy once 14-15(?) if he wanted to know abt. sex wld tell him. He thought he already knew all abt. that ...

March 25, 1915:
... Further perversions uncovered:
Intercourse w. wife per anum several times. Also she has taken his organ in her mouth once. He has put tongue in wife's mouth & she in his, but neither liked it much. He has not put mouth to her genitals.

Dreamed about his wife & twin. Wife was nude. [Dr. Emerson's own written comment: (Bisexual. Longing for irresponsibility of bro.)]

Considerable jealousy between wife & mo. [mother] Wife won't have mo. in house ...

March 29, 1915:

Depressed & Dizzy—

Last night dreamed of a burglar getting in the back way. He tel. for police ...

When he went home Sat. found Mrs. W. on sofa—unresponsive—

Thought of masturbating came once to mind—went out again. Repressed.

Felt better in warm bath, naked, saw own body. Narcisistic. [sic] "When I have those feelings I don't have any sexual craving at all." Autoerotic ...

April 1, 1915:

Went to sleep in his chair & dreamed he was in Essex, old home, at shipyards. He had some long narrow boards which someone else seemed to want. He took them upstairs to a carpenter's shop & hid them. [Homosexual overtones? Or "long narrow boards" merely my linguistic/fantasy equivalent of "penis"?]

April 2, 1915:

History of courtship: taking arm—arm around waist—pulled down in lap—hand on breast—kiss (symbol of engagement—she kissed too) further fondling—masturbating—lit match to look at her genitals—ejaculating—marriage—took month to penetrate—wife refused to get breakfast for him the morning he finally broke hymen—never felt ready for marriage & responsibility.

After m. 6 yrs. in Washington one Summer alone ... Can't remember first, but often thought & sometimes spoke of separation or divorce. Wife is cross-eyed. Never really loved her. Felt honorbound to marry, after a while. When engaged she put her hand in his trousers & was surprised to feel his erection. She thought it would be little. No formal engagement nor words said.

April 3, 1915:

... "I think I never had the primary emotions," i.e. 'love' because father & mother did not love each other. Mo. was a factory worker, fa. a physician, & looked down on her. He always said all the good qualities came from him & bad from her. Mo. always had to get up &

build fires, do heavy work, etc. He & bro. felt it wrong in fa. Has tried to do diff. w. [differently with] his wife.

April 5, 1915:
Sometimes begin in one room end in other. Sometimes down stairs end up. Sometimes while waiting for her to come to bed & finish it would tremble violently. Would withdraw & wait 10 or 15 min. before going on—maintaining erection—did everything he could to prolong the pleasure...

April 7, 1915:
Dreamed Walter E. S ... .[classmate] was not able to go yachting because he had cut his finger so his wife had to steer & run it. Dreamed he was at some sort of chemical meeting & Gov. Walsh came & sat on the arm of his chair. [It is possible to read homosexual overtones into the above].

Wife used to get terribly mad because he wouldn't impregnate her. Used to try to hold him to her by grim force. Would quarrel abt. this. Wouldn't speak to him for a week once.

April 8, 1915:
... Remembers seeing mo. look at man undressing before open window. He felt ashamed. Mo. let him suck her breasts when he was 9-10...

April 14, 1915:
... Dizzy spells persist. Can remember no dreams.
The analysis of one dizzy spell & blurring of vision led to the imagery of a pretty girl lying on the floor w. legs apart waiting for coitus. As this image formed itself in his mind he noticed the trembling, a peculiar feeling in knees, & sensations around penis, leading usually to an erection...

April 21, 1915:
... Ever since he began to masturbate has done it on an average 3 or 4 times a week; often every day; sometimes 2-3 times a day...

April 23, 1915:
... Dreamed a plumber told him the way to stop a leak in a pipe was by hammering the hole together by the head of a nail.
Dreamed he was tying a bandage tight around the arm of a friend; or having a bandage tied tight around his arm.

Asso. [association] led to thinking of bandaging penis to prevent semen coming out...

May 11, 1915:
... Does not think phantasies had anything to do w. pleasure of sucking & masturbating as a boy. This came later...

Changed from sucking "cocks" to manipulation at advice of older boy. Didn't like it so well at first. Advantage, later, lay in its being possible alone & oftener...

May 14, 1915:
Dreamed there was a lion outside the house which he was trying to shoot ... Asso. brought out the fact that the lion symbolised Mrs. W. also his own masculinity, also the dream showed his feminine tendencies. In corroboration of this idea he said that he had tried when having c. to imagine how it would feel to be the woman...

May 26, 1915:
Last night dreamed Dr. Gill of M.I.T. advised him to sell his house etc. as taxes would eat it all up. Afterwards dreamed some boys were trying to get in the house. They did finally & went through opening & closing doors. He didn't want them to get to the back of the house because Mrs. W. & Louise were there undressed & he didn't want these boys to see them. So he started after them. Just as he got to the back & was about to see the boys he woke, startled, feeling a little glad it was only a dream.

June 7, 1915:
... Has responded sexually to a lot of men lately. To affect him they must be usually young & fair...

June 22, 1915:
... Sexual thoughts don't trouble much now. Come & go. All symptoms disappear when playing ball w. the boys.

1930s

"SEX VARIANT WOMEN"

*In 1941 Alfred Kinsey wrote Robert Latou Dickinson, "It was
your own work which turned my attention ... some 10 or 12 years ago
to the purposes of research" in the field of sexuality. Yes, Kinsey was
crediting Dickinson—not Havelock Ellis, Magnus Hirschfeld, Freud
or Jung—with first setting him on his ultimately revolutionary path
in exploring human sexuality.*

*Kinsey's attribution, startling today, would not have raised many
eyebrows forty years ago. By 1941 the eighty year old Dickinson had
become a gynecologist and researcher of international renown,
bracketted with his contemporary Margaret Sanger for pioneering
achievement in changing attitudes about contraception, abortion and
gender, especially within the medical community. Of the two, Sanger
was more controversial in her assumptions and more radically
outspoken in her tactics. Dickinson was a more genteel team player
wedded to a strategy of producing social change by "boring from
within." Which may be one reason that Sanger's name remains widely
known while Dickinson's has been almost wholly forgotten.*

*Yet he deserves rescue from his near oblivion. To quote Kinsey
again, Dickinson "had initiated the process of preparing his profession to deal with the sexual needs of modern America."[1]*

*I myself had never heard of Dickinson until I stumbled upon the
uncatalogued boxes of his personal papers stored at the Countway
Medical Library at Harvard. During the weeks I researched those
papers, the single most exciting find was a lengthy, unpublished
gynecological study Dickinson and his associates[2] made in the 1930s,
tentatively entitled "Sex Variant Women." The study was based on
detailed case histories of thirty-nine lesbian women, and the voluminous notes extant in the Dickinson Papers include "statistical"
analyses of the women's psychological and experiential profiles, in
addition to the researchers' attempt to generalize beyond those
immediate findings. My guess is that the chief reason Dickinson
never published the study is related to the high standards he held for
precision research and his awareness that despite the effort and care
he had taken, the final results of the "Sex Variant" study remained
too sketchy to withstand scientific scrutiny. The subject of "sexual
variation among women," he apparently concluded, awaited the
further development of research techniques and the availability of*

more wide ranging data before worthwhile generalizations could be offered.

Still, in the course of their work Dickinson and his associates did manage to accumulate a hefty amount of material, and some of it still seems of sufficient value to the modern researcher to warrant publication. I photocopied a fair proportion of the entire manuscript, but I reproduce here only a small segment—enough, I hope, to stimulate other researchers to examine the entire work and to give it the comprehensive review I believe it warrants.

The following are seven of the thirty-nine case histories Dickinson and his colleagues wrote up, along with their tentative conclusions.*

SUSAN N.

This is another experience with early rape—at 13—extremely painful, necessitating a week spent in bed, which is rather a record for shock. Had no other physical relations with men. The homosexual technique is not the most usual, consisting primarily of lying above, with clitoris pressure rhythms between symphysis, and finger friction also thus. These relations were carried on with one partner for 5 years, and with 4 or 5 other girls twenty minutes, two or three times a week.

PAMELA D.

This English aristocrat, now 40, was chaperoned until she was 16, then in the war tried to give pleasure to men, several men, but got little in return. Desperately in love with a nurse during the war, very active in kissing her breasts and masturbating her (never mutual, lasted two years). At 20 first heterosexual relation with old friend who wanted to marry her. Repeated relations. After the war with three different women. "I resorted also to self masturbation and thus had first orgasm. At 25, with father's mistress, kissed a friend's clitoris and she masturbated me." Later, lonely, drank, had affairs with men and women. With men not successful physically. From 27 to 31 in small business and affairs with several women. At 34 fell in love with negro actress, who was indifferent, so married American society man who was bisexual and practically impotent, now for six happy years with this woman.

GLADYS H.

One of the 3 or 4 in this series with only homosexual physical experiences, this girl was attracted by breasts since 13 and given to mouth to mouth caress, and body pressures general. There is the story of "instinctive" genital oral caress with two girls. Her breasts are flat,

*This article appears for the first time.

the nipple becomes prominent and erectile, with follicles present but not prominent. The majora, 7 cm., and vulva not over the average; the minora moderately protruding and elastic (4 cm. spread) with accessory labia and a thick corrugated prepuce, the clitoris erectile, 4 by 5. The hymen shows nicks to base, but will admit but one finger two joints. The uterus is small and retroverted in the third degree. The libido is between, not near the periods. Here the story of an early supposedly complete sex act by a boy cousin and no male entry since is borne out by a nicked hymen but admission into the vagina of only one finger. The age given as three may be inexact, even with a boy of 13. The accessory labia are those of repeated traction, by the Dickinson category, which is manual in previous findings and not admitted by this "wary" young woman.

ALBERTA X.

Given to extensive experimentation, intensely passionate with women, able to obtain orgasm in two minutes or two hours, at times almost daily for months, this woman is an artist who thinks men "badly designed" and that homosexuality has made her what she is. A lover at sixteen gave no distress and taught her "all the tricks" and was experienced, but though there was no distress, she failed to experience orgasms, which first occurred at age twenty-four and with a woman. "Kissing breasts, genitals, mutual masturbation and mouth—about it we had a lot of instinct." She is now twenty-four, athletic but of female build and female type pelvis; her breasts are normal, with 3.5 erectile aureola and some pigmented areas around the right nipple . . . .

KATHLEEN M.

The business woman of thirty began, while studying art, to sleep with a boy, but the relation meant nothing to her; coitus started painfully, and she was ignorant about contraception. Thereafter began to have homosexual relations with a famous Lesbian actress, an aggressive bisexual. Kathleen did the kissing of the vulva instead of using the hand, and the actress had the orgasm. She was soon dropped, as was the habit of the actress. On the rebound, Kathleen tried coitus with an old friend, but without evoking any response. For five years thereafter had relations with a woman, both using lips and tongue (on vulva), Kathleen having orgasm. Faithful to one woman for three years, she was then disillusioned, drank, played to get girls with whom she slept and then dropped; most of these girls were experienced in homosexual practices. The yielding was complete, the method oral, lying of the side; kissing and caressing the breasts and the whole body. She would not let her partners touch her. A psychologist advised relations with men; [a man] slept with her, after which she had vaginal bleeding for two months (No examination records explain this, such as a small vulva, spasm of a thick vagina, or an encircling muscular band). Kathleen is not an athlete, however.

For two years now she has had mutual relations by mouth, sleeping with her partner every night, having orgasm about twice a week. Her lover, Gladys, likes genital kissing, but prefers the breast, and shows prominent nipples, erectile and corrugated, thick labia with erectile clitoris—labia moderately protruding (from above mouth caress).

SUSIE K.

This thirty-year old Negress, a popular contralto, was a bareback rider as a girl, and a bed-wetter to the age of ten, when she began to menstruate. At eleven she was "hurt terribly" by coitus with a boy of sixteen, but bore a child before she was thirteen. At fourteen more painful coitus and a second pregnancy. Sex play with another girl began at eight years of age, and was active by age twelve, preferably in coital postures. She now prefers homosexual monogamy. "My clitoris is two inches long", she claims, "and enlarged it's three inches and the thickness of a little finger. It's grown half an inch in the last year". She is able to "insert my clitoris in the vagina" and produce orgasm in other women in a most desirable fashion. She enjoys caressing other women's breasts but does not want her own breast touched. "I never could masturbate myself. I love to have a woman go down on me. No man in the world could rouse me. I loathe the idea of anything going inside me, even a douche." Her preference is for two or three homosexual relations a week, of twenty to forty minutes duration.

MARVEL W.

Again a story of bed-wetting and spanking; menses began at age ten; boys began advances at nine. When twenty years of age, at college, with a girl, had mutual manual vulvar orgasm, for two years, off and on, during vacations. Later the same type of relations with an older woman, in the same fashion, during three years. At twenty-six had normal sex relations with a man, which were painful at first; she was not interested in marriage. At thirty-two, while living with a girl-lover, she had relations with two or three men, in one case for a year. Thereafter, fell in love with Ellen T. and with her began to use mouth. Marvel can have orgasms several ways, by caressing the breast, almost by making love. While she prefers the mutual oral-vulvar method, she cannot make it "work" with Ellen. Says she has fantastic erotic dreams of men and girls—a statement seldom appearing in this series.

SUMMARY

Orgasm and sexual satisfaction with women is reported by these 39 women in nearly every instance. Although most had had bisexual experience, only one fourth of this class reached orgasm with men. Having tried both, they preferred women, both as sexual partners and as loving comrades.

Autoeroticism is reported in only one fourth, or one half to a third as often as in other studies of sex life of women.

Menarche was at average age, with a group of early onsets.

Marriage took place with nearly half, two thirds of these marriages showing pregnancies.

The average age of homosexual beginnings was 20 years, or later by 2 years than their average start of heterosexual relations.

Penalties of excessive or unduly frequent periods are not in the picture, and painful periods infrequent, while cervix catarrhs and inflammations are strikingly absent. All this is contrary to the general belief in view of the next two findings.

A very high frequency of evidence of *erotic feeling* is demonstrated on local examination. Two thirds show flush, wetness and erect clitoris in this particular small group, with an equal frequency of quick erectility of the nipple, nodular breast structure occurring very often.

The external genitals are large with the special hypertrophies of various parts that accompany frequent, vigorous sexual stimulation and activity. The labia minora protrude particularly often and the surface of the glans clitoris is long from front to rear, with three times as many large glans as in general groups. No intersex genitals were discovered. No definite findings could be classified as peculiar to homosexual practices.

Notes

1. Kinsey's words are quoted in James Reed, *From Private Vice to Public Virtue: The Birth Control Movement and American Society Since 1830* (Basic Books: 1978), pp. 192-3. Along with the Reed book, I've relied heavily on Linda Gordon, *Woman's Body, Woman's Right: A Social History of Birth Control in America* (Grossman: 1976) for background information. Judging from their bibliographic references, however, neither Reed nor Gordon seems to have known of (or utilized) the Dickinson manuscript materials presented here, though Reed apparently did have access to other portions of the Dickinson Papers at the Countway Library of Medicine.

Katherine Bement Davis was one of Dickinson's associates during some of his work on "Sex Variant Women". See her 1929 study, *Factors on the Sex Life of Twenty-Two Hundred Women,* which was reissued in 1972 by the Arno Press. For additional information on Davis, and a great deal more besides, see Estelle B. Freedman's brilliant essay, "Sexuality in Nineteenth Century America: Behavior, Ideology and Politics", *Reviews in American History,* vol. 10, no. 4. (December 1982).

1932

IN DEFENSE OF HOMOSEXUALITY

The following excerpts are from a lengthy essay in The Modern Thinker *for June, 1932. It was one of numerous replies attacking "The Riddle of Homosexuality," by W. Beran Wolfe, which had appeared in the April 1932 issue of that magazine. The sophisticated insights of the essayist—writing fifty years ago—should remind us again, that not all enlightenment dates from Stonewall.*

IN DEFENSE OF HOMOSEXUALITY
by "Parisex"

(The pseudonym for Henry Gerber, one of the founders of the Society for Human Rights, an early gay rights group.)

After reading the article by W. Beran Wolfe, M.D., in the April issue of *The Modern Thinker,* one cannot but deeply sympathize with the inverts for being the world's eternal scapegoats....

Now that the inverts have almost escaped the stake and prison, the psychoanalysts threaten them with the new danger of the psychiatric torture chamber. The chief fallacy of psychiatry and similar trades is that it puts the cart before the horse. If we may believe the psychoanalysts, it is not modern machine civilization, at great variance with nature, that is conducive to neuroses, but civilization itself is the norm, and anything else, even nature, is perverse and neurotic. Nature, which has struggled along valiantly these million years, is now being told by the Freuds, the Adlers, the Jungs, and their slavish followers, that its manifold sex urges are abnormal, and that civilization, that recent upstart, is the only norm of life; that if one reverted to good old mother nature he would quickly be accused of no less a crime than seeking to flee from reality. What about the homosexual fleeing from reality? As to [their] social responsibilities, I am not aware of [homosexuals] having been exempted in the late war, neither do I see on the tax blanks where the unmarried homosexuals pay less than the heterosexual who is not fleeing from reality; nor do I know of any place of employment where the homosexual is not required to work as hard for his pennies as the heterosexual worker.

And is not the psychiatrist again putting the cart before the horse in saying that homosexuality is a symptom of a neurotic style of life? Would it not sound more natural to say that the homosexual is made neurotic because his style of life is beset by thousands of dangers? What heterosexual would not turn highly neurotic were his mode of love marked "criminal," and were he liable to be pulled into prison every time he wanted to satisfy his sex urge—not to speak of the dangers of being at all times exposed to blackmail by heterosexuals who prey upon him, and the ostracism of society? While Dr. Wolfe unhesitatingly affirms the question whether homosexuality can be cured; how, where, and for how much this can be done, the deponent sayeth not. I doubt if there ever was a cure of a genuine homosexual .....The few cures reported were brought about by alleged heterosexual suggestions to the "patient" to get married.

It is highly improbable that an intelligent homosexual could be "cured" by suggesting to him the blessings of monogamy. ... Too much pessimism, of course, is uncalled for, but anyone acquainted with the real life of homosexuals or heterosexuals will have to admit that many heterosexuals lead a happy life, but also that homosexuals live in happy, blissful unions, especially in Europe, where homosexuals are unmolested as long as they mind their own business, and are not, as in England and in the United States, driven to the underworld of perversions and crime for satisfaction of their very real craving for love....

The fact that scientific information concerning the nature of homosexuality is almost unobtainable is not due to the ignorance of the medical profession but to the public policy of suppressing anything truthful about homosexuals. The truth about homosexuals is suppressed in the same degree as the knowledge of birth control, for homosexuality, of course, is but one of the many natural forms of birth control.

It is ridiculous to assume that the whole Greek nation was neurotic because homosexuality was practiced there with the sanction of the state. Homosexuality even exists among the primitive tribes and among animals, though this fact also has been suppressed. It must be more than neurosis if a certain natural trait persists throughout all ages and still carries on after the most cruel and fatal persecution of those so inclined....

One cannot enforce a law against natural cravings. Taboos always result in bootleggers of love or drink. The very fact that it takes so many laws to enforce monogamy at once labels it only an ideal but not a natural institution. One never hears of laws compelling people to eat!...

We are told that inversion is not a matter of biology or physiology, but is acquired by social conditions and determined by "early childhood experiences." We are shown the proof of this by the statement that homosexuals as children, "in the vast majority" of cases, occupy an ordinal position in the family—that is, they are almost always the oldest or youngest child, that the father dies early (in the boy's case) and that the resulting coddling of the boy by its mother ultimately makes the boy homosexual. Suppose this is true: How then will psychiatric therapy of the "individual homosexual" effect a cure? Supposing such a cure possible, supposing further that each homosexual could be prevailed upon to submit to this cure (which is preposterous) the fact would still remain that in every generation there would be another crop of homosexuals, simply because boys still continued to be first and last children, losing their fathers and mothers early in life....

Homosexuality has existed from the beginning of time, in all sorts of social regimes and conditions. It is a constant human quality. ... Why? There has to be a reason somewhere, and that reason must be one of utility, of human value, else it could not survive. If the homosexuality of geniuses does not prove that homosexuality is a higher order, it certainly does prove that homosexuality is not exclusively an affliction of gutter snipes, maniacs, and thugs....

The extermination of homosexuality, even if it were possible, might result in a very jagged hole in the fabric of society and its culture; might, in fact be a costly experiment.

But there is a yet more complex problem attached to this therapeutic cure of homosexuality. Dr. Wolfe gives the impression that homosexuality centers around actual sexual intercourse, that it is exclusively absorbed with intercourse and the act itself. But there are all shades and degrees of homosexuality, from Platonic, spiritual attachments down to the sexual. Where is the psychiatrist to draw the line here? Will he cure the homosexual who is literally sexual, and permit to exist all the varying shade of attachment between similar sexes, attachments that verge close to the sexual border and are yet beyond it? There is no hard and fast distinction between friendship and love—friendship can and does deepen into love. Therapeutic methods, developed to their ultimate capacities, would, it seems, cast suspicion on friendships existing between members of the same sex, however non-homosexual those friendships might really be. Such a state of affairs might inconvenience many people, including hetero-sexuals; including also Dr. Wolfe, of course....

After all, it is highly futile for Dr. Wolfe to worry about neurotic homosexuals when the world itself, led and ruled by the strong heterosexual "normal" men is in such chaotic condition, and knows not where to turn.

It is quite possible that if called upon, the homosexuals in this country would put up the money to send Dr. Wolfe to Washington to examine these great big "normal" men, who guide the destinies of millions, to find their "neurosis" and to cure it.

1933

THE NEW DEAL:
SEX IN THE C.C.C. CAMPS

Soon after Franklin Delano Roosevelt took office as president, he established the Civilian Conservation Corps (C.C.C.). It was designed to provide immediate relief for the multitude of jobless young men who had been thrown out of work by the onset of the Great Depression. The men were set to work on a variety of public projects and housed in a number of camps around the country.

Although the New Deal is not one of my areas of special expertise as an historian, I've read fairly widely on the subject, teaching it at one point in my academic career. Nothing I read contained even an oblique suggestion of homosexuality in the C.C.C. camps. Knowing that boys will be boys (or ten percent of them, anyway) this "gap in the data" seemed suspect. Yet, the documents excerpted below are the first I know of actually to establish the existence of gay sex in the C.C.C. camps. I found them in the Institute for Sex Research in Indiana (the Kinsey Institute); the materials were not catalogued in the Institute's official file. Kinsey's co-author, Wardell B. Pomeroy, revealed in his book Dr. Kinsey and the Institute for Sex Research *that the Institute received information (some solicited, some not) from a wide, unorthodox range of correspondents. It seems reasonable to deduce that "BA" (see text) and the others who forwarded the information about life in the C.C.C. camps were part of Kinsey's wide-ranging network. No internal evidence in the documents suggests that the veracity of the material need be questioned. The absence of verbal tags of disapproval suggests that the observers had been schooled to appreciate the objectivity required by their role, or that they were themselves participants.*

THE NEW DEAL:
SEX IN THE C.C.C. CAMPS

Camp 1:
Source of data: Record kept by BA [code name]. BA was a man of forty-seven known to have had considerable experience in sex relations with men and boys. He was intentionally planted in the camp under an agreement with him that he would make all the sex contacts he could and learn all he could and keep a record which he

would turn over from time to time. An appointment as a "Local Experienced Man" was obtained for him and he secured an assignment in charge of the camp supply room and warehouse. This gave him considerable freedom of time and movement and brought him into contact with all of the boys. He ate with them but slept in the warehouse alone except there were two or three extra cots which could be used by visitors or anyone invited. He had privacy at night and could have in daytime by locking the door and if necessary claiming he had been away.

The camp authorities were not aware of the arrangement and if they knew of his sex activities they said nothing. There were no unfavorable comments or trouble.

BA's wife (he had no children) staid [sic] in the nearby town. He had a car and frequently went into town evenings and was free to spend nights there. This facilitated contacts and gave him a stand in with the boys because he could give a ride into town and back to whomever he desired. He had sufficient influence with the camp authorities that he could often obtain better or easier work assignments for the boys and could favor ones in issuing [sic] supplies etc., etc. He also maintained a kind of small loan business with the boys— without interest. He lost small amounts in it. His pay was small but he had a small private income and he made some money from men for arranging dates with the boys. He did not pay any boys for sex relations.

Period covered: about 6 mo.

Camp strength: at start 200 boys, at end 172, average 186. Range in ages: 18 to 26 by regulation but many boys lied about their age and got in some as low as 15. There were few above 22. Most of them were 17 to 21.

Geographical origin: Recruited from farms and towns in Texas. None from cities.

Number approached by BA: to extent that they knew his intentions 104 (there was no selectivity. He approached all that he had opportunity to.)

Number who refused: 39 (Some of these permitted feeling of their genitals but not their exposure).

Number who permitted masturbation and fellatio by BA: 65

Number who made the first advances: 20 (Probably most of these had heard about it from others. Some openly and frankly asked for it.)

Camp 2 [unlike camp 1, no "source of data" is cited]:

Homosexual. Investigation did not begin until about 2 mo. after the camp was established and there are no data on its prevalence before that date.

One enrollee of 22 initiated a sex contact in the camp latrine with a man who was visiting camp. He had had experience with males before enrolling.

A comment on the tan on the shirtless torso of another enrollee of 19 by a visitor while he was working in a group in the woods caused him to fall behind the others when they moved on. When alone the man renewed his comments and ran his hand over the back and shoulders of the boy who threw his arms around the man, made coitus like motions and tried to expose the man's genitals. The man made him stop but invited him to meet him in town that night and took him to his room for the night. The boy's sex desires were uncontrolled and insatiable. He wanted both active fellatio and passive pederasty.

Another boy who was contacted in a saloon town said he had had coitus with girls before enrolling but no relations with males. He was seduced by a man he met in a saloon after enrolling. There had been subsequent relations with the same man and others and he was willing to have intercourse with anyone. He had always been well paid by the men.

Another enrollee of 18 had had both heterosexual and homosexual contacts before enrollment. After the acquaintanceship had progressed to a point where he had confidence in the other he told of his relations with one of the camp foremen. He proudly claimed that he had seduced the foreman. An attempt to check his statements from the foreman were not successful but other facts bore them out and it is believed they were true. The foreman was about 60 with a wife and a large grown family.

The wife lived in another part of the state and he seldom went home. He was a large, well-poised man with an unusual faculty for getting along with boys and controlling them; inspiring confidence in them and getting them to work. He had an excellent reputation with boys and officials and was rated high as a foreman. About twice a week the foreman would take the boy out in the evening and either drive to some secluded spot or to a cabin in a tourist court. There would be passionate petting with some oral contacts ending with vigorous active anal coitus by the foreman. The boy, who understood the situation better than is usual, said he was in love with the foreman and the foreman was with him. His frequent discussion of the situation left no doubt that there was a strong attachment. Subtle questions of the foreman got nothing from him. He avoided the whole topic of sex and created the impression—intentional or otherwise—that the subject of sex was distasteful to him. Another enrollee of 20 said he had heard of such activities in camp but had not had experiences himself but was willing to have them, particularly if he got paid.

Another of 19 was introduced by one of the above. He had had female coitus before enrolling but no homosexual contacts. He was seduced in camp by the boy who introduced him. He had had 5 experiences with men in town and was willing to have more. He expected to be paid. All of the above boys together with others with whom there were casual conversation and chance remarks agreed that there was a great deal of sexual practices between males but the estimates of the number of boys involved varied from 10 to "half" (ie. 100). The observer's [identity not known] own estimate having the advantage of all the others' observation and estimates together with his own was 40% or about 80. This included relations between boys of which there was a great deal.

Several of the boys were known to have "regulars" in town—men whom they met frequently and secretly. One would stand out in front of the camp quite openly every few evenings and be picked up by the same man in a good car and not return until late at night. There was a good deal of joking about him but he kept by himself and ignored it. Quite a number had plenty of spending money the source of which was a mystery. Several foremen and officers commented on it.

As an example of the difficulty of getting the real facts about sex behaviour and the chances of missing things the observer was not aware of the sex activities of the camp Supt. [Superintendent] until about 2 years later in spite of his familiarity with the camp. The Supt. then told the observer of them. He had similar relations in 2 other camps of which he was supt. They never became known or at least there were no repercussions. He was rated a top supt. and his camps were particularly free of disciplinary troubles e.g. organized kicking about food, loafing, refusal to obey orders etc. He was approaching 60, a large, good natured hearty man who had married a woman about 10 years younger a year or so before he first entered camp. She lived in another part of the state and they met about every 2 months. Their relations with each other seemed happy and satisfactory. No record whether it was the first marriage for either. He was a graduate engineer and people often wondered why he continued the camp job when he could earn more in other jobs and at home.

He observed the boys carefully and when he saw one who appealed to him and who he thought would be susceptible he assigned him as his clerk. If the boy did not respond to his careful approaches he found an excuse for replacing him with another. The Supt. slept in a room adjoining the office or another adjoining room. Relations consisted of almost nightly fellatio on the boy by the Supt. with swallowing of the ejaculate. He thought it kept him vigorous and acted as a tonic. Orgasm by the Supt. once or twice a week preferably by fellatio but he was not very particular. Generally the boy became tired of it in a month or two and quit and was replaced by another. He paid them well.

Camp 3:
Location: Over 100 miles from a railroad and town. Some small rural communities closer. Enrollees recruited in Texas.

Source of data: Observation and statements of a nearby resort owner and 3 enrollees.

Near the camp was a small store with 6 or 8 cabins which were rented to summer campers. A small farm was operated in connection. The owner was about 50 and had been running the place for at least 10 years. Was married but had no children. No contraceptives had ever been used. He bore a good reputation in the neighborhood.

One of the camp foremen who was about 40, married and with several children and a former Boy Scout Executive, used to rent one of the cabins for a night giving as the reason to get away from the noise and get a good night's rest. One night the owner noticed a boy go into the foreman's cabin and not come out. Next time the foreman took a cabin the owner watched and a boy entered. The owner listened outside and heard them having sex relations. The foreman continued the practice all summer.

The owner had had male sex relations in his younger days but had given them up when he married. The foreman's actions gave him the idea and he had no difficulty in establishing relations with—all told— 9 boys—ages 17-21. Boys frequently visited the store to buy candy, soda pop, etc. so it was easy to arrange contacts. The boys involved were given unlimited credit at the store so they considered the liaison a good bargain. The act was consummated usually in a cabin but sometimes in an outbuilding and consisted mostly of fellatio with more or less petting and some anal coitus. When possible they stripped and went to bed. Sometimes 2 of the boys slept together in a cabin with relations. Probably all of them knew of the others' relations with the owner; certainly 5 did. Sometimes the act was performed by the owner and 2 or 3 boys together. On one occasion a visiting man, the owner and 3 boys spent about 3 hrs. in a cabin in the act. On another a man spent a night with a boy and the owner was with them for over 2 hrs. The boy had 7 orgasms. A man, a fisherman who rented a cabin for a few nights threw some hints to the owner who responded in kind and an agreement was reached whereby the owner arranged to have a boy visit the man. The man remained a month with almost daily or nightly visits by various boys.

1935

"OUR BISEXED HERITAGE"

This brief, highly eccentric article dates back some fifty years and until now has never been reprinted. Entitled "An Analysis of Homosexuality" and bearing the byline "Ray W. Harden," the article appeared in the July 1935 issue of Sex Knowledge, *which despite its alluring title, was a rather sober publication. About the author, Harden, nothing seems to be known: none of the standard reference works in sexology contains a single mention of him. Perhaps "Harden" was a comically chosen pseudonym. I lean to the theory that he did in fact exist, and was brought down—officially silenced— at an early age because of his audacious views. (A politically convenient theory, without a scrap of evidence to support it.)*

I found Harden's article while ploughing through a huge, and hugely tedious pile of old periodicals. Even on a quick first reading, the piece brought me up short. It struck me as a bizarre melange of theories at once daring and silly, repellent and prescient; an article distasteful in many particulars, but nevertheless captivating in its overall unorthodoxy. Some of the views Harden expounds are, on the face of it, foolish, such as the connection he draws between semen and gender identity; others are offensive, such as his pronouncement that lesbianism results from the arousal of the "man-element". Yet at the article's center—if you can bear wading through the surrounding nonsense to reach it—lies a discussion of androgyny (Harden's term was "bi-sex") that strikes me as startlingly contemporary, the more so for having been promulgated in the mid-Thirties, a period not known for speculative ferment about sexual matters.

Harden's main thesis is that "originally" (meaning in prehistoric times) all human beings were androgynous. Only much later, and for reasons unknown, were sharp distinctions drawn between "maleness" and "femaleness," and with disastrous consequences: our potential humanness left unexplored and our range of expressiveness curtailed. Even today such hypotheses are considered outlandish, associated with the "extremist" views of such "fringe" types as Elaine Morgan.

Harden went on to argue—with a confidence and optimism not commonly heard today—that humanity's disastrously wrong turn not only could be, but would be, reversed. History was cyclical; it would turn again, restoring our long lost "bisexual life and power." And it would do so because of the impetus that the "despised homosexuals" provided. They were the "true pioneers", Harden insisted, in the struggle to reclaim humanity's essentially androgynous nature.

AN ANALYSIS OF HOMOSEXUALITY
by Ray W. Harden

Before we allow ourselves to become overwrought upon the subject of homosexuality, it might be well to consider this phase of human behaviour [sic] in the light of nature and also to take an age-long view of its development. For minds normalized to present day standards, the only erotic attraction considered natural must take place between a male and a female. Perhaps this was not always so arbitrary—and perhaps it may not continue always to be so in future as evolutionary changes progress, bringing developments, perhaps even structural, along bi-sex lines.

To determine more fully the possibilities behind this idea, we might, with profit to our understanding, consider what "male" really means—and also "female."

To begin with, the words themselves are strikingly similar. We merely add two letters, "f-e" to distinguish one from the other. The root of "fe" means to compensate or to "worth [sic] with."

There are deep philosophic meanings concerning the male and female elements in cosmic nature, which may be dealt with to a fascinating degree in another article. Suffice it to state the fact that to be wholly male or female is an impossibility. Every plant and every creature, including the human, is bi-sexed, fundamentally.

If you doubt this, consider as one very convincing example the breasts of a male. There you always find two undeveloped milk nipples. Also, in the exterior female sex organ we note a small replica of the penis, and this the seat of pleasurable feeling in copulation.

There are hundreds of other indications showing that each individual is both masculine and feminine. In fact, philosophical anthropologists assure us that there was a time in the far-prehistoric past on this earth, while the forms we now know were in the process of formation—perhaps under the very design of the Deity himself— when sex was so evenly balanced that each individual body carried within itself complete, the functions of both sexes.

As time went on, they tell us, some became so "lopsided" in this regard that they tended toward much greater strength in their male attributes while others over-emphasized their feminine qualities. Gradually, age after age, this divergence increased until those who were most abnormal (speaking bisexually) were forced to seek another body which had attained excessive development on the sex side which they themselves had almost lost.

Of course, for a bi-sexed body to grow so weak in its male powers as to require the co-operation of a body intensely masculine (and correspondingly weak in its female aspects) would tend to rapidly tropy [sic] in the sex which, already weakened, it now ceased to exercise at all, within itself.

A reconstructed picture of that transition period, which doubtless occupied millions of years, would be the observance of bi-sexual bodies having the preponderance of female qualities, seeking to obtain semen (which they no longer possessed the ability to secrete to any practical extent) from other bodies in which there was an overproduction of semen.

These specialists in supplying semen—at the expense of their own feminine half, finally became so overwhelmingly masculine, that they ceased to recognize or remember that they had ever possessed female characteristics.

Of course incalculable periods of time would be required to bring this development down to our present strictly one-way sex condition. Yet there is sufficient evidence remaining, even now, to show that both sexes are present in every body, despite the extent to which one or the other has apparently wholly disappeared. Even in human psychology there is evidence which drops out whenever a man or woman refers to the wife or husband as the "better-half."

This theory offers the only consistent explanation of the hermaphroditic "throw-back" known to medical investigation in support of the theory.

The ecstacy produced by sexual communion would be seen as having grown up from that sense of satisfaction and relief which would naturally have been experienced by one bi-sexual, upon receiving from another the magnetism, the activities and secretions in which "he" or "she" had grown distressingly deficient. Sex attraction, likewise, would be precisely what it is, as a result of an age-long practice of bi-sexuals admiring those amazingly developed in the very attributes which were well-nigh extinct within "himself" or "herself."

Homo-sexual tendencies are more understandable in this light. In fact, the condition termed homo-sexual is in reality an extreme case of that which is present in moderation, in all people. Every woman has some interest in viewing the nude body of another woman, whether she expresses it in contempt and disgust or admiration and desire for contact. And of course this same is true of men.

Sex interest may be quite subconscious in some, and is only termed "homosexuality" when it reaches a degree sufficiently active to be recognized.

Furthermore, the man who admires boys and men sexually, is not really a case of "male attracted to male." Rather it is a slightly awakened submerged female nature within "him," responding to the outward male expression of the other, an effect which, from the viewpoint of our theory, is after all, quite natural.

On the other hand, the Lesbian is simply a case of the man-element aroused in a "woman" and directed toward the feminine qualities in another woman whose masculine qualities are more completely inert.

The subject grows a bit more involved when we follow it to discover the fact that a woman who loves an effeminate man, is as much a homo-sexualist as her Lesbian sister. It is the masculine part of her nature aroused and directed toward those qualities in the man which cause him to be considered effeminate. Of course the same reasoning applies to the case of a man in love with a masculine-type woman.

When sex acts are practiced between those of the same sex (as we now arbitrarily divide it) this always means at least a temporary relinquishment of the "typed" sex by one of the parties concerned, and the adoption, in its place, of the qualities of the sex which is recognized and dormant within.

Deep students of cyclic law assure us that the human body will regain, in time, its bi-sexual life and power. In that case, the despised homosexualists are today's pioneers on this very long and very dark road. They are now what they are because of the stirring within them of nature itself, beginning its evolutionary work. Of course they are abusing the principle, but what else can be expected when the whole subject is buried in misunderstanding and not even open for discussion.

With the growing light upon sex matters, bravely offered in sincere publications, humanity shall yet gather courage to look at the subject squarely. Then indeed, great improvement and undreamed of benefits will begin to accrue.

1936

DEGENERATES OF GREENWICH VILLAGE

The following excerpts are from an article in the December 1936 issue of Current Psychology and Psychoanalysis.

A New Yorker who returned to his native city after an absence of two decades was astounded at the changes that had come over New York and, in particular, Greenwich Village. A few weeks before he returned, police had raided a large, brightly-lighted cafeteria in the heart of the Village. The place had been infamous for the past few years as the meeting place of exhibitionists and degenerates of all types. Sight-seers from all parts of the city made pilgrimages to view these misfits on parade.

... Greenwich Village, which was once a happy, carefree abode of struggling young writers and artists, inhabited by many of America's literati, is now a roped-off section of what showmen would call "Freak Exhibits."

... True, many well-known people still live in it—and like it ... But one is made far more conscious of the unfortunate misfit characters who frequent Village rendezvous and make themselves conspicuous on the streets.

... These exhibitionists lack the substance to make themselves stand out in a crowd—hence to appease their childish vanity they resort to the unique method of "dressing to display themselves". ...

The poseurs can usually be distinguished from common mortals without difficulty. Sometimes it is a continual habit of carrying a book that looks "heavy" (and which is never read). Sometimes a violin case or an easel is lugged about. ...

Villagers of this type congregate at various places. There are many glaring restaurants serving unbelievably bad food. ... There are cellar restaurants, dimly lighted with candles, that somehow manage to pass board of health inspections. And there are the perennial "studios", insect-ridden, filthy, dimly-lighted.

Several "lecture-dance halls" in the Village cater to this type of New Yorker—and his cousin from the Bronx and Brooklyn. Under the guise of cultural study, these meeting places muster a season's calendar of "lectures" and "social events." The one dominant theme on their lecture schedule is Sex. ...

Forming an important division within this group are the sexual inverts—members of the third sex. Persons with abnormal sex habits flaunt their traits in the Village. One sees many of them—the boy assuming the usual feminine characteristics and obligations, the girl the Lesbian, who apes her brother.

"Lady Lovers," as they are termed on Broadway, are plentiful. Girls, many in their teens, with their "wives", rove both the dark streets and alleys and the well-lighted avenues arm-in-arm. Often it is difficult to tell whether these creatures are boys or not. Clothed in mannish togs, flat-chested, hair slicked tightly back and closely cropped, seen in a restaurant or bar room, one often ponders minutes before hazarding a guess as to "its" sex. Faces thin, often hard, voices low as a man's, their features have masculine characteristics, although few shave. Make-up is not used in an obvious fashion as it is by most women.

Boys, usually known as "pansies," are seen with make-up; heavy mascara, rouge and lipstick. In high-pitched voices, these exhibition-ists smirk indecent suggestions at each other.

The center meeting place has been, for a long time, a cafeteria. It is a large place—one of the largest self-service restaurants in town. Brilliantly lighted, fully exposed to two streets, it operates day and night. Here, sipping coffee and munching sandwiches, is the most curious restaurant gathering to be found in all America. The Park Avenue deb with the Wall Street boy friend nibbles cheap pastry and stares and jibes at the "show". ... Wide-eyed school girls and boys from neighboring parts of the city gape at the unbelievable sight— boys with rouge on!—and drunken parties end their carousing here. An occasional brawl started indoors is ended outside.

There is a wide-spread use of strange slang among some of these human misfits. Once I heard one say: "That queen over there is camping for jam." I was puzzled. Investigation showed that neither royalty, the wide open spaces nor the household delicacy were involved. The statement meant that a ringleader (queen) of a group of homosexuals was making a play (exhibiting-camping) for a young boy (jam-virgin).

The use of drugs is fairly common among these people. Mari-juana is a favorite. ...

At Village parties, attended by members of the three sexes and their friends, cheap liquor and marijuana are consumed in large quantities. On West Third Street is a dilapidated tenement known as the Love Stable. One room "apartments", cooking privileges in-cluded, are [rented] for a few dollars weekly. Many rooms are tenanted by several people.

At many of these Village parties, held on and near Third Street, promiscuity, sexual exhibitions, physical degradation are quite "the thing." These words are too feeble to convey a picture of the abnormal activities.

But there are other "nice" places, newly decorated, in good taste, serving cheap food and good liquor ... I think of a place that is well known, near Sheridan Square. ...

At the tables may be seated a score or so of Lesbians. They talk quietly, in deep, low voices. Their outstanding characteristic is their jealousy. They are vicious with the green-eyed god of envy. If one's "girl friend" is seen talking with another, if idle rumors tell of "unfaithfulness" there is apt to be as mad a hair-pulling, face-scratching and punching scene as could be found in a month's tour of alley brawls. A real Kilkenny cat fight. Black eyes are often in evidence.

Many of these creatures are actually paid for displaying themselves in night clubs to sensation-hungry guests. They revel in their own peculiarities, and are never so happy as when they have a good audience. They are possessed by one craving: to be noticed. They have never grown up.

1948

BOY PROSTITUTION—35 YEARS AGO

Cash for sex. If prostitution is not the world's oldest profession—some would opt for sorcery—it nevertheless ranks near the top of the list. The more I've thought about the subject, the more convinced I've become that a set of issues and values long ignored, yet of profound significance to the gay male community, lie embedded in the phenomenon of hustling. Angered by the recent [1982] spate of headlined scandals (some of suspect authenticity) about "widespread rings of organized prostitution," I've decided to bring out one portion or a longer essay on hustling I've been writing, and get it into timely print.

Excerpted below is an article, "Nightmare Alley, U.S.A." by Selwyn James, from the March 1948 issue of Salute, *one of a host of popular pulps of the day. Don't let the article's tawdry tone and suspect moralizing throw you off—lead you to discount it as a piece of inconsequential sensationalism. Our most recent outbreak of "exposes" is no less superficial and sleazy—and consequential.*

It's worth noting how little tone or content—moralistic rhetoric and bathetic themes—have changed in thirty-five years among those who would "save our children." The Salute *article of 1948 and the Jerry Falwell literature of 1982 provide almost identical accounts of the sordid lives and tragic fates of those who sell their bodies and, in short order, their souls. The "moral concern" expressed for our nation's youngsters continues to ring with the same patently phoney, repellent tone.*

Still, I think it would be a mistake—and a dangerous one—for the gay male community to respond to such sensationalism with campy hilarity in private or with blanket denials in public. Male prostitutes under the age of 16—i.e., "boys"—do exist in the gay world. Should any skeptics remain, they might try strolling any night of the week along that same 42nd Street-Eighth Avenue area—now popularly known as The Minnesota Strip—described thirty-five years ago in Salute. *Evidence abounds, and to deny it only facilitates the work of homophobes out to discredit all gay people; exposes ourselves even more to denunciatory and distorting labels—as "molesters", "monsters, "complicitors", "dissemblers"; encourages us to fall into their traps, to fight the wrong battles. What are the "right" battles just now,* *in the face of the mounting campaign to defame us? Do other, more promising tactics and options exist? Not many. What we can try to do is counteract calumny with authentic facts and with our own lists of questions and demands. The fact, for example, that in those gay places currently being singled out as the most notorious hangouts for boy prostitutes in New York City—the Gaiety Male Burlesque, the Follies theater, Dallas, Haymarket (since closed), Rounds—one would be hard put to find anyone under the age of sixteen, because owners and managers, far from encouraging (let alone "organizing") congregations of underaged boys, are usually rigorous in demanding I.D.s. Along with presenting such counter-evidence, we need to demand proof of the authenticity of our adversaries' evidence. And, since we suspect it is partly trumped-up, proceed from there to raise questions about what is really going on behind the current defamatory campaign.**

To make such "demands" requires political clout, sustained pressure from a unified community strong enough in numbers and purpose to exert genuine power; a near-laughable prospect, I know, tantamount to a copernican revolution in sensibilities. Unifying, organizing and sustaining gay political commitment has been a rare feat, especially in New York. To hope for such a coalescence around the issue of "boy-prostitution" is day-dreaming. The issue of boy love has proven explosively divisive, and that of boy sex only marginally less so. It is fantasy to expect that more than a handful would gather round a banner proclaiming the wonders of boy prostitution. The vast majority of us wouldn't want to, finding no acceptable grounds for defending the phenomenon in the abstract, let alone for "demanding" such specific reforms as the legalization of gay-male prostitution for the 15-and-unders.

But is it accurate or necessary to see the issue (as most do) in those terms, to place it under so self-defeating a rubric? To do so, in my view, is to adopt the homophobic formulations of the scandalmongers. The true and critical issues at stake have little or nothing to do with the "morality" of boy-prostitution. That's a blind, a red herring cynically and skillfully tossed into the spotlight to deflect us from recognizing the deeper threat that lurks in wait.

—"For what reasons, at whose initiative and to achieve what ends have such gay establishments as, say, the Follies, been falsely libelled—and in a national press blitz, no less?"—"Why have comparable gay gathering spots elsewhere around the country

---

*See, "Hunting Sex Perverts, p. 148.

suddenly been singled out for raids and defamatory campaigns about their 'perverse activities'?"—"Why have a large number of other and varied gay 'scandals', that of the congressional pages being the most notorious, suddenly surfaced in a simultaneous outporing of publicity?" Those are the critical questions.

Boy prostitution is a decoy issue, one that too many gays have accepted at face value, falling prey to that most ancient of ploys: divide and conquer. Our attention has been diverted, our energies diluted, our political fragmentation accelerated, our community's goals and values further muddied, by our failure to distinguish between actual issues and the emotionally overcharged misrepresentations of them. Boy-prostitution is being highlighted, pushed front and center in the media, out of the shrewd calculation that it is the best possible opening shot both for dividing the gay community and for building up loathing against us in the country at large— softening up mainstream public opinion for anti-gay policies that might lie just ahead.

Yes, the phenomenon of under-sixteen-gay prostitution exists, although almost certainly to nowhere near the extent that it does among heterosexual minors. Yes, you as a gay person, personally may find the very idea of "child prostitution" immoral, disgusting, infuriating—whatever. But recognize it for what it is: a Trojan Horse concealing in its belly a full-scale, gruesome repression. The "horrors of child whoring," real though they are, may eventually seem penny ante in comparison with what looks to be coming down the pike.

Perhaps this historical document may help us as we try to refocus our view of the socio-political terrain. The last time the country was harrangued with large scale "revelations" about "childhood prostitution" was the late 1940s through mid-1950s. Soon after the propaganda barrage began, McCarthyism burst into full flower, wielding a reckless scythe that indiscriminately—and permanently—devastated thousands. Maybe this time around it will go down in the history books as Falwellism. Whatever the name, the carnage will be widespread, destroying many of us. Early alerts and mobilizations do not guarantee that it can be headed off or even minimized, but such, at least is the hope.

NIGHTMARE ALLEY, U.S.A.
by Selwyn James

The handsome, shabbily dressed youngster was about 14. He stood outside the crowded penny arcade, watching the faces of the Saturday-night funmakers. He was shivering. Then, as he saw a middle-aged man casually approaching, he turned to stare at a tankful of pet turtles behind the plate-glass window. "Cute, eh?" the man said. "Sure are," the boy replied, and grinned shrewdly. They chatted awhile, and then as the crowd swirled about them the man bent down and whispered something close to the boy's ear. The boy nodded. They walked off together.

An hour later the lad emerged from the man's furnished room, in his hand a $5 bill.

An airtight case of seduction? Hardly. This boy was a prostitute—with a six-month background of uninterrupted experience. He was one of dozens of twisted, money-mad kids who daily offer themselves to homosexuals along New York's Nightmare Alley—a 200-yard block of once-glamorous 42nd Street, between Seventh and Eighth Avenues.

Twenty years ago this was the heart of Broadway's illustrious theatrical district. Today it is an outdoor community center for the city's dregs. Here, under the glaring movie marquees, in the gaudy fun palaces, subway arcades and jammed bus terminals, are hustlers, pimps, sexual perverts, dope peddlers, drunks, gamblers, thieves and bums.

But of all the social tragedy and moral ruin to be found on this street, that of free-lance child prostitution is the most heart-breaking, the most urgent. Nor is it a purely local problem. It is nation-wide in scope. These unfortunate kids can be seen plying their sordid trade in the nightmare alleys of every sizeable city in the U.S.

Their ages range from a pitiful ten to about 18. Most are victims of low-income homes shattered by death, divorce, or irresponsible parents. Many flock to 42nd Street from the appalling slum areas of Greater New York. Others are runaways from as far off as Montana and Texas. Still others are reform-school escapees—tough, wily boys to whom hustling is only a new twist in delinquency.

Lacking normal home and family life, they all are demoralized, unhappy, roaming the trackless sands between childhood and maturity. Deep down they harbor a fervent wish to conform to established ethical standards. But meanwhile they flounder in a lonely world of their own, in which depravity is normal, common decency unknown.

About 20 percent of them have no homes at all. In summer they sleep on rooftops or in Central Park. When cold weather strikes, they bunk down in hallways, flophouses, cheap hotels and Y.M.C.A.'s, or at the homes of "clients." Or they hitch-hike to Florida resort towns. Their income often is supplemented by blackmailing clients, most of whom are men between 40 and 60; rolling drunks in dark streets; stealing food from cafeterias; looting parked cars, and hawking marihuana [sic] cigarettes on a percentage basis.

Possibly excepting a few older youths, none of the lads is homosexual. On the contrary, they openly express disgust for the grisly profession they have adopted, and some even admit to being physically revolted by what they do. Yet they are as cynical and unprincipled as their adult female counterparts. They are prostitutes because prostitution offers big monetary rewards. With clients paying from two to five dollars, a boy can net as much as $35 a week.

"Show me another way to make five bucks in an hour," comments a tow-headed 12-year-old from nearby New Jersey. "It's easy dough—I'd be crazy to go back to shining shoes," says a chubby 15-year-old Brooklynite. If these lads are typical, however, they will abandon 42nd Street inside six months. The reasons are not necessarily heartening:

They may cultivate regular clients (an enviable achievement) whom they meet by appointment elsewhere, or they may migrate to greener pastures in some other city. They may be picked up by the police as wayward minors, or they may graduate to more remunerative crime, such as robbing stores and warehouses. Parental awareness of their unexplained funds and day-long absences from the home may result in stricter discipline, less personal freedom. They may voluntarily give up their wretched Jekyll-and-Hyde existence because of a guilty conscience; or, if they are runaways, homesickness may draw them away.

Drives by the New York Police Department to clean up this blighted street take place about twice a year. Shoeshine boys and all other loitering youngsters are warned away. Truant officers pick up some of them. A few youths may be arrested for vagrancy. The effeminate, powder-and-lipstick type of homosexuals may spend an uncomfortable night in jail. And the pimps, hustlers and dope peddlers drop from sight. But none of this has a lasting effect. A week or so later, when the heat is off, 42nd Street resumes its former seamy character.

1948

BOYS AND BOY-LOVING

I discovered this anonymous letter, which was sent to Dr. O. Spurgeon English, a well-known Philadelphia psychiatrist and author, in the files of the Institute for Sex Research (The Kinsey Institute). From internal evidence, it seems to have been written by an Englishman. I read it as a rhapsodic special interest plea.

BOYS AND BOY-LOVING

A few words in defense of homosexuality after reading your book "Emotional Problems of Living." It seems to me that the homosexual fills [a] necessary and constructive position in society. For many years I have been connected with the Scout movement (and with [the] Boys Club Movement) and I have come to the conclusion that a heterosexual cannot run youth movements of any kind (except when he is paid for it, as a schoolmaster, and then only with the aid of a severe discipline). The reason is that a scout troop or a boys club needs a basis of affection between man and boys, and this a heterosexual cannot give. Heterosexuals usually have no interest in anyone's children except their own—not always then—and I have often found them to be actually frightened of boys. A successful scoutmaster or club leader of long standing is sure to be a homosexual (and I venture to say the same of a successful school-master—if the public found out the truth about Mr. Chips they would soon clap him in jail!). The only other scoutmaster in my district who has run a troop successfully as long as I have possesses (I happen to know) a large collection of his little friends photographed while bathing in the nude. I don't know whether he goes any further with them, but I can guess! And I have seen the County Commissioner (he doesn't know—it was in the dusk) kissing one of his little scouts. But these men do lead constructive and useful lives, they train boys and advise them and give them many happy hours. That they have to relieve themselves at intervals with certain selected boys I regard as no crime. The labourer is worthy of his hire! They would not be human if they did not. Why, only a certain specialized type of man can give his life and heart to boys and to penalize him for satisfying the sexual urge with them is cruel! What else can he do? He has no interest in women.

You say that the homosexual is ruthless in his seduction of children. However, it is the ruthless ones who get caught and they defeat their own ends, for the boys detest them. Twice during my career a rival homosexual has turned up in my district and endeavored to attract my band of boys to himself. But they all deserted him in a very short time and I found that they regarded him with positive hatred. "He's too cheeky—he's too dirty," they told me. This from fauns who rejoiced in phallic gambols with myself was surprising, and I could only account for it on the supposition that my rivals had wanted sexuality without love. That wan't good enough for the lads. A boy wants to be liked for himself and not merely because he possesses a genital apparatus. He will (if he is the right type) do anything for a friend, but he hates to be made use of.

For myself I divide boys into 3 classes. My division is derived from long experience and may prove surprising to you Freudians, for it seems to show that not every boy passes through a homosexual phase—and then where is your theory that homosexuality is a fixation of immaturity? I make it a rule never to touch a boy for at least six months, until I am able to classify him.

First, are the innocents, the sexually undeveloped boys. They are very often winsome and childlike and easily able to arouse the tender feelings. I give them (when suitable) kisses but nothing more, for sexuality frightens them and to make sexual advances to them would lose me their friendship. Whether they form the majority of boys, I am unable to decide. At one period you will find that your troop contains a majority of innocents; at another period you will find there isn't one!

Second, are the heterosexual boys. I suppose you would say there are none, but I have found plenty of boys who never pass through a homosexual phase at all but are interested in girls all through their childhood, especially in the country where they frequent the co-educational village schools. And the lengths these village boys of 9, 11, 13 go with the village girls of the same age is surprising! I would say that the majority of them have experienced full coition before they are 13. They are annoying creatures to a homosexual, for they are highly sexed and like being masturbated, but will do nothing in return. They have no interest in the male member of another boy of the same type or of a grown adult, but—I will come to this in a minute—they are excited by a homosexual boy. I would judge that the great majority of boys are either innocent or heterosexual.

Third, are the homosexual boys. (A) Those who pass through the homosexual phase. I have usually met with this type among town boys and I judge that is due to their being segregated from girls, as they are in the town schools. I have only known one country boy who passed through a homosexual phase—and he was running after girls at the same time. (B) The true homosexuals. You can tell them at once for they have an intensely exciting effect on the other boys. I can remember one in particular who caused a veritable explosion of passion. Twice he caused me to lose control over the troop; for one and all they rushed to assault him—even the innocents were carried away. I could do nothing with them. I still had a few "ideals" at the time and I was appalled. He was 13 when he was introduced into the troop and the effect was exactly as if one had introduced a bitch on beat [sic] among a crowd of dogs. (He was a handsome little thing, with a good figure.) At the first camp he went to, the others flew at him in a body and stripped him naked! If I had not rescued him they would have masturbated him. At the second camp there was a similar incident in which the others took his trousers off. After that I investigated for myself and found him to be a most violent homosexual, passionate and amorous. He remained homosexual till late adolescence and probably still is—he went into the Navy. Even at 17 he still retained his mysterious attraction over the others, for there was another stripping incident at that age. This boy had the most erectile penis I have seen on a lad, but the other boys who remained homosexual till I lost touch with them in late adolescence had just the same effect on their comrades. They were always losing their trousers in gambols with the others. The boys who pass through a homosexual phase are also assaulted, but much more mildly. They have not the intense exciting effect of the true homosexuals. This goes to show that homosexuality is innate and not a fixation in maturity.

To return to your other argument—you say that homosexuality is not aesthetic. Between adults (men) I agree, anyone would be repelled by the spectacle of a couple of hairy brutes fondling each other. But boys are, except for one point, practically indistinguishable from girls. When a passerby comes across my tribe of boys bathing naked in the Avon, you can see by the fatuously delighted smile which spreads across his face that he regards the spectacle as supremely aesthetic!

Finally, to dispose of the absurd remark that if all were homosexual the race would cease to exist. Heterosexuals and homosexuals are complementary. Heterosexuals have little love for children and are glad to pack them off to be looked after by someone else. I sometimes think that the family system is a mistake and everyone would be much happier if the heterosexuals restricted themselves to begetting children and the homosexuals brought them up! The unhappiness of institutional life is no reply to this, as orphanages, etc., are usually run by paid heterosexuals, with deplorable results.

Looking back, I would not exchange my life as a homosexual for any other for it has been very happy. No one can ever deprive me of my memories of sunny days by rivers with the happy laughter of the lads splashing in the water, or the long walks with their feet pattering by my side, and their eager laughing voices. No one can take away the memory of the kisses of that curly headed innocent whom I loved best, or the mad abandon of those hours when I gamboled with a naughty naked colt. I have read somewhere that the dead live on in the memory of their past lives. I desire nothing better.

THE VILEST OF RACKETS

The excerpts below are from the lead article of the April 1950 issue of Esquire *magazine. Entitled "The Vilest of the Rackets," it was written by Lloyd Wendt, at the time a* Chicago Tribune *writer and co-author of two books,* Lords of the Levee *and* Bet a Million Gates.

Though the article is self-explanatory, it is important to note that its sympathy is confined to sexually "normal" men falsely accused of "the shameful crime" of homosexuality, and does not extend to gay men unconscionably entrapped by plainclothes policemen, a familiar NYC phenomenon temporarily put to a stop by Mayor John Lindsay. For a fuller account of the forces behind Lindsay's policy decision, see The Politics of Homosexuality *by Toby Marotta (Boston: Houghton Mifflin Co., 1981; Chapter 2.)*

THE VILEST OF RACKETS

THE VILEST OF RACKETS

Our studied refusal in the past to discuss homosexuality has led to the shocking success of a shakedown racket so heinous it is rarely mentioned in print. Annually, this vilest of rackets takes a fortune from the pockets of more American men than most of us realize. And, just because of our hush-hush attitude toward the whole subject of homosexuality, the police are unable to do anything about it, for public prejudice has, up to now, been unwittingly on the side of the criminals.

What's all this got to do with you? This, among other things: There are hundreds of innocent victims of this racket. They are innocent because they are sexually "normal" men; they are victims because they're afraid to complain to the police. And don't think it couldn't happen to you!

The racket is an almost perfect crime from the viewpoint of the hustlers who practice it. They are seldom caught, and almost never prosecuted. The police know many of their leaders, some of whom "earn"—if we may use the word—splendid incomes as a reward for their criminality. Detective-bureau files in all big cities contain plenty of information on them. But few of the facts ever get before a judge and jury.

There is only one way to stop the racket, say experienced law-enforcement officials. That is by publicity. No man familiar with the technique of the sex-perversion shakedown need ever be a victim. Every man is a potential dupe if, through public ignorance and apathy, the foul business is allowed to continue ...

Police officials estimate that the perversion shakedown is engineered at least once a day in many of the large cities of the country. The Chicago police report two hundred arrests of such racketeers every year. New York, Cleveland, Boston, Detroit, and Los Angeles have been plagued by the thing for years. The arrest records are hardly an adequate indication of the prevalence of the crime. However, complaints are received in only a small proportion of the cases.

The extortion scheme works in several ways, for large or small stakes, but the basic pattern is pretty consistent. Let's take a look at one of the gangs in action.

Not long ago, a rugged foreman in a Gary, Indiana, steel plant, quit his job to see the country on the $15,000 he had saved. He got no further than a Chicago saloon. There, over a couple of beers, he flashed a roll of bills and talked about his plans. His talk drew the attention of a spotter for a shakedown gang. The two men struck up a quick friendship, and soon the spotter invited the now drunken foreman to his room for a drink.

The burly citizen from Gary hardly knew what happened next. A curly-haired boy appeared in the room out of nowhere, and without his having the faintest idea how it had happened, the foreman suddenly found himself maneuvered into a compromising position with the boy. What's more, "a policeman" flashed his badge and, in choice gutter language, loudly denounced the victim as a pervert. "You're under arrest," he said. He pointed to the spotter, the man who had originally invited the poor foreman into the room. "This man," he went on, "is our witness." The foreman stood helpless in his disgust and horror. The youth was obviously effeminate; a cop and a witness had caught two men in what looked like an incipient homosexual act. The Gary man felt sick as the big policeman hurled abuse at him.

Dazedly, he accompanied the cop out of the house and into a parked automobile, which looked exactly like a police squad car. The "witness" came along with them. The car started off, and then the witness began to plead with the policeman. "Please," he said, "be lenient, won't you? Sex perversion's a kind of disease. Give the bastard a break!"

The brawny foreman shuddered, but he began to have hope.

Maybe he could get clear of the filthy affair. They were driving toward the Chicago police headquarters at Eleventh and State, and the foreman talked fast. He was innocent, he insisted. He had been framed. If they would let him go, he'd make it right with them.

The spotter took up the foreman's cause again. He pointed out that the Gary man's reputation would be forever ruined if they dragged him into police court. A block from the police building, the big cop relented. He repeated again what he thought of perverts, but consented to forget the whole thing. All he'd wanted, he said, would be $5500 for bond—plus a little fix money.

The foreman agreed eagerly. The next morning, back in Gary, he drew $6500 from his bank. Two weeks later he had paid out his entire $15,000 to the blackmailers, but they kept on asking for more money. Finally, in desperation, the foreman visited a government agency, which interested itself in the matter because of the fact that extorted money, in an amount over $5000, had been transported across state lines. Within a few days all three hustlers were identified, but the case collapsed when the victim refused to appear in court. He wanted no public connection with proceedings from which some might infer that he was "queer." The racket gang was clear. The most the government agency could do was to provide an estimate of the hustlers' illicit earnings to the Bureau of Internal Revenue.

Incredible as it seems, this racket succeeds day after day, year after year, in most of the large cities of the country. A Boston hotel owner is estimated to have paid more than $200,000 to extortionists prior to his death. A mid-western university professor mortgaged his $17,000 home to meet payments before he finally complained to officials. A California bank officer embezzled money to pay off a gang and went to prison for his crime, but refused to prosecute the shakedown artists responsible for it. And were all these men, and hundreds of others who have suffered, sex perverts? Is that why they paid and paid and paid? Not at all! Why, then, do so many innocent victims take their losses in silence?

There are several reasons, all of them rooted in a general ignorance of the nature of the racket.

The victim invariably assumes that the pretended officers are genuine. He shares and fears public contempt for homosexuals and believes he will be suspected of depraved behavior regardless of any defense he may attempt. The loathsome and humiliating situation in which he finds himself leaves him helpless and vulnerable to any suggestions that seem to offer escape from embarrassment. ... The bulk of the crimes are against the ordinary guy who happened to be caught alone in a public washroom or at a secluded spot on the beach or in a park.

If an advance selection is made, the gang looks first for a potential victim with money. If his physical appearance is of the kind often ascribed to homosexuals, he should prove to be an especially good prospect. A single man is preferred above one who is married, since he will be more suspect. A leader in boy's activities is often selected, because the charge of perversion can be particularly terrible for such a man. But the racket can touch anybody at all—literally anybody.

1950

HUNTING SEX PERVERTS

In the two seminars I teach at City University, "The History of Radical Protest Movements" and "The History of Sex Roles and Sexuality", we discuss the feminist and gay movements. At one point I alluded to the Family Protection Bill. Blank stares. The what *bill? Two of the students out of forty-five vaguely recalled hearing* something *about it, but were at a loss to say just what.*

Ignorance concerning the bill is not confined to students at CUNY (whose average age, incidentally, is twenty-five). The national media have done almost nothing to publicize the bill's provisions— or, for that matter, to call attention to a number of other ominous governmental initiatives and interventions, such as the denial of immigration rights and legal aid servic ̇s to gays and the hardened line against allowing gay people to join the armed forces. The media have *given considerable attention to that fount of homophobia, the Moral Majority, but have not sufficiently detailed and emphasized its bottom-line goals: to put the patriarchs firmly back in power, women back in the kitchen, children back in Bible class, blacks back in line— the unemployment line—and gays back into closets (air-tight ones, to encourage asphyxiation).*

The gay press has done an immeasurably better job than have the national media in keeping us informed of the Far Right's agenda. Unfortunately, only a fraction of the gay population reads the gay press. Of those who do, I've heard any number shrug off the Moral Majority's goals as too "farfetched" to warrant alarm: "Mainstream America would never buy so repressive a program. Besides, we gays are now too well-established, have too much money, political clout— and allies—to be easy prey for repression."

Perhaps. But I keep hearing those Jewish voices in Germany in the Thirties: "We're too well-integrated into society, too powerful in our influence, to worry unduly about the frothings of the lunatic fringe." Knowing the fate of the Jews, we're denied the comfort they took in conventional safeguards—or in human "reason" and "compassion." Still, the ostriches among us have a fallback position: "all that *took place in Germany. This, after all, is the United States. It couldn't happen here". Wrong. It already has—not merely repression, but murder. Ask American Indians. Ask blacks.*

True, there has never been in this country a systematic, explicit, state-sponsored program for the mass repression and extermination of gay people. Yet the necessary prelude for such a policy—official denunciation and harassment—have long been present; homophobia, along with baseball and apple pie, are among the few constants in our history. Harassment ebbs and flows. In the twentieth century the highest tide came in 1950-55, when Senator Joe McCarthy spearheaded a drive to eliminate "perverts" and Communists from government positions, to break their "stranglehold" on the State Department and other federal agencies.

Try mentioning the McCarthy witch hunt and purge to your gay friends. If your spot poll is anything like mine, the most common response you'll get it a vague flicker of recognition—along with a rebuke for always being so heavy. I doubt that such equanimity could be maintained if gay people would read the actual words spoken in Congress (and elsewhere) thirty years ago, the startlingly sweeping, unqualified denunciations of our "degeneracy." Proceeding on the tired and admittedly pedagogical cliche that "knowledge is liberating" and can convert somnolence into wakefulness, I'd like to introduce you to some small portion of the vitriol against us which poured forth in the early Fifties.

I've chosen to excerpt a single document from the period—in my view, the key document—one which fully enunciates official sentiments and "solutions" of the day. It's entitled "Employment of Homosexuals and Other Sex Perverts in Government," and is a report issued by the Senate Investigations Subcommittee in 1950. In Gay American History, *Jonathan Katz mentions the report as "a major document of the 1950s antihomosexual witchhunt era," but doesn't reprint excerpts from it, choosing to publish instead the summary accounts that appeared in the press. I think the truly malevolent flavor of the report can best be savored in excerpts from the document itself. The actual words the Senate subcommittee employed, and the attitudes revealed, cut like razor blades. They need to be read and reread—not to cause needless alarm but, hopefully, to stimulate needful vigilance.*

The virulent attitudes against gay people expressed in the 1950 report may have subsided somewhat today. Certainly more Americans currently hold a more benign view of us than did thirty years ago. The critical question is how many more—and also how stable the "new" view is. My own opinion is that homophobia remains deeply entrenched among large portions of the population. The Moral Majority shares that assessment. I think we need to face squarely that whatever progress we've made in recent years is fragile and reversible. What has been "given"—permitted, tolerated—can be taken back. And, in fact, not much of substance has been given. Yes, we're allowed to dance until dawn in our big-city clubs, to crank out our own periodicals, to run gay candidates for office, to assert openly the validity of our alternative lifestyle. Some would argue that such "privileges," though desirable, are ultimately inconsequential—little more than calculated concessions to the profits to be derived from encouraging gay consumerism among the more privileged (meaning mostly gay white men). In the meantime, most gay people are still denied such fundamentals as job security, an end to discrimination in housing, the right to raise their own children. None of these needs has as yet found widespread legal protection, neither through legislative statutes nor court decisions.

Protection remains elusive and distant. Even should the halcyon day arrive when we succeed in obtaining across-the-board anti-discriminatory legislation, we shouldn't delude ourselves into regarding such an achievement as definitive, etched in concrete. Having such legislation on the books could do many things—but not everything. It could provide us with legal channels for the petition of grievances. It could curtail official bigotry, put roadblocks in the path of local efforts to enact discriminatory policies. It could serve as a buffer (since courts and legislative bodies tend to move slowly) against volatile shifts in public opinion.

But it's well to remember that laws are subject to interpretation, circumvention and repeal. They are a useful tool for achieving equal treatment and opportunity, but no guarantee of it. If laws can prevent the open expression of bigotry, they cannot prevent it from going underground, from finding subtle new extralegal forms of expression. As blacks have painfully learned over the past two decades, not even legislation on the federal level can do much to modify or monitor the hatred of the heart.

Although protection under the law will turn out to be limited, it goes without saying we'd be delighted to have it. As of now, we've succeeded in getting only a handful of state and local ordinances passed that protect our rights to any degree. This is worth stressing, as we congratulate ourselves on the gains of the past decade. Almost all those gains have been entirely extralegal in nature. They rely wholly on sufferance—on the tolerance of public opinion, that most whimsical guarantor of security. We're right to pride ourselves on our new visibility, but should avoid equating it too glibly with a widespread, solidified acceptance of our "alternate lifestyle." That equation could be a function of wishful thinking—confusing a possibly transient and limited shift in public tolerance with a profound reversal in traditional moral values.

The evidence is hard to read, lending itself to opposing interpretations. The reality of a federal gay rights bill being introduced for the first time in history in Congress encourages the belief that we've achieved a substantial level of acceptance, and that a floor has been set below which they would never again dare to push us. Contrarily, the emergence of the Moral Majority, with its demonstrable power to sway critical votes, makes the ground we stand on seem alarmingly shaky; one fears that even a muted sign from Reagan—a sign, say, that he'd lend quiet support to passage of the Family Protection Bill—could plunge us into an engulfing abyss. So long as the mood of the country remains elusive and volatile, it might be well to err on the side of pessimism, to keep our guard up. Few seem prone to that stance. Instead, the dominant mood in the gay community seems a compound of apathy, naivete, and Coueism—"Every day in every way we're getting better and better." Too many seem lulled into a false sense of security by what on the surface—but not in the statute books—have been dramatic "changes" of late in public acceptance. Should a sweeping, summary reversal take place, we'd be ill-prepared or equipped to handle it. The American Civil Liberties Union can be counted on to raise hell. The majority of Americans can't.

Which returns us to the example of the McCarthy witch hunt thirty years ago. To put it mildly, the American public was late in recognizing the senator's misrepresentations, later still in reining in the excesses of his punishing minions. One might counter that we learned much from that experience. I wouldn't count on it. Americans have notoriously short and selective memories; a mere ten years after Vietnam, we're rattling the sword again in Central America. We can't count on the average American's ability to retain the lessons from the past because few have ever learned them—other than those versions filtered through the superpatriotic prism of standard high school texts and teachers. I'd count instead on the average American's historic susceptibility to demagoguery, religiosity, and jingoism. I'd count on the schizophrenic split that has always marked our national character: the split between our rhetorical defense of "individualism" and the strong contradictory pressure to conform. Now and then, conformist pressure sweeps all before it; a righteous conviction takes hold that there is only one way to be "a good American."

The Fifties was one such period. The Eighties may prove to be another. On delicate balance, I think it will not. But should the Moral

Majority's well-financed momentum continue to build, we have little countervailing power to offer against it—too many gay people remain closeted, too many of those who are out remain indifferent to politics, their energies "elsewhere" absorbed, eyes closed to the potentially venomous volatility of public opinion. Just how venomous that opinion can be—how ruinous, once triggered—is well illustrated in the tone and recommendations of the 1950 Senate subcommittee report excerpted below. Perhaps reading it will alert more of us to the thin line we walk, to the possible hazards that lie ahead.

One footnote. Among the seven senators who served on the subcommittee was Margaret Chase Smith of Maine. Is her name familiar? For many decades, Smith enjoyed a national reputation for independence and compassion—a famed "liberal." Senator Smith could have disqualified herself from serving on the subcommittee. She did not. She could have submitted a dissenting view, in whole or in part, to the report. She did not. She entered no demurral of any kind to one of the most scurrilous official documents (and ensuing reigns of terror) in our history. I call this a "footnote." But I suspect for those in the gay community prone to placing special faith in "liberal" support, the footnote may prove a more dramatic eyeopener than anything in the report itself.

81st CONGRESS SENATE DOCUMENT 2nd SESSION
No. 241

EMPLOYMENT OF HOMOSEXUALS AND OTHER SEX PERVERTS IN GOVERNMENT

INTRODUCTION

The primary objective of the subcommittee in this inquiry was to determine the extent of the employment of homosexuals and other sex perverts in Government; to consider reasons why their employment by the Government is undesirable; and to examine into the efficacy of the methods used in dealing with the problem ... . A number of eminent physicians and psychiatrists, who are recognized authorities on this subject, were consulted and some of these authorities testified before the subcommittee in executive session. In addition, numerous medical and sociological studies were reviewed.

Information was also sought and obtained from law-enforcement officers, prosecutors, and other persons dealing with the legal and sociological aspects of the problem in 10 of the larger cities in the country . . . .

In this investigation the subcommittee tried to avoid the circus atmosphere which could attend an inquiry of this type and sought to make a thorough factual study of the problem at hand in an unbiased, objective manner . . .

For the purpose of this report the subcommittee has defined sex perverts as "those who engage in unnatural sexual acts" and homosexuals are perverts who may be broadly defined as "persons of either sex who as adults engage in sexual activities with persons of the same sex." . . . This investigation is concerned only with those who engage in overt acts of homosexuality or other sex perversion.

The subcommittee found that most authorities agree on certain basic facts concerning sex perversion. . . . Most authorities believe that sex deviation results from psychological rather than physical causes, and in many cases there are no outward characteristics or physical traits that are positive as identifying marks of sex perversion. . . .

Generally speaking, the overt homosexual of both sexes can be divided into two general types: the active, aggressive or male type, and the submissive, passive or female type. The passive type of male homosexual, who often is effeminate in his mannerisms and appearance, is attracted to the masculine type of man and is friendly and congenial with women. On the other hand the active male homosexual often has a dislike for women. He exhibits no traces of femininity in his speech or mannerisms which would disclose his homosexuality. This active type is almost exclusively attracted to the passive type of homosexual or to young men or boys who are not necessarily homosexual but who are effeminate in general appearance or behavior. The active and passive type of female homosexual follow the same general patterns as their male counterparts . . . .

Psychiatric physicians generally agree that indulgence in sexually perverted practices indicates a personality which has failed to reach sexual maturity. The authorities agree that most sex deviates respond to psychiatric treatment and can be cured if they have a genuine desire to be cured . . . .Persons afflicted . . . should be considered as proper cases for medical and psychiatric treatment . . . .However, sex perverts, like all other persons who by their overt acts violate moral codes and laws and the accepted standards of conduct, must be treated as transgressors and dealt with accordingly.

SEX PERVERTS AS GOVERNMENT EMPLOYEES

In the opinion of this subcommittee homosexuals and other sex perverts are not proper persons to be employed in Government for two reasons: first, they are generally unsuitable, and second, they constitute security risks . . . .

Perverts lack the emotional stability of normal persons . . . there is an abundance of evidence to sustain the conclusion that indulgence in acts of sex perversion weakens the moral fiber of responsibility. . . . The presence of a sex pervert in a Government agency tends to have a corrosive influence upon his fellow employees. These perverts will frequently attempt to entice normal individuals to engage in perverted practices. This is particularly true in the case of young and impressionable people . . . .One homosexual can pollute a Government office . . . .

SEX PERVERTS AS SECURITY RISKS

The conclusion of this subcommittee that a homosexual or other sex pervert is a security risk is not based upon mere conjecture. That conclusion is predicated upon a careful review of the opinions of those best qualified to consider matters of security in Government, namely, the intelligence agencies of the Government. Testimony on this phase of the inquiry was taken from representatives of the Federal Bureau of Investigation, the Central Intelligence Agency, and the intelligence services of the Army, Navy and Air Force. All of these agencies are in complete agreement that sex perverts in Government constitute security risks.

The lack of emotional stability which is found in most sex perverts and the weakness of their moral fiber, makes them susceptible to the blandishments of the foreign espionage agent. It is the experience of intelligence experts that perverts are vulnerable to interrogation by a skilled questioner and they seldom refuse to talk about themselves. Furthermore, most perverts tend to congregate at the same restaurants, night clubs, and bars, which places can be identified with comparative ease in any community, making it possible for a recruiting agent to develop clandestine relationships which can be used for espionage purposes . . . .

EXTENT OF SEX PERVERSION IN GOVERNMENT

An individual check of the Federal agencies revealed that since January 1, 1947, the armed services and civilian agencies of Government have handled 4,954 cases involving charges of homosexuality or other types of sex perversion. It will also be noted that the bulk of these cases are in the armed services as is indicated by the fact that 4,380 of the known cases in Government involved military personnel and 574 involved civilian employees . . . . The military services, unlike most other Government agencies, traditionally have been aggressive in ferreting out and removing sex perverts from their ranks and this is bound to make for a larger number of known cases in the services . . . Many of the civilian agencies of the Government [have been] either negligent or otherwise failed to discover many of the homosexuals in their employ . . . .

HANDLING OF THE SEX PERVERSION PROBLEM IN GOVERNMENT

. . . The subcommittee has found that many civilian agencies of government have taken an entirely unrealistic view of the problem of sex perversion and have not taken adequate steps to get these people out of government . . . . In many cases the fault stemmed from the fact that personnel officers and other officials . . . handled the problem in accordance with their individual feelings or personal judgments in the matter . . . [There were those] who adopted . . . the false premise that what a Government employee did outside of the office on his own time, particularly if his actions did not involve his fellow employees or his work, was his own business. That conclusion may be true with regard to the normal behavior of employees in most types of Government work, but it does not apply to sex perversion or any other type of criminal activity or similar misconduct . . . .

CONCLUSION

There is no place in the United States Government for persons who violate the laws or the accepted standards of morality, or who otherwise bring disrepute to the Federal service by infamous or scandalous personal conduct. Such persons are not suitable for Government positions and in the case of doubt the American people are entitled to have errors of judgment on the part of their officials, if there must be errors, resolved on the side of caution . . . . This conclusion is based upon the fact that persons who indulge in such degraded activity are committing not only illegal and immoral acts, but they also constitute security risks in positions of public trust.

The subcommittee found that in the past many Government officials failed to take a realistic view of the problem of sex perversion in Government with the result that a number of sex perverts were not discovered or removed from Government jobs, and in still other instances they were quietly eased out of one department and promptly found employment in another agency . . . .

Since the initiation of this investigation considerable progress has been made in removing homosexuals and similar undesirable employees from positions in the Government. However, it should be borne in mind that the public interest cannot be adequately protected unless responsible officials adopt and maintain a realistic and vigilant attitude toward the problem of sex perverts in the Government. To pussyfoot or to take half measures will allow some known perverts to remain in Government . . . .

Christopher Street, Issue 60, 1982.

1951

WHEN IS AN "H" NOT AN "H"

The prestigious American Association of Marriage Counselors met in annual convocation in New York City on March 9, 1951. Breaking precedent, it set aside one session on the program to discuss the "growing 'H' problem." I should explain that "H" was common parlance among the experts of the day—a sort of discreet short-hand—for homosexuality. Similarly, "Ht." was used for heterosexuality, "M" for masturbation, "C" for coitus, etc. Apparently nothing dared speak its name thirty years ago.

Predictably, the dominant tone of the "H" session was homophobic. Yet some dissenting voices and—surprisingly, for 1951—some unorthodox views were expressed. Moreover, despite the decorous resort to "H" or "Ht.", all the participants spoke English, not Scientese. Any non-specialist can read through the transcript of the session without having to consult a specialists' dictionary. In contrast, today's "scientific" authorities typically speak and write in an intimidating technical language, sexologists being among the worst offenders.

The triumph of jargon has had deplorable consequences. Much of the recent technical research literature on homosexuality employs an arcane vocabulary that makes the data inaccessible to most readers, as well as preserving it from the careful scrutiny and challenge of those who know the subject best—gay people themselves. Debate on the merits of this new literature is largely confined to an inner circle of mostly non-gay specialists. This insularity hardly seems to trouble them. To the contrary: Judging from the self-congratulatory tone of the experts' debates, they apparently hold to the view that discourse should be confined to professional sexologists. Perversely, at the end point of that logic lies the assumption that being gay—unless one also happens to be a trained specialist—is a handicap, a disqualification for understanding gay life. "Objective" commentary requires distance and disengagement; the less direct the exposure, the less chance of "contaminated" observation. In this bizarre—and commonplace—scenario, experience, and the ability to decipher it, are placed at odds; being gay and understanding what it means to be gay become incompatible. The bottom-line message is a familiar one: the experts know best.

Many of the country's leading therapists, counselors, and sexolo-

gists attended the AAMC's 1951 session on the "'H' problem."
(Wardell Pomeroy, Kinsey's co-author, was one who did not; too little
was known about homosexuality, he said, to warrant the sort of
confident generalizations such a meeting would be likely to en-
courage). Most of the sessions were refreshingly free of jargon—yet
also replete with confidence. The AAMC had some reputation for
unorthodoxy, but as the "H" session made amply clear, the
reputation was inflated. Most of the experts expressed views derived
from the current mainstream model of homosexuality as pathology;
the "disease" model commanded overwhelming allegiance.

But not unanimous allegiance—some dissenting voices were
heard, notably that of George W. Henry.[1] His benign, laconic
skepticism may seem timid today, but in the rigidly conformist
climate of 1951, his remarks were strikingly (and to traditionalists,
alarmingly) unorthodox. In challenging, however tentatively, the
ingrained assumptions of the day about same-gender sexuality,
Henry and a few other participants cast seeds of doubt that
foreshadowed and encouraged the more forceful, broadly gauged
dissent that was to emerge two decades later.

These early voices of dissent deserve recognition. Chiefly for that
reason I include (with only a few deletions) nearly the complete
transcript of the AAMC's "H" session, which I found at the Kinsey
Institute. The AAMC transcript, far from being in need of condensa-
tion, is if anything too elliptical, apparently because the original notes
were subsequently pared down.

CASE PRESENTED BY E. MUDD:

In 187 cases in the Philadelphia Marriage Council there was only
one case of H which was a problem. This was a college couple in their
20s. Male was Jewish; he had been overseas for 3 years in the war. The
female went to the Philadelphia Council five times pre-maritally;
male one time. Female said male had H tendencies and that he
considered himself H. Male was formerly engaged to another female
but broke this because of the H. The female stated she did not want to
be a virgin all of her life. Male went to a psychiatrist in the Army but
did not have time for much talk about the H with him. The male had
overt H but had no overt Ht, but wanted marriage and a family.
Mudd referred him to a psychiatrist. Psychiatrist reported that he was
not neurotic; he was definitely H; marriage not indicated. Both male
and female had a job in the same summer camp where the female saw
letters between the male and a male H friend. The friend became
jealous over the female and therefore, the male broke his engagement

with her. Three months later: A letter received by Mudd saying that they were married secretly. Later they came back to Mudd for an interview. They reported a good adjustment although the Ht was less agreeable to the male than H. Male has H as frequently as Ht but the wife does not know of it. Cm 2 to 3 times per week.

Moved to California. Mudd thinks there is a fair possibility of the marriage working for some time.

CASE PRESENTED BY LESTER DEARBORN:

Dearborn divided H into three classes: 1) Invert; 2) Acquired; 3) Substitutive. He has three classes of bisexuality: 1) H more frequently than Ht; 2) H [equal to] Ht; 3) H less than Ht.

It is possible to have overt H with Ht phantasy [sic]. It is possible to have H activity without being a homosexual.

The case presented was a married male born and raised in New England. Masturbated from 13 to date. At 14 he had H once with an older male. He then had no more H until 20. Feared masturbation from 20 to 23. Ht with three partners at 23 to correct H. No orgasm except in masturbation with H phantasy. He carried on C [coitus] and H for ten years; two children resulted. Again resolved to break H after his H partner died. No H for seven years. C irked him and he threatened suicide. He was an acquired H because his appearance and history so indicate. Dearborn was convinced that he was not a "true H" and Dearborn felt H would be damaging to him unless he found a "suitable partner" ... Several months later subject reported he was much better, with no H tendencies. Four years later marital relations reported as still better—no H. Same report given another 4 years later.

Dearborn: 1) established the patient's self-respect; 2) established confidence in the patient's ability; and 3) broke down the making of resolutions which patient would inevitable break.

CASE PRESENTED BY WALTER STOKES:

Stokes regards H as a very significant factor in the family. It damages feeling of security, etc., in the family. 2% of the population are overt H; 50% of the population are latent H. There were 3,000 overt H roped in by police in Washington (no times mentioned). McCarthy says 2,000 H employed in State Department. Washington is reputed to have many H colonies. McCarthy and J. Edgar Hoover presecute the H—both are bachelors in late 40s. No one damns H as much as the latent H. The Washington legislators instead of putting them in penal institutions put them in St. Elizabeth's Hospital for treatment and cure. The H is a psychosis and a deep-rooted personality problem. They are the most difficult type of psychotherapy problem.

The case reported on is of a male who was in the Armed Service and was having H three times a week. He has had 550 therapeutic hours of treatment so far and expects to have 250 more hours with Stokes. The male continues his overt H but has stayed out of legal difficulties. He took testosterone in the Army for one year with no results. He was 35 years old at first interview and had had 70 H overt partners ... He has no close relationship with any of them. He is attracted to the masculine type. There is often fellatio with no climax. No anal intercourse. He has felt guilty about M [masturbation] but not about H. He had C at age 25; was mechanically potent but his attitudes are not Ht. He entered into this relationship on the basis of curing a female of her neurosis. He was born in the country and lived there until 7 years old. Now employed in an important personnel job in Washington. Has had a religious background. Is the oldest of three children. Has a high-school education. He has moved around a great deal in order to make H contacts. His relation with his mother has been bad. His mother told him his genitals were horrible and would not even let him wash himself. She made him pants without pockets. He developed paralysis of his right arm because his father insisted he play ball; he hated his father. He was afraid to M with his left hand. He is antagonistic toward females because a girl cousin told on him when he experimented with her. He felt males would not do such a thing. Sin and Sex were stressed at home. A seven-year-old cousin was killed by a train. He knew his cousin had had Ht play and was told his cousin was "bad." From 5 to 10 he was interested in wearing female clothing. He saw his father and mother have C when a child which frightened him.

Dreams after three years of analysis: 1) On road to a tunnel, met a big cat at the tunnel. He was in rags. Cat bites off his arm (mother threatened to cut off his penis once). 2) See someone go down a hole and play with alligators snapping around.

He now masturbates with his right hand, has climax, and has had no overt H for two years. Has developed relations with females and can think of vagina but not of a female face (because of stern mother).

Kinsey says [in his pioneering 1948 book *Sexual Behavior in the Human Male*] that H should be accepted as is M; not much can be done about it. (Albert Ellis[2] contradicted this).

Stokes advised against marriage and to stay out of the hands of the police.

Laidlaw explained that [Wardell] Pomeroy was not at the meeting because he felt their research on the H was not far enough advanced to make statements.

Dr. George W. Henry: Laidlaw introduced him as "the man who has had more clinical experience with problems of H than any psychiatrist in America today."

Henry says he is confused about the terms H and bisexuality, because actually there are infinite gradations between the theoretic male and theoretic female, whereas the above terms sound specific. He agreeswith everything [however contradictory? M.B.D.] already said.

Laidlaw to Henry: In your book, Sex Variants, you infer [sic] that H is psychopathic.

Henry's answer not gotten [by whoever took the notes].

Stone: Is there any relation between small organs and H?

Henry: Not necessarily except because of fear of being inadequate in Ht.

Stokes: What is wrong in a family which influences a person toward H?

Henry: Parents contribute more than other individuals toward maladjusted males, who are more vulnerable and deviate from the norms more easily. Lack of security contributes to sexual maladjustment, fear of M, etc. (when talking Henry spoke of the penis as "it").

Mace: Can you trace H to a specific pattern?

Henry: No.

Stone: Quoting Ford and Beach;[3] "H is present in all cultures; in 64% of societies H is condoned." How much is generic and how much is acquired?

Henry: You will have to ask the Lord.

Mace: We often hear of a boy who as a result of H relations with an older male becomes H (I don't really think it alters his pattern). Have you had evidence that [tendency?] toward H have been awakened by an H assault.

Henry: I agree there is no way of being certain that patterns will be altered. Many who protest vigorously at first later become H. Male Prs [prostitutes?] often become more H than Ht.

Dearborn: Are physical characteristics indicative of H?

Henry: Not necessarily.

Stokes: Quotes English figures that there is no proof that physique is related in any way.

Kleegman: Cites Landis study of 300 cases of females with three overt H cases with mesomorphic [body] structure. Actually in private cases the opposite may be true. What is your experience with marriage where one partner is more H than Ht?

Henry: Marriage has little chance for success, although frequently a female will get along better with a male who is a little feminine than one who is very masculine.

Woodward (in regard to the Mudd case [see above]): How would having children alter H tendencies?

Henry: There is no definite answer. There are few who can take on the responsibilities of children without spoiling the marital adjustment.

Stone: Are latent H psychopaths? Stokes said 50% of the population are latent H; there, 50% of the males are psychopaths.

Stokes: I agree.

Ellis defines psychopaths: Can H be labelled psychopathic?

Henry: Cannot go by text-book definition.

Woodward: Are H tendencies developed in the happy, good home?

Henry: Yes.

Stone: No one has mentioned the female.

Henry: Everything can be said about the female which has been said about the male except the "female is not so much trouble in society."

Ellis: Are H predispositions psychologically innate?

Henry: The best guess is yes. There are some constitutionally predisposed.

Ellis: Is the predisposition hormonal? 90% of hermaphrodites were surgically diagnosed. Where is the evidence that H is genetic?

Henry: We cannot be sure. Hermaphrodites are exceedingly rare ....It is possible to determine which gonad is present but did that tell you how that gonad was functioning?

Ellis: There is only one set of gonads present, etc.

Henry: There is so much uncertainty about hormones that no one can tell.

Folsome: Hormones have power but not direction ...

Laidlaw: Do you consider H entirely due to environmental conditions?

Folsome: Yes ...

NOTES

1. George W. Henry and his associates published a two volume study in 1941 entitled *Sex Variants: a study of homosexual patterns.* Dr. Henry's research was

based on two hundred male and female volunteers, mostly of a "professional class" and mostly New Yorkers. Of the two hundred, forty of each sex appeared in the study—"personality measurements, anthropological data, pedigree charts, X-ray photographs, and gynecological reports."

2. Ellis is still a prominent sexologist and still churns out book after dogmatic book. I haven't had the stomach to wade through his recent volumes, but I've been told he has adopted a somewhat less homophobic line of late.

3. The anthropologists/psychologists whose book *Patterns of Sexual Behavior* was among the earliest and most important challenges to the reigning medical model of homosexuality as "disease."

DR. KINSEY AND MR. "X"

The letters excerpted in this article are between the great sexologist Dr. Alfred C. Kinsey and a European businessman herein referred to as "Mr. X." The latter gave me permission to publish the correspondence with the sole stipulation that his anonymity be maintained. As he is still actively employed by a conservative foreign firm, the use of his real name could threaten his livelihood.

The correspondence between the two men runs to nearly 400 typed manuscript pages. The original letters are housed (but have not been made available to researchers) at the Kinsey Institute in Bloomington, Indiana. I would never have become aware of their existence—let alone come into possession of a complete set of photocopies—had it not been for the forceful intervention on my behalf by C.A. Tripp, author of The Homosexual Matrix *and for many years one of Kinsey's closest associates. Indeed, following Kinsey's death in 1956, Tripp saw to it that the correspondence with X continued. He took Kinsey's place in the interchange and—substituting cassettes for letters—has continued contact with X to the present day.*

Thanks to the generosity of both men, those cassettes, too, have been placed at my disposal, but I've not drawn on them for the following article. I confined my selections solely to the Kinsey/X correspondence of 1951-55, and primarily for two reasons: unpublished Kinsey letters are likely to arouse the most interest; and far less editorial work was entailed selecting excerpts from typed pages than from untranscribed cassettes.

Now and then, some editorial intervention has been necessary. A glance at X's letters makes it apparent that he's an enthralling correspondent—yet also a man who only partially mastered English as a second language. To clarify X's meaning I've sometimes had to fiddle with spelling and syntax (ellipses and brackets denote the spots)—while trying not to over-tamper, obliterating the special charms of his idiosyncratic prose.

Kinsey's side of the correspondence is by far the more spare, often a mere thank-you note acknowledging receipt of one of X's lengthy letters. Yet even from the beginning Kinsey would sometimes respond with animation to X's accounts—drawn out by their rare amalgam of astonishingly frank reports on sexual adventuring combined with acute general observations on the different sexual mores encountered. Kinsey's expansiveness grew with the years, especially after the two men finally met in person. When Kinsey travelled to Europe in 1955 X offered himself as guide, and proved a remarkable one: socially adroit, sexually encyclopedic. The private "tours" he arranged for Kinsey put to rest any lingering doubts the Indiana scientist may have harbored about the veracity of the more sensationalistic portions of X's letters. Seeing was believing. Kinsey now fully grasped that X's lengthy reports constituted a "World Guide to Gay Male Life", and one unparalleled in sophistication and scope. X's letters were at once a scrupulously gathered storehouse of "raw data" and a shrewdly gauged set of interpretative generalizations—ones few professional anthropologists (had they cared, or dared) could match. Clearly X was a man doubly blessed: keen appetites, keen insights.

Honoring my pledge to protect his anonymity, I'm only able to say that when X first wrote Kinsey in 1951 he was an unmarried man nearing 40 from an upper-class Scandinavian family. These are bare biographical bones indeed, yet I hope provide some context for evaluating X's comments. Ultimately, the importance of the letters lies in their content—and that is easily grasped.

X was initially prompted to contact Kinsey after reading the French translation of his epochal book, Sexual Behavior in the Human Male, *which was first published—to a now famous uproar— three years earlier in the United States. Datelined Tangiers, Morocco, July 27, 1951, X's introductory note to Kinsey was uncharacteristically short but typically forthright:*

Dear Professor,

I won't say: "excuse me taking the liberty of approaching you personally," because you are seeking for the sake of science a clear picture of our human sexual comportment and you consider probably every new 'case' one brick more on this big building you are erecting; but myself, I want to do as much that others are not going to suffer under the misconception of this chapter of life as I had to do.

X went on to congratulate Kinsey "with a good deal of gratitude" for his pioneering work and to offer to put at his "entire disposal with all the knowledge I tried to gather ... out of my own or out of comparison with others in all the countries I have travelled through."

Within two weeks, Kinsey responded with a gracious note thanking X for his offer of help. "For the most part," Kinsey wrote, "our data are secured by direct interview with our subjects." (See Wardell B. Pomeroy's fascinating book, Dr. Kinsey and the Sex Institute [*Harper & Row: 1982*] *for a detailed description of the interviewing procedures Kinsey and his associates—Pomeroy being among the most prominent—used when gathering and evaluating data.) "But there is some value," Kinsey wrote, "to case histories that are written out for us, and if you care to do that for your own history, I can assure you that the material will be appreciated. ... In addition ... we should be glad to have a record of your comments and observations on Africa."*

Kinsey's prompt, warm reply was all the encouragement X needed. Within a matter of days he sent Kinsey a lengthy report—the first of what would ultimately grow to a remarkable and massive sequence. I feel privileged to publish here samples from that sequence. Though lamentably brief, the samples do at least span the entire period during which the two men corresponded (1951-1955) and contain material from both men's letters. I've drawn the excerpts chiefly from X's descriptions of male/male sexuality in those countries—Morocco, Italy, Greece, Nazi Germany and Turkey— which he knew best and about which he wrote most cogently.

The letters are chronologically arranged. The opening selection is taken from X's first full-length letter to Kinsey.

Tangiers, Morocco/September 1951
X TO KINSEY

... I have been with them [the Arabs] now for more than three years and I venture to say that those Arabs who would decline to have something to do with you [sexually] could be counted on your fingers ... Due to the Koran the male intercourse is not allowed but in practice it is so well known that it belongs in a certain way to the Arabian picture of life as it made a indelible feature of the Greek life of the 5th century B.C. The sexual behavior of the great majority of the Arabs is again not to be compared with our own one and is animal like without any refinement. Even kissing not always "allowed." The most normal way for them is the anal coitus very often also used in their intercourse with their women or girls or prostitutes. The answer was [to the question "Why men?"]: more pleasure because the sphincter is tighter, the danger of V.D. lower and seldomer the viewpoint [prospect] of no-pregnancy. I never found in my life not only a single individual but a whole group a whole population absolutely egotistic and egocentric in their way of sexual relations.

For us very often the deepest satisfaction is bound to the knowledge that the other part is at least as much enjoying the being together as one self. The Arab thinks only of himself, is erected immediately and has not the long gap between erection and final orgasm. Any for-or-afterplay is not desirable to him. Religious necessary washing after each intercourse [begins] at the very moment the ejaculation has taken place; peculiar ideas about the pure or un-pure [nature] of sperm can become another disturbing moment. But what makes Arabian life for an European with these inclinations so unusually temptuous is the fact that every Arabian atmosphere is full with sex, potential sex. To pass an Arab has almost automatically the consequence that he turns around and ... read in your eyes before you even thought of the possibility of taking him into sexual consideration. I met 10 year old boys—shepherds—which were offering themselves to me in a kind of competition with each other. I saw many of them playing with each other. The standard rule is that the older takes the younger one. The character of a male social life gives of course many possibilities to this inclination. It's a very natural sexual life, whenever they feel like doing something they do so, either masturbating as very youngsters, or very often if [in] the country with animals, or in town wherever and whatever is available no matter if male or female. The almost impertinent sexual self-assurance they have I experienced best when an Arab with a long beard and doubtless more than 70 years asked me to come with him but [at] the same time asked me what I'm going to pay him. If married or not does not make much difference. Affection I found among the many 100s of cases I know as good as never...

Bloomington, Indiana, September 20, 1951
KINSEY TO X
[*After thanking X for his letter, which had included a long account of X's own "case history," Kinsey wrote:*]
... I am particularly interested to know how the Nazis handled the homosexual question. We have the legal documents and we have some of the published acts but very little first-hand information from any of our subjects on the way in which the laws were enforced. If you want to write me at greater length on that point, it would be very valuable..."
[*In his case history, X had described being picked up by the Gestapo in 1937 and spending two years in prison. Accused of being homosexual, X had pleaded not guilty of that* "but of an abnormal sexual attitude: at least I had to avoid castration or dangers like that

in the moment where you admitted to be an incorrigible homosexual type....

During the trial I became entirely clear upon myself, that there was nothing to change in me and that [what] was un-natural for them was natural for me. The day of the sentence I masturbated in a kind of self-desperation in the way of: this damn sex business has brought you here, now take it, do it all the more. This uncontrolled attitude changed soon in a make the best of it and I started reading, learning languages following up encyclopaedies etc. Even Spengler's [historical works] was in the prison-library available! Masturbation once a week. Loveletters to other prisoners—I was in confinement for one year....

After one year transfer to forced labour camp with 100s of other prisoners. Immediately were sexual relations taken up; our room with 34 prisoners, had exactly 9 active couples of homosexual persons—also convicted for this reason—and ca. [about] 4, 5 other couples where one party was 'normal.' After some months these conditions were found out by the authorities and everybody was separated from his friend and red marks on the respective beds shown for special controls by the guardians"].

November 16, 1951
X TO KINSEY
Dear Professor,
Thank you so much for your kind letter, dated 10/20. I'm very relieved to know that everything reached safely the port it was bound for, especially pleased to learn that my notes were of use to you. ... My thanks also for your reprints which I read with the greatest interest...

Before I write you more upon the Nazitime and its horrors to so many 1000s of us, let me take up some points of your articles. ... I would easily commit myself to pick out among 50 Europeans—but not Spaniards or Italians—the ones who have an inclination of this kind [gay]. There is always something, no matter whether only a certain humility in the eyes, a peculiar way of holding the hands or moving the shoulders, not to speak about the more evident signs of clothing. Some sudden utterances of joy or surprise can give away the whole so well hidden personality's sexual basic structure. And most of our kind in Europe quite apart from eventual sympathy or antipathy like to open the visor at least for a second and that's enough for the esoteric knowing of this group. It is a kind of Cain's mark....

A Russian soldier explained to me that in the army even death punishment is given for the 'crime' of homosexual activities and in Russia herself also heavy penalties threaten the civilian.

As you know, in Germany existed also in the time of the German Weimar Republic the law against homosexual activities. But as soon as SS took over power interpolations were made.

Clubs were *en vogue*, big balls were highly frequented by male dancers female dressing. The cabarets made allusions, the movies even started [to] use the matter as a spicing attraction. The literature flourished with products out of this field and sportive magazines, nudity clubs sent out their advertisements. All the dozens of male clubs of the "Wandervoegel" were a excellent occasion and breeding place for all ones who were inclined to the homoerotic atmosphere. This was the inheritance Nz. [Nazis] took over in '33....

So we went to jail. The judicial procedure if it was employed and not only was handled by the Gestapo, showed the most undignified scenes under the name of the "German people".... The most delicate and intimate details were discussed, the judges took to a language that made redden the defendant more for that reason than for his shame he felt for the crime accused of. I [remember] with [what] wonderful gesture the prosecutor formulated the sentence and climbed up to the climax of moral indignation when he said; " ... [X] had wallowed himself in the muddy pool like a pig..." Really, I had when I thought under these words on the fine bodies of my mates only a pitiful inward smile.

Out of a very often most refined Oscar Wilde-type became a prisoner number [deleted] with—not in prison but in the camps—a special sign with regard to his abominable crime. I met priests, lawyers, physicians, authors, businesspeople in leading positions, artists. ... it was seldom that you met apart from some gardeners, barbers and bakers types of the lower classes ... Only church and half-an-hour airing out in military discipline gave you the view of other human beings. Nevertheless relations between neighbors—via the pipes or with the help of threads or after a certain time of experience with the help of the "waiters"—developed and I never received so many love letters in my life as in this time! I know of many relapses between prisoners, be it in the dispensery, be it in the corner of a floor, be it in the short minutes an old-timer showed a newcomer the necessary manipulation for his manual work he had to do. I had one case where an acquaintance of mine went as far as that to act sexually during church service with the man next to him. Many cases of the 'normal' ones discovered their latent innate [sic] inclination of this character.

The attitude of the guards and "higher" personnel differed very much; the older ones did not consider this group of prisoners as criminals, the younger ones were partly curious to make contact with this funny species, partly did they represent the Nazi opinion of this theme and treated us worse than the murderer. The leading figures showed the full contempt for this aberration as it had to be shown accordingly to the Nazi evangelium. The co-prisoners again varied strongly, inferiority-complex made them very often [?] to an unsupportable room mate. Many ridiculed, specially the more effeminate ones, many were as rude as possible to counter-balance this suddenly too unknown tune of prison language. In the camps different methods were employed: Sometimes 175 were all put together, sometimes they were deliberately separated and even given to the control of coprisoners. There were some cases of agents provocateurs even in jail. ... The propaganda took advantage of every case that gave a good loot, many industrials, many directors of big concerns disappeared and with them their fortune. A particular feature of this time is that the persecution of the Jews very likely does not show many cases of Hs. [Homosexual] Personally I found only very few Jews who were Hs.

Bloomington, Indiana, November 23, 1951
KINSEY TO X
I have received your letter of November 16. We are very much indebted to you for the additional information you send along. It makes an important addition to our files, for we have had relatively little information on how the Nazis had handled the homosexual question, although we do, of course, have all of the official documents.

We are tied up primarily with our forthcoming volume on the female [*Sexual Behavior in the Human Female* (1953)]. I am sure you will be interested in it when it comes out for it gets to a lot of basic material which is necessary for understanding either the male or female.

I wish there was some way for us to meet, but I see no chance of my traveling in your part of the world for some time to come. Let us keep in touch, however, and perhaps some day our paths will cross. Meanwhile, I wish you the best of everything.

Morocco: December 20, 1951
X TO KINSEY
An Arab boy keeps very often with another Arab mate sexual

intercourse in the form of mutual anal contact. Often also only reciprocal masturbation. That refers also to relation between European and Arab boys of the same age. (Speaking about 11-17) Very many have in the same time relations with girls of their own race or of the other one. In all those cases is no question of money involved. As soon as a difference of age exists, the financial point gains importance; the older boy, 18 with 15, has to pay. That is independent of colour. The same situation occurs for the man with the boy or the younger ... But in the conception of the Arab on the street also subconsciously in the mind of the "civilised" one (they certainly are much more civilised than we in passed times!) the European is free ... [and] powerful. That's why he has to pay at any rate. This traditional opinion is certainly the soundest basic explanation for this phenomenon.

But they try from their end to give some other reasons too: The European coming to their countries get something that he can't get in his own country. (Only partly justified, correct that he can get it much easier without conventional complications). One other often heard point is that pleasure we are supposed to have in this event is said to be bigger, [a] very silly objection as the Arabs are as much looking out for the European as we for them and as their whole sexual behavior points in this direction. The "traditional viewpoint" weighs so much, that it does not make any difference who is looking for whom, it is always the European who has to pay. In this connection it does not make any difference either whether the European is the older or the younger. ... it is he that has to pay...

The woman is still an absolute inferior being and not an equal or better adequate companion to the man. The character of the Arab society is that of a male one. The astonishing fact uttered that among the Arabs is less love than among us. The relations between man and woman can be of so incredible superficial character that we simply can't understand it. Often the sexual intercourse takes place without more than the opened fly. The point of being married or not does not concern actions very much. It often happens that their own wife is "taken from behind." The reason probably the higher tension of the sphincter specially in connection with the just mentioned viewpoints makes this method more desirable. I tried to find out why the Arabs react so violently to the slightest touch of their own back; usually the first area they are groping around. What we arrived at was that the back is the very male realm nobody has to touch without offending the bearer or owner of this domain of male strength and beauty par excellence. Another strange feature is that the daily life of the Arab male is filled with caress among themselves; going hand in hand is quite common, even the arm around the shoulders of the other guy is usual. Kissing on the cheeks not seldom, lounging and caressing in general the rule.

Bloomington, Indiana, January 8, 1952
KINSEY TO X
... The information that one gets from a traveler or from persons who have lived in the country without making an actual survey from a good portion of the population must inevitably reflect their own viewpoints. For instance, we have extended notes from persons who have lived in Arabian countries for long periods of years, and find that the Arabian people are very much restrained and have practically no extra-marital sexual activity and with homosexuality practically unknown. This reflects the restricted experience of such an observer. Other persons have suggested that homosexual activity is more common than any type of non-marital heterosexual activity, and this I am inclined to believe although I am still uncertain what the averages would be until we can get something approaching a real survey of a good sample. Your own notes in the meanwhile, add considerably to our material.

Certainly the things you report in your last letter are in accord with some things I have from other sources and your discussions of their attitude toward payment for sexual relations is very interesting. If you have time to write us further, I shall appreciate it and hope that some time we may be able to do more for you...

Tangiers, Morocco, March 17, 1952
X TO KINSEY
It's quite a time that has passed, since I received your kind letter of January 8, 1952. But all my own affairs were in such a pending state that I did not feel in the mood for writing. Let me go back to your letter: it really amused me to learn that some people have lived with the Arabs and arrive at statements as the ones quoted by you; where have those men their eyes and ears? Of course, I can't claim to give you any exact figure-basis, but I can assure you that my judgment is built upon my many own experiences, compared and filled out by literature and based on so many conversations I had with Arabs on this topic.

Yet I have to admit, that there are great differences between the several tribes, the town-people and the countrymen, the population

of Tangiers with its doubtlessly special conditions and the people of
Marrakesh. But—these are differences that certainly can be generalized and you have done so [in K's book] with your grouping in
City-and-rustic-population: just the same happens here. I was up the
mountains in the Spanish Zone and found quite a reluctance to my
insinuating demands, people are proud and reserved and hard-
working. On the other hand the men from the Rif-area are even
known among the other Arabs as specially preferring the intercourse
with young boys. And those Rif-mountaineers are extremely handsome, fierce and masculine looking in their whole appearance. I had
not long ago a visitor here, a Swiss woman, and when we walked
down the street and she saw some Arabs, their hands linked into each
other, she broke disgusted out: "are all those Arabs homosexual?"
Now then, this observation will become a statement, as soon as she
arrives at home, and there we are at this kind of report you speak
about. You certainly heard about the Shleus, a special Berber tribe
from the Atlas mountains; it is absolutely known among Arabs and
non-Arabs, that those guys can be bought by everybody. Here in the
Moroccan, certainly also Algerian, area, I dare to repeat my previous
assertion, that first of all: extramarital activity is undeniable,
secondly, whether that will be hetero-or-homosexual relation depends just on circumstances; very often the choice will be directed by
the material reason. Out of my own experience I would today
formulate it this way: out of 100 Arabs 98 would say yes, 10 of those
would later refuse, if not given the possibility of anal intercourse, 30
of the 98 would decline to kiss or to be kissed, the great majority
accept oral satisfaction (or femoral), 5 would after having had anal
contact offer the same to you this time passive and 2 out of the 98
would suggest anal intercourse in the passive role as the most suitable
one to themselves. That here in this corner of Africa.

After three years I must consider it almost impossible to find any
relationship that gives friendship and sexual satisfaction...

Milan, Italy, October 31, 1952
X TO KINSEY

I'm sorry I can't be of any help to you with respect to the Lesbians.
Personally I'm absolutely indifferent to this type and at any rate not
at all attracted. All my friends, all my many acquaintances feel more
or less the same way about it. We all have our work to do, then in the
spare hours we will not lose a chance to find what we are actually
looking for. People as artists... who are put together on work with
female partners think different and enjoy to have the female element

in their life in this un-dangerous form. Also some types I know who for one or the other reason are fond of night clubs and have to live a more socially bound life told me the same, that they enjoy to be together with those women, who also frequent the same places and make it unnecessary to struggle around with the hs. women.

The Milan is quite different type than the Roman or the Napolitan. The Italians kept their individual features designed by a historic background ... nobody knows better than you how much the environment has to do with the development of the sexual behavior of the individual. Let me sketch for you the picture. ... the male is growing up ... usually surrounded by a lot of older ones ... he sleeps in the bed where the parents are making love, where beside the older boys are investigating what sex is for, a not at all so mysterious mystery. He sees the older ones with erections in the morning and in their joking remarks about it. He lays around as a kid with other kids and where ever they are chasing around they will find in some quiet corners some people making love.

He will also notice that the grown ups touch their genital parts continuously and adjust it, that they speak with proud [pride] about a *cazzo grande*. Then he will find glamour in the streets of Naples where the big hotels are located and where the ships for Capri are leaving. He will learn that it is easy to enter this realm just by having what a man has to have to be authorized to say he is a man. He will learn of friends who made a fortune in this city, and he will see some other ones who suddenly quit their job and show up with some fine clothes and go to the movies and about big parties and wonderful dinners and trips into the country. Brothels are expensive if one does not make enough money, the physical urge exists—so what? It's also typical for Naples that you will, in contradiction to Torino, not find so many queens in the general street picture, but you will notice 100's of males who make you understand that they would be ready. In Torino I found it distasteful to see at the station, where the main point had switched into the railway station, half a dozen of all aged queens who were fawning around some soldiers, who came there in whole groups only for this purpose, worse than any streetgirl would ever do it. Torino a town with a rich and well-to-do population created quite a different type of hs. than here. The Neopolitan has certainly to be ranged as bisexual type just like the Arabs with whom they have anyhow so much in common.

Also here Sailors play a special part in the sexual game: they seem to be considered by everybody as personal property of hs. milieu. I have not heard of any case where a refusal was known. I dated one sailor and he could not show up so what he did was to send me a representative to tell me that he was impeded; the meaning was that I take his comrade. With the Arabs happened just the same: sometime some of them introduced me to their brothers or friends because they were for one or the other reason not available, and it was not always agreeing with their choice. It is really as trivial as that.

There is still this point with the kissing that puzzles me; maybe I found more details to add: almost all of my acquaintances did not kiss, neither did they in the intercourse with women. It must be that kissing really falls into the more sentiment-bound realm as one of the chaps told me and that it is therefore banned from the only-sex contacts.

In the meridional zone [Naples] you find much more anal tendencies than in Milano or the north. I think to be right in the general statement that the Italians in general have very well shaped and big male organs; at any rate much bigger than the Arab as an average has.

I should not omit to tell you that in those rooms where I occasionally went to with my partners were always holy pictures on the walls and usually just above the very bed where so un-holy things took place.

Milan, Italy, December 22, 1952
X TO KINSEY

I was astonished that here in the north quite in contradiction to the southern parts is anal intercourse not desired. An almost general refusal to kiss or to be kissed and an almost absolute granting to oral intercourse or manual activities. Also in their marital status they do not as a rule kiss or to enjoy in general all the delaying steps in our procedure on the way to final orgasm. I was twice refused to use the tongue as perfectly un-exciting. There is a funny feature: I found— especially soldiers—quite a few who told me openly that they are masturbating pretty often...

The typical latin attitude [is] to have a fiancee that only might be kissed and touched in the upper parts of her body leads to the final result, when the guy has said good night to his girl he either goes—if he has money enough to a brothel or that he masturbates. If some hs. cross his path in this state of things, he will of course accept his activities too. Now—there is an other group that told me just as sternly: masturbation? Never. What does that mean to us? Without having a body and a female one under me I don't enjoy anything. Masturbating I only did as a *ragazzo*, but not as a man. That might be in accordance to the also mentioned trait, that they do not like to keep record on those things or cultivate a special literature in this line: no theory counts, only the vital concrete experience ...

Bloomington, Indiana: July 14, 1953
KINSEY TO X

... The material in your letters continues to be excellent. It has given me a totally new idea concerning the situation in Italy. It would be of great help if we could get together some day and we shall watch for the opportunity. ...

Greece: 1953
X TO KINSEY

... What I met in the parks were some ingeniously interested guys just to have fun, some others I took by surprise—even in the literal sense of the word—sleeping on benches I work them slowly up to a better presence! Nobody thought me crude in doing so and everybody agreed. Those about ten cases of the parks the majority not inclined to accept oral activities but wanted anal intercourse. In two cases I achieved anyhow to impose my will and the lads agreed afterwards that they hadn't thought of getting so much pleasure out of this method. I'm not very much in favour of having anal intercourse in the open air. Positions are too ridiculous and also too uncomfortable. It's something that I began to like more and more but in bed. Maybe [the Greeks] are not in such high an extent beautiful as the Italians are but they show often more kindness, also money asking or accepting is done in a nicer way ... not to forget in this comparison that Athens is ... much more on a tough cash basis at least in public places.

On a short [train] stop I was absolutely struck by the beauty of a guy who waited with some friends to see the train pass. I showed him my admiration and the whole group of about six guys laughed and shouted with excitement ... they said in Greek to each other that I was rather good looking! That I say here to show that the Greek has a feeling for male appearance. It's the southern attitude; the body is nothing to be ashamed of; on the contrary, it's something that can give you a lot of pleasure. No difference what the body belongs to. To me it is always anew a deep pleasure to see those soldiers hand in hand, laborers too,[embracing] each other in all dirt and sweating, men wheresoever embracing each other. Things you will never find in the countries of the North here in those surroundings you can make love just as you take a cup of [tea]. It was astonishing how many turned around or made some remarks, or gave me understanding glances.

I can well say that in the most of the conversations I had with the guys one statement was repeated time and again: we prefer anal intercourse also with women. Athens—as world town—showed not this reluctance as the other places as to oral activities But kissing also here very seldom practiced ... When I asked the proper Greeks if they had not quite a good deal of own countrymen who live with them ... they agreed ... but mentioned also that everything in this direction is quite hidden.

I went for a weekend down to Rhodes, the little island which has seen so much—all times and nations and races. A charming place that reminds me of Tangiers. There are stationed a lot of Greek sailors. I picked up about ten of them ... Another group could not understand that I was not willing to take them all but wanted to have to do only with two of them. With two other ones I went to the beach and we had a good time there. One of them waiting for his turn. There was always a lot of fresh joking going on and things are taken very natural....

Now American sailors, certainly the freshest and cleanest one can find or imagine ... they are cold and without the slightest sex. They are sexy made up and are at the same time the most unsexy men. All their joking is so ingenious or on the other hand so childish, their touching each other could in the same second also become a punching, they have not a single bit of this sexual nature, this animal beauty and animal bestiality, that in fine shades can be seen on the Italian. And don't forget one trait which is important too: how many Italian men are crying, crying out of an abundance of feelings...

There was a small trait that pleased me [with the Greeks], almost all of them asked me "what's your name", and with this little question was entering some more personal element in the relation; it was not as with most of the Italians almost an unpersonal encounter in which only counts the facts that one of the two has a male organ and the other a mouth or sphincter ... especially at Rhodes, but also in Athens, when I passed a party in some little bar with 5-6 sailors and some civilians there was a big hello and I had to join them, when they ask me what I liked best and I stated the Greek pseuli—what means the male organ—there was even a bigger hello and everybody wanted to make dates with me for the next two hours. It's a very charming and open joking with a slight stroke of more heart in it than I met at the Italians.

Denmark: 1954
X TO KINSEY

I [have been] in Denmark and it was quite interesting to observe the difference in the behavior of those Northerns and also on the other hand to see how similar everything is that is called sex. . . . Most of my partners belonging to the same classes as here were willing to kiss and showed also in the whole more pleasure to get involved in technical variations. But there was nobody who wanted to have anal intercourse neither in the passive or active way.

Cinemas are not found there. What takes place has to happen at only the few warmer months . . . at the beach,etc. All the public WC's [toilets] are now in an impeccable shape: no holes anymore; the police took care of that. But the urinals are still important milestones on the way to hell or heaven. . . .

There is something in the northern behavior of making love, that makes it more pleasant to the hs. partner, the act is not only just a physical relaxation, but some feelings enter into the act, they—and that's a very essential point—enjoy it more and the best word might be: enjoy it deeper, than southern colleagues. Also a general feature was that more of them are willing to engage in own activities with the hs. playmate. . . .

In Denmark are a good deal of "boardinghouses for boys" who came in conflict with the law; the stories one hears are horrible, and if only half of it is true it's bad enough. Not a few "teachers" had regular anal intercourse with the youngsters, but achieved in many cases by force, sadistic excesses were not seldom. The boys were in a high degree masturbating, the elder ones 16-19 had mostly relations with the younger ones.

Greece,Egypt and Turkey: September 12, 1954
X TO KINSEY

. . . Everything I had seen, felt, experienced in North Africa I found again in Egypt and what I had observed in Liberia I recognized to a high degree in the surroundings of Upper Egypt; and also just as well corresponding to the situation in Senegal or Sudan.

I think we are perfectly agreeing that one has to take into account in any judgement of sexual behavior the general as well the individual environment of the persons in question, this strong sun in Egypt, the deep difference of the poor, the unbelievable crowdness on any spot where they are living together, the general undeniable innate melancholy—a take-it-easy attitude—certainly also born from the fatalism of their religion, have their influence on the sexual comportment.

Greece: I started off for Greece in the beginning of August. I arrived in Athens in the evening. Immediately I went to the well-remembered places and found a sailor; we went to a big park. Anal intercourse was what the sailor liked. But he also kissed and caressed. Already in this first Greek contact I felt a certain difference between Greek and Italian: the urge to have sex seems to be stronger, more ingenuous; in the two days I met more men who had sex with me without asking for money than in the whole year here in Italy; out of the thirteen cases in this time were five who were kissing and participating in sexual mutual activities.

This first evening I had four anal intercourses and four oral ones. Among which the last one was an American, tall as a giant and standing in the men's room masturbating himself. When I entered he left his job to me and finally said "Thanks a lot." That I book as a feature of national difference. It's seldom that a Greek or Italian will say thank you for this kind of cooperation! In my hotel were two Americans; and I have to add; where ever I saw American "queens" they are worse than those of any nation, because also in this field you people present the "super" of everything.

It is amazing how highly developed the Greeks "leading capacity" is: one short look and the guy turns around and knows exactly what it all is about. But this quality doubtlessly is even more spread out among the Arabs or the Egyptians. A place like this big park in Athens can't be easily found any other place: it's certainly one of the sexiest gardens I know.

The officer informed me that the Air Force is widely known to foster quite a few hs. "compulsive" as well as—of course much more: "faculative" types. (That was also confirmed to me by another Greek well-to-do-hs.)

Turkey: First of all I was struck by the general dirtiness of this land. Arriving at one o'clock a.m. was not much time left to get into investigative night excursions. I just ran into some 5 soldiers who really reacted positively, but intended to go with me—all 5 of them. Now knowing the general conditions yet, neither the possibilities of finding some adequate place nor the habits of robbing sexual partners I had to renounce. The big bunch of soldiers is absolutely "misleading", and one can stare at them without any understanding from their end. Sailors are more receiving and I met a nice morning in a public park two, who both wanted and had sex with me; both anal and with much enthusiasm. I thought most of them making love very good speaking from a technical viewpoint. They try to enjoy this act as much as possible. Their technique is anal intercourse. No kissing, no touching, no interest in oral activities and not even accepting [excepting?] their organs. Their behind is a holy realm—just as all the other Arabians I know, certainly the influence of the traditional partly religious attitude in this aspect. One could not speak about any refinement or "building-up" procedure but the actual intromission is skillfully performed and ejaculation as long as possible repressed. That in difference to the Arabs.

I want to stress: they [the Turks] are not aware in the way an Arab is. There are quite a few who have tasted the forbidden fruits and they are showing their interests in a frightening way no regard to surrounding; where ever it will be, they try to drag you against a wall and think in their limited birth-ostrich-policy, now even more blinded by sexual desire, nobody will see anything. Reckless and thoughtless they want to arrive at their satisfaction. (Some Egyptian soldiers went even further and got their rifles ready when I did not want to continue the game!)

A disgusting trait you have to notice is the touching of their organs all the day long; I saw even men, who had their trousers in this region mended. Sailors—in the most dirty white uniforms I have ever seen—have dark stains in this area, the same the soldiers, many civilians show the same signs. The whole clothing is without any sexual undercurrent. Beauty is seldom and I was tempted to say to myself: when the Turk is at his best he is Italian like. There are some wonderful looking men and women, but that is the breed of old race and general culture and can't be booked a general feature. I had a total of 16 contacts, of which were 14 anal. It's certainly the way they prefer most.

As little sexy the atmosphere in Turkey is, as much is this the case in Cairo. In Egypt the slightest mental touch is enough to induce the right reaction—it does not even need the physical touch! What surprised me most: very many country-types up to certainly 60 years old showed first of all a very unusual size of their organs and furthermore a surprisingly strong erection.

I wonder whether heteros. run also into so many ridiculous scenes as we certainly do: in Cairo I discovered one evening a big motorpool with some guards walking up and down. I approached them and after a short while we agreed to climb on one of the trucks and to have sex. So it happened. Hardly finished with the first, showed the second one up, and I also noticed that they had woken up the rest of the whole gang who had slept until then in their tent. Nobody minded anything and the second one enjoyed just as much the situation with the spectators as the first one without them. Then I thought more adequate to jump down from the truck and make some dates with those guys for the next day. Far from that, they insisted that the whole gang has its rights and the money for this doubtful pleasure should be paid in advance! I had already during the whole action to watch with one eye my clothes because I had noticed some arms and hands slipping through the canvas cover of the truck in a dangerous nearness to my pockets. When I refused to continue, rifles were loaded and I faced this desired dream of many hs. to be raped by a whole regiment! It was a long struggling and shouting "to help" till I could liberate myself from this assault of male "rut".

In Cairo saw a few real hs.; among the natives it's just as seldom as it was among the Arabs in Morocco. I had to smile when I saw how about 6 waiters of a restaurant reacted when a terrible made-up queen—probably French—showed up and swayed through the rooms. Everybody signaled immediately to the next one and a big relishing smile was alighted on everybody's face; it was not at all deprecating, maybe a little bit pitying that one shows so open what one is made for, but more dominant was the idea: I would like to have that! I could have had much more sex, if those guys were not of such an unbelievable negligence of our customs: to yell in plain daylight, to follow you in groups of two and three. What can a European do in those cases than to show the cold shoulder? I observed a group of laborers—masons—in their rest hour; sitting on the ground they had one teenager among them. He was literally offered around and anybody played with him partly as a mother with her child, sometimes more as a father with his boy just caressing him a bit, but just as much also as a lover with his counterpart. The boy—one of those astonishing editions of miniature men in a perfection I never saw on white—reacted perfectly at ease and even with a certain coquetery.

I saw again very clearly the road they are going: embracing, sleeping together, exchanging so freely signs of caressing, easily excited until erection, showing that to each other, speaking to each other about that topic, being very close to nature as far as procreation is concerned, not inhibited by education principles of the olders.

The law is against hs. for the time being not inforced. But young dictators have always to find new slogans to please their subjects.

I noticed that many of the Egyptians, just as the Arabs in the other parts of Africa, are arriving [coming] very quickly, even so quickly that one does not realize it. Usually I was also missing the groaning or other signs of real convulsive outbursts of achieved Satisfaction.

Bloomington, Ind.: March 30, 1955
KINSEY TO X
. . . . I am again impressed by your capacity, not only as an observer but to interpret the social significance of the situations you are recording. It is a remarkable record you are accumulating for us.

I still have no plans worked out for my trip to Europe this year but I shall let you know as soon as they are worked out. Certainly I hope we shall have a chance to meet then.

Damascus, Lebanon: August 18, 1955
X TO KINSEY
. . . It's right that the taxi drivers are the key to sexual life almost in all the middle East countries. I noticed that already in Tangiers. The driver comes in contact with everybody; tourists ask him every question and he gets used to reading the mind of his customers. How many girls separate from other groups in which they are coming to the holy land to get into a car with a strong Arab driver and to engage in unholy activities. Deduct the exaggeration and unexactness of the "reporters" [and there] remains an impressive daily figure of pre- and extramarital coitus performed in this way. And the same is of course valid for homos. men.

No doubt can be that for the Latin as for the Oriental man sex is essentially always awake. Natural carelessness in quite an open way must lead in many cases to even closer contacts. The meal, the drinks, are in a good many of cases absolutely provocating sexual activities Daily language is full of allusions from the sexual life. But to come back to the drivers and their assertions. It's right that I found everybody of them ready to have a trip with me. It was even in Jerusalem and in Beyrut [sic] like that; they stopped and tried with all persuasion to get me in their car. Of course it's not quite free from business reflections. But if somebody opens the door and says come in I have to f. you, so that in the first line sexual urge and afterwards he might think of also gaining something with this pleasure he had sought.

My conclusion after having passed through the Arabian lands is that they are to me the most attractive in Tangiers—and in the same time the most unsatisfactory in the act. Their sexual demands here in the East are highly developed and after two jerks they are at ejaculation. There were many of them who had techniques and liked to engage in a fine build-up. It's mostly done in a crude way but that has for me a high degree of excitement. They throw you in a corner, try to push you around in a position that suits them and can't come quick enough to the actual part of the body they like most: the behind.

That certainly is the preferred way and only a few want oral methods. They also with women have anal intercourse. They are hugging and caressing but seldom kissing. And several times I got this answer, that the country people will never engage in kissing but town men start now by and by to get used to it and to demand it. But if so, it's again rare to have the man kissing another man. There we are pretty close to the Italian comportment.

When asked about real compulsive homos. types I got un-animously the answer—in Jerusalem maybe 3, maybe 4 in the whole town, but not more! But just as promptly was admitted that all the rest has nothing against making love with a man in the masculine part. I learned about some younger chaps who get really married with the older ones, who also buy them officially from their parents and look after the house; they dress them and treat them very womanlike. It's down in South Arabia, Hedjas [a town].

I think it is very interesting what one man told me: "very few of us are homosexual but in our youth it often happens that we have contacts with elder ones who use us as a sexual outlet—that changes very soon and we start ourselves. Quite a few of the priests invite you, and after a not bad dinner you can't refuse them the favor they ask you for—more seldom but it happened to me and others occurs that with the nuns—if anybody of our people heard that somebody had had sex with me and he in the masculine part, it would be impossible for the rest of my life: whenever I had to speak up in community this man would come forward and say: how can you open your mouth, you who has got my seed—we would be deeply ashamed, whilst we know very well that for you is that [sexual acts] all the same—but most of us like it very much to have sex with men—there are some tribes also today where the boy gets married to the elder man."

Bloomington, Ind.:September 14, 1955
KINSEY TO X

...I am increasingly surprised at your great capacity to get around into all sorts of places and to interpret what you see and how people are reacting, with the acumen that you show. It is too bad that you did not get into scientific work where your capacity to become ac-quainted with diverse cultures could have been utilized. You would have done excellently as an anthropologist....

1955

DON'T CALL US "QUEER CITY"

*For some insight on the alternate claims that San Francisco is a
dead end or a mecca for gay people, I thought a little historical
perspective on what it was like a mere twenty-five years ago to live in
that city might make the ingrates a bit more grateful and the dewy-
eyed a bit more aware that Utopia is a temporal phenomenon.*

*"Don't Call Us 'Queer City" was the actual title of the article
reprinted below (in its entirety) when it first appeared in the April
1955 issue of the magazine* Men. *It was written (or rather "told to" a
journalist named Terry Hansen) by Lt. Eldon Bearden, then chief of
the Sex Crimes Squad of the San Francisco Police Department.*

DON'T CALL US "QUEER CITY"

The two men entered the San Francisco park on top of Nob Hill
from opposite ends. The night was warm and sultry—a rarity in the
wind-whipped city. Flashy cars lined the curbs bordering the park—
Huntington Square. Their owners dined and danced in the Fairmont
and Mark Hopkins, two of the city's most fashionable hotels.

Inside the park the two men wandered aimlessly along the bench-
lined pathways. Positive no one else was in the park, the two, by
prearranged signal, darted into a bush-clustered area.

The homosexuals didn't notice the bulky shape of a police
inspector step from behind a tree and cross to the bushes. Neither did
they see another man suddenly leave the sidewalk on California
Street and gingerly pick his way up the side of a bank to a point where
he could watch the pair.

After a brief surveillance, the two police inspectors moved into
the open area protected by the shrubbery.

Spotting them, one of the homosexuals spun around, knife in
hand. He slashed at one policeman. The officer sidestepped the
vicious swing and clamped a beefy hand on the man's wrist, hanging
on until the knife dropped to the ground. Both suspects were taken
into custody.

In other parts of the city, other teams of plainclothesmen and
uniformed policemen were rapidly moving in on the homosexuals.

Two inspectors, Frank Murphy and Lloyd Kelly, walked into the lavatory of a hotel.

Murphy flung open the door. One occupant, a slightly built man, ran past him, trying to escape. He ran into the arms of Kelly. Murphy wasn't so lucky. The man still inside was a 220-pounder. He grabbed the inspector by his tie and yanked him forward and downward at the same time bringing his knee up and catching Murphy in the groin. The blow sent the big policeman spinning across the long room.

The attacker barged out of the lavatory and leaped down a short flight of stairs. He got no further. Kelly, who'd handcuffed his quarry, dived through the air and crashed on top of the man's shoulders. Both fell to the floor. The two men began pounding one another with head-busting blows.

Despite the intense pain racking his body, Murphy got up and went to his partner's assistance.

When the battle had ended, Kelly nursed a bad cut beneath his left eye. His coat was half torn off his body. Nevertheless, he and Murphy were satisfied. They had two more violators in custody.

This was the situation in San Francisco recently. Instead of being known as the "Golden Gate City," San Francisco was being tabbed "Queer City," or a haven for homosexuals. My orders from Chief Michael Gaffey were, "Get rid of this offensive mess."

It wasn't an easy job.

Homosexuals had flocked into the city from all parts of the United States. They were everywhere. They filled the bars in the city's cheap "Tenderloin" district, off Market Street, in the city's mid-section. They thronged together in the city's parks and squares. It made no difference whether the park was in skid row or in the better areas, like on top of Knob [sic] Hill, or Union Square, which is bounded by Powell Street and Geary, Stockton and Post Streets.

Even policemen can have a difficult time detecting the "queens" in their female clothing. During our vice drive against the homosexuals, a bartender in one of the swank hotels called the police. He was suspicious of two women sipping drinks at the bar.

When our two officers arrived, they thought the guy was slightly out of his head calling them. One of the girls was a chesty redhead; her companion was a sleek-looking little blonde, appropriately filled out in the right spots.

However, the bartender stuck to his guns until the police finally took the women into the Hall of Justice for a closer examination. The bartender had been right: The "girls" were men.

On the second night of the drive, Inspectors Kelly and Rudy

Kopfer found a prominent business executive involved with a homosexual. Kopfer and Kelly followed the executive out of the hotel and stopped him on the street.

When the inspectors identified themselves, the man began struggling. The two were clutching his coat when the man squirmed out of the apparel and started running down the street. A short distance away, Kopfer and Kelly caught him. A wild free-for-all developed. Kopfer had his wristwatch broken and his clothes ripped; Kelly sported mean-looking purple bruises on both shins.

Another suspect who also was bisexual, was brought to our offices on the fourth floor of the Hall of Justice for questioning. Midway in the quiz, the poker-faced man leaped up out of the chair and broke for the window, partially open. I snagged him just as he was about to dive to his death.

We didn't arrest everyone we caught in the raids. If we found a married man and it was his first offense, we took his name, address and description, then let him go with a warning.

One man we arrested was a refugee who'd suffered under the Nazi terror reign in Germany. After he was jailed, we learned of his refugee status and that he could be deported if found guilty. We went into a huddle with the judge and district attorney. Eventually the charge we'd brought against him was dismissed.

Police in any large city realize the problem of how to cope with the homosexual is a difficult one. Many laws are vague on the subject.

In my state, California, nothing can be done to the bar owner whose establishment has become a second home for the sex deviate. California police have attempted for years to have a law invoked so that tavern owners who cater to such persons can lose their liquor licenses.

But the California State Supreme Court has ruled several times that a homosexual has as much right to be in a restaurant or bar as any other adult human being.

1956

THE GAY "STRANGLEHOLD" ON THEATER

Tip-Off *was one of many scandal mags popular in the Fifties—precursors of today's more explicit* National Enquirer. *In its April 1956 issue,* Tip-Off *published an article entitled "Why They Call Broadway the 'GAY' White Way," which is herein reprinted almost in its entirety. Despite its pretense to being a daring expose, the article's "revelations" amounted to little more than a compendium of gossip already widespread at the time; as someone who came out (sexually) in the mid-Fifties and had also become involved with the theater world, I can attest to the commonplace rumors then current about "queers" controlling the assignment of parts and the fate of careers. If memory serves, the "news" that many gay people worked in theater would hardly have come as a surprise. What would have, was* Tip-Off's *claim that we had a "stranglehold" on the entire entertainment industry—not simply the stage, but film, television, radio and (no less!) the circus.*

Therein lies this article's chief historical interest. It's a significant period-piece not because it "revealed for the first time anywhere" that theater was, more than most professions, a magnet for gay people, but because of its exaggerated description of their control over the entire world of performing arts—and for its ugly tone (the "growing cancer" of the gay menace, etc.). Not only does the article sound the alarm, it also demands a "cure": gays must be rooted out, the arts cleansed of their sinister influence. "Even one of the most popular children's shows on TV," Tip-Off *indignantly reports, had become infected. That word: children. Long before Anita Bryant, hucksters and homophobes of all kinds had discovered that the specter of sex with children created maximum terror. To this day the homophobes still wield that mythic weapon. Thirty years after* Tip-Off *sounded its demagogic alarm—and in the face of innumerable published studies in the interim concluding unanimously that child molestation is an almost exclusively heterosexual phenomenon—Save the Children! remains the most powerful slogan for rousing the homophobic minions.*

THE GAY "STRANGLEHOLD" ON THEATRE

The handsome young actor arose, shook hands with the assistant casting director of the network and smiled nervously as the pink-cheeked man behind the desk gave his fingers a meaningful squeeze and said: "I think you might be just fine in the part, but I would like to see you again before making up my mind. I think you must be a bit nervous coming in here like this and you might feel more relaxed and natural over a cocktail at my place."

The actor pocketed the card bearing the assistant casting director's private telephone number, said goodbye and walked to the elevators, where he stood lost in private thought. He could destroy the card and forget about the job, or he could phone later, play along with the other man and probably land the part.

PLAY BALL OR STARVE

This situation—or others similar in nature—occur each day in all phases of show business; situations in which aspirant young actors and actresses are faced with the choice of "staying on the good side" of homosexuals in key positions in their fields or risk permanent unemployment.

"Some of the biggest people in the business are 'gay' and make no bones about it," one Broadway actor told Tip-Off, "Three shows which were on Broadway within the past year were completely dominated by deviates in key spots who hired 'cooperative people' wherever possible."

One wealthy and famous producer insists that his entire crew be "gay." Thus, he always engages one of two big-name costume designers known to be members of the cult, one of two choreographers of proven caliber and so on down the line. Only name stars, technicians, and musicians may work without play.

"A few years ago," the actor continued, "there was a millionaire producer in the business who has since died. I happened to have snared a part in one of his shows which was beautifully written and seemed a sure hit. Because he had a 'yen' for a young writer he had met ... [he hired him to script the show] ... paying him $500 a week. He ruined the book and the show flopped, but so did the young writer—for the producer.

"This particular man's wife was also a bit on the weird side and used to hang around backstage during rehearsals to ogle the chorus girls. The ones that didn't smile back and accept her luncheon invitations found themselves looking for work the next time her husband was casting a show."

BIG NAMES HAVE OBLIGED

Homosexuals have gained such a stranglehold on the theater, those in the know contend, that quite a few big stars on Broadway and in Hollywood have at one stage or another in their career, been forced to "play the game" in order to get work. A young actor, currently considered "the hottest thing in the theater," looks like a genuine he-man, but is actually strictly for the boys and dates a notorious Lesbian actress merely as a front.

"Even the circus has been strongly infested with the limpwrist set from time to time in past years," one well-known Broadway agent confided ... And the newest of the "big money angels," heir to a mercantile fortune, is ecstatic over the opportunities the theater offers him as a "backer."

The star of a recent Broadway hit insisted on passing on every other male member of the cast, to be certain that he would "be among friends" and last summer actually became a bridegroom in a mock marriage ceremony which took place at Cherry Grove on Fire Island. The "bride," was a fellow with a blonde moustache! An actor, it so happened.

Within television and radio there is a thriving "lavender" set which tries, whenever possible, to find work for those willing to put their all into their work. Foremost among these are a top exec of one of the major networks, who happens to be married; the husband of one of TV's best teams; and the conductor of a popular TV band.

Three or four evenings of each week a tour of the Third Ave. bars in the Fifties could well lead any aspiring young radio and TV actor to success, should he happen to meet the middle-aged producer of one of the most popular afternoon TV-radio shows. Only a year ago a young man he met in a Third Avenue bar was hired as a $350-a-week writer—a position he held for 13 weeks, by which time our producer friend had found a suitable replacement.

Some time ago there was the report of a TV hot shot who was virtually cured of his liking for young men when he was badly carved up with a switch-blade knife when he propositioned the wrong young man in a Harlem after-hours club. The case, which police listed as a "mugging," was kept out of the papers at considerable expense to the network.

Both AFTRA and the newly-formed TV Authority have become interested in the growing cancer within the radio-TV industry, but many veterans in the business say that they have discovered the situation too late in the game and that a full expose could wreck the industry and destroy sponsor confidence in the networks.

Tip-Off doesn't agree. Why this article is being printed is because we believe that this condition, when recognized in its early stages can be cured. Facts must be told, so that the diagnosis will be correct; a diagnosis that will result in immediate treatment. It's worth trying, so let's stop playing ostrich-in-the-sand, and be sensible.

"HOW THE KING COLE BAR
AT THE ST. REGIS GOT 'DE-FAGGED"

There was an outpouring of glossy, popular magazines published during the 1950s priding themselves on catering to the interests of Real Men: angling or deerhunting; hair-raising tales from the Foreign Legion about the mutilation of savage tribes, and the victory celebrations ("Bizarre, Erotic Adventure!") which followed in the alleyways of the Casbah; reports from "insiders" on the real reasons the authorities clamped down on burlesque houses in Manhattan, forcing them to move their operations to Union City, New Jersey— along with consumer reports on the quality of the current Union City offerings. That kind of thing...

Rave magazine was among the better-known of the genre. In the issue of March 1956 it printed an article meant simultaneously to draw attention to the recent infiltration of "an unusually revolting species of pest" (i.e., "fags") into some of the city's best-known clubs, and to pay tribute to Detective Ray Schindler—"The Master De-Queerer," as Rave dubbed him—the one man capable of "making the pansies flee." The article details the tactics Schindler used in cleansing the St. Regis's swank King Cole Bar. Or, as Rave put it in a banner headline introducing the piece:

FLASH! FOXY RAY SCHINDLER,
**Super-sleuth-extraordinary, scours swanky
New York bar of fags! Here's how...**

"HOW THE KING COLE BAR
AT THE ST. REGIS GOT 'DE-FAGGED"

The hoity-toity St. Regis, one of New York's most expensive hotels (owned and operated by Vincent Astor), was up to its distinguished neck in trouble. To be specific, an unusually revolting species of pest had invaded the hotel's classy King Cole Bar. The pest was composed of that breed of humanity variously referred to as queers, fags, fairies, pansies, and so on and on and on.

Every day, around cocktail time, they would begin to drift and flutter in, and presently the room would be filled with their simpering, twittering voices as they discussed their peculiar fairy gossip, coquetted with one another and spun new fag romances.

The St. Regis management was not only revolted, the management was speedily going nuts. The King Cole Bar was getting the name of a queer joint. The regular, respectable clientele was staying away in droves. The very existence of the great, wealthy hotel itself seemed threatened.

And yet there didn't seem to be a single damn thing the management could do to correct this deplorable state of affairs.

Why had pansies suddenly started to sprout in the King Cole Bar? No one knew. It had just become, almost overnight, the place for the smartest fags and their lovers. Yet the management could not kick them out. The King Cole bar was, by law, a public place, open to all. And homosexualism itself is not a crime; it is the active practice of homosexualism that is against the law. Needless to say, the queers in the King Cole Bar were not actively practicing homosexualism. They were just talking about it.

Feverishly wiping the sweat from its aching brow, the St. Regis management put in an emergency call for Private Detective Ray Schindler.

Ray Schindler was, and is, probably the biggest-shot private detective in the U.S. Growing up with the old, famous William J. Burns Detective Agency, Schindler soon made a name for himself as a super-wily sleuth, noted for the subtlety and originality of his methods.

He had dealt with murderers, with con men, with blackmailers, with erring husbands, and mischievous wives. He had never yet dealt with fags. No doubt that is why, when the St. Regis management put their problem up to Ray—how to get the queers out of the King Cole Bar and keep them out—his first move was a mistake.

Ray's first move was simply to hire a half dozen husky, loud-mouthed, uncouth assistants—big, rude, slobbish types. Every day around 5 p.m. he and these craggy characters would shoulder their way through the crowd of fawning fags and begin to pass insulting remarks in a loud, offensive tone of voice. This was supposed to wound the pansies' delicate feelings and send them scampering out, never to return. The plan was an utter flop. The fairies fell in love with the big tough types. They doted on the bar more than ever.

Now Ray Schindler had to start all over again.

The next afternoon he entered the King Cole Bar with three quiet, efficient-looking assistant detectives. Taking over a table at the end of the room, they swiftly set up a fingerprinting apparatus. Every time a fag finished his drink at the bar, the bartender would bring the glass to Ray. With the skill of highly trained technicians, he and his assistants would dust the glass with powder and take an impression of the fag's fingerprints. The fingerprints would be numbered and carefully filed away in an impressive steel cabinet that Ray had brought with him.

A high-priced lawyer with queer tastes, lover of one of the pretty boys, faced Ray indignantly. "You've got no right to take the fingerprints of my clients!" he shouted. "I'm warning you, you'll have to answer for this!"

"Tut-tut," said Ray, or words to that effect. "I'm not asking your so-called clients for their prints, but there's no law to prevent me taking them from the glasses they've used. You see," he went confidentially, "the police have given me a list of crooks who happen to be fags. Well, this seems to be a fine place for fags. When I've got the prints of all the people who come here, the police will match them with theirs. There should be some interesting results."

The effect of this announcement was dramatic. With shrill cries of consternation and fairyish alarm, the King Cole's unwanted guests fled for home and mother.

A few indomitable queers and their protectors remained, however. Ray disposed of them with one masterly stroke. This time he came to the bar with one assistant carrying a huge newspaper-type camera. Ray joined the pansy group at the bar; the assistant edged around so as to get a good shot of their faces; and bang, there went the flashbulb.

The same lawyer protested, "It is absolutely illegal for you to take our picture without permission!"

"I'm not taking your picture," Ray said suavely. "I'm having my picture taken. I'm going to send prints of it around to my newspaper friends to show them what a swell joint I come to. If you and your friends just happen to be in the picture, that's not my fault, is it?"

The lawyer considered the implications of this statement. He was then observed to turn pale. "Boys," he said to his pretty friends, "let us get out of here."

But a few minutes later he came back. Sidling up to Ray, "Listen, man," he whispered. "Tear up the negative of that picture and I promise you'll never see any of the—well, ah—any of the boys here again."

1958

RADIO LEADS THE WAY

My aim with these documents from the fifties has been to provide a cautionary tale: a reminder, in these days of potentially dangerous backlash, of how embedded homophobia is in our culture—and how it can erupt in sudden, fierce, destructive outbursts; a reminder of our need to remain vigilant against the possibility of the Eighties turning into a duplication of the Fifties.

The Morality Tale of the Fifties would not be complete, however, if I left the impression that everything and everyone in that dank decade was drenched in homophobia. There were voices raised against the then-current consensus of homosexuality as "disease" and "disorder". Some of those voices prefigured with surprising prescience attitudes and arguments not widely held until the Seventies. It seemed a good idea to end this series on the Fifties with a sample of that altogether more cheerful—and infinitely more rare—positive view.

The best such example I've come across is a taped recording of a two part radio program entitled "The Homosexual in Our Society," broadcast on November 27, 1958, by station KPFA-FM, Berkeley, California. Some of the views expressed during that roundtable discussion were timebound. More surprising is that by far the larger part of the broadcast consisted of enlightened testimony remarkable for the period. By 1958 the worst of the McCarthy onslaught was over, a comparatively more progressive climate had begun to set in. It was somewhat easier to speak out against the rampant conformist terror than earlier in the decade. Not that many did. The KPFA forum was hardly typical radio fare of the day, and the views of its participants were decidedly on the fringe of mainstream thought. It took considerable imagination and courage for the panelists to speak out on homosexuality as boldly and as unstereotypically as they did. Would that their straight/"liberal" counterparts were doing as much today.

I've abridged the transcript, but have tried to include each speaker's main points. Three people participated in the first half of the discussion: Harold L. Call, editor of the Mattachine Review; *Blanche M. Baker, M.D., psychiatrist; Mrs. Leah Gailey, housewife and mother.*

The four participants in the second half of the discussion were Karl Bowman, a psychiatrist; Dr. Frank A. Beach, Jr., a psychologist, co-author of the pioneering (1951) anthropological study Patterns of Human Sexuality; *Morris Lowenthal, an attorney; and Dr. David H. Wilson, of the University of California School of Criminology.*

Both segments were moderated by Elsa Knight Thompson, of the public affairs department of station KPFA.

RADIO LEADS THE WAY

Moderator: Mr. Call, you are the editor of the *Mattachine Review,* a publication put out by the Mattachine Society. Is that correct? Could you tell us something about what the Mattachine Society is and what its general purposes are?

Harold Call: Yes, the Mattachine Society is an incorporated, non-profit organization that is engaged in examining and doing something about the problems that face the homosexual in our country today. ... it is a membership organization ... The magazine is national, in fact it circulates also in 18 foreign countries. ... Right now we have about 117 members ... The interest in our subject is very great, but people are loathe to join. All of the members are over 21 years of age.

Mod.: But the magazine itself would have a wider coverage than that?

Call: Yes, about 2,500 copies monthly.

Mod.: Perhaps [Dr. Baker] can tell us what the state of knowledge is, scientifically speaking?

Dr. Baker: ... There are many, many outstanding theories ... For instance, there are those physicians who feel that this is definitely a neurotic problem. Many feel that it is a glandular problem. Many feel that it is hereditary ... Now, for myself ... I think that homosexuality may have many different kinds of causes. ... And I do not look upon homosexuality as a neurotic problem, but more a basic personality pattern reaction. Just as some people prefer blondes and others prefer brunettes, I think that the fact that a given person may prefer the love of the same sex is their personal business. Now, that doesn't mean that homosexuals may not become neurotic. I think that they often do, because society is so hostile to them and their own families do not understand them, so they are subject to a great many pressures and a great deal of unhappiness ...

Mod.: Would you say that yours is a minority attitude where the medical profession is concerned?

Dr. Baker: I suspect that it is pretty much a minority. ... the actual viewpoint is pretty generally hostile. ... Now, in America, we have too much the attitude that a person is either male or female. As I find it, all the people I work with are mixed—male and female. When there are certain experiences in early childhood it tends to throw a person more toward the male side or toward the female side, and subsequent patterns develop from that.

Mod.: You mentioned, Mrs. Gailey, that you had become a member of [the Mattachine] Society because your son was a member.

Mrs. Gailey: That's true ... I think my first reaction would be a universal one—it was a shock. Here was ostracism facing me, ostracism for me and for my son. I loved my son—I wasn't about to put him out of the family circle just because he happened to have a different sexual attitude. So, I decided I would try to understand it. You know, the big part of fear is the unknown. As soon as you start to understand, some of the fear leaves ...

Dr. Baker: One of the first things that I do, in working with a person who has homosexual tendencies is to begin the process of self-acceptance in him. And as he accepts himself he becomes more relaxed and more comfortable ... these problems are not just a matter of the homosexual's problems, but are the problems of anyone that deviates from the accepted standards. I believe that holds true not only for sexual problems, but for anybody who differs in their viewpoints even. ...

Mod.: Dr. Baker ... do some of these people wish to be able to rid themselves of this particular approach to life?

Dr. Baker: Most of them that come to me want to get rid of it. And it is, of course, a pretty difficult thing to do—I think it is practically impossible. I always tell them that if they have a heterosexual component large enough to function with, it will come into being and they may be able to marry or have a love affair with a person of the opposite sex. But in so many cases they don't have that potential ... I'm happy to say that I have among my friends a great many people in different professions—artists, teachers, doctors— who have made remarkable adjustments to themselves as individuals ... I very much agree with the late Dr. Alfred Kinsey that homosexuality is one of the heritages from our mammalian ancestry. The animals all have homosexual reactions—it doesn't take much observation to know that. So, I believe we are dealing with something that is pretty basically part of our human heritage and that we have been trying to stamp out. My emphasis is: let us accept it and develop the wonderful things associated with it. Because so many homosexuals are very versatile, gifted people, and I feel that society should make them proud members, and that giving encouragement brings out much in the way of hidden resources.

Dr. Beach: ... the fact that biological factors are involved, it seems to me, is beyond dispute. I hope that I'll have a chance to develop that because I don't want to leave the impression that I'm saying that homosexuality per se is inherited ... so far as we know homosexuality has been present throughout human history and this would suggest some very pervasive source of influence. Certainly we might pose the question as to whether or not homosexuality is part of man's heredity. ... The evolutionary evidence, based upon observation of other mammals, suggests that this may be the case ... so far as I am aware, exclusive overt homosexuality does not occur in any species except man. I believe that this is probably due to the fact that human sexual behavior, like all other kinds of human behavior, is very heavily influenced by individual experience in learning, much more so than the behavior of any other species ...

Mod.: Dr. Wilson, I believe that you function on two levels in this discussion: as an attorney and also as a psychiatrist. Have you something to add?

Dr. Wilson: ... Passing a law in no way affects the amount of homosexuality or the amount of homosexual behavior. ... it doesn't affect the amount of homosexuality as such. ... the law is passed against the act, not against the existence of homosexuality ... if the law doesn't work, we should carefully reappraise the situation. ... Passing more stringent laws doesn't affect it, taking the laws off seems to make no difference. There is a basic bio-psychological factor involved that makes [them], with or without laws ...

Mod.: Why does society feel threatened?

Dr. Wilson: ... I think the most logical theory is that there is some unconscious, unknown fear of homosexuality in everyone, and this fear is transmitted to the social group. ... This is not a logical fear because homosexuality itself is not dangerous or destructive. ...

Dr. Bowman: ...Homosexual acts, carried out in private by two willing adults, no force used, no physical harm carried out, should not be a crime. ... The American Law Institute in May 1955 voted to recommend that sodomy between consenting adults "be removed from the list of crimes against the peace and dignity of the state." ... Judge Learned Hand ... spoke for the revision. He said that criminal law which is not enforced is worse than no law at all, and he said that after having previously voted the other way he now had decided that sodomy is "a matter of morals—a matter very largely of taste," and not something for which a person should be put in prison. I mention all this because I think many persons listening might assume that this was some new and original and sort of crack-pot idea of the discussants here, that had not received much consideration elsewhere.

Dr. Wilson: ...the problem is more than one of merely voicing our views here and suggesting changes. There is this tremendous backlog of prejudice, of feeling, unconscious and conscious feelings. ... It is going to take time—it is going to take education. This is a start, the mere fact that it can be aired publicly is a start in the right direction ...

1960

THE INTERNATIONAL HOMOSEXUAL CONSPIRACY

The following excerpts are from an article "Homosexual International" in the September 29, 1960, issue of Human Events, *a weekly Washington, D.C., newsletter that claimed to reach some "40,000 business and political leaders" with "the news behind the news from the Nation's Capital."*

The author of the article, R. G. Waldeck (nee Rosie Goldschmidt, 1898-), was further identified in its lead-in as "Countess Waldeck, a Ph.D. from Heidelberg University and an American citizen" who was a "political writer and novelist." In the days of the Weimar Republic in Germany, Countess Waldeck was known as "Frau Ullstein" (of the famous magazine publishing family) and among her many books, "the best known" were Europe Between the Acts, Athene Palace, *and* Lustre in the Sky.

Though the editors of Human Events *may have over-valued R. G. Waldeck's credentials, her article does reveal a sophisticated intelligence—however gainfully ill-employed. Which is to say we should keep in mind the old chestnut: "never underestimate your enemies."*

THE INTERNATIONAL HOMOSEXUAL CONSPIRACY

On March 25, 1952, Mr. Carlisle H. Humelsine, Deputy Under-secretary of State, told the House Appropriations Committee that the State Department had ousted 119 homosexuals during the previous year.

Popular reaction to this sensational piece of news ranged all the way from righteous indignation on religious grounds to a pseudo-liberal attitude of "tolerance."

... the main reason why ... the elimination of the homosexuals from all Government agencies and especially from the State Department is of vital urgency is that by the very nature of their vice they belong to a sinister, mysterious and efficient International.

... This conspiracy has spread all over the globe; has penetrated all classes; operates in armies and in prisons; has infiltrated into the press, the movies and the cabinets and it all but dominates the arts, literature, theater, music and TV.

And here is why homosexual officials are a peril to us in the present struggle between West and East: members of one conspiracy are prone to join another conspiracy. This is one reason why so many homosexuals from being enemies of society in general, become enemies of capitalism in particular. Without being necessarily Marxist they serve the ends of the Communist International in the name of their rebellion against the prejudices, standards, ideals of the "bourgeois" world. Another reason for the homosexual-Communist alliance is the instability and passion for intrigue for intrigue's sake, which is inherent in the homosexual personality. A third reason is the social promiscuity within the homosexual minority and the fusion it effects between upperclass and proletarian corruption.

The Tie That Binds

There are various theories concerning the origin of homosexuality. Some attribute it to a glandular predisposition; others to a hereditary one. According to modern psychology the homosexual is a victim of arrested emotional development which makes it impossible for him to sublimate a childhood experience of identification with and jealousy of the mother. All agree that, as the feminine element marks, more or less subtly, his gestures, his contours, his voice, a complicated mass of obscure hates, frustrations, inferiority feelings and guilt feelings mark his humiliated soul.

In other words, the homosexual would be an unhappy and unstable human being, even if he were not forced to "live in falsehood and perjury" (Marcel Proust). Still, the opprobrium and the dangers weighing on him add greatly to his instability. More or less consciously he hates a society which makes him feel "different" and which, judging his deepest desires as shameful and punishable, forces him to conceal, deny, camouflage them.

This many-grounded vulnerability in itself, Harden* understood, made the homosexual a bad security risk. And he also understood this aggravating factor—namely that the mysterious laws which rule this condemned portion of humanity are more binding on its members than any national, spiritual, social loyalties.

... the Homosexual International began to gnaw at the sinews of the state in the 1930s. Until then it just nibbled. I have before me notes I took years ago about that nibbling stage. Still very new to politics, I

---

*Maximilian Harden, the magazine editor whose 1907 articles implying "improprieties" in the lifestyles of Count Moltke and Prince Eulenburg, advisors to the German Emperor, led to a prolonged scandal.

was amazed to discover that the "*Cherchez l'homme*" pointed to a much more powerful factor in international affairs than the "*Cherchez la femme*."

With fascination I watched the little Sodoms functioning within the Embassies and foreign offices. Somehow homosexuals always seemed to come by the dozen, not because they were cheaper that way but rather because a homosexual ambassador or charge d'affaires or Undersecretary of State liked to staff his "team" with his own people. Another reason was that the homosexuals really do look after their own ...

Homosexuality And Communism

The alliance between the Homosexual International and the Communist International started at the dawn of the Pink Decade. It was then that the homosexual aristocracy—writers, poets, painters and such—discovered Marxism. Why did this bleak doctrine charm people who up to now had posed as decadent aesthetes? No doubt, the same sentiments which motivated the Communist conversion of intellectuals in general—such as opposition to Nazism and Fascism, visions of the end of capitalism and the need of a faith—played a part in the Communist conversion of homosexual intellectuals. But particular emotions gave it an additional fervor.

Political Intrigue

... the Homosexual International works into the hands of the Comintern without any special organizing effort. This does not mean that every homosexual diplomat or official is a Communist or even a fellow traveler. Still, this dangerous mixture of anti-social hostility and social promiscuity inherent in the vice incline them towards Communist causes. That's why agencies in which homosexuals are numerous excel in the sort of intrigue and doubletalk which, apparently objective, somehow always coincides with the party line.

Natural Secret Agents

There is another even more sinister aspect of homosexuality in high places. It is that homosexuals make natural secret agents and natural traitors. This conclusion is to be drawn from a theory developed by Professor Theodor Reik in his "Psychology of Sex Relations." Briefly, this theory is that the fantasy of sex metamorphosis operating in most homosexual affairs which causes him to play the role of the other sex causes him also to enjoy any job which gives him the chance of playing a double role.

The classical example is the famous espionage case of the homosexual Colonel Alfred Redl of the Austro-Hungarian Military Intelligence who, during the decade preceding World War I, delivered Austrian military secrets to the Russians and denounced his own agents to them. He got an immense kick out of playing the role of both the traitor and of the one whose lifework it is to apprehend and punish traitors.

A Political Problem For Psychologists

It is one thing to demand the elimination of the homosexuals from Government agencies and another thing to really eliminate them. Unless the screening is done by careful and experienced psychologists, it will result in ludicrous errors such as homosexual family fathers getting away with it while honest-to-God bachelors come under suspicion.

There is another reason why careful experienced psychologists are of the essence. It is that homosexuality has many gradations, and that the security risks they represent vary. It would be unfair to throw them all into the same pot, but it needs an expert to tell the harmless from the dangerous ones.

At best the elimination of homosexuals from Government agencies is only one phase of combating the homosexual invasion of American public life. Another phase, more important in the long run, is the matter of public education. This should be clear to anyone who views with dismay the forebearance bordering on tenderness with which American society not only tolerates the infiltration of homosexuals everywhere but even allows them to display their perversion in public.

An Educational Task

... the chief educational task would be to combat the "love-and-let-love" line which, peddled by the pseudo-liberal fringe, claims that sexual preversion [sic] does not prevent a man from functioning normally in all other contexts and that it was just like Senator McCarthy to "persecute" the poor dears in the State Department. This line is fatal in that it lulls society into a false sense of security....

1963

GROWTH OF OVERT HOMOSEXUALITY IN
CITY PROVOKES WIDE CONCERN

The article below appeared in the New York Times *on December 17, 1963, and is self-explanatory. I would only point out that the article and the attitudes it reveals are less than twenty years old.*

Note in particular the disproportionate amount of space which the Times *gives to the gay-is-illness theory of Doctors Bieber and Socarides. (For a public squabble I had with the two doctors a dozen years later, see pages 286-292). The "new tolerance," in other words, is indeed frighteningly new. "Frightening," because a mere two decades is not sufficient time for any shift in moral values to become reliably established.*

The problem of homosexuality in New York became the focus yesterday of increased attention by the State Liquor Authority and the Police Department.

The liquor authority announced the revocation of the liquor licenses of two more homosexual taverns that had been repeatedly raided by the police. The places were the Fawn, at 795 Washington Street near Jane Street, and the Heights Supper Club at 80 Montague Street, Brooklyn.

The city's most sensitive open secret—the presence of what is probably the greatest homosexual population in the world and the increasing openness of its manifestations—has become the subject of growing concern by psychiatrists and religious leaders as well as of law enforcement officers. One division of the organized crime syndicate controls bars and restaurants that cater to the homosexual trade. Commenting yesterday on the attack on such places and the attention being directed at their habitues, Police Commissioner Michael J. Murphy said:

"The police jurisdiction in this area is limited. But when persons of this type become a source of public scandal, or violate the laws, or place themselves in a position where they become the victims of crime they do come within our jurisdiction.

Mr. Hostetter said the Heights Supper Club had a signal light system "that warned the boys to stop dancing with one another" when a newcomer was suspected of being a policeman.

The Fawn has a back room to which an admission was charged and where as many as 70 to 80 deviates had parties on Friday and Saturday nights. Most of the patrons were males, but on occasion police found women dancing with women.

There were 19 police visits this year resulting in summonses and complaints of a noisy jukebox, disorderly premises, insufficient lighting and dancing without a cabaret license, and an arrest for degeneracy.

Out Of The Shadows

[Homosexuality] is a problem that has grown in the shadows, protected by taboos on open discussion that have only recently begun to be breached.

The overt homosexual—and those who are identifiable probably represent no more than half of the total—has become such an obtrusive part of the New York scene that the phenomenon needs public discussion, in the opinion of a number of legal and medical experts.

Two conflicting viewpoints converge today to overcome the silence and promote public discussion.

The first is the organized homophile movement—a minority of militant homosexuals that is openly agitating for removal of legal, social and cultural discriminations against sexual inverts.

Fundamental to this aim is the concept that homosexuality is an incurable, congenital disorder (this is disputed by the bulk of scientific evidence) and that homosexuals should be treated by an increasingly tolerant society as just another minority.

This view is challenged by a second group, the analytical psychiatrists, who advocate an end to what it calls a head-in-sand approach to homosexuality.

They have what they consider overwhelming evidence that homosexuals are created—generally by ill-adjusted parents—not born.

They assert that homosexuality can be cured by sophisticated analytical and therapeutic techniques.

More significantly, the weight of the most recent findings suggests that public discussion of the nature of these parental misdeeds and attitudes that tend to foster homosexual development of children could improve family environments and reduce the incidence of sexual inversion.

Experts View Differ

Estimates [of the number of homosexuals] range from an avowedly conservative 100,000 by one leading psychiatrist to a probably exaggerated 600,000 by the homosexual president of the Mattachine Society of New York, the organization dedicated to education of the general public on "the problems of the sexual deviant."

Some experts believe the numbers of homosexuals in the city are increasing rapidly. Others contend that, as public attitudes have become more tolerant, the homosexuals have tended to be more overt, less concerned with concealing their deviant conduct.

In any case, identifiable homosexuals—perhaps only half of the total—seem to throng Manhattan's Greenwich Village, the East Side from the upper 40's through the 70's and the West 70's. In a fairly restricted area around Eighth Avenue and 42nd Street there congregate those who are universally regarded as the dregs of the invert world—the male prostitutes, the painted, grossly effeminate "queens" and those who prey on them.

In each of the first three areas the homosexuals have their own restaurants and bars—some operated for them under the contemptuous designation of "fag joints" by the organized crime syndicate.

They have their favored clothing suppliers who specialize in the right slacks, short-cut coats and fastidious furnishings favored by many, but by no means all, male homosexuals. There is a homosexual jargon, once intelligible only to the initiate, but now part of New York slang. The word "gay" has been appropriated as the adjective for homosexual.

"Is he gay?" a homosexual might ask another of a mutual acquaintance. They would speak of a "gay bar" or a "gay party" and probably derive secret amusement from innocent employment of the word in its original meaning by "straight"—that is, heterosexual—speakers.

The homosexual has a range of gay periodicals that is a kind of distorted mirror image of the straight publishing world.

The Gay Magazines

Thus, from the Mattachine Society and other serious homophile organizations, the homosexual can get publications offering intellectual discussion of his problems.

Newsstands offer a wide range of magazines and papers designed to appeal to inverted sexual tastes. These include many of the so-called body-building publications presenting, under the guise of physical culture, photos of scantily-clad, heavily muscled men, and others peddling outright homosexual pornography in text and illustration.

In summer, the New York homosexual can find vacation spots frequented by his kind—notably parts of Fire Island, a section of the beach at Jacob Riis Park, and many others.

In fact, a New York homosexual, if he chooses an occupation in which his clique is predominant, can shape for himself a life lived almost exclusively in an inverted world from which the rough, unsympathetic edges of straight society can be almost totally excluded.

Spokesmen for the Mattachine Society complain bitterly against alleged entrapment of homosexuals by plainclothes policemen sent into homosexual haunts. The homophile groups have won some support from civil rights groups in their campaign to outlaw the uncorroborated testimony of an arresting officer as proof in cases of entrapment for soliciting.

Open To Entertainment

The tendency of homosexuals to be promiscuous and seek pick-ups—a tendency recognized by the gay[1] writer, Donald Webster Cory, in his book *The Homosexual in America*—makes them particularly vulnerable to police entrapment.

First Deputy Police Commissioner John F. Walsh says the Police Department has limited itself to an effort to suppress solicitation in bars, public lavatories and Turkish baths and any approaches to minors by homosexuals. No attempt is made, he says, to enforce the theoretical ban on private homosexual conduct between consenting adults.

Found Everywhere

Inverts are to be found in every conceivable line of work, from truck driving to coupon clipping. But they are most concentrated—or most noticeable—in the fields of the creative and performing arts and industries serving women's beauty and fashion needs.

Their presence in creative activity is not, as an old myth fostered by homosexuals would have it, because inverts tend to have superior intellect and talent. Most students of the subject agree that the significant factor in homosexual colonization of some of the arts is that men who would find difficulty in winning acceptance from fellow workers in more prosaic activities naturally gravitate toward solitary, introspective endeavor.

The list of homosexuals in the theater is long, distinguished and international. It is also self-perpetuating.

There is a cliquishness about gay individuals that often leads one who achieves influential position in the theater-and many of them do—to choose for employment another homosexual candidate over a straight applicant, unless the latter had an indisputable edge of talent that would bear on the artistic success of the venture.

Not Immune To Women

There is a popular belief that homosexuals are immune to sexual attraction by women. Dr. Irving Bieber, director of the most recent extensive study of homosexuality, disputes this view and cites the presence of large numbers of inverts in occupations that bring them into close personal contact with women to prove the reverse.

He asserts that homosexual men receive sexual stimulation from women. But, because their capacity for normal erotic expression has been crippled psychically, Dr. Bieber believes female attraction produces a reaction of fear and search for homosexual outlet.

The tendency of high-fashion designers to produce styles that minimize or suppress womanly curves—styles that can be worn really well only by hipless, bosomless mannequins—has often been interpreted as an expression of homosexual hostility toward women. In Dr. Bieber's opinion, it is, rather, another expression of fear.

Family Ties Studied

In a nine-year study, "Homosexuality—A Psychoanalytic Study of Male Homosexuals" that won international attention last year, Dr. Bieber, associate clinical professor of Psychiatry, New York Medical College, and nine associates in the same field published evidence that the roots of homosexuality lay in disturbed early family relationships.

In almost every homosexual case they found some combination of what they termed a "close-binding, intimate" mother and/or a hostile, detached or unresponsive father, or other parental aberrations.

"The father played an essential and determining role in the homosexual outcome of his son," the Bieber group reported flatly. "In the majority of instances the father was explicitly hostile.

"We have come to the conclusion [that] a constructive supportive, warmly related father precludes the possibility of a homosexual son: he acts as a neutralizing, protective agent should the mother make seductive or close-binding attempts."

The group reported that 27 percent of the homosexuals under

treatment by the group achieved a heterosexual orientation.

"Our findings are optimistic guideposts not only for homosexuals but for the psychoanalysts who treat them," the report concluded. "We are firmly convinced that psychoanalysts may well orient themselves to a heterosexual objective in treating homosexual patients rather than 'adjust' even the more recalcitrant patient to a homosexual destiny."

The organized homosexuals dispute the validity of psychiatric findings on deviants. They argue that the medical students of the problem see only those homosexuals who are disturbed enough to seek treatment. Therefore, they say, findings based on that sample cannot be applied to the majority of "adjusted" homosexuals.

To this, Dr. Bieber replies that during his wartime service, he interviewed intensively about 75 homosexuals discovered by military authorities. Among these involuntary subjects for study he found no basic differences in their psychopathology from that of the voluntary group under treatment, except that the former were more defensive and resistant to recognizing their deviancy.

Hostility A Key Factor

Dr. Bieber differs from some of his colleagues on the probable effect of a sudden—and highly unlikely—removal of all the legal and social hostility to homosexuality.

"Public acceptance, if based on the concept of homosexuality as an illness, could be useful," he says. If by a magic wand, one could eliminate overnight all manifestations of hostility, I think there would be a gradual, important reduction in the incidence of homosexuality."

He believes that wiping out negative attitudes would contribute to healing homosexuality rather than creating it.

But he does not approve the attempts by organized homosexuals to promote the idea that they represent just another minority, since their minority status is based on illness rather than on racial or other factors.

He notes the contrast between this attitude and that of Alcoholics Anonymous, which is based on recognition of alcoholism as a disease and the determination to do something about it.

Dr. Charles W. Socarides, a New York analyst with wide experience in treating homosexuals is worried about the drive by homosexuals to win social acceptance for their deviancy as a kind of "normal abnormality". "The homosexual is ill, and anything that tends to hide that fact reduces his chances of seeking and obtaining treatment," Dr. Socarides says. "If they were to achieve social acceptance it would increase this difficulty."

Confronting these generally accepted scientific conclusions that homosexual development can be both averted and cured is the strange, ambivalent attitude of the homosexuals toward themselves, as reported by Randolf Wicker.

He is a young man in his middle 20's, under his real name a free-lance writer, who founded the New York League of Homosexuals, now merged with the Mattachine Society. He asked 300 homosexuals to answer two questions: "If you had a son would you want him to be homosexual?" and "If a quick, easy cure were available, would you take it?"

Eighty-three per cent indicated basic dissatisfaction with the life of a homosexual by saying they would not want a son to follow that path. Only 2 per cent answered the first question affirmatively and the rest said they would leave the choice up to the hypothetical son.

But an overwhelming 98 per cent told Mr. Wicker they would not change, even if the change were easy. Why? The 44-year-old president of Mattachine gave the answer.

"I have been a homosexual for 30 years," he said. "I have none of the social and emotional background of the straight world—no history of normal dating. I would be lost in the world of hetero-sexuals."

1. The *Times'* willingness to use the word "gay" in 1963 stands in curious contrast to its resolute refusal to do so ever since.

1964

A FRIEND AT COURT

In our concern with documenting the gross injustices inflicted on gay people through time, the occasional friend who stood out against the homophobic tide might be overlooked—but mustn't be. One such friend was Chief Justice Baxton Craven of the United States District Court. He was not a man entirely free of the prejudices of the day (for example, in his stress on "rehabilitation"), but his important, and previously ignored, decision in the case of "Perkins v. State of North Carolina" reveals not only an uncommon humanity but an uncommon sense of humor as well. I'm grateful to Perry Deane Young, co-author of The Dave Kopay Story *for having brought this significant judicial statement to my attention.*

A FRIEND AT COURT

Max Doyle Perkins Petitioner, v. State of North Carolina, Respondent. Civ. No. 2234. United States District Court W.D. North Carolina, Asheville Division. Heard Aug. 21, 1964. Decided Oct. 5, 1964.

On January 8, 1962, Max Doyle Perkins and Robert Eugene McCorkle were jointly indicted by the grand jury of Mecklenburg County, North Carolina. It was charged that they "did unlawfully, wilfully, maliciously and feloniously commit the abominable and detestable crime against nature with each other." McCorkle pleaded *nolo contendere,* received a sentence of five to seven years, served a portion of it, and has been released. Perkins, after conviction by a jury upon his plea of not guilty was sentenced to a term of not less than twenty nor more than thirty years. The disparate sentences were passed by the same judge.

Perkins was convicted of a violation of N.C.G.S. sec. 14-177, which reads in its entirety as follows:

"If any person shall commit the abominable and detestable crime against nature, with mankind or beast, he shall be imprisoned in the State's prison not less than five nor more than sixty years."

The statute is copied from the first English statute on the subject passed in the year 1533 during the reign of King Henry VIII. It was adopted in North Carolina in 1837 with only one difference. The words "vice of buggery" which appeared in the ancient English statute were omitted and instead there was substituted the delightful euphemism "crime against nature, not to be named among Christians." It then read in its entirety:

"Any person who shall commit the abominable and detestable crime against nature, not to be named among Christians, with either mankind or beast shall be adjudged guilty of a felony and shall suffer death without the benefit of clergy."

By 1854 Christians had become more articulate and less clergical. The phrases "not to be named among Christians" and "without benefit of clergy" were deleted from the statute. Finally, in 1869, the death penalty was limited to murder and the like. The punishment for crime against nature was limited to sixty years maximum. Since 1869 the statute has remained unchanged—in itself a shocking example of the unfortunate gulf between criminal law, and medicine and psychiatry.

The evidence against Perkins tended to show that his criminal conduct consisted of *fellatio.*

What is "the crime against nature"? The statutory history shows that beyond question it was "buggery" at common law. According to the great weight of authority, as well as the far better reasoned cases, the conduct of Perkins (*per os*) was not buggery at common law. Yet, in State v. Fenner, 166 N.C. 247, 80 S.I. 970, (1914), the North Carolina Supreme Court misinterpreted both the statute and the common law in holding that the statute covered sexual acts *per se*[1]
. . .

If the statute were a new one, it would be obviously unconstitutional for vagueness. The former concern for the feelings of those reading the statute has yielded to the necessity that an indicted person know of what he is charged. Euphemisms have no place in criminal statutes. But this is not a new statute, and it has been interpreted many times by the North Carolina Supreme Court. Although the court has said it means much more than it meant at common law or an enactment during the reign of Henry VIII, its decisions have made equally clear that crime against nature does not embrace walking on the grass.

The prohibition of cruel and unusual punishment contained in the Eighth Amendment of the United States Constitution applies to the states through the due process clause of the Fourteenth Amendment. . . . The Court said "the exact scope of the constitutional phrase 'cruel and unusual' has not been detailed by this Court. ... The Amendment must draw its meaning from the evolving standards of decency that mark the progress of a maturing society ..."

Does the mere duration of sentence—twenty to thirty years—make it "cruel and unusual" within the prohibition of the Constitution? The Attorney General of North Carolina, although requested to do so, has not called to the court's attention any sentence under this statute in excess of five years where the offenders were both adult males.[2] It may be judicially noticed, certainly within the last decade, that sentences imposed on adult homosexual offenders in North Carolina courts, absent special circumstances, seldom if ever exceeded the five year statutory minimum. The moderation of North Carolina judges in this respect is probably the reason why the Legislature has not long since felt required to amend the statute. If the usual five year sentence is "right," then twenty to thirty years is "wrong." Certainly twenty to thirty years is unusual. There can be no justification for such disparity of punishment. But the sentence is within the astounding statutory limit of "not less than five nor more than sixty years," and it is well settled that within statutory limits even the harshest sentence, absent exceptional circumstances, is not cruel and unusual within the meaning of the Constitution.

Is such an exceptional circumstance present here? The co-defendant in the same indictment who pleaded *nolo contendere* was sentenced to five to seven years; whereas Perkins who pleaded not guilty and subjected the court to affording him trial by jury was sentenced to twenty to thirty years. It is easy to suspect that Perkins may have been punished for insisting upon his right to trial by jury. Indeed, court-appointed counsel concedes that Perkins may have been punished in part for pleading not guilty. But the inference is of doubtful validity. Perkins and his co-defendant, McCorkle, were apparently quite different in background and in previous homosexual conduct.[3] Although the difference is not enough to justify the extreme disparity of punishment, it is enough to cast doubt upon what otherwise might be inferred: that his not guilty plea inconvenienced the court and that he was punished for it.

... court-appointed counsel testified that he had sufficient time to prepare the case for trial. Since he neither interviewed defendant's proposed witnesses nor caused them to be subpoenaed, the inference is inescapable that counsel, after talking with state officers, became so convinced of Perkins' guilt that he considered making any defense an utter futility and therefore attempted none ...

In the instant case, *none* of Perkins' witnesses were brought into court. Nor did court-appointed counsel interview them or otherwise investigate to determine if there were a defense ...

Plainly counsel was not afforded reasonable opportunity to investigate and prepare for trial. In light of these attendant circumstances, there was "such expedition as to deprive" Perkins "of the effective aid and assistance of counsel."

It will be ordered that the petitioner be released within sixty days unless the State elects to try him again.

In all probability, Perkins will be tried again, found guilty, and resentenced.

Putting Perkins into the North Carolina prison system is a little like throwing Brer Rabbit into the briarpatch. Most doctors who have studied homosexuality agree that prison environment, including close, continuous, and exclusive contact with other men, aggravates and strengthens homosexual tendencies and provides unexcelled opportunity for homosexual practices. For the confirmed homosexual, imprisonment can accomplish no rehabilitative function; instead it provides an outlet for the gratification of sexually-deviate desires.

Is it not time to redraft a criminal statute first enacted in 1533? And if so, cannot the criminal law draftsmen be helped by those best informed on the subject—medical doctors—in attempting to classify offenders? Is there any public purpose served by a possible sixty year maximum or even five year minimum imprisonment of the occasional or one-time homosexual without treatment, and if so, what is it? Are homosexuals twice as dangerous to society as second-degree murderers—as indicated by the maximum punishment for each offense? Is there any good reason why a person convicted of a single homosexual act with another adult may be imprisoned six times as long as an abortionist, thirty times as long as one who takes indecent liberties with children, thirty times as long as the drunk driver—even though serious personal injury and property damage results—twice as long as an armed bank robber, three times as long as a train robber, times as long as one who feloniously breaks and enters a store, and 730 times as long as the public drunk?

These questions, and others like them, need to be answered.

NOTES

1. How the error occurred is documented in James R. Spence, "The Law of Crime Against Nature", 32 N.C. Law Rev. 312-316.

2. Six weeks before the hearing the court requested that the state determine from the Director of Prisons what percentage of offenders, if any, were serving sentences in excess of five years. The Attorney General advised that no such records were kept.

3. This oblique comment apparently refers to the fact (as I've learned from another source) that Perkins was dressed as a woman when arrested.

1965

AMERICAN INDIAN TRANSVESTISM

In 1979 I published an article in the spring/summer issue of the Radical History Review *on "Hopi Indian Sexuality."* I based it on some unpublished early twentieth century documents I'd discovered while doing research at the National Anthropological Archives of the Smithsonian Institute in Washington, D.C. The material seemed to me unusually provocative: it raised a number of important questions about sexual behavior in general, not simply about the Hopi; some of the documents, moreover, cast doubt on the competence and candor of previous studies—confirming my sense that traditional (heterosexual-dominated) anthropology has long avoided data relating to sexuality of any kind, and especially the "deviant" kind.*

In order to intelligibly pose *(certainly not "answer") the significant questions I felt the documents raised, I embarked on a self-help course of intense reading in the literature on Pueblo culture. That done, I still felt woefully inadequate to the task at hand. I'd never before studied American Indian culture and history in any depth, and the attempt made me more aware of my ignorance. And so we—the editors of* RHR *and myself—came up with the idea of inviting two specialists in Pueblo culture—Professor Eggan of Chicago and Professor Clemmer of California State—to comment both on the documents themselves and on the questions I finally managed to formulate as to their possible "meaning."*

Both men accepted the invitation, and their commentaries were printed in the same issue of the RHR *that carried my article. The comments were not exactly friendly. Eggan and Clemmer categorically stated that all the significant questions about Hopi sexuality had long since been satisfactorily answered by specialists in the field. (I had read the specialists and not found them "satisfactory.") They rejected just as categorically, and with a bit more temper, to the suggestion in my article [see p. 97] that a more general indictment of anthropology was perhaps in order for its endemic avoidance of matters relating to sex; quite untrue, the professors insisted. The debate between us became heated and eventually spilled over into a second formal exchange, printed in the Fall 1980 issue of the* RHR.

---

*I have reprinted a greatly shortened version of the essay in this volume; see p. 97.

One of the many points in contention in our non-dialogue was the extent and meaning of cross-dressing among Hopi men (I had found scant references to cross-dressing among Hopi women).[1] In our second exchange, Professor Eggan did off-handedly acknowledge that some meager evidence existed of "occasional transvestites in Pueblo society" at an earlier period. He went on to reassure us that "none has been present in recent history."

Eggan was wrong, but at the time I didn't have enough evidence to challenge his assured, unequivocal assertion. Now I do. While at the Smithsonian I came across material on the Hopi dating from much later (1965) which did contain specific references to cross-gender dressing and behavior. Unfortunately, I hadn't filed the 1965 data with the earlier documents; in truth, by the time the RHR controversy rolled around, I'd entirely forgotten the 1965 material and rediscovered it only recently, while making an abortive attempt to re-sort my chaotic files. Too bad I didn't have it at hand in 1979-80; it might have proved useful ammunition. Might have. More likely, Messrs. Eggan and Clemmer would have treated the new data with the same hauteur and contempt they employed in dismissing the earlier data.

Fortunately, a new generation of anthropologists seems to be emerging, one more willing to acknowledge the sex-negativism of their discipline in the past and more concerned with filling in the huge gap in anthropological literature on matters pertaining to sexuality. For evidence of this new attitude, interested parties should have a look at Kenneth E. Read's Other Voices *(1980), and Carole Vance's "Gender Systems, Ideology, and Sex Research: An Anthropological Analysis",(Feminist Studies, Spring 1980). They, if not the Eggans, will, I think, be interested in the documents excerpted below.*

A few words of caution—especially for those who, like myself, are not specialists in Pueblo Indian culture. What on the surface seems roughly similar behavior can, in fact, signify very different meaning within different cultures. Glib analogies ("Oh, so the Hopi had drag queens too!") cannot responsibly be drawn; nor can Hopi "cross-gender" behavior be "understood" simply by linking and equating it to our own cultural reference points and definitions. We do not even know to what degree—if any—Hopi transvestism was a variant on the "berdache"—that relatively familiar figure found in a number of American Indian cultures. We know less about the berdache than is often assumed—for example, whether cross-dressing and cross-role-playing were ipso facto *evidence of an active homosexual orientation. Donald G. Forgey's "The Institution of Berdache Among the North*

American Plains Indians" (Journal of Sex Research, *February 1975);*
Harriet Whitehead, "The Bos and the Burden Strap: A New Look at
Institutionalized Homosexuality in Native South America"in Sherry
B. Ortner and Harriet Whitehead, ed., Sexual Meaning: The Cultural
Construction of Gender and Sexuality *(Cambridge Univ.: 1981) are*
among the best summaries of the known information currently
available.² But the recent researches of the openly gay anthropologist,
Walter Williams of the University of Southern California, promise to
broaden and change our understanding of the berdache considerably.
[His completed study, The Spirit and the Flesh, *is now—1986—in*
press.] I hope the material will prove of some value to Williams—and
to those few other brave souls in the social sciences—willing to engage
such subjects and to explore their implications.

Interview with Grace Chapella and Alma Tahbo, August, 1965.
Interviewer: Joann Kealiinohomoku. Location of both tapings at
Chapella home, Polacca, First Mesa, Arizona.

Interviewer: I want to ask question—you say that boy grinds corn
w[ith] you. And I remember when we were at Gallop they had that
Navaho corn grinding song. Do Hopis have a corn grinding song?

Alma: They used to ... not any more.

Int.: What was the idea—the men would do it [sing] while the
women were grinding corn?

Alma: Yeah, the men ... were singing and ... then they all get up
and all danced together.

Int.: A corn grinding dance?

Alma: Uh huh. [affirmative] Oh! Some would be grinding, and
some not grinding; they would be dancing ... That was long time ago
... Nobody has grinding stones anymore.

Int.: None of the mesas?

Alma: Yeah. There's just about one house—over at Shungo-
povi—that has a grinding stone. Everybody comes over to grind.

Int.: And they dance too?

Alma: Nobody does the dancing anymore. That was such a long
time ago and it just died away I guess.

(Discuss modern commercial machines. [Grace] Chapella has a
shed outside their home [with] corn grinding machine ... and she
hires a man to run it. Notice this cultural change, with a man running
the machine, whereas formerly corn grinding was strictly an activity
of women, with the exception of transvestites ...)

Grace: ... It was fun to do corn grinding dance. Girls who were
waiting to grind danced, and so did the boys dance.

(They say that Grace doesn't remember any of the songs, but an "Aunt" does. More than one song. Grace says the "ladies had their own songs," Alma says it was "tiresome grinding." "You have to work all day . . . grind . . . toss to the next grinding stone . . . when gets to fine finishing stone it coughs up like flour . . . [Nowadays, we] grind even before weddings . . . the young people . . . just fix all the things at their house and then go over there and just sit all day. (That is, the girl takes the required things to the boy's home.) Some . . . go to groom's house and make blue corn bread there, but nobody grinds. They don't even have any grinding stones.)

Int.: Yes, and you even have a man . . . (question whether he is considered man/woman since doing woman's work)

Alma: He had to do it . . . he belongs to them and he's doing it. (He is a relative?) I used to do it, but my "Aunt" took over . . .

Int.: . . . and you got $27 for it? A beautiful piece of pottery?

Grace and Alma: Oh yeah.

Grace: At that time, you know, it breaks in burning it. I guess that's what happened, because it looks like it (i.e., the hole) on the bottom a little ways from the edge . . . there's a little piece of hidden rock, it's plastered . . .

Int.: The pottery of the "man-woman"—that is in your house also?

Grace: Yes.

Int.: But the trader gave you each money for it. (i.e., Grace and her sister took the pottery to the trader together, and the trader wanted to buy it because he recognized that his "aunty" had made it. They bargained and eventually the trader paid both girls. This must have been about 50 years ago, or more, for Grace was a young married woman with one baby.)

Int.: Because it was made by his aunty, except he wasn't his aunty. What do you call somebody like that? If they're not a man . . . and well, they are a man but they act like a woman? Is there a word for that?

Grace: They say that "she" can make better paper bread than the ladies. Thin (this is the one who made the pottery) "she" grinds . . . teaches the girls how to grind, make paper bread, that "she" was a good worker.

Int.: "She" was a Hopi, wasn't she, and "she" wanted to marry a Tewa boy? (yes) Has it ever happened that a man married a man in the Hopi?

Alma: No, it's just in their thoughts.

Int.: Is there a name for a person like this? It's not he and it's not she.

Alma: Yes there's a name for it. The Hopis call it [word omitted in manuscript]. This means "a man that wants to be like a girl." The Tewa call it [word omitted in manuscript]. That means "woman-man."

Int.: Are there any women who want to act like a man?

Alma: Yes—just like some of these girls we call tom-boys.

Int.: But do they ever want to marry another girl?

Alma: No. They are that way in their actions.

Int.: With a tom-boy they usually outgrow it. But is there a case where they don't outgrow it, but just keep on acting this way all their life?

Alma: Yes, because the men are married, like their old uncle. (She has missed the point of my question.) His actions was like one of the women all the time. And he died like that. He thought he wanted to be—his actions want to be like that of a woman, he acts like a woman, and he talks like a woman. He had lot of cattle but he knows that he has cattle and that he has to go after them, to herd them ...

Int.: Did he dress like a woman too?

Alma: No.

Int.: Because this other one you were talking about (the pottery-maker re: above), he did dress like a woman.

Grace: Yes.

Int.: They actually called her "aunty" even though she was a man. They treated her like she was a woman?

Grace: This is what they used to think.

Int.: Wasn't "she" about the age of your own mother? Your grandmother?

Alma: My little grandson—if he comes up here and I'm baking bread he comes over ... and the children are playing he'll say, "I'll be the grandmother," "You be the children." "She" tries to take the place of the mother, or be the sister or the grandmother. I hear "her" so many times like that.

Int.: You mean Mark?

Alma: Yes. He talks like a girl. He'll be cleaning the house, and cooking the meal, and that's all he think about—the part of the girl.

Int.: Does this worry you?

Alma: No. I don't care. We tease him about it, but he doesn't care either.

Int.: Do you think he'll be able to grow up and be a normal man?

Alma: Yes. I don't think it's anything to worry about. It's just in their action ... and from their family, you know—Mary's family. See, their old uncle was like that, and their nephew was like that.

Int.: Did they ever marry?

Alma: No ... The nephew ... he's still a young boy, at the age of about 21 or 22. He isn't married yet. And see this Mark is in the same family line ... he's like that. I think it's in the family line. And there's one boy—he's about my age too. (She is probably mid-forties.) He was like that too. He was young when we were still kids ... we used to grind all the time every day (i.e., grind corn) ... and he used to wear one of these gathered skirts ... made out of hickory cloth. He used to have a nice little basket, carried corn in that. He used to play around with us all the time. We made bread, he comes around and makes bread with us. His actions are more like girls, you know.

Int.: Did you like him? Did you play with him?

Alma: Oh, we liked him.

Int.: You didn't think something was the matter with him?

Alma: No, uhuh. There's nothing the matter with them. It's just their actions ... maybe they just wish that they were a girl. Just like a girl that wants to be more like a boy. Just like her (referring to her daughter Deanna, a mother of a three-year-old girl.) Now she's changed a little more. About two or three years ago, she was more like a boy. I mean her mind was more like a boy.

Int.: But as she grows older she grows more interested in women's things ... But these men, I think, are a little different because they don't ...

NOTES

1. But see the recent article on the berdache by Evelyn Blackwood, "Sexuality and Gender in Certain Native American Tribes: The Case of Cross-Gender Females", (*Signs*, 1984).

2. Additional information is in Gilbert Herdt, *Guardian of the Flute* (McGraw Hill, 1981); and Edward S. Schiefflein, *The Sorrow of the Lonely and the Burning of the Dancers* (St. Martins, 1976).

PART TWO:

Essays

1972

THE LITERATURE OF HOMOSEXUALITY

Emerson once remarked that "people would stare to know on what slight single observations those laws were inferred which wise men promulgate and which society receives later and writes down as canons." After months of reading the "scientific" and "movement" literature on homosexuality, I'm convinced that no one is in possession of sufficient knowledge at this point in time (though almost no one concedes this) to warrant the confident generalizations heard on all sides—and especially on the scientific side. The deepest morass is in discussions of the "cause" of homosexuality, on which much of the scientific literature concentrates—though homosexuals, sensibly, are learning to eschew the question as presently unanswerable, as a political tactic designed to perpetuate barbaric legal and social discriminations, and as a convenient intellectual outlet for heterosexual condescension. It's currently possible to cite expert opinion "proving" that sexual orientation results from prenatal hormonal programming, the psychodynamics of the family structure, or an innate bisexual potential variably activated or repressed according to individual experience (such as confinement in prison) and social climate (in our country, sex-negative and homophobic).

The Columbia psychiatrist, Robert Liebert, in an article, "The Gay Student: A Psychopolitical View", points out that "to discover psychodynamics ... is not to be confused with discovering psychopathology."[1] Even if the experts could agree on the causes of homosexuality, they would not have thereby demonstrated that it is a "sickness." The medical criteria employed to establish the presence of "disease" relate to measurable physio-chemical phenomena. Not only has such pathology not been adduced for homosexuality, but the behavioral traits often employed as substitute proofs of illness—self-contempt, protective clowning, guilt, dependence and passivity—have been drawn primarily from clinical sources, from homosexuals who present themselves for "treatment." These traits are far less characteristic of homosexuals not in treatment and in any case reflect a pattern of, dependence and passivity—have been drawn primarily from clinical sources, from homosexuals who present themselves for "treatment." These traits are far less characteristic of homosexuals not in treatment and in any case reflect a pattern of "victim" symptomatology regularly found among all oppressed minority groups.

Most scientists bring to their research a culturally derived model of "normal" behavior that influences the nature of their findings. The model, basic to the Judeo-Christian heritage, assumes that human development, psychosexual as well as physical, follows ascertainable curves: certain instinctive biologic forces propel all individuals through similar "stages" which (unless "destructive" environmental forces intervene) culminate in the "healthy" end product of genital and monogamous heterosexuality.

The model is a moral, not a scientific construct, as even a cursory glance at cross-cultural data reveals. Ford and Beach in *Patterns of Sexual Behavior* and Wainwright Churchill in *Homosexual Behavior Among Males* may, as some anthropologists argue, have exaggerated the extent of homosexuality and the degree of its social acceptance in other cultures. But even if so, the Judeo-Christian model can hardly accommodate the evidence that Arab women in certain Red Sea areas take black female lovers, that among the Keraki anal intercourse is thought essential to the health and character of the growing boy, and that prominent Siwan men in Africa lend their sons to each other for purposes of sodomy.

Kinsey is reported to have said "the only kind of abnormal sex acts are those which are impossible to perform." Distinctions need to be made between sexual "acts" and sexual "identity," but as Ernest van den Haag has written, "homosexuality is as natural as heterosexuality and not less, even if less frequent; nor would homosexual acts be 'unnatural' if confined to the human species (which they are not). Religion and art are, and the wearing of shirts ... Moral distinctions are not made by (or in) nature, but about it—they are parts of culture, and must be justified within it."

The tendency of the psychiatric profession is to brand as sick that which is merely unconventional. Differences of all kinds have come to be equated in our society with "deficiencies," and deficiencies—for we are rigorously rational and ameliorative—must be "explained" and "cured." Sexual deviations have come in for far more scrutiny than have deviations from other behavioral norms—like not wanting to own an automobile. The causes and cures of homosexuality have been pursued through time with missionary and almost comic zeal. Same gender love and lust have been variously ascribed to possession by devils, to self-abuse and to neurological or glandular disorders; and its "cures" have ranged from being burned alive, to chastity, to "transference," to electric shock. If the causes of shifting social reactions to sexual deviation had been studied with anything like the fervor invested in searching for the causes of deviation itself, we may have had relief long before now from punitive laws and moralistic vocabularies. When did we last hear a debate on whether heterosexuality, *by its nature,* involved promiscuity and child-molestation, or whether heterosexuals are easy to identify by appearance and behavior, or whether, through proper treatment, they can be "converted"?

The gay liberation movement that has surfaced in the past three years is understandably angry at this history of social ostracism and "scientific" didactics. The movement has already spawned a considerable literature. Some of it, like John Murphy's *Homosexual Liberation* is gently inoffensive, though I would guess that many gay liberationists will discover, as did many blacks in the early phases of *their* struggle, that courtesy and earnestness succeed neither in maximizing outside support nor in accommodating internal rage. Still other works, like Lige Clarke and Jack Nichols' *I Have More Fun With You Than Anyone,* are merely self-congratulatory, nonchalantly bypassing the myriad issues which other liberationists find enigmatic and troublesome.

Peter Fisher, in *The Gay Mystique,* raises some of those issues, often with charming and lucid insouciance. In taking on psychoanalytical theories of homosexuality, he casually asks "Why is the 'active' role in anal intercourse an indication of 'phallic fixation' while the 'active' role in vaginal intercourse is a sign of 'genital maturity'? Why is it 'oral fixation' if a man [performs fellatio with] a man, but a 'harmless regression' if a woman does so?" And "just where is the homosexual who also enjoys heterosexual intercourse fixated?" Fisher argues that the individual with the narrowest range of sexual experience is the one most "fixated"—which puts at the top of the list "the heterosexual who never strays beyond genital intercourse."

In offering "exclusivity" as a new norm against which sexual "abnormality" might be measured, Fisher's book represents the radical challenge to traditional sex roles more characteristic of the gay liberation in its first two years (1969-70) than currently. Before the famed "Stonewall Riot" in 1969 (in which a New York City police raid of a gay bar was met with resistance for the first time), the homophile movement in this country and its chief organizations, The Mattachine Society and The Daughters of Bilitis, were small and discreet.[2]

The new movement inaugurated by the Riot, was initially typified by the Gay Liberation Front, an organization stressing fluidity and spontaneity, anti-authoritarianism and decentralization. It also stressed that sexual liberation, gay and otherwise, had to be fought for in conjunction with a variety of social reforms. This meant alliance with radical representatives of other oppressed minorities (like the Panthers) and rejection in general of a "bourgeois" life style. In calling for basic inquiries into sex, love and gender, G.L.F. seemed to embody Herbert Marcuse's prophetic suggestion in *Eros and Civilization* [New York: 1955] —some 15 years ago—that homosexuals, because of their explicit "rebellion against the subjugation of sexuality under the order of procreation" and their implicit rejection of genital tyranny, might provide a social critique of immeasurable significance. No such expectation seems justified by recent developments. Today, G.L.F. no longer exists as an organization—though many of its impulses do survive in scattered consciousness-raising groups and small collectives. The history of its disintegration and the gradual secession of those who believed in more orderly procedures and more single-minded concentration on gay civil rights, can be followed in a number of recent books. The best is Arthur Bell's witty, vulnerable *Dancing the Gay Lib Blues,* but valuable additional information is in Donn Teal's *The Gay Militants,* Jack Onge's *The Gay Liberation Movement,* and the collection of interviews with activist leaders gathered by Kay Tobin and Randy Wicker in *The Gay Crusaders.* The two best sources on the somewhat different emphases of the lesbian movement and life style are Sidney Abbott and Barbara Love, *Sappho Was a Right-On Woman,* and Phyllis Lyon and Del Martin, *Lesbian/ Woman.*

In the New York area, the most influential homophile organization is now [1972] The Gay Activists Alliance, a structured Roberts-Rules group that considers political ideology divisive—and therefore irrelevant—and is, in the words of its constitution, "completely and solely dedicated" to effecting changes in the present, to "implementing and maintaining" gay rights.[3] Dennis Altman's *Homosexual* traces this shift in emphasis and grasps all the strands thus far to appear in the emerging fabric of the gay liberation movement. It is also the only work that bears comparison, in terms of sustained analysis and theoretical complexity, with the best to appear from the Women's Liberation movement—from Shulamith Firestone, Kate Millett, Alice Rossi, Naomi Weisstein, Robin Morgan, Roxanne Dunbar and Anne Koedt. (In its new incarnation, it should be remembered, the gay movement is barely three years old.)

Altman recognizes that current divisions within the movement may well represent healthy diversity—and in any case serve expressive if not instrumental ends. He tries to understand each position and to abstain from accusations. Though G.A.A. may seem "middle-class", "reformist", even "sexist to those in the radical wing of the movement, it is doing essential work in civil rights and consciousness-raising, and while the far left Revolutionary Effeminists may seem "adventurist", violence-prone and opaque to members of G.A.A., they are formulating basic questions on gender.

Nor does Altman's generosity of spirit come at the expense of intellectual rigor. He manages to combine the two chief approaches—the autobiographical and analytical—that have thus far characterized the literature of homosexuality, without succumbing to the occasional exhibitionism of the former or the frequent overstatements of the latter. Indeed he surpasses the best thus far available in either genre. His personal testimony is as moving as Merle Miller's *On Being Different* but not as sentimental; and although Altman's command of the research literature is as firm as that of any social scientist, unlike most of them, he openly acknowledges the gaps in the evidence (and we have more gaps than fill), resisting the familiar impulse to raise speculation to the dignity of fact, repudiating the notion that one can "command" quicksilver.

Altman also repudiates the easy assertion sometimes found in gay liberation circles (indeed throughout the counter-culture) that promiscuity and the ability to appreciate varieties of human eroticism are the equivalents of liberation. In doing so, he perhaps shies too far away from the possibility that selective promiscuity and cycles of erotic variety may be necessary concomitants of any relationship free of possessiveness. At any rate, this touch of primness in his book, if that is what it is, seems a by-product of his refusal to celebrate in Dr. Pangloss fashion the imminent arrival of the best of all possible worlds, one in which "no special or different feelings [to quote Peter Fisher] exist between homosexuals and heterosexuals."

Altman knows that centuries of oppression have left identifying marks, that many homosexuals bear deep hostility to straight people, and that in ways we may not yet fully understand, we homosexuals have unique testimony to offer on the human condition. Since basic inquiries, moreover, originate on the margin, not from the center, we should be cautious—for society's sake as well as our own—in announcing that our lives are identical with everyone else's. As other oppressed minorities have learned, it may not be possible (at least at this moment in time) both to proclaim that we are "just folks" and to develop our outsider's special insight into socio-sexual norms.

In place of easy celebration Altman presents the gay liberation movement with a difficult even stern set of challenges. He asks homosexuals to remember that if Freud's belief in the inherent bisexuality of human beings is correct (and like all assumptions about sexuality, that one, too, is subject to revision)[4], then homosexuals must add to the slogan "everyone is gay," the concession that "everyone is also straight"—and in addition, must attempt to realize that fact in their own lives. Only thus can homosexuals fulfill what may be their historic function: to undermine our culture's damaging insistence on sexual exclusivity.

Altman also challenges the sexual liberation movements to remember that there are basic racial and class inequalities in American life, and if gay (or black or female) separatism now seems an essential stage in consciousness-building, it is not in itself the optimal goal, that eventually—and the difficulties here can hardly be overestimated—a coalition of the oppressed must be forged. Finally, Altman challenges gay liberation to resist the temptation (spawned by the desire for quick self-confirmation) to replace an older set of myths about sexuality with a new one. He warns that "to generalize is to lose the texture of reality"—a warning hardly applicable to homosexuals alone. Kinsey sounded the same note two decades ago when he pointed out that "nature rarely deals with discrete categories." It is human beings who invent those, forcing a variety of experience into neat classifications—thereby eliminating its enigma.

Sixty years ago, in *Corydon,* Andre Gide wrote, "How strange! One has the courage of one's opinions, but not of one's habits." Now that we are learning the courage of our habits, perhaps we might also find the strength to question our opinions.

The New York Times, December 10, 1972

Notes

1. *Change,* October, 1971.

2. For a detailed reading of the pre-Stonewall homophile movement, see John D'Emilio, *Sexual Politics, Sexual Communities: The Making of a Homosexual Minority in the United States, 1940-1970* (University of Chicago: 1983).

3. GAA is now(1985) defunct. Its perspectives are most closely approximated currently by the National Gay Task Force.

4. See my detailed discussion of this issue in "Bisexuality", p. 249.

"THE FAGGOT"

Two plays about gay life have recently opened in New York. One, "The Faggot", would seem to have everything going for it—an experienced cast, fine physical facilities at The Truck and Warehouse Theater, and the much-acclaimed talents of composer, lyricist, author Al Carmines. It's more than a failure. It's an affront.

The second play, "Coming Out!", would seem to have everything going against it—a cast of ten, only one of whom has had any professional experience, an unknown author, Jonathan Katz, an untried director, David Roggensack, a rudimentary theater, and an agit-prop format that conjures up advance visions of a Chinese ballet honoring The Grain Harvest. Coming Out! is not a complete success, but its impact is profound.

Much, as always, is in the eye of the beholder. Much—not everything.

Admirers of "The Faggot" have told me that like all belated converts I've become the Truest Believer (in gay liberation), that I judge Al Carmines' play not on its own light-hearted terms but in accord with some presumed standards of "progressive" politics. Maybe. We do all need a laugh. If it happens to be at our own expense, if it confirms the social stereotypes that have made our lives as gay people a laugh a minute, well then, here's to those other lighthearted entertainers: Stepin Fetchit, Charlie Chan and the Bloody Injun. Self-exploitation, I suppose, is preferable to the other brands: *we* get to keep the cash.

Chastised, I paid "The Faggot" a second visit, asking for nothing more this time than "a lighthearted good time." I did laugh at two routines, and chuckled at a couple more. I wondered what the scene about Catherine the Great's *partialismus* to the male horse was doing in a musical about gay life, but fell into the crowded aisle when she sang of "my lover half-centaur—and the other half centaur, too." If only "The Faggot" stuck to dizzy routines a la "Dames at Sea" or "Little Mary Sunshine", we could casually ignore or enjoy it, chalk it up to a revival of camp consciousness—the gay contribution to the epidemic of nostalgia currently sweeping the land. But it doesn't. It pretends to a kaleidoscopic view of gay life. It insists on treating issues that have serious implications for millions of people—and does so in terms of tinkly tunes, perky choreography and cartoon realities. In the process it trivializes everything it touches—gay love or loneliness, problems of age and youth, monogamy and promiscuity, jealousy and devotion.

"The Faggot's" cheap parodies will help to perpetuate stereotypes that a serious movement has been attempting to eradicate—at the cost of jobs and apartments, jail sentences and beatings, broken noses and rape. A transvestite in "The Faggot" trills the line, "revolutions are never good news for queens ... where everything is permitted, nothing is extraordinary." Would that we currently faced such an alarming prospect. Would that Carmines had heard another transvestite, Sylvia Rivera, bellow at gays for their indifference to the plight of those beaten and jailed because of openly insisting on being "extraordinary." Sylvia could have told him that musical caricatures of gay life are not good news for revolutionaries.

It's a little late in the day for cutesy-poo. Do many gays—for reasons ranging from police harassment to identity confusion—continue to feel desperate about the quality of their lives? Well, "The Faggot" tells us, "some people just like being desperate." A young man in the musical, with an idiotic smirk as broad as his bow tie, sings to us cheerfully of his devotion to misery, thereby reducing homosexual anguish to a joke, a reduction that heretofore I thought we could safely rely on the straight world to make.

As for gay domesticity, there is everybody's favorite Picasso painting, Gertrude Stein, and her "helpmate" Alice B. Toklas, everybody's favorite cook. They sing along merrily about the joys of "Ordinary Things"—like corn and beans. Bizarre enough in itself, this cloying view of the shared lives of two remarkable women becomes still more startling when we remember that it was Al Carmines, in his brilliant 1968 musical "In Circles," who once found, with almost magical aptness, the visual and musical equivalents for Stein's subtle, quirky, stylized inventions. In "The Faggot", Carmines manages to make her sound like Maria von Trapp, thereby raising what is perhaps the evening's only interesting question: "Whatever happened to the Al Carmines of 1968?"

The show relentlessly issue-hops. Does aging present special problems for gays in a youth-dominated culture and sub-culture? Yes it does, Carmines answers. Why? Because older people get bored! He drapes five of the dreary middleaged complainers over their habitual bar stools and has them bleat about "the same old bars, the same old boys, the same old pains, the same old joys." Given their semi-catatonic selfpity, it comes as something of a surprise when they manage to rouse themselves at the entrance of "The New Boy in Town." But they do so only to go through routines of seduction so patently self-degrading and offensive, that our sympathies go out to the New Boy, sadistic little teaser though he is.

"The Faggot" has been called a musical version of "Boys in the Band," but that is a gross injustice to Mart Crowley's once-daring, witty play. Even in its moments of melodramatic selfpity and sentimentality, "Boys" dealt feelingly with real aspects of the then dominant gay life style. "The Faggot" is a smug cartoon version of that same style. Seeing it, you'd have no idea that gay life in 1973 is in any way different from what it had been in the '50s—except in the absence of all authentic emotion. Crowley disclosed real pain; Carmines, only unrelieved triviality. With friends like "The Faggot," the gay movement needs no enemies.

To gain some understanding of the current mood in the gay community, and of the history of oppression that has led up to it, one must see "Coming Out!" The play's achievements are sufficiently honorable and substantial to make extravagant claims in its behalf unnecessary. It is not a theatrical or literary milestone. Its importance is as a political artifact, not art—the difference between exemplifying a historical moment and creating one. I could have done with fewer moral strictures against "mating like dogs in heat" and more celebration of erotic pleasure. And I would have liked more on bisexuality—that is, less about gay *versus* straight, and more on the dawning possibilities of being gay *and* straight. Still, gay and straight alike will profit infinitely more (at half the price) from a viewing of "Coming Out!" than from "The Faggot."

The one deals in lives, the other in stereotypes. The one stirs, the other lulls. The one provides a context for struggle, the other an excuse for ignoring it. The one suggests the need for unity and commitment, the other for bikinis and cocktails. The one demands an end to oppression, the other helps to reinforce it. Where "The Faggot" is a belated memento of the older view of gay self-depreciation, "Coming Out!" marks the moment when "a yes has come into it."

The New York Times, July 22, 1973

When the above article appeared in *The New York Times,* it produced a deluge of mail. The *Times* printed some of it on two subsequent Sundays (July 29 and August 12). The letters raised important points about the relationship between politics and art that transcended the immediate controversy, and accordingly I reprint them below. I include also my own follow-up response—not printed in the *Times;* they had tired of the debate and felt (probably rightly) that I'd already had my say.

To the Editor:

In responding to Martin Duberman's broadside attack on my musical play, "The Faggot", let me first say that I have both respect and affection for him—not only for his superb documentary theater piece, "In White America," but also for the kind words he has had for my work in the past. I also respect and think I agree with his stand on gay liberation and I admire his forthrightness and the enormous sense of compassion which emerges from his article.

However, although I agree with Mr. Duberman's political position regarding gay liberation, in the case of "The Faggot" he is not dealing with a political position paper, but rather with a personal, idiosyncratic, quirky, highly subjective theater piece. This is the crux of the disagreement between Mr. Duberman and myself. I do not believe politics is art and I believe a confusion of those two human activities is a dangerous and ultimately catastrophic misunderstanding.

Mr. Duberman is really accusing me of not being politically acute in "The Faggot." To this I plead guilty. I plead guilty because I believe it is precisely this obsession with political models that is the bane of American life today and the bane of its liberation movements.

Politics is finally a concern with strategy—the use of certain facts or images to gain a desired end. I believe that strategy has nothing at all to do with art. I am not concerned with the "image" gay people or straight people would like to project. If I wanted to deal in those images, I would be in advertising, not theater. However my work offends I can assure him that there are four questions I did not ask in writing "The Faggot":

(1) How will "The Faggot" affect the gay community?
(2) Does it adequately explain the gay life to "straights"?
(3) Does it help the gay cause?
(4) Is it politically liberated and correct?

No, Mr. Duberman, these are questions I did not ask and, if I had asked them, I would consider myself unworthy to aspire to the name of artist.

I spent five years in a theological seminary filled with earnest young men and women who believed that their earnestness was sufficient redemption for the world. Therefore, I am afraid that I am inoculated against the kind of seriousness that is more concerned with doing what is politically correct than with what is quick with life and truth. My domain—if I have one—is that crack between ideologies where contradictory, frustrating, unideological, stinking and thrilling humanity raises its head.

My drag queen in "The Faggot" is not a representative drag queen. She is an individual with no causes to espouse except her own unshakable existence. My desperation dancer is not concerned that his desperation seems slighting to Mr. Duberman's sexual ideology. He is telling the story of one life—his own. My bored and depressed middle-aged homosexuals are not interested in pretending that they are not bored and depressed middle-aged homosexuals in order to gild the image of gay liberation. In short, Mr. Duberman, my characters are themselves with their and my very personal pain and joy in relating to this world.

No matter how benign, no matter how humanitarian, no matter how compassionate, no matter how just, those who would have any artist trim his vision to fit a sociological or political need for the "right things being said" are the corrupters of art. As a political entity, I am committed to gay liberation and many other liberations. As an artist, I am committed only to the absolute human truth as I see it. And that truth is far more complicated than any party line, however noble, could ever be.

Mr. Duberman asks where the Al Carmines of 1968 is. In 1968, Mr. Duberman, I wrote only music. And I used music to underline, accentuate and, I am afraid, occasionally undercut the lyrics of those with whom I wrote. I did not write words because I was intimidated by people like you, Mr. Duberman—people sheathed in a point of view like heavy armor. And then I discovered that I, too, had a point of view—a shriek against all those causes that demanded blind commitment and believe that certain messy facts can be conveniently left out if they blur the desired image. I do not believe that, because gays have suffered, they are perfect. I do not believe that, because we struggle, we cannot laugh at ourselves. And I do not believe that gays, as well as everyone else, have to deal with self-glorification, self-righteousness and pomposity. I write of both the squalor and the glory of homosexuality, of both the confusion and the clarity; of both the ludicrousness and the holiness of the sexual life.

I have spent a lifetime trying to see what I see—rather than what leftists, rightists, gays, straights, old or young tell me I ought to see. I don't believe the only acceptable plays about homosexuality are those which wallow in self-pity or sound the call to arms. I believe there are ways of being black, or a woman, or gay, or anything else which are not comprehended in even your compassionate militancy, Mr. Duberman.

As for the accusation that "The Faggot" deals with serious issues in terms of "cartoon realities," well, yes—if given the choice, I would rather be Herblock than Max Lerner. And that, perhaps, is the real difference between Mr. Duberman and myself.

AL CARMINES
New York City

To the Editor:

I would like to comment on Al Carmines's response to Martin Duberman's review of Carmines's "The Faggot" and my own play, "Coming Out!" The Duberman-Carmines debate raises publicly for the first time some basic questions about a new, developing gay culture; the answers will affect its future character.

Carmines assumes an absolute opposition between politics and art, coming down totally on the side of "art"—an ivory-tower view I believed had gone out with the glorious 1950's. I thought we were all agreed by now that there is a necessary and intimate interconnnection between such formerly disparate "fields" as art, sexuality, and politics.

Carmines seems to think his play is not political or ideological. In fact, "The Faggot" could not even have reached Off Broadway, much less be advertised in the subways, if the militant gay liberation struggles of recent years had not forced Americans to consider that previously unmentionable subject.

"The Faggot" is also political in that it adds to the oppression of gays; it trivializes our experience and reinforces stereotypes, as well as failing to indicate any of the social pressures which have led to homosexual self-hate and desperation.

Carmines explicitly states that he does not care what effect his play has on straights or the gay community or liberation movement. From his position on high, "artist" Carmines will not stoop to such work-a-day concerns. In this context, Carmines's lip service "to gay liberation and many other liberations" sounds like empty liberal rhetoric. The Rev. Carmines's elitist, art-for-art's-sake philosophy, by denying the social and human effect of his art, is finally irresponsible.

I do not feel there is any antagonism between the artistic and the political. I find most exciting that art which is explicitly political and engaged and, yes, highly creative, an art which is an act of defiance against a society oppressive to gays, women, blacks, American Indians, orientals, old people, young people, working people, etc., etc.

There exists at this particular time in our history what seems to me a marvelously inspiring and challenging role for the homosexual artist: to create a new, liberated gay culture which is both of high artistic quality and reflective of the new consciousness being created by gay liberationists. While there is certainly room and necessity for many kinds of gay art, I hope that more gay culture will come to embody this new gay awareness, including a sense of the social situation of homosexuals, anger at our oppression, and joyous self-affirmation.

JONATHAN KATZ
New York City

To the Editor:

Al Carmines's response to Martin Duberman is a fine statement of what it means to be an artist. Carmines—an independent, an outlaw, a rebel, call him what you may—is fighting for the integrity of his soul, if I may use an old-fashioned word. In essence, he is saying, "World, capitalism, little people and big, don't break my critical canons—as a man and as an artist."

LUCAS LONGO
New Haven, Conn.

To the Editor:

I find Martin Duberman's review of Al Carmines' "The Faggot" lamentably shortsighted; what he fails to grasp is Carmines' idea that the best way of getting beyond homosexual stereotypes is not by ignoring them but by exploding them.

Carmines breaks through, with humor and lyric sensibility, those very cliches he sets up, and the audience, rather than being put down by the experience, is permitted a reshuffling of the cliche-cards, and therefore a new awareness. Duberman does both the audience and the gay movement a disservice when he confuses the solemnity of gay rhetoric with gay pride, and thinks of laughter as the enemy.

MICHAEL GRUMLEY
New York City

To the Editor:

Not only must a theatrical work about gay life staged in 1973 necessarily have a political dimension, it must even have political consequences because of its effect on a large audience. The dimension here is the negative one of omission. If you don't challenge the present view of homosexuals, you reinforce it.

"The Faggot" is unsatisfying not because it's totally inaccurate but because it's incomplete. No one doubts that many homosexuals are miserable or bored, and no one asks to see a fake, projected image of the happy, problemless homosexual as a theatrical subject. However, it is disappointing that Carmines is willing to leave out the most significant scenes in his panorama of the gay experience, those encounters with prejudice that show why many homosexuals have become accustomed to despair.

ALFRED CORN
New York City

To the Editor:
How, in the midst of the dynamic social, political and sexual revolution, no less the gay movement, which is germinating all around us, does Al Carmines presume to be liberated without being politicized?

As Jonathan Katz's "Coming Out!" clearly indicates, and Martin Duberman's political sensitivity reveals, being gay should presently connote explicit articulation and action in regard to the phenomenon of gay oppression. Liberation means having your head and body together and in concert with gay brothers and sisters undertaking the very psychological and political creation of gay actualization.

Carmines might profit from a scrutiny of the life and works of the most successful song and dance man of the modern theater—Bertolt Brecht, the totally politicized man and playwright.

DR. FRANK S. GALASSI
Asst. Professor of Theater, Borough of Manhattan Community College, Brooklyn, N.Y.

To the Editor:
While I disagree with Al Carmines' apparently blanket dichotomy between "art" and "politics," I also disagree with Martin Duberman's suggestion that, when drama transforms human oppression into a circus, it loses its political punch and moreover becomes crassly insensitive to human pain.

The clown is both a comic and a tragic figure. We laugh at him, or her; and maybe in the laughing, we hide our tears. Perhaps it's because we are the clown—gay, straight, rich, poor, black, white, male, or female. And because we can't quite deal with the reality of the tragic. It's been said that humankind can bear but so much reality. A function of art is sometimes to help us get as close to the reality as we, the audience, can—and then to leave us, suspended with our own consciences and capacities, by which we determine the next move.

(THE REV.) CARTER HEYWARD
Union Theological Seminary
New York City

To the Editor:

I find Al Carmines' response to my *Times* article grandiose and irresponsible. Placing the crown of Artist on his head, Carmines announces himself above the fray, exempt from the consequences of his own acts.

"The Faggot," for starters, is *not* Art, is not "quick with life and truth," engaged with those interstices "between ideologies where contradictory ... stinking and thrilling humanity raises its head." Carmines' exalted view of his own musical play bears as little resemblance to the one-dimensional cartoons actually on the stage as those cartoons do to the realities of gay life ostensibly being portrayed.

The claim that "The Faggot" is art is only slightly less bizarre than the pretense that it is not politics. Carmines apparently believes "politics" is something confined to legislators and agitators. Such naivete is dangerous. The vacuous plastic creatures he has put on the stage reinforce negative social attitudes about gay life; these, in turn, re-inforce oppression and discrimination. If Carmines can't see this, he's alarmingly innocent. To mislabel that innocence "Art" is to compound ingenuousness with affectation.

Martin Duberman
New York City

COMING OUT

(My keynote speech at the founding conference of the Gay Academic Union)

A seemingly absurd phrase has been haunting me since I began to prepare these welcoming remarks several weeks ago: "Honored Rabbi, dear parents, relatives and friends ... " It's the opening to the speech I delivered, age 13, to the congregation of Sinai Temple gathered to celebrate my bar mitzvah, the ceremony in the Jewish religion that marks the rite of passage to manhood. When the "honored rabbi" phrase first popped into my head, I laughed at it, thought it bizarre—typical of the way disaffiliated, inappropriate images continually break into the logical processes that we like to believe dominate our minds and lives. Then at some later point I realized that the phrase was not inappropriate, that like many "illogical" intrusions it had managed to make connective sense out of feelings and events widely separated in time.

For today, too, is a rite of passage. Not for me alone, but for us together; not into manhood or womanhood as those states have been traditionally defined; not sanctified by supernatural doctrine; not blueprinted by centuries of ritualized behavior; not greeted by kinship rejoicing and social acceptance; not marked by the extension of fellowship into the established adult community—nonetheless a rite of passage of great significance, for the society at large as well as for us. For what we're saying here today is that we do not accept standard formulas for gender identification and standard norms for sexual behavior. We're saying instead what Herbert Marcuse suggested some fifteen years ago in *Eros and Civilization*; namely, that so-called "sexual perversion" could be the cutting edge of rebellion against "the subjugation of sexuality under the order of procreation, and against the institutions which guarantee this order." In protesting genital tyranny, in rejecting the notion that same-gender love and lust affront the laws of nature, we are placing ourselves in the forefront of the newest and to my mind most far-reaching revolution: the recharacterization of human sexuality.

It is in this spirit that I welcome you: not simply as fellow gay women and men, but as fellow revolutionaries.

This two-day conference inaugurates an effort to integrate the truths of our personal and professional lives. It signifies an historic, perhaps unique moment: the point in time when gay women and men decided, on a large scale, to organize themselves around their professional activities, to use their professional skills and identities in the fight against homophobia—their skills as sociologists, biologists, historians, et cetera, their identities as scholars, educators and students. Our personal experience provides the sensitivity, our professional expertise the tools, for taking on the function of critical philosophy that Herbert Marcuse envisioned for us.

This conference, we hope, marks the beginning of the long march through those particular academic disciplines and institutions with which we find ourselves affiliated. Marching is notoriously hard work. And institutions are notoriously resistant. Neither dedication nor competence, moreover, guarantees success. In the short run, they probably guarantee heightened resistance. Because we challenge the exclusive heterosexual lifestyle by which the majority in this country all at once defines biologic truth, social necessity and personal essence, our work will be difficult and frustrating. Because we are asserting our own worth and our special perspective, the work can be joyful.

Self-worth, however, is not a function of self-congratulation. If we mean seriously to challenge sexual stereotypes, we cannot assume any automatic truths. If we wish to inaugurate a profound debate on sexuality, we cannot set the topics or terms, nor announce in advance the nature of the conclusions. Nor can we afford to dismiss out of hand information or arguments that might discomfit our own theoretical models—we cannot, that is, if "liberation" is to be more than a slogan and "revolution" more than a posture.

We're right to insist that heterosexuality, as well as homosexuality, needs explaining; but that means broadening the inquiry, not putting an end to it. We're right to insist that if some day sexual behavior is shown to have a hormonal or genetic component, we will have gained insight only into how certain patterns get formed, not whether a particular pattern is "good" or "bad". The latter is a moral judgment and reflects social mores; it hinges on cultural, not scientific imperatives. It is up to us to make that distinction clear but not to prevent or discount the research that makes such distinctions necessary. It's our function as students, scholars and teachers to reevaluate current evidence and to provide new evidence, but it can never be our function to suppress evidence—not under the most severe ideological pressure nor in the name of the most sublime political advantage.

The potential role we might play as scholars and critics is the subject of this conference's first day of panels and workshops. I'd like to say a few words as well about tomorrow's topic, "Coming Out in the University."

I realize, of course, that everyone has to decide this matter in terms of his or her own timetable and circumstances—and absolutely free from external coercion. I realize, too, that my own experience in coming out will be of limited use to others. As a tenured full professor teaching in a New York City school, I operated, as it were, out of a maximum security situation. Knowing my experience may be untypical, I want to speak with great caution about what I take to be the risks and gains of coming out.

There *are* risks. First, the risk of losing jobs, or never being hired for them—a particularly potent consideration in today's desperate job market. I doubt very much if I would have come out if I hadn't had job security, and I can only say that I'm in awe of the courage of those students and untenured faculty who are coming out in increasing numbers; indeed, the untenured among us—those with the most to lose, as the world measures loss—have been setting the pace for their more privileged and protected colleagues.

The second risk in coming out is one we all share, tenured or not. And that's the risk of laying ourselves open to simplification, of giving the straight world the opportunity it often seeks to reduce our varied personalities to a one-label category. Within every movement, moreover, the need to stress common intersections and to fight against common oppression always involves some minimizing of individual inclinations. No one likes being labeled or minimized. Sometimes we have to remind each other, as we work to forge a movement, to emphasize our commonalities, that individually we are a good deal more complicated than the sum of our sexual experiences. More often we have to remind the straight world—eager as it is to believe that same-gender sexual attraction is symptomatic of retardation or disease.

Finally, there's the risk that a public avowal of being gay will be treated as merely confessional, as a self-indulgent, vaguely unclean bit of exhibitionism. Our culture has long told us that it's "exhibitionistic"—or worse—to discuss our private lives, and we've internalized the negative judgment. But "exhibitionism" may be the wrong word for what is in fact an impulse to end bifurcation and pretense, to understand honestly and to share honestly. The fear of being called "exhibitionistic"—or worse—has proven a potent mechanism of social control, a device for preventing new kinds of communication that might threaten accepted definitions of humanness—and thus accepted relationships of power.

The risks of coming out are real, and only a Pollyanna would deny them. But they seem to be inescapable aspects of becoming political, risks that must be run because of the overriding necessity of openly uniting with others—no less frightened, complex and private—to end the common oppression.

Besides, the risks, at least to my mind, are far overbalanced by the gains. In coming out, in joining together, we learn that we are not singular freaks but part of an emerging community—one that includes some heterosexuals, (mostly women) along with gays and bisexuals—a community willing at last to talk about what we all want to hear, to demystify the desperate secrets, to end the separation in ourselves and in our culture between private and public voices. It's a community willing to embrace variations in sexual behavior as enrichments to be enjoyed, not shameful fantasies to be concealed.

Movements for social change reflect process as well as ideology; they're shaped as much by how fellow workers treat each other as by how they front on the world. The movement to combat homophobia and sexual stereotyping has already had its share of internal feuds and divisions. Perhaps this can't be avoided, given the diversity of our lives, our differences over tactics and goals and, above all, the fact that we, too, are products of the same set of social values against which we struggle—values that confuse maleness with machismo, femaleness with docility, bisexuality with indecision and sexuality with orgasm. We represent a variety of lifestyles and that variety requires expression. It may not require mutual recrimination and contempt. We can at least try to proceed as friends reinforcing each other's confidence, instead of as adversaries assailing each other's deviations. The former builds community, the latter perpetuates powerlessness. The one does the work of the revolution, the other the work of the oppressor.

In saying this, I don't for a moment mean to subscribe to sappy slogans of "love, love, love." The expectation that all gay people should "love" one another seems to me as destructive of individual impulse and choice as the larger society's insistence that no gay people can love one another. My hope is that we can serve as a genuine alternative to the sexist models that dominate our culture; that we will refuse to talk of human beings—gay or straight—as single impulses, fixed essences, judgeable objects; that we will offer, in opposition to the current vision of homogenized humanity, our celebration of human diversity.

The goal is utopian, and must partly fail. But only utopian goals, I believe, will allow us partly to succeed.

THE COURSE OF THE GAY MOVEMENT
(The concluding speech I gave at the 2nd Annual Conference of the Gay Academic Union.)

I think almost everyone left last year's conference high—pleased we had become visible at last to each other and to the society at large, delighted at the numbers and talent that had turned out, optimistic (some more cautiously than others) that we were well launched in an effort to meet our stated goals of opposing all forms of discrimination against all women and all gay people in academia, of providing support for individual academics in the process of coming out, and of promoting new approaches to the study and teaching of the gay experience.

It's a year later. How are we doing? And where do we go from here? As I've attended sessions and talked to people over the past two days, I've come away feeling more confused than at this time last year. Others seem to share my mood of uncertainty, even upset. Some of that is to the good—part of our maturing process as an organization, and a tribute to the high level of discussion and intense seriousness of purpose that have dominated the sessions. We've put away most of the slogans. We've gotten down to the tough and vital issues of commonality and difference. We've begun to tailor our expectations to our real situation. As some of the grander rhetoric has faded, we've started to hear actual voices.

I've been disappointed that so few from the tenured ranks on our campuses have attended—fewer, I think than last year. I go through the usual apologia in my head: older gay people, brought up in a desperately homophobic climate, are simply too cowed, too brainwashed, too self-hating, to make a move in their own behalf. But I can't summon up the apologia as often as I once could. More and more instead, I remember Lord Acton's comment: "Beware of too much understanding lest you end by too much forgiving." We've heard much over the past two days about differences in life style and perspective between gay men and lesbian women, and how these present real obstacles to forming a community. But we've heard almost nothing about the obstacles created by differences in generational perspectives.

The problem is largely within the gay male community—for the simple reason that there aren't many older lesbian women with money, power, privilege, position. Anyone who has worked with any gay organization over the past few years will tell you that even when total anonymity is guaranteed—when donations, for example, are carefully laundered—it's been possible to raise only pitiful sums from those gay men who have the most to give—doctors, lawyers, professional chiefs. Even anonymously, even indirectly, even marginally, these men have refused any identification with or any contribution to the gay movement. I think I'd be less depressed about this if I thought I saw much hope of it changing.

I don't mean we should write off the *entire* generation. And I don't mean we should harass or "expose." I do mean that we probably have to face the fact that in a very real sense a generation of gay men has largely been lost to us—that they have been superbly, probably irretrievably indoctrinated and cowed by the patriarchial culture. If community is to come, the work and rewards alike are going to belong to the young.

Turning to GAU itself, its main activities this year on the male side—which is all I can comment on—have been social events and consciousness-raising sessions. I know how necessary and useful those activities are. For most people consciousness-raising is a needed prelude to active political commitment. And continuing social contact is a valuable device for keeping that commitment humane—oriented to the needs of people rather than to the dictates of ideology.

But I do want to suggest that the amount of time and energy the men have put into social events and consciousness-raising has been excessive, even self-indulgent. Let me explain. My feeling is that most of us, almost by definition—college educated, middle-class, white—are already over-privileged as compared with the majority of our gay brothers and sisters. I also think most of us are in better shape psychologically than we sometimes care to admit to ourselves. The argument that we "have to get our heads together before we can do any political work" can become a standing rationale for doing nothing: our psyches are somehow never quite ready, our motors never quite tuned up. I think this has a lot to do with American perfectionism, and even more to do with male selfishness.

In a city like New York, I don't think we can legitimately claim that we need GAU primarily for social/sexual contacts. "True enough," some say, "but only in GAU can we meet people like ourselves." I distrust that rationale. I think it falsifies the available range of our social options—and the cross-class lines of our sexual tastes. But I can understand why the rationale appeals. It allows us to evade responsibility for the fact that we've given most of our energy this past year—true to our training as men—to ourselves: to perfecting even further our "self-awareness"; to tending still more our already well-tended psyches; to broadening still further not only our social, but our career contacts and professional opportunities. Like all academics, we're in danger of talking too much and doing too little. And talking, moreover, about a limited set of issues. I've heard almost nothing during the past year, or in this conference, about the real, serious, oft-evaded divisions within the gay community—within the society at large—based on class and race.

Perhaps we've done what we had to do for a year. But if so, a year, I suggest, is enough. It's time we did more work in the world. Time we used our already extensive expertise and self-knowledge, our already extensive privilege, to work for the larger gay community. Time we made more of an effort to implement the purposes we bravely formulated last year. As matters now stand, we're in danger of simply becoming an organization that gives a conference once a year. And at that, a conference modeled rather closely on those genteel gatherings we're already familiar with from our respective professional caucuses. We've started to play it a little too safe, to concentrate on the mainstream, to avoid more controversial aspects in the gay style of living and loving.

There's been considerable contempt and intolerance towards those gay people whose style is outside the mainstream—towards those into the S/M scene, for example, or towards transvestites and transsexuals. Apparently few of our members—to judge at least from their outer appearances and declarations—are so inclined. Thus no real effort has been needed to keep "fringe" styles and topics out of sight. But many of our members did declare themselves to be bisexual (not myself, I should add—lest I be accused here of copping a personal plea). If the complaints and rumors of the grapevine are true—and I've heard them often enough to believe they are—something like a deliberate effort has been made to exclude bisexuals and ignore issues of concern to them.

To put it mildly, I find this unfortunate. It means we're involved in playing a version of the same game the larger society plays with us, namely: "either do it our way or be prepared to find yourself ostracized." It comes down to the same contempt for individual differences that we deplore in the culture as a whole. If we try to humiliate those who deviate from *our* norms, how do we protest when those who adhere to the heterosexual norm choose to hound and humiliate *us?* I don't see how we can affirm the rightness of same-gender love and lust—and then add the qualifying clause: "so long as your love and lust is directed *exclusively* towards people of the same gender." To my mind, we must oppose any prescription for how consenting adults may or must make love. I don't care whether we're talking about enemas or toe-sucking, I say no one—and I mean no one, not the U.S. government, not the psychiatric profession, not the churches, not Matthew Troy*, and no, not the GAU—has the right to tell us what we can or cannot enjoy.

I hope I haven't overstressed the negative. If so, I've been untrue to my own feelings about GAU's accomplishments and potential. But I did think it important to bring out into the open some tendencies within the organization which have bothered me (and others) and which threaten to sap its potential.

I believe these are tendencies only and that thus far they've been far overbalanced by the fine work GAU has done in helping us find ourselves and each other, and in at least beginning the work of combating what Wilhelm Reich called "male armor"—that is, those dictatorial, hostile/aggressive, elitist/authoritarian, emotionally des-sicated or defended qualities within ourselves (and in the larger society) which keep us *from* ourselves.

Despite all the differences in point of view which have emerged during the conference, despite all the real obstacles we face in trying to achieve a community, I think we have the right to a certain amount of self-congratulation and pride. Not only have we come together—we've stayed together. Not only have we tried to combat homophobia and sexism in the culture—but within ourselves. If I've been among those most critical of GAU's activity—or lack of it—during the past year, these last few days have given me a renewed sense of the enormous amount of talent, energy and guts we have among us. If we are not yet a "community," there can be no doubt we have the human resources ultimately to create one strongly unified in its common purpose even as it is richly diversified in its style and texture. To that double end, hopefully, we will rededicate our energies.

*The New York City Council member who had pledged to work to get "Intro 2", the then-pending civil rights bill for gay people, passed "if we didn't rock the boat with street demonstrations, etc."—and then having gotten that agreement, proceeded to vote against the bill.

BISEXUALITY

The bisexual ideal is increasingly touted as the standard against which all who aspire to *bona fide* membership in the Sexual Revolution must measure themselves. The psychiatrist Robert E. Gould, speaking as a heterosexual, has recently published an article in *The New York Times* professing his newfound conviction that "if there were no social restrictions on sexual object choice, most humans would be functioning bisexuals." Phil Mullen, speaking as a homosexual, has expressed a similar view in an article in *The Gay Alternative.* "We gay people," Mullen has written, "have often been heard to argue that the lives of straights would be richer if they could only respond sexually and emotionally to others of their own gender. Our gay lives, by the same token, would be richer if we could open up to ... heterosexual love ... Now that we're finally learning that gay is good, we'll have to start learning that gay isn't good enough..."

My own feelings pretty much coincide with those expressed by Gould and Mullen. Yet I'm less sure than they are that everyone's nature is bisexual. And I worry that that assumption—seemingly on the side of human liberation—could prove tyrannical, could become the latest in a long series of "scientific" party lines used to intimidate and control "deviants"—in this case exclusive homosexuals *and* exclusive heterosexuals. The scant literature available on bisexuality does little to clarify my confusion or down my fears. For most of my life I've been made to feel guilty (both in and out of therapy) about my homosexuality. Now, under the sting of new cultural imperatives, I'm learning to feel guilty about the *exclusivity* of my homosexuality. Since guilt is the common denominator (and since I'm Jewish), I suppose one reasonable conclusion is that no shift in social attitudes will appease my unquenchable instinct for self-castigation.

Most of my homosexual friends regard my admiration for bisexuals as suspect. They view self-designated bisexuals as people suffering from a failure of nerve, an unwillingness to take on the still onerous, still stigmatized image associated with being homosexual. If I try to argue against their view (half-convinced of the accuracy of both), they retort that I've merely found a new tactic for asserting superiority—my "openness" to new explorations, information, etc., rendering my gayness provisional in a way they feel is inconsistent with integrity. When I explain that bisexuality is, at most, an aspiration, not in any sense a present reality for me, they shift to the accusation that I'm some latter-day Horatio Alger, forever fixated on Self-Improvement for its own sake. The nerve having been hit, I then respond that *they* are fixated on self-congratulation, though calling it self-affirmation. A bristling standoff. And as I've said, I don't see much, if anything, in the official literature on bisexuality that would help us resolve these issues.

The little "objective" data we do have comes mostly from three sources: biology, anthropology and history. The evidence from all three disciplines seems to me remarkably scanty and often contradictory: lodged either in data that are comparatively new, as in ethnobiology and human behavioral genetics, and thus not yet adequately replicated; or else in historical data that are irrevocably old, and therefore inherently incapable of being replicated.

Since I am an historian and not a scientist, I'm far from confident that I can successfully separate out the few "facts" current researchers in biology are willing to agree upon. Approaching the complex territory through Freud, the Founding Father of bisexual theory, is difficulty enough. I gather Freud believed bisexuality was a biological universal—a sort of endoplasmic potential inherent in all cells, tissues, organs, creatures. Since he also believed that psychology reflects biology, he assumed that bisexuality is present in the thinking and feeling processes of all human beings as well—even if not ordinarily part of their overt behavior. More than forty years ago the analyst Sandor Rado, in his essay "A Critical Examination of the Concept of Bisexuality,"[1] presented what has since come to be regarded as the classic rebuttal of Freud.

Rado concentrates his fire on the sloppiness of Freud's conceptualization. According to Rado, Freud used the mid-nineteenth century discovery that the urogenital systems of both sexes have a common embryonic origin as the basis for unwarrantable speculations of a far broader nature about an innate human predisposition to psychosexual bisexuality. He had, according to Rado, confused "bipotentiality of differentiation in the early embryonic stages" (to quote Rado's charmladen prose) with hermaphroditism, the possession of two complete reproductive systems in the mature organism. Only when a dual reproductive system is present, Rado insists, can the term "bisexual" appropriately be used.

It seems to me a narrow semantic point. Even when conceded, it doesn't move us very far along. Strictly speaking, Rado is certainly correct: what he calls "true hermaphroditism"—a bisexual reproductive capacity—is never found in human beings, or, more precisely, is almost never found: a few rare conditions exist that are characterized by genital ambiguity, a mixture of ovarian and testicular anatomical structures, or, as occasionally occurs in the male, by degeneration of the testes. Rado is also right that the absence of this characteristic in human beings is in contrast to its presence in several other species on the phylogenetic scale; for instance, in the garden worm, which can produce both eggs and sperm (John Money and Anke Erhardt, in *Man & Woman, Boy & Girl,* call this trait "simultaneous bisexuality," a term that hardly helps clarify the issues). Certain species of fish exhibit what has been labelled "sequential bisexuality". For example, the Mexican swordtail spends part of its life as a male, making sperm, and part of its life as a female, making eggs. Terminology aside, no comparable processes can be found in human beings. So Rado wins his modest point: bisexuality defined as a dual reproductive system is not characteristic of human beings.

But little is accomplished by conceding this. Such a narrow linguistic definition of bisexuality is irrelevant to the phenomenon of bisexuality as commonly perceived, discussed and practiced— namely, as same-gender love and lust alternating with or simultaneous with attraction to the opposite gender. Among the few generally agreed-upon propositions I've been able to find in the biological sciences is that human behavior—unlike that of garden worms and swordtail fish—is a function of culturally learned norms more than instinctual imperatives, which means that *despite* the absence of dual reproductive systems we are capable of seeking pleasure and relatedness wherever our socially conditioned psyches cue us to look for them. Sometimes this takes the form of emotional and sexual involvement with people of the same gender. Sometimes it takes the form of identification with the *behavioral* traits of people of the opposite gender—of mimicking supposedly "masculine" or "feminine" mannerisms or dress, a complex appropriation of the available stereotypes.

So if we do not find the capacity for hermaphroditic reproduction in human beings, we decidedly do find, using other definitions (and using our eyes and ears), bisexual behavior. And apparently this is true for all mammals, not merely for humans. The zoologist and physiologist R.H. Denniston has an essay in Judd Marmor's *Sexual Inversion* in which he categorically declares that "frequent homosexual activity has been described for all species of mammals of which careful observations have been made [and] it has little relation to hormonal or structural abnormality."

The standard response to views like Denniston's is to say that he equates and confuses homosexuality with "dominance behavior"— the ritualized, hierarchical forms of submission (among males) in which actual anal penetration rarely takes place, and orgasm never. Dominance theory has long held sway among behavioral scientists, but in recent years has come under increasing challenge, the challenge not unrelated, I think, to the increasing numbers of women scientists; as their numbers and influence increase, I expect we'll see an ever widening set of reevaluations of longstanding scientific "truths," since many of those so-called truths have merely been uncritical reflections of the patriarchal values of male scientists. (Women scientists, like women everywhere, so at least I find, are much less frightened of homosexuality than their male counterparts.) The work of Suzanne Chevalier-Skolnikoff as regards dominance theory is a case in point.

In her study of the stumptail monkey,[2] Chevalier-Skolnikoff has come up with findings that support Denniston and explicitly refute the principal findings of the dominance theorists. Defining a "homosexual" interaction as one involving "prolonged" (fifteen seconds or more) genital stimulation of at least one of the monkeys, she automatically excludes "most mountings that function mainly as dominance behavior, since these mountings rarely involve prolonged genital stimulation." Of the five female monkeys in the group she studied, four were, for various lengths of time, involved in "homosexual" behavior. Among the males, she observed eight different methods of stimulation, including "extensive" manual and oral variations, as well as "dorsal mountings with pelvic thrusts and anal intromission." Homosexual intercourse, moreover, took place in essentially the same position assumed in the common heterosexual interaction—and this even when heterosexual options for sex were readily available.

As we have learned (or should have learned) from the criticism levelled at the work of Konrad Lorenz, Robert Ardrey and Desmond Morris, extrapolations from animal behavior to human behavior tend to be simplistic and misleading. We can tell plainly enough when two male stumptail monkeys are pleasuring each other (in eight observable positions, no less), but we can't be sure whether the frequency or "psychological" content is affected by the artificial environment of the laboratory; that is, whether and how the feelings of the monkeys relate to their behavior (and, by analogy, to our own); whether and how the feelings of scientists observing those prodigious instances of fellatio and sodomy affect their "objective" reporting of the events; whether, indeed, the behavior of the stumptail monkeys has *anything* to do with that of, say, macaque baboons, let alone with that of the inhabitants of New York City.

John Money's research on transsexuals[3] strongly suggests that human sexual behavior is primarily a function of social learning, not biological wiring, that it arises in response to the models, cues and injunctions dictated by the environment. Although the anatomical and chromosomal equipment of a given transsexual are entirely intact—check out as "correct" against all the scientific indices of gender—the psychological conviction of the individual that he or she has in fact been misassigned overwhelms all the supposed mandates of biology. "I am a woman trapped in a man's body" takes precedence in a male transsexual over all the physical evidence: XY chromosomes, testicles and penis, prostate gland and gonads, high androgen levels and hairy chest. Neither psychotherapy nor electric shock, neither the insistence of doctors and priests nor the pleas of family and friends, makes any dent in the determination of a transsexual to convert his or her anatomy to conform to the inner conviction that he or she was intended to be the opposite of what heredity and anatomy seem to suggest. Additional and dramatic evidence of the overwhelming importance of social learning in determining sexual identity are found in cases where children are deliberately socialized into sex-role behavior that contradicts their biological equipment. Money and Ehrhardt recount the story[4] of a seven-month-old male infant whose penis had been severed through a surgical mishap. The infant was reassigned as a "girl," vaginoplasty (genital reconstruction) was performed, and the child was dressed and treated from then on as "female." By age four and a half, the mother reported that she'd "never seen a little girl so neat and tidy . . . She is very proud of herself, when she puts on a new dress, or I set her hair." In other words, having been reared in a traditional manner as a female, the child, in spite of her biological constitution, had comfortably adjusted to her self image as a girl.

Anthropology provides still further evidence that sexual behavior results largely from cultural, not genetic, imperatives. Even a cursory glance at other cultures confirms the dependency of our own psychosexual patterns on parochial and largely tacit social dictates. More than twenty years ago, Ford and Beach, in their classic work *Patterns of Sexual Behavior,* revealed that 49 of the 76 societies they surveyed (64%) regarded homosexuality as a normal sexual adaptation. (They were referring to male homosexuality; 17 of the societies did sanction female homosexuality, but in anthropological research, as in everything else, female behavior is less visible—or less studied). The 49 cultures vary considerably in the kind of homosexual behavior sanctioned, the degree to which it is formally institutionalized, merely encouraged or actually prescribed.

Among the fierce Kukukuku people of the New Guinea highlands, the ingestion of semen is given a magical status, is considered essential to virile growth—and is accordingly prescribed for all preadolescent and adolescent males. Among the Keraki of New Guinea, the prescription for health in the growing boy includes regular anal intercourse with an older man. Among the Crow Indians of North America, anal intercourse is unknown—but oral/genital contact is frequent. Among both the Koniag of Alaska and the Tanala of Madagascar, "transvestite" males (berdaches) are usually regarded as shamans, persons in possession of supernatural power, with whom sexual contact is thought to confer a variety of blessings. Among the Melanesian people of the Southwest Pacific, transvestism is unknown, but acceptable sexual practices include homosexual partnerships between adolescent friends (even brothers) and between adolescents and older men (including their fathers' friends).

It's important to note that in all these examples—and they can be multiplied many times over—it is *bi*sexual behavior under discussion, not exclusive homosexuality. The expected, approved, even prescribed homosexuality in these cultures is not found to the exclusion of heterosexuality. It is expected—the berdache or shaman may be a partial exception—that if there is same-gender sex there will also be opposite-gender sex: sometimes simultaneously, sometimes alternately, sometimes progressively (that is, gender choice shifting completely from adolescence to adulthood).

The anthropological data allow for many near-generalizations in regard to same-gender sex. We can say that it is *usually* connected with puberty rites and/or has some religious significance; that it *usually* involves anal intercourse rather than oral/genital contact; that it *usually* occurs prior to marriage and child-rearing; that a considerable difference in age between the partners is *usually* found. Given the paucity of field studies to date, and the unwillingness of most anthropologists even to address these issues, the one potentially universal generalization that seems to emerge is that homosexuality is rarely, if ever, found *in opposition* to heterosexuality. The same near-universal seems to emerge from animal studies, among the few exceptions being Konrad Lorenz' famous geese, among whom he observed lifelong male pair-bonding.

But what is apparently true for most non-human animals and for most "primitive" human cultures is not true for our own, for the culture of the Judeo-Christian West. Historically, however, this hasn't always been true. In ancient Greece, exclusive homosexuality (*or* heterosexuality) among males (again, we know little about female behavior) was apparently a rarity[5] and was, at least on the evidence of the plays of Aristophanes and Menander, a subject for mockery. It's possible, too, that we associate exclusive homosexuality with the West simply because the phenomenon has been so little studied in Eastern cultures.

All generalizations about sexual behavior in the past ought to be tentative, since all are based on limited evidence. For the West itself, the history of sexual mores is poorly documented and the documents are susceptible to wide differences in interpretation. As the anthropologist Steven Weinstock has put it, "incidences are easily demonstrated, but attitudes can only be surmised." There are really only two books in English that broadly survey the subject with any competence: G. Rattray Taylor's pioneering mid-fifties work, *Sex in History,* and Arno Karlen's more comprehensive *Sexuality and Homosexuality.*[6] Taylor's book is graceful and witty, but is burdened with a theoretical superstructure that is derived from the rigid categories of psychoanalysis and now seems overinterpreted and outdated. Karlen's book is more than a little homophobic in attitude, but does provide an abundance of detailed information.

Among Karlen's most firmly held views is that "we must scrap the biologically rooted concepts of bisexuality and latency." On the same theme, Taylor waffles strangely. Not once, but twice, he states that "homosexual elements are present in everyone." Yet throughout his book Taylor never ceases to equate homosexuality with "abnormality." How a quality present in everyone can be considered abnormal is never clarified—though the whimsical implications of the converse proposition are certainly tempting: "Normality is that quality which can be recognized by its absence in everyone."

While denying that bisexuality is biologically rooted, Karlen presents us with copious evidence that bisexuality has been widely practiced throughout history. Though perhaps counterintuitive, no necessary contradiction is involved: obviously it's possible for a behavioral pattern to be common and yet not biological in origin—driving a car would be one example. Such behavior, we say, is "learned". Fine. But why, through time, have human beings been so prone to "learning" bisexual behavior? If biological imperatives have not been the cause, they have apparently not been a deterrent either; there is no evidence of a biological mechanism that inhibits the capacity to take physical pleasure and emotional comfort from people of either gender. Respecting sexual preference, "nature" would seem to be neutral; in other words, we are or we aren't bisexual depending on whether our culture does or does not encourage the activity.

There is ample evidence for arguing that bisexuality has been so pervasive an aspect of human history that, statistically, we would have to rank it among the few constants of "human nature"—on a par with waging war or using intoxicants. Even Karlen, so hostile to the notion of any inherent capacity for bisexual responsiveness and so careful to warn that evidence about the sexual behavior of people in earlier times is scanty, says that on one matter we can pronounce "with confidence": "for centuries or even millenia before the Greeks, many peoples from the eastern Mediterranean to Sumeria worshipped a goddess whose rites included both heterosexual and homosexual intercourse"—among others Artemis in Ephesus, Aphrodite in Corinth, Astarte in Phoenicia, Ishtar in Babylon, Isis in Egypt, Anitis in Persia, and Bendis in Thrace.

Even Sandor Rado, like Karlen unsympathetic to Freud's notion of a biologically rooted bisexuality, stated in his essay of some forty years ago that for as far back as we have records of human behavior, we have evidence of bisexuality. (We only have records, of course, for about 1% of human history—the last ten thousand years; before that human beings lived in nonliterate hunting and gathering societies.) Rado found traces of bisexuality in the Upanishads and the Old Testament, and he refers to certain Egyptian gods as being "notoriously bisexual." Still more curious, given his vigorous argument against biological bisexuality, Rado locates the source of persistent bisexual behavior through history in "primeval, emotional needs of animalistic man." This is, to say the least, a confusing statement. If "primeval emotions" bear no relation to biology, perhaps biology should no longer be looked upon as the source of our "instincts." Or at the least, we should no longer allow "instinct" to carry the linguistic weight it currently does of an "emotional imperative."

Those "experts"—from psychiatrists to historians—who pronounce so confidently against the suggestion of biological underpinnings for bisexual behavior have the responsibility to provide (or at least attempt to provide) some form of social analysis as an alternative explanation for the frequency with which bisexuality has appeared through time and across cultures. They have not taken up that responsibility. Instead, they have focused on the tangential question of *when* bisexuality ceased to be commonplace. Even in regard to that question, their comments have been brief and glancing.

Rattray Taylor, for example, stresses the critical dividing-line of 500 B.C. Before that date, he argues, homosexuality was characteristic of the whole early Mediterranean world—"wherever the leading deities were feminine." Thereafter, a "remarkable psychological change" took place; sexual activity in general became more inhibited and repressed, and homosexuality decidedly less acceptable.[7] In his influential book, *Homosexual Relations Among Males,* Wainwright Churchill argues that "the ancient Hebrews before the Babylonian Exile [circa 700 B.C.], like their neighbors, accepted homosexual practices and even accorded status to male temple prostitutes." Subsequently, "for reasons that remain obscure," homosexuality became increasingly taboo. Perhaps it was the punitive sodomy practiced during the Exile (which gave anal intercourse a bad name). Perhaps it was the "supernationalistic fervor" that seized the Hebrews subsequent to the Exile; in Talmudic writings sodomy became associated with "the way of the Canaanite, the way of the Chaldean—the way of the 'heathen'". Such "foreign" customs were initially denounced as a form of idolatry and then, by the time of *Leviticus,* as an "unnatural abomination" to be punished (in the case of males) with death. (Homosexuality was disapproved of for females, too, but penalties for lesbianism were instituted only later.)[8]

The vicissitudes of the reputation of the poet Sappho (612-558 B.C.) illustrate the gradual triumph of homophobia over the bisexual ambience that earlier characterized the Mediterranean world. In her own day, as Dolores Klaich documents in her book *Woman Plus Woman: Attitudes Toward Lesbianism,* Sappho's poems were celebrated throughout the Greek world, coins that bore her image were minted, statues erected in her honor. In other words, no stigma was attached to her lesbianism (or perhaps bisexuality; the existence of a husband and, what is more probable, a daughter, are disputed). But by the time of Theodosius the Great—that Christian emperor who massacred 7,000 people at Thessalonica—and the Council of Constantinople (390 A.D.), edicts were issued declaring homosexuality a capital crime; and in the wake of them, Sappho's poems were consigned to the flames, all but a few fragments lost forever to the world.

Any attempt to generalize about sexuality in the ancient world involves, of course, an absurd compression of a wide variety of lifestyles spread over some thousand years of human history.

Moreover, scholars dispute the extent and characteristics of bisexual behavior at every point in history. Rattray Taylor, for example, agrees with most scholars that among the aristocratic class in Periclean Athens "every man was expected to take to himself a boy," and a boy not chosen was a boy disgraced. Yet he disagrees in insisting the relationships were confined to the kind of quaint Victorian roles of Inspirer and Listener that I very much doubt Socrates and Alcibiades would have recognized.

Such examples of contradictory opinions abound in the limited literature on the subject. Definitive interpretation at this stage in our knowlege can be for now only illusory. We must content ourselves with scattered glimpses of the diverse, and somewhat mystifying styles which characterized bisexual behavior in antiquity:

In the fourth century B.C. a picked band of male lovers fought against Philip of Macedon at Chaeronea and died to a man. In Sparta, a boy who had no lover was punished—and a boy who picked a poor lover over a rich one was fined. Julius Caesar's diversity of sexual tastes earned him the reputation as "the husband of every woman and the wife of every man"; yet even Caesar was scandalized by the harems, containing concubines of both sexes, that Mark Antony kept in Rome—perhaps because Caesar did not believe pleasure should be institutionalized. Although we know that lesbianism was practiced in Greece, we do not know to what extent. Among the few bits of extant evidence are the fragments of Sappho's poetry, Plato's comment in the Symposium that the existence of lesbians, like that of male homosexuals, was to be explained naturally, as part of bisexual creation, and Plutarch's remark that "at Sparta love was held in such honor that even the most respectable women became infatuated with girls."

If the definition of bisexuality is broadened beyond "sexual lust and love for the same gender" to include non-sexual identification with the "behavior" of the opposite gender, the phenomenon of cross-dressing also becomes a matter of historical interest (and debate). In *The Glory of Hera,* Philip Slater describes "the prevalence, in puberty initiations and other *rites de passage,* of exchange of clothes between the sexes." One such rite was the nuptial ceremony. In Greek custom and myth—the two are difficult to separate—we find cross-dressing particularly associated with the wedding night. At Argos, for instance, brides donned false beards; in Sparta the bride's head was shaved and she put on men's clothing; at Cos the procedure was reversed: the husband wore women's garments to receive his bride.

Why? We don't know—though theories are easy to multiply: to

ensure potency with the opposite sex; to neutralize its power by assuming its outer guise; to express appreciation for its "otherness"; to unravel its mysteries—or surrender to them. Concern about the experiences of the other gender—however clouded the source of that concern—is exemplified in Greek myth as well as custom. The story of Tiresias, the male seer who spent seven years as a woman, is merely the best known of many ancient legends depicting men and women who changed sex during the course of their lives. The Greek deities also numbered several bisexual or androgynous figures, the most famous being Hermaphroditos. Rattray Taylor has pointed out that in late Greek art Hermaphroditos is portrayed as an effeminate youth, but that in the earlier period he appears "either as a bearded and virile figure with breasts or a massively maternal figure with prominent male sex organs. The figure represents not a neutral cancelling of sexual powers but the fullest possible expression of both aspects of sexuality."

In Rome, too, cross-dressing was a familiar practice. Will Durant (in *Caesar and Christ*) describes the sons of the rich in the 1st century B.C. who "dressed and walked like courtesans, wore frilled robes and women's sandals, decked themselves with jewelry, sprinkled themselves with perfume, deferred marriage or avoided parentage and emulated the bisexual impartiality of the Greeks." (Alas for today's unisex pioneers of the "new" who, in thinking they're inventing a world, may be merely representing another shift in an age-old cycle— a shift so long delayed this last time around that those applying weight to the edge are perhaps entitled to their claims of originality.)

In his book *Sexual Life in Ancient Rome,* Otto Kiefer comments that "everything relating to sex was regarded as completely natural, and was approached far more simply and innocently than it is now." The comment is suspiciously sweeping and bland, but Kiefer does draw the needed contrast between the acceptance of diverse sexuality in the ancient world and the repression of it—even of the inner wish for it—in the Christian era that followed, and that continues to influence thought and behavior. Which is not to say the Christianized West came merely to exemplify sexual repression; the bawdiness of Chaucer's poetry is alone enough to remind us that stereotyped and static generalizations absurdly compress (and thus hardly do justice to) the diversified patterns of a thousand years of Christian history (no less than to the thousand or more years of "pagan" history preceding); to remind us, too, that human behavior rarely coincides with whatever may be the publicly proclaimed moral code of the moment.

Yet it does seem that official disapproval of the pleasures of the sensual life was often fierce, even obsessional, during the Christian centuries—as exemplilied in the "penitential books" and in the ferocious punishments ordained during the Inquisition, when its handbook, the *Malleus Malleficarum,* explicitly stated that "all witchcraft comes from carnal lust." Moreover, the triumph of Christianity marked (in Karlen's phrase) "the West's full transformation from a shame culture to a guilt culture, in which prohibitions are fully internalized and man is ruled by conscience rather than by others' disapproval."

It hardly needs demonstrating that the guilt, the internalization of sexual prohibitions, remains very much a part of our culture—despite the signs of a countervailing movement. Both the continuing repression and the incipient liberation from it were recently exemplified in a controversy in the pages of *The Chronicle of Higher Education.* After the *Chronicle* published English Professor Louie Crew's article describing his sense of heightened freedom after coming out publicly as a gay man, it printed, two issues late, the outraged response of Albert J. Maier, Comptroller of Marquette University in Milwaukee. In a tone reminiscent of the *Malleus,* Maier denounced the publication of Crew's article as "a blunder of unforgivable magnitude ... a sign of the general moral decadence." He went on to characterize homosexuality as "one of the most vile blasphemies against God," following through—with the understatement of a papal bull—by warning Louie Crew that "someday he will be called upon to give an accounting of the stewardship entrusted to him by our Creator." Maier left no doubt as to the Lord's verdict: "a one-way ticket to hell."

Should we dismiss Maier's remark as the ravings of an isolated bigot? Not when "sophisticated" New York City has yet to pass a minimal civil rights bill protecting homosexuals against discrimination in jobs and housing.* Not when a recent [1975] Supreme Court decision declares that private acts between consenting adults are subject to state regulation. Not when a recent poll revealed that some 70% of the citizenry disapprove of gay people teaching in primary and secondary schools. I have no statistical poll, but only my own impressionistic hunch that at this particular moment in time there is still less acceptance of bisexuality than of exclusive homosexuality.

I think it's easier for exclusive heterosexuals to tolerate (and that's

*Eleven years later, in 1986, it finally did.

the word) exclusive homosexuals than to tolerate those who, rejecting exclusivity, sleep with individuals and not genders. It's easier because in the Cartesian West we've long been taught to think in "either/or" categories, to believe that one is male *or* female, boss *or* worker, teacher *or* student, child *or* adult, gay *or* straight. To suggest, as practising bisexuals do, that each of us may contain within ourselves all of those supposed opposites we've been taught to divide humanity into, is to suggest that we might not know ourselves as well as we like to pretend. It's to suggest, too, that the roles by which most of us define ourselves—the Tarzan/Jane, Doctor/Nurse dichotomies that are so tacit and pervasive—represent transient, even ludicrous social values, limitations imposed on us by the culture in which our world-view has evolved.

Such suggestions provoke insecurity and distress. Few people welcome distress, including most gay people. In the years I've been active in "movement" politics I've heard considerable disparagement among homosexuals of the "confusion" and "cowardice" of their bisexual brothers and sisters. Gay people, struggling to accept their self-worth, don't like hearing that once one mountain's been scaled, another may lie directly ahead.

Bisexuals, in short, seem at the moment very much between the devil and the deep blue sea. And in their struggle for the right to define their own lifestyle, there isn't much legitimizing comfort to be drawn from the blurred data emerging from the social sciences. Biology (though not biologists) seems mute on the subject, while anthropology and history provide considerable evidence of the widespread incidence of bisexuality through time and across cultures—but not without also providing evidence that in *our* culture most people have been exclusively or predominantly heterosexual.

The safest conclusion to be drawn from the fragmentary evidence available seems to be that human beings will behave sexually as their culture tells them they should behave—and both the social cues and the behavior have varied widely through time. *Why* societies have differed so radically in their behavioral norms is almost as mysterious as why people have usually accepted such parochial "programming" as the equivalent of universal truth. I don't mean that answers to these conundrums are impossible to come by—Freudians, Marxists, Feminists and others have all had their say—but only that the answers offered to date seem partial and polemical.

Besides, as any good utopian knows, the past need not be seen as a binding model for the future. Even if it can be conclusively demonstrated that exclusive heterosexuality has been the dominant sexual mode throughout the history of the West, that does not mean it will or should remain so. Even if additional research consolidates and clarifies the argument from biology, there would still be many who would argue against biological determinism—in the name of the continuing evolution of the species, and out of an awareness that "unnatural" human intervention (building cities, inventing flying machines, etc.) has always been salient in the evolutionary process. As the psychologist Pam Oline once said to me, "What if more *were* known about the connections between body chemistry and certain predispositions? Would that knowledge tell us automatically how to behave?"

Whatever the answer to that question may be, the few studies done on bisexuality[9] agree that in the United States it's currently more visible and assertive than ever before. And in tight little circles within tight little islands like Manhattan, bisexuals are even being hailed as exemplars of a brave new world. But hostility towards bisexuality is on the rise, too, and from both gays, who tend to view it as a "cop-out" and from straights, who tend to feel threatened (women less so than men). Faced with crosscurrents of adulation and contempt, it's not surprising that bisexuals are beginning to exhibit an initially defensive, progressively offensive chauvinism of their own. In this connection, I am reminded of an ex-student of mine, who went to live in a small commune after he graduated from Princeton. Its members were paired heterosexually, but the women in the commune were also having sex with each other. They began to bait the men as "hung-up Puritans" because of their reluctance to do likewise, finally driving the man I knew, desperate to get his credentials in the counterculture, to having a homosexual experience that was entirely unsatisfying and which has so far kept him from further experimentation.

"Well," someone might say, "that's the way it has to be for a while, as we try out, often disastrously, possibilities that in the long run will prove enriching." Fine, agreed. But the long run is a difficult hike to embark on and pointing a gun in someone's face may not be the optimal way to get him to put on his track suit. Besides, it can be argued that sexual orientation becomes so "fixed", so thoroughly imprinted at so early an age, that most adults, even if they had the will, would be unable to activate what some insist is a universal bisexual potential. Why *some* adults can and do is one of the many mysteries.

"The long run" at any rate, at least as I optimally envision it, will allow for more, not less, diversity. We don't want to exchange one set of harnesses for another; not, that is, if we believe the rhetoric many of us have been spouting about the specialness of every human being. I think the future will see more people relating bisexually, in at least the minimal sense that they will regularly enjoy the pleasures of having sex with someone of a formerly excluded gender, though still preferring that their "core" relationship be heterosexual, or homosexual, as the case may be.

But D. H. Lawrence's "credo" (as published in *Studies in Classic American Literature* some 70 years ago) puts it best:

That I am I.

That my soul is a dark forest.

That my known self will never be more than a little clearing in the forest.

That gods, strange gods, come forth from the forest into the clearing of my known self, and then go back.

That I must have the courage to let them come and go.

That I will never let mankind put anything over me, but that I will try always to recognize and submit to the gods in me and the gods in other men and women.

New Times, June 28, 1974

NOTES

1. His essay is conveniently reprinted in Judd Marmor's indispensible anthology, *Sexual Inversion* (Basic Books: 1965).

2. *Archives of Sexual Behavior,* vol. 3, no. 2, March 1974. For confirmatory evidence of the influence women scientists have had in the decade since this essay was written, see, among others, the field studies by primatologists Jane Goodall, Diane Fossey, Jane B. Lancaster, Sarah Blaffer Hrdy, and most recently Meredith F. Small,, ed., *Female Primates: Studies by Women Primatologists,* (Alan R. Liss: 1984). The new views that have emerged in the field of primate studies are conveniently summarized in *The New York Times,* September 18, 1984.

3. *Sex Errors of the Body* (Johns Hopkins: 1968); *Transsexualism and Sex Reassignment,* co-edited with R. Green (Johns Hopkins: 1969); *Man & Woman, Boy Signatures,* co-authored with Patricia Tucker (Little, Brown: 1975). See Janice G. Raymond, *The Transsexual Empire: Making of the She-Male,* (Beacon: 1980), for a critique of Money's views.

4. *Man & Woman, Boy & Girl,* p. 119.

5. See Boswell, *Christianity, Social Tolerance, and Homosexuality,* (University of Chicago: 1980) for a revisionist challenge to this view (and my review of his book on p. 329).

6. In the decade since this essay was written, some additional commentary has been published (e.g. Reay Tannahill, *Sex In History*).

7. See Boswell, *op. cit.* for a persuasive new (1980) challenge to this view.

8. G. Rattray Taylor, "Historical and Mythological Aspects of Homosexuality," *Sexual Inversion,* Judd Marmor ed. (Basic Books: 1965); Churchill, *op. cit.,* pp. 75, 200.

9. For a convenient summary of recent studies up till 1977 see Roger W. Libby's "Addendum" (pp. 253-256) to this article as reprinted in *Marriage and Alternatives: Exploring Intimate Relationships,* Roger W. Libby & Robert N. Whitehurst eds. (Scott, Foresman: 1977). For example, Blumstein and Schwartz have reported that 61% of the males and 32% of the females they interviewed (in a study which included a wide ranges of ages and socioeconomic groups) recount some homosexual experience—a substantial increase since the Kinsey studies of some thirty years ago. (See Blumstein & Schwartz, "Bisexuality", *Journal of Social Issues,* 33 (2), 1977.) In Laud Humphrey's 1975 study, *Tearoom Trade,* he found that in casual male/male homosexual encounters in such public or semi-public places of assignation as men's rooms, 54% of the men involved were married—moreover, he found no evidence that their marriages were unstable. Such studies, like all scholarship that breaks new ground, is subject to legitimate cavil. As the sociologist Roger Libby has emphasized, these early "piecemeal efforts of sex researchers from several disciplines have not resulted in a unified body of knowledge as basis for a theory of sexual identity." The studies further suffer—along with most discussions of the subject in the popular media—from confusion and imprecision in terminology (for example, the blurred lines between sexual acts and sexual fantasies, or the blurred descriptions of "male" and "female" sex role behavior). Finally, the new studies rely almost entirely on notoriously unreliable "self-report" data, and are more given to merely tabulating the number of same-gender orgasms than speculating about their meaning (or more accurately, given the wide diversity in age, race, class, etc. of the participants, their meanings). Yet at least a start has been made in studying such formerly taboo topics, and there is general agreement among such researchers that "bisexual" behavior is decidedly on the rise. The most significant discussions on bisexuality to appear since I wrote this article ten years ago are: the four issues of *Journal of Homosexuality* devoted to Bisexuality: "Bisexual and Homosexual Identities", vol.9, nos. 2&3 (Winter 1984); "Bisexual and Homosexualities: Critical and Clinical Issues", vol. 9, no. 4 (Summer 1984); "Bisexual and Homosexual Identities: Critical Issues", vol. 10, nos. 3&4 (Jan. 1985); and "Bisexualities: Current Research", vol. 11, no. 1&2. (March 1985).

CONSENTING ADULT

"Dear Mama,

" ... I have something to tell you that I guess I better not put off any longer ... you see, I am a homosexual. I have fought it off for months and maybe years, but it just grows truer ... "

With these words, written by 17-year-old Jeff Lynn in 1960 to his mother, Tessa, Laura Z. Hobson begins her new novel*, a milestone in the history of social attitudes if not of art.

Most of the book's success hinges on the complexity of her two main characters, Tessa and Jeff, mother and son, and also on its decision—unique in the literature about homosexuality—to tell the story from the parent's point of view.

Jeff is not the docile mama's boy so dear to the psychiatric literature. Nor is he the proud young revolutionary of counter-myth, but rather a self-sustaining, somewhat inelastic solitary, absorbed first in sports and then in science—and wholly apolitical. When, at the end of the book (by then a 30-year-old doctor), Jeff does "come out," the novel is at its least plausible, in part because little in his character or experience has prepared us for the event, and in part because, at about the same point in the narrative, Hobson walks him into the sunset with another Fine Young Doctor. Having worked almost too hard through most of the book to avoid assigning Jeff any stereotypic "gay" attributes, Hobson then capitulates entirely to the counter-stereotypes of settled self-pride and monogamous love.

It is politically valuable and sociologically accurate to learn that the gay male world has its strong silent types too (though a switch in sexual orientation would not make John Wayne any the more appealing). It is also politically valuable and sociologically accurate to learn that some gay men (and perhaps more gay women) do settle into, and seem to prefer, a life of domestic fidelity. But in *Consenting Adult* these truths tend to obscure others. If Jeff is meant to be viewed to any degree as an emblematic figure—and of course he will be— then our awareness of the range of gay experience and personality will have been valuably expanded in one sense only to be contracted in another. His rugged temperament, his professional success, his monogamous love life are suspiciously close to the official model of what constitutes a healthy heterosexual. Jeff's qualities seem drawn

---

*Which in 1985 was aired as a much-discussed television special.

to the specifics of Tessa's—and perhaps most mothers'—fantasy needs (including Hobson's, apparently: there's nothing in the novel to suggest any differentiation between the points of view of character and author). Yet these needs, derived from the traditional culture, are currently under serious challenge as indices of "maturity" or guarantors of personal happiness.

It never crosses Tessa's mind that current erotic and emotional norms may no longer be functional for gay—or straight—males. Nor any recognition that both are beginning to know it. Where gays have long tried to pass by mimicking straight styles in "manliness"(rigidity in socio-sexual roles, and an emotional range running from A (Aggression) to D (Dormant)), the reversal has begun to set in: gay men affirming the value of their expressiveness, straight men lamenting their comparative constriction. Only some men, and only sporadically; but any movement in this direction is tantamount to the end of the ice age.

Tessa and her son are hardly in the vanguard of this cultural shift. At times they seem in the rear guard. Tessa is squeamish about sexuality of any kind; she finds recent novels "repugnant" in their sexual explicitness and thinks their readers "Peeping Toms." And she is proud that Jeff "almost never sought sex as sex."

Yet some gay people—quite contrary to the Jeffs—are beginning to argue that the pejorative term "promiscuity" has served as a means of social control, a way of denigrating the pleasures of sexual variety, of holding us all in guilty bondage to parochial Judeo-Christian norms. These gay people are taking up the argument that emotional commitment and sexual desire are not equivalent states, that we are creatures with a variety of impulses that should be deliberately cultivated rather than suppressed and punished.

In this context, Tessa and Jeff are mainstream "integrationists": they want society to give up its "false" estimates and exaggerations and open wide the doors. Beyond that, they see little need for change—certainly none involving "new models of maleness" or redefinitions of "love" and "commitment." Like most of us today, Tessa and Jeff struggle to achieve less self-loathing from within and less condemnation from without. Like most of us, their initial response to homosexuality is that it is a monster to be exorcised—the "horror of it," the unendurable horror, Tessa cries, when Jeff's letter first arrives. She rushes out to consult doctors, read books, find explanations, embrace "cures." Her liberal background gives her something of a headstart: she automatically rejects religious notions of "sin" or "evil." But that same liberal background, with (in 1960) its automatic allegiance to psychiatric models, raises instant panic within her about "disease," "abnormality" and "psychic disturbance."

She is numb with relief, then suffused with hope, when a psychiatrist tells her that most authorities agree a "successful outcome" (i.e., heterosexuality) can be expected in about 25 per cent of the "cases" that undergo treatment. Willingly—gratefully—she foots the psychiatric bills year after year awaiting some clue that the coveted transformation has occurred. Then, gradually, she begins to wonder why the psychiatrists keep talking of episodes in Jeff's life as "valuable material"—"as if he were being measured off like yards of cloth from a bolt of goods." She begins to wonder about the other 75 per cent: is it possible those who don't achieve "cure" will find that analysis has added to their already pronounced sense of worthlessness, their already heavy burden of failure and exclusion?

As she reads on and on in the literature, she finds disturbing discrepancies in the theories of the "highest authorities." And then—a decade down the tortuous road—she starts hearing about a new body of research, a new group of therapists, an emerging rejection among some of the "highest authorities" themselves of the notion that homosexuality is an illness or a character disorder. No one, she finally decides, has a satisfying explanation for homosexuality. She begins to understand that the very emphasis on causation has been a form of derision (why haven't scientists been studying the possible aberrance of exclusive heterosexuality—or the certain aberrance of homophobia?). She comes to feel that we may be "at some new threshold about the age-old subject," and that the only good therapist is the rare one who helps to question set formulas and reduce self-hatred. Slowly, Tessa's frame of reference shifts; from feeling "if only Jeff could change," she comes to realize that it is she who has to change—and the world. She sees that if she continues to view Jeff as her tragedy she must inescapably become his.

Tessa's progress is willed, splendidly willed. As the product of a certain class, generation and culture, schooled to view homosexuality as a desperate curse, change for her could come in no other way (not initially, at least, not until understanding begins to grow). Unlike her hip, radical young son-in-law in the book, for whom acceptance of homosexuality is natural and easy, Tessa has to claw out every inch of gain. This is precisely the poignance of her story—and the measure of her achievement.

She (and her creator) will be derided, perhaps, as "mere" liberals. Well, would that we had more of them—more of the "merely" decent who push themselves to change, who recognize that we're "at some new threshold" and do their best to cross it, even if that best entails some visceral resistance to a full awareness of the seismic nature of the shift at hand. Those who are tempted to sneer at Hobson's inadequacies will have to be sure that they are not doing so as a convenient way of evading their own responsibility to match the author's courage and meet her novel's central moral challenge: to try to understand and respect that which is different.

The New York Times, July 6, 1975

POSTSCRIPTS:

(1) Dear Mr. Duberman,

There is in existence today, a knowledge called Aesthetic Realism. Your study of it should be considered mandatory in your research on sexual behavior in the U.S. Your recent review in the literary section of *The New York Times,* dealing with Laura Z. Hobson's book titled *Consenting Adult,* deeply affected me. I happen to be a mother of a son who changed permanently from homosexuality, through the knowledge of Aesthetic Realism.

The events you described in Laura Z. Hobson's book, were very similar to my life as a mother of a homosexual son. I also saw homosexuality as a disease, abnormality, and psychic disturbance. My son and I, spent many fruitless years in psychiatry, vainly trying to resolve this problem. Aesthetic Realism gave me back a son I could respect and be proud of. It succeeded where psychiatry failed. I am deeply grateful to it's founder Eli Siegel, for giving my family and myself renewed hope and happiness for our lives.

Aesthetic Realism sees all homosexuality as arising from a wrong attitude to the world. A mother does contribute to the cause: She allows a son to conquer her, and when he does, he has contempt. She encourages him to feel women look both silly and easy and therefore less desirable.

What is large in the way Aesthetic Realism sees homosexuality, is that it makes the way one sees the world as a central thing in one's life. To care less for women, is to care less for reality. In homosexuality, what is different from the self, is not respected. As one learns to respect reality, the need to be homosexual becomes undesirable. ... If you'd like to know more, my colleagues and I can arrange to meet with you for further questioning. At present, I am an Aesthetic Realism consultant in training. My hope is to teach mothers a method that can prevent them from making the painful mistakes that caused so much distress in my life.

Respectfully yours,
[A.S.]

(2) Steven Dansky* in *The Soho Weekly News,* Thurs. July 17, 1975:

... Martin Duberman makes clear that he believes that *Consenting Adult* is a major achievement, but he can't refrain from using spurious value judgments against Hobson by saying that her characters were "counter-stereotypes of settled self-pride and monogamous love."

His attack on monogamy made me think of a faggot couple struggling to find some dignity in their attempted commitment against an entirely hostile culture. Duberman throws meaningless epithets of "moralism" or "Judeo-Christian hangups" at a risk-filled struggle that few attempt, even fewer are able to succeed at. We live in a culture that only pretends to support monogamy, badly at that, but truly is most threatened by any devotion which two people show for each other.

Duberman's futile effort to be radical only becomes doubly vague. He suggests that promiscuity may be a positive force for social change. He favors the "pleasures of sexual variety," whatever that may mean. Duberman calls for faggots to be part of the sexual revolution vanguarded by such people as Hugh Hefner and Al Goldstein. Are they to be considered the real threat to patriarchal power? Is *Screw* providing the impetus for Duberman's ideological formulations? No, he is more sophisticated than that: he cites Marcuse, the Marxist-Freudian—what a combination. Duberman posits the theory that "the so-called sexual perversions may well turn out to be the cutting edge of social transformation." How insulting to faggots. What perversions is he referring to? Child molestation? The ever-increasing rape of young women by their fathers? Sexual sadism? Terminal sex?

In his review, Duberman never once mentions the word sexism. He carefully avoids the painful realization of Tessa: sexism is what it's all about. Why does Duberman do this?

*A self-designated Revolutionary Effeminist and one of the founders of that group's *Double-F Journal.*

Obviously, to avoid the necessary personal changes that are required of men.

When he proposes revolution, what revolution is he referring to? Is it socialism? Anyone who read the July 9 *New York*

When he proposes revolution, what revolution is he referring to? Is it socialism? Anyone who read the July 9 *New York Post* would have been struck by the headline: "Reports Nixon Still Is Mr. Nice Guy To Mao." The article said that Mao regretted the Watergate scandal because it resulted in the tragic ruin of Nixon's career; it occurred because of an atmosphere of "too much freedom of political expression in the U.S." That ain't my revolution.

Why doesn't Duberman unzip his pretend-radical-spokesman suit and reveal his true identity, the opportunist-liberal-on-the-make? Hobson has the guts to name the enemy. She's no liberal who needs his imprimatur.

When Elizabeth Barrett died, Edward Fizgerald, a bachelor recluse who translated Omar Khayyam, said that her death was greeted with a sigh of relief. At seventy-seven Robert Browning wrote a reply which I partially quote: "Surely to spit there glorified your face,/Spitting with lips once sanctified by hers."

Maybe I shouldn't be so vitriolic. But who will be there for the mothers such as Elizabeth Barrett? Or Rose, Ruth, Myrtle, or Ella? Or the sons, Steven, John, Robb, or Ken? When one feminist defended women's right to a Great Love, I thought it was my right too.

July 17, 1975
Dear Stephen Dansky,
... I had to tell you how angry your "review" of Marty Duberman's review made me.

I was glad to see you relating to the human side of *Consenting Adult* because I think it's fairly hard to do and Marty didn't do very well with it. But your attack on him in the rest of your piece is really misguided and, I think, slanderous. The revolution he was talking about is the same one you're talking about, the revolution against sexism. You have to be very mean spirited not to see that in his review. His attack on monogamy is part of a general (too general, for my tastes) attack on the kind of liberalism Hobson exemplifies and the same kind you hate yourself. I don't remember seeing any praise of Goldstein or Hefner in his review? Where did you get that?

And note that the "so-called perversions" are exactly that, so-called in his review. Aren't you being deliberately dense?. . . .

George Whitmore [Poet and author, *The Confessions of Danny Slocum*]

(3) Christopher Hobson [son of Laura Z. Hobson] in *The Detroit Gay Liberator*:

Laura Z. Hobson, the author of *Gentleman's Agreement,* has written a novel called *Consenting Adult.* The adult in question is the mother of a young homosexual(although it is also, somewhat parenthetically, the homosexual himself). As the jacket copy and advertisements for the novel announce, this book is unlike previous ones about homosexuality, "because they all dealt primarily with homosexuals themselves, with their problems, their point of view, while this one takes the opposite stance entirely and focuses on the parents and family of the homosexual, their pain, their fears, their point of view."

This approach is supposed to be courageous. In the *New York Times Book Review,* Martin Duberman, an historian who is homosexual, called the novel "a milestone in the history of social attitudes. . . " That a homosexual who has evidently been influenced by the gay movement could react to this book in this way is a mark of the decay of the movement, its failure to transform homosexuals' consciousness in a lasting way.

Consenting Adult on the surface is a sympathetic statement, pro-gay and pro-gay liberation. In fact, however, the author has constructed a novel hemmed in on all sides by restrictions necessary to make homosexuals and homosexual liberation acceptable in terms of liberal middle-class values. Gay liberation is reduced to a standard nearly anyone can accept, the right of a homosexual who is socially "desirable" in every other way to be accepted by middle-class society, assuming his/her homo-sexuality is relatively unobtrusive. But even within these limits, the novel is not what it pretends—it applies a method of special pleading which takes all the rough edges off heterosexual prejudice and results in a self-flattering fantasy of liberal heterosexuals' behavior. And on the basis of this it constructs a view of social change which is also a fantasy, implicitly anti-homosexual. . . .

SEX AND THE MILITARY: THE MATLOVICH CASE

Leonard Matlovich, tech sergeant in the Air Force, had been relieved of his duties in 1975 after coming out publicly as a homosexual. The Langley Air Force Base hearing in late September was the first round in a protracted struggle for reinstatement, a struggle which ended (at least temporarily) in 1981, when Matlovich accepted a cash settlement in exchange for giving up litigation. Simultaneously, the Armed Forces further tightened its exclusionary policy against admitting any known homosexuals for military service. The New York Times agreed to pay my expenses to cover the Matlovich hearing at the Langley Base in Virginia, though cautioning there was scant chance they'd publish any article I might write on the case; but in the upshot they did.

LANGLEY AIR FORCE BASE, HAMPTON, VIRGINIA, SEPT. 1975:

If there has ever been a son of mid-America, it is Lenny Matlovich. He believes in God, duty, his country, monogamy, competition and hard work. He volunteered for three tours of duty in Vietnam because "that's where my nation needed me." He erected an 18-foot flagpole in his front yard. He voted for Goldwater. He always did more than his share on the job, pushing himself to excel—and then took on additional jobs. He was never comfortable with sexuality; in his conservative Catholic family, "anything relating to sex was not discussed." His politics were right-wing: when the Air Force became integrated, he protested being housed with "niggers." He considered Walter Cronkite a "flaming liberal."

That is, until two years ago, when Leonard Matlovich, aged 30, lost his virginity. To a man.

One doesn't want to claim too much for the transforming power of sex—or even of self-acceptance—but if the causes can't be neatly charted, Matlovich today is clearly a different man from the superpatriot of a few years back. He is now deeply ashamed of the stand he took against integration, and his eyes water when he notes the irony that blacks at Langley have formed his chief support group since he publicly came out. On the front door of his apartment a placard reads, "Trust in God—She Will Provide."

Some of his earlier values remain intact or only marginally different. He still disapproves of those who would "destroy the country." He would still "turn in immediately any gay individual harming security." He says that if he had the choice—and he is adamant that homosexuals never have the choice—he would rather be straight (when he first realized he was gay and before coming out, he "cried a lot, prayed a lot," begged the Lord to "make me like everybody else"). He still believes in monogamy, still hopes to find the "one right person." He still insists that duty impelled his decision to come out: he had sworn to uphold the Constitution, with its guarantees of equal rights for all citizens. He still loves the Air Force and is still optimistic that he will be allowed to serve in it.

The board of inquiry convened here at Langley in late September for a week-long "fact-finding hearing" (the Air Force's preferred phrase for "trial") has ended with the recommendation that Mat-lovich be discharged, but he plans a string of subsequent appeals. The final outcome of those appeals will not, it seems to me—after sitting in on every session of the hearing at Langley—hinge on the human or legal merits of the case, but on certain assumptions about sexual behavior—the causes and permissible limits of erotic expression—that dominated (albeit unintentionally) his first hearing and seem likely to dominate subsequent hearings, however concealed by the rational mode of courtroom discourse.

Before attending the hearing I had expected and hoped to see a simple morality play, having already cast the leading heroes and villains. The event has proven more complex. The defense witnesses did not embody all available enlightenment and persuasiveness, nor did the prosecution prove to have a monopoly on condescension and confusion.

On the very first day of the trial the chief attorney for the defense, David Addlestone, conducted a *voir dire*—an examination of the jury to determine its impartiality. The jury—the board of inquiry—consisted of five majors and colonels. Each was questioned separately, out of hearing of the others, and it seemed to me that all—give or take the usual quotient of human evasion—were candid, even earnestly so, in their responses (though the higher the rank, the more monosyllabic the replies). Four of the five said they had read little or nothing about homosexuality. All five felt that their religious training (Protestant, in every case) had not influenced their views on homosexuality.

That was the first time I blanched. True, Roman Catholicism and Orthodox Judaism have been more explicit and virulent in their homophobia, but it's also true that until very recently all institutional religion in the West has uniformly viewed same-gender sex as sinful. That these Air Force officers insisted to the contrary did not seem to me part of a deliberate intention to deceive but rather a lack of self-consciousness about the sources and extent of their own ideology.

I say this because they revealed that ideology with almost ingratiating innocence. In response to particular questions relating to the "immorality" or "sickness" of homosexuality, the board, taken as a whole, was decidedly more inclined to the former view—suggesting a greater adherence to the traditional religious rather than the traditional psychiatric model of homosexuality (though a full 50% of all answers were some version of "I don't know").

The "liberal" civilian press corps tut-tutted a great deal among themselves over the officers' equivocation, ignorance and bigotry, and I joined in the general derision. Still, "I don't know" isn't the worst state of mind with which to approach some of the formidable questions about sexuality that came up at the hearing and that are currently at issue in the culture—assuming, of course, that the officers' uncertainty wasn't feigned. My own impression is that it was not. Which isn't to say they sounded enlightened, but only that in their unenlightenment they're in the mainstream of public opinion and that some of them, in certain particulars, seemed a little in advance of it. It's too easy to ascribe the verdict in the Matlovich case to the "retrograde mentality" of the military—too easy because this interpretation far too casually disparages "them" and far too conveniently congratulates "us." Through some limited private soundings I learned that at least 3 members of the board agreed during the deliberations that Article 125 of the Uniform Code of Military Justice (which forbids "any unnatural carnal copulation") was "ludicrous, antiquated" and perhaps unconstitutional. If the Article indeed offended their sense of what is just and reasonable, one might argue they acted with insufficient courage in abiding by the narrow parameters which the Judge had set. But it would be more difficult to argue that homophobia pure and simple was responsible for their decision to recommend Matlovich's discharge.

What was most fascinating about the trial, what gives it a larger significance, were the broad questions raised during the hearings (and the attempts to answer them) about our current assumptions regarding gender identification and sexual orientation. The defense attorneys called a number of expert witnesses whose testimony provided intriguing insight into the range of scientific opinion on sexual behavior. What does science currently claim to know, the specialists were asked, about the "causes" of homosexuality? (Three of the board members, during the *voir dire*, ascribed it, without hesitation, to "environment"). Is there a critical point at which sexual orientation becomes fixed? If so, is that point during gestation? Within the first few years of life? During adolescence? Later still?— Never? Are erotic patterns, once fixed, subject to change? If so, marginally or totally?—and as a result of what experiences? Is "bisexuality" a modish fantasy or a biological reality? What is "perverse" in sexual behavior, and what is "normal"? Does society have any stake in insisting on the maintenance of certain standards of sexual "morality," and if so, through what agency should intervention proceed?

The experts testified on these questions with a good deal of conviction, impressive erudition and a notable paucity of "I don't knows." Much information was elegantly packaged and dispensed, various "myths" challenged, new "truths" revealed. Those rooting for Matlovich were greatly heartened. A more humane world seemed indubitably on the way. And yet ... some of the new truths seemed less than conclusive, some of the certitudes seemed to conflict with each other, the will to do good was sometimes more apparent than the hard evidence needed to prove that good must be done. The testimony of John Money was the most significant case in point.

The famous head of the psychohormonal research unit at Johns Hopkins, author of a dozen books and hundreds of articles, president of the Society for the Scientific Study of Sex, John Money was the most commanding figure to appear as a defense witness. Austere, lucid, formidably at ease, he performed with the taut resolve and polished reserve that transport all fans of Sherlock Holmes into instant rapture. The courtroom seemed full of such fans. By the end of Money's testimony, there wasn't an empty notebook in the room— or an unscrambled brain. The one moment when I felt any rush of sympathy for the prosecutor was when—a weak smile on his face, his shoulder tilted deferentially—he asked Money the addlepated question, "Is it true that the closer one is to genius, the more likely one is to be homosexual?" Money flashed a charming smile. "I don't subscribe to that theory" (said Holmes to Watson).

What Money said he did subscribe to is worth attending in some detail, for his views carry enormous (though not uncontested) weight in the scientific community. And they have also—thanks largely to the semi-popular book *Man & Woman, Boy & Girl,* which he co-authored with Anke Ehrhardt—been widely disseminated in educated circles generally. Money's research in endocrinology and his studies of transsexualism have had special impact on the ancient controversy over the comparative influence of nature (the biological givens) and nurture (the social expectations) in determining personality structure.

The thrust of Money's testimony seemed on the side of pre-destination—physiological, not divine. At one point he went so far as to say that "once the die is cast hormonally, it cannot be reversed." Unfortunately, he never made clear what "it" referred to: the establishment of "gender identification" ("I am male"; "I am female") or the development of "sexual orientation" ("I am erotically aroused by members of the same—or opposite—sex"). His references veered between the two without specifically mentioning either. "Prenatal hormones," he said early on, "can predispose bi- or homosexual development" (a reference, clearly, to sexual orientation). Later he declared that we are "psychologically undifferentiated or neutral" until roughly 18 months of age (a reference, apparently, to the onset of gender identification). At yet a third point, he claimed that "by adulthood, we don't have the potential any longer to be other than what we are—homosexual, bisexual or heterosexual" (a matter, again, of sexual orientation).

A trial, of course (even when called a "fact-finding hearing") is essentially a political, not a scientific, occasion. Legal strategy, the pressure of the moment, the eagerness to be helpful, the lack of opportunity to expand and qualify remarks, all encourage simplification and even misstatement; indeed, they may be in evidence in direct proportion to the witness's humanity. All that said, Money's apparent emphasis during his testimony on the paramount importance of biology came as a considerable surprise to anyone familiar with his writings on the subject.

If Money meant that the "die" of gender identification cannot be reversed after a certain age, then what he said on the stand was consonant with his published findings. His work with transsexuals (those convinced, contrary to all anatomical and genetic indices, that they are members of the opposite gender) has persuasively demonstrated that after age 5, at the very latest, an individual's psychological conviction about his or her gender cannot be changed—just as he has also shown that in an *infant* the "die" *can* be recast (in one of his most famous examples, a male baby accidentally castrated was not only successfully reassigned as a female, but, under the pressure of stereotypical socialization, became a little girl obsessed with cleanliness, hair ribbons and dolls).

But if Money meant to imply during his stated testimony that the die of *sexual orientation* cannot be recast, then he would have to square that statement with the anthropological data he has himself often cited, data which suggests that we all have "a bisexual capability which is either *culturally* encouraged or suppressed." Money's emphasis on the stand on the congenital and the predetermined is important I think because it reflects a general resurgence, a renewed acceptability in our culture, of the belief that biological considerations are the basic ones in any explanation of human behavior.[1] This shift in cultural consciousness—it is nothing less—is especially startling in a country which for so long has insisted on the malleability of behavior and has touted "change" as a cardinal social value (even as a test of personal authenticity).

Like most "revolutions in consciousness," this latest one seems less a breakthrough into the previously unknown, than a retreat to the recently forgotten. The vocabulary ("bias on the neutral substra-tum"), the units of measurement (neonatal "startles") and the techniques (pituitary grafts), all seem miracles of modernity. But thus far the modern mountain has brought forth only the proverbial mouse—sorry, rhesus monkey. And it seems to be squeaking an ancient tune. For in fact many of the assumptions about sexual behavior that are suddenly prominent again are the same ones that guided the earliest—only a hundred years ago—self-conscious theorizing about sex. In the late 19th century, almost all sexologists agreed that male homosexuality (women as usual were rarely considered) had a constitutional base; behavior was inborn, not acquired. Before Freud, almost no one (the French psychologist Binet may be the one important exception) stressed the possible importance of environmental factors. Considerable disagreement did exist as to which constitutional factors were most salient and which secondary symptoms most revealing. Among the favored "causes" were "embryonic malformation," "degenerated genes," a "woman's brain," epilepsy and anemia, climate and altitude, masturbation, an absence of spermatazoa and the presence of genital nerves around the anus. Among the most telltale symptoms were small glans, a smooth rectum, a penchant for dirty books and luxurious living, left-handedness, an inability to spit and whistle.

Despite these disputes over the distinguishing organic and somatic marks of male homosexuality, almost universal agreement prevailed that the "condition" itself was incurable; one couldn't be cured of that which was innate; nor should one be punished—and this marked a human advance—for that which was involuntary. What could be expected of the afflicted was that they remain celibate (a position Norman Mailer, that revolutionist of modern consciousness, has more recently flirted with in *The Presidential Papers*). Should will power prove insufficient to the task, the 19th century physician could recommend such popular devices of the day as the spiked penile ring—guaranteed to discourage any threat of tumescence.

Far removed from 1975 and the climate surrounding the Matlovich case? Hardly. Not only did the hearings demonstrate that the congenital theory of homosexuality is rapidly gaining ground again, but the government's attorney actually invoked the 19th century remedy. "Sergeant Matlovich," he asked, "would you sign a contract never to practice homosexuality again?" Matlovich blanched in disbelief—then declined.

On the fourth day of the testimony Dr. Wardell Pomeroy, Kinsey's associate and co-author, took the stand. A man of less intellectual brilliance than John Money, Pomeroy's presence— warm, rumpled, grandfatherly—was altogether more benign. His testimony coincided with Money's on many counts—but was most provocative when it did not. The two agreed on much: that Matlovich the individual was stable, bright and self-assured; that the great majority of homosexuals did not wish to "convert" heterosexuals; that they are not prone to "molest" children; that they stand up as well (or badly) as anyone else under pressure.

When asked whether they viewed homosexuality as "unnatural" or "immoral," both men concurred that the terms had to be clarified before the question could be considered. "Strictly speaking," Money said, "anything that occurs in nature is 'natural'—and homosexuality is recorded among all primates." He aptly redefined "morality" as "ideology"—the value set and rules of behavior that characterize a given culture at a given time. "In our civilization since Christianity," he conceded, "we've chosen to define homosexuality as immoral," but "society is now in the process of making up its mind whether this longstanding stigma any longer makes sense—just as it has recently made up its mind to take mad people out of dungeons and to stop treating lefthandedness as a disease." (Another witness, Michael Valente, Professor of Religious Studies at Seton Hall University, testified to the shift currently taking place within the churches themselves; not only are they moving away — at a glacial pace — from the view that homosexuality is immoral, but away from the Augustinian/Thomist tradition which holds that all sex is tainted with evil, the evil merely counteracted—not nullified—when the partners intend procreation.)

Pomeroy amplified on possible definitions of "normalcy." The statistical norm simply means "what is common"—what more than half the people do. By that standard—using the familiar Kinsey finding that about 40 percent of all adult American males have had a homosexual experience to orgasm—male homosexuality is on the borderline of "normalcy" (although Pomeroy now thinks the 40 percent figure may have been too high, at least in 1948). If we use as our gauge, "What do we as mammals do?" then the verdict on homosexuality is "normal"—since it is "ubiquitous" among mammals. According to our Judeo-Christian cultural values and legal definitions, homosexuality is judged to be abnormal—but both attitudes and laws are changing.

The Money/Pomeroy approach to the questions of "normalcy" and "morality," I would have thought, would strike most reasonable or reasonably well informed people as so obvious as to be banal. So I thought, that is, until I started reading some of the reasonable, well informed press commentary on the hearings. To take only two (prominent) examples: Edwin A. Roberts Jr. in *The National Observer* and William Safire in *The New York Times* have written columns which all at once express sympathy for Matlovich the individual, declare the Air Force misguided in not retaining him, and make pronouncements about "normalcy" that exude all the confidence and most of the prejudices of the Council of Constantinople (381 A.D.).

"The acts that homosexuals indulge in," Roberts writes, "confound the natural purpose and structure of sex." If among "acts" he wants to include kissing, fellatio and anal intercourse, a fair number of Roberts' heterosexual friends should be keeping their eye out for notices of excommunication. Safire, in his column, is not a whit less confidently categorical: "Homosexuality is a sin ... to practice it is to break all moral codes." To men so parochial and ethnocentric, it's probably futile to point out the high incidence of homosexuality recorded in the historical and anthropological literature—the conclusion, for example, of the anthropologists Clellan S. Ford and Frank A. Beach that 64% of the societies they surveyed regarded homosexuality as a normal variable. The information would make as much impression as the news that ancient Greece also had a "moral code."

Since both Roberts and Safire have publicly declared that they advocate civil rights for gay people, I shudder at the likely sentiments of those who regularly lobby and vote against bills which would extend those rights. At one point during his trial Matlovich exclaimed, "It's hearts we have to change!" Alas, no expert has yet found the lobe specific for heart-change, nor even the endocrine gland that bathes it.

In one area, as I said, Pomeroy and Money disagreed in their testimony. A critical area, involving the central question, "When and how does sexual orientation become fixed and to what degree can it thereafter be changed?" Money claimed to have found "a great deal of evidence" to support the view that prenatal hormones play a significant role in "predisposing postnatal sexual behavior." Pomeroy said he has found almost none. Neither man was pressed during the hearings for details, but Money did point to research on pregnant women under stress as indicating one way that hormonal imbalances could be created and the child's later sexual orientation affected.

But as Naomi Weisstein, professor of psychology at the State University of New York at Buffalo and herself engaged in basic brain research, pointed out to me when we talked over Money's statement, almost all women (and most men) in this culture are under considerable stress much of the time. What critical density has to be reached before which specific behavioral results can be predicted? And what other hormonal levels—and behavior—are or are not affected? Not only is the stress variable difficult to isolate and measure, but even were it possible to do so, we would still have to explain why so many "stressful" pregnancies apparently produce heterosexual offspring.

It also needs to be noted that hormonal research is in its infancy. Because the available data are minimal and contradictory, dogmatic statements about the effect of hormones on behavior are suspect. Besides, hormone levels in a given individual seem to vary according to environmental circumstances; a study of American soldiers in Vietnam, for example, showed a sharp drop in testosterone levels. We are apparently dealing with a fluctuating process, not a fixed state. As Tripp has written in *The Homosexual Matrix,* "the idea that definite chemical substances might account for homosexuality incorrectly assumes that heterosexual and homosexual responses are discrete and that they differ in some fundamental way. On one level, it might be easy to postulate such differences—but not differences which would be compatible with how easily a homosexual response can develop and can coexist with heterosexuality." To add the words of another student of endocrinology: "What is really needed is for some good, controlled studies in man—or some well deserved silence in the absence of them." In the interim, Pomeroy's skepticism seems warranted.[2]

Which is not to preclude the possibility that subsequent ex-
periments may establish a significant or even controlling role for
prenatal hormones in programming postnatal sexual behavior. Nor
does such a possibility, as I see it, pose any necessary threat to gay
people (as many seem to feel). The possible discovery that hormones,
or other aspects of our biochemical and genetic inheritance, may be
responsible in whole or part for establishing sexual orientation,
carries no automatically negative judgment. That is, if—and it's a big
"if" in a culture as insistent as ours (despite rhetoric to the contrary)
on homogeneity—"differences" are not equated with "deficiencies."

One reason gay people—and women and blacks, too—have been
so distrustful of the current resurgence of interest in "innate"
differences, is their awareness that in the past such "discoveries"—the
homosexual's presumed inability to whistle and spit, the female's
presumed lack of interest in sex, the blacks' presumed smaller cranial
capacity—have been spawned not by science (as claimed) but by
ideology, by the need to justify and extend the existing patterns of
power. Knowing the repressive uses to which "scientific" findings
have been put in the past, many gay people have understandably
decided that the safest tack for the present is to refuse to be drawn into
any discussion of the "causes" of homosexuality.

I myself feel that stance is neither safe nor wise. Even if we grant
that scientific discoveries do emerge from a particular social context,
it doesn't and needn't follow that they must always be put to
repressive uses. Even if scientific inquiry often has reflected and
served the interests of those already in control of social resources, it's
difficult intellectually to justify a demand for an end to scientific
inquiry *per se*. To do so would put us in the company of those who
brought on the Scopes trial.

What we (gays, women, blacks, *et. al.*) can do is play a double
watchdog role—point out, first, that subjective assumptions significantly influence scientific findings and the use to which they are put;
and second, continue to insist that "differences," if cultivated rather
than suppressed, are a potential source of personal and social
enrichment.

That watchdog role needs to be maintained not only against the
biological view of sexual behavior currently gaining in popularity,
but also against the older environmentalist position which itself
continues to sprout new variations. Pomeroy, for example, reported
during his testimony on research currently in progress on the "play
groups" of pre-adolescent boys, research which he thinks may

demonstrate *one* way homosexuality becomes established. According to this view, when a boy is excluded from his play group because of, say, poor coordination, he may develop an erotic interest in the very group that excludes him.

It is as easy, and necessary, to be skeptical of this latest wrinkle on the environmentalist side of the argument as of the biological—easier, since nurture theory has held sway for so long, been used so destructively and, recently, been challenged so sharply. The inadequacies, for example, of the "binding mother/absent father" theory of male homosexuality most closely associated with Drs. Irving Bieber and Charles Socarides, have lately become so apparent that the theory has been all but relegated to the dump heap—though not in time to save a generation of parents from disabling guilt and a generation of sons from the tortures of the talking cure.

Unlike Drs. Bieber and Socarides, Wardell Pomeroy is neither homophobic nor judgmental. His research is worth noting, not to recommend or disparage it but only to demonstrate that the search for the "causes" of homosexuality continues unabated on both sides of the nature/nurture controversy. And does so with infinitely more zeal than has ever characterized any investigation into the origins of homophobia—or heterosexuality. In this last regard Naomi Weisstein suggests (as has Dr. Jean Lipman-Blumen) we look to the fact that in our culture women have long been deprecated; it may thus be *natural* for men to grow up erotically and emotionally drawn to people of their own gender. Starting from this perspective, what would need explaining is why and how some men do *not* become homosexual, why and how some men surmount the serious psychological obstacles the culture places in the way of developing respectful and loving feelings toward women.

In any case, where John Money feels "that by adulthood, we don't have the potential any longer to be other than what we by then are," Pomeroy believes that sexual orientation is never wholly fixed—that within limits, the range of our erotic interests can be changed at almost any point in the life cycle. And the possibility for change, he believes, is in direct proportion not to the individual's age but to the degree he or she accepts the sexual orientation already dominant. In elaborating that view during his testimony, Pomeroy referred to the familiar Kinsey scale of 0 to 6—0 designating an exclusive heterosexual, 6 an exclusive homosexual, the others some mix of bisexual experience. Pomeroy believes it's impossible for a 6 to ever become a 0, or vice versa. And he wryly recalled that he had long ago challenged those psychoanalysts and behavioral therapists who claim "cures" involving total transformation to produce a single such case. The challenge has never been taken up.

Short of such a complete reversal in erotic patterns, however, Pomeroy believes that considerable realignment is possible: a 0 can become a 5, a 6 can become a 1. It is, as he put it, like adding right-handed dexterity to left-handedness—not switching completely from one to the other. But to accomplish that, one must first be comfortable with left-handedness; the degree of self-acceptance about what one already is, directly affects the ability to become something more. A heterosexual man disassociated from his sexuality can be compulsive about proving and re-proving that he is, indeed, "all man." In that state of mind, obsessed on inadequacy, he is not receptive to other internal impulses.

In listening to Pomeroy, I was reminded of the number of gay men who have told me that since coming out they've developed—for the first time in their lives—erotic interest in women. I'm reminded, too, of the number of women I know who, after becoming active feminists, adopted a bi- or homo-sexual lifestyle. My own anecdotal evidence has recently had some indirect statistical confirmation. In their book *Male Homosexuals,* Martin Weinberg and Colin Williams, research sociologists at the Institute for Sex Research, have concluded that gay men who are publicly "out" are less rigid, fixated and anxious—have fewer inhibitions of all kinds—than those who remain closeted. When fear and shame occupy the core, there isn't much energy available for exploring the periphery. Being constantly armed and at attention doesn't exactly inspire others to make friendly advances, or oneself to receive them.

Needless to say, all such "findings" by sexologists should be taken with a ton of salt. Societies typically tend to produce "expert opinion" that clarifies and consolidates already acceptable assumptions about how the world works. Though specialists usually view themselves as pioneers driven by "the need to know," fearlessly exploring the frontiers of Truth, the typical role they play is to confirm, not challenge dominant social attitudes. Only the greatest in each generation—often to their own surprise, sometimes contrary to their own expectations—re-examine experience in a sufficiently original way to unsettle familiar notions. (Even they, it could be argued, are responding to social cues—to the microcosmic ones, those needs in the culture so new and tentative that they elude all but the most sensitive antennae). Moreover, it's only with the passage of time that we can distinguish with any confidence between approaches that marked a genuine passage to the "newness" and those that—however novel the packaging—serve essentially to rationalize existing arrangements.

At this confused moment in time, we can confidently say only that growing numbers of Americans no longer find serviceable the traditional formulas used to categorize sexual behavior and the conventional morality used to judge it. We can also say that new—in at least the minimal sense of not having been recently fashionable—explanations and norms have begun to assert themselves. What is much less clear is why the argument from biology—one among several competing views—has jumped to sudden prominence; why, despite the paucity of evidence, the theory of the importance of prenatal hormonal influence on postnatal sexual orientation has captured so much attention and allegiance. If, as I think, it's not a case of the theory persuading through the sheer weight of evidence, then how else do we account for its growing appeal? By looking at the set of values that would be confirmed if the biological view triumphed.

To step back a bit:

Until recently we have—perhaps more than any people in history—stressed our ability to shape our destiny according to whatever design we deemed desirable. This has been true of us at least since the decline of Calvinism (with its emphasis on pre-destination and man's *in*ability)—a decline completed by the end of the 18th century but probably underway from the day of the first settlements, when it seemed, in this vast solitude of space, that man could indeed start anew, unimpeded or regulated by previous rules. Certainly during all of the 19th century and for most of the 20th, it seemed axiomatic that "we" (meaning white males) could become whatever we wished to become. Neither human history (the accumulated force of tradition) nor human biology (the genetic givens) was seen as a significant counterweight to human will. Divine Intention did, to be sure, carry weight; but in sending us out to people an "empty" continent, He had made manifest *our* specialness and *His* decision to renovate the world. We have thus been, through time, the most optimistic—and most petulant—of people; convinced of our birthright to do as we pleased, we have treated any effort to thwart our will as an affront to Nature. That frame of reference has shifted dramatically in the last decade—most notably under the hammer blow of our defeat in Vietnam, most recently [1975] under the prolonged insecurity of an economic recession. We've lost confidence not merely in our ability to "renovate the world" but to control our individual lives. As a result, the conviction that change is a difficult process, and radical change a dangerous one, may have greater currency in our society at present than at any previous time in our history. And as judged by the emergence of a movement like Werner Erhard's training institute, "est", many are now willing to reaffirm Dr. Pangloss's vision: Whatever is, is right.

It's comforting to be granted respite from that relentless American injunction to "arise anew," to transform ourselves yet again in response to yet another set of social dicta about what is optimal behavior. Both John Money and Wardell Pomeroy, despite their different emphases, are encouraging us—all of us, regardless of sexual orientation—to be whatever we are rather than to become what someone else tells us is desirable. Which is to say, both are on the side of self-acceptance—and diversity. This is a humane shift in emphasis, a shift away from an inflated sense of self-mastery and from a demeaning conformity to social expectations. It may well mark a profound passage in national consciousness: an end to our inordinate confidence in Will and to our missionary zeal to homogenize the planet; a belated and welcome dilution of American arrogance.

As with every passage, there's some sense of loss, and foreboding. When Matlovich heard that the verdict had gone against him, he held up a Bicentennial 50-cent piece with the inscription "200 years of freedom." "Not yet," he said, "maybe some day, but not yet." Can we believe "some day" might still arrive if we lose *entire* confidence in human capacity for self-transformation? The question should be considered without reference to the immediate issue of sexual orientation—for it transcends it.[3]

The New York Times Magazine, November 9, 1975

Notes

1. A trend greatly accelerated since this article's publication, as exemplified in the recently emergent school of sociobiology. Still more recently, a counter-reformation has begun to assert itself. (See especially Stephen Jay Gould, *The Mismeasure of Man* (Norton, 1981); and R.C. Lewontin, Steven Rose & Leon J. Kamin, *Not in Our Genes* (Pantheon: 1982)). Even the granddaddy of sociobiology, Edward O. Wilson, in his latest book, *Biophilia* (1984), seems to have modified his position on the extent to which human behavior is "innate", pre-natally determined.

For more on sociobiology, see William Paul, James D. Weinrich, John C. Gonsiorek and Mary E. Hotvedt, *Homosexuality: Social, Psychological and Biological Issues* (Sage: 1982).

2. See Noretta Koetge, "The Natural Causes of Homosexuality: Philosophic and

Scientific Inquiry," *Journal of Homosexuality,* special issue, volume 6, no. 4, (summer 1981); and also John Gagnon's brilliant review of *Sexual Preference* by Alan Bell, Martin Weinberg and Sue Kiefer Hammersmith, (*New York Times,* December 13, 1981). For more on the debate within the American Psychiatric Association which led to the vote to drop homosexuality from the "disease" category, see Ronald Bayer, *Homosexuality and American Psychiatry,* (Basic Books, 1981). As regards the latest turn in the cycle of biological explanations for homosexuality, see the report in the *New York Times,* September 21, 1984 of a study done at SUNY, Stony Brook, about a "special" hormonal response pattern purportedly found in homosexual men.

3. For an update on the status of gay people in the military, see the article by Steven Kulieke in the *Advocate* on the Dronenberg case (September 18, 1984).

POSTSCRIPT

When the article on Matlovich appeared in The New York Times Sunday Magazine *on November 9, 1975, it inaugurated a spirited dispute, with particularly angry responses coming from the two psychiatrists—Dr. Irving Bieber and Dr. Charles W. Socarides— whom I had singled out as tenacious supporters of untenable views. The* Times, *on Dec. 28, 1975, reprinted the exchange of letters between Dr. Bieber and me, but not several others which seemed to me more weighty in their insights and arguments. Accordingly, I'm reprinting them here.*

A.

In just two sentences, Martin Duberman ("The Case of the Gay Sergeant," Nov. 9) made three misstatements about my work, clumsily attacked psychoanalysis and attempted an inept, *ad hominem* thrust against Dr. Charles Socarides and me.

He confused data with theory and inaccurately referred to our findings on the fathers of male homosexuals. A research team of 10, including myself, found that the fathers were mostly detached and hostile, not absent. Had Mr. Duberman read our book he would know that, of the 106 homosexuals studied, only three had absent fathers. He would also know that not one subject had had a loving, constructive father. In 1969 Evans and, independently, Snortum *et al.,* using our questionnaire to study samples of nonpatient homosexuals, found the same parental configuration. Over the past 12 years I have personally interviewed more than 900 homosexual men, and all the information gathered continues to support our original findings. The data are incontrovertible, though some colleagues have differing theories as to causal variables. I have concluded that given a good father-son relationship no boy develops a homosexual pattern.

Mr. Duberman has erroneously associated Dr. Socarides with our study. As it happens, he worked independently and did not know of our research until it was published as a book. Dr. Socarides is not affiliated with our sponsoring organization, the Society of Medical Psychoanalysts.

The view that our study has been relegated to the dump heap is wishful thinking. It won a research award from the American Psychiatric Association in 1964, was later translated into Spanish, is now being translated into Italian, and Basic Books, Inc., has just issued another 1,000 copies—developments that do not suggest an ignominious end.

As to psychoanalysis, he warns against "the tortures of the talking cure." If he got that idea from an unfortunate personal experience, he would do well to give it another try. I would gladly recommend any number of competent, painless analysts.

Mr. Duberman refers to Dr. Socarides and me as homophobic, a description he would likely attach to anyone who views homosexuality as other than a variant of normal sexual behavior. This is a typical *ad hominem* technique when avoiding a more cogent engagement with substantive issues. Mr. Duberman is a historian, a pursuit that does not qualify him to make authoritative judgments in another field where he is strictly a layman. A homosexual adaptation does not, in itself, provide the background and training required of experts in the biology and psychology of sexuality.

IRVING BIEBER, M.D. New York City

Martin Duberman replies:

Dr. Bieber is being deliberately naive. He knows perfectly well that "binding mother/absent father" has become standard shorthand for describing the theory of homosexuality with which he and Dr. Socarides are identified. "Binding" and "absent" are umbrella terms—like "homosexuality"—that should indeed be broken down into their component parts when intricacies of definition are under discussion; that was not, however, the purpose of my essay. Bieber is being equally evasive in stating that I "erroneously associated Dr. Socarides with our study." I did not say in the article that the two men worked together on the same book. I said that they are associated with a common set of findings—namely, that a particular family configuration will produce homosexual children. Like Dr. Socarides, Bieber continues to insist that those findings are "incontrovertible." To which I can only say that he must have given up reading the medical journals after he won that prize.

Bieber feels that a "layman" has no right to express an opinion on the subject. Who are the laymen? Leaving aside the legion of fellow specialists who have challenged Bieber's data, it is surely time to ask whether gay women and men might not themselves qualify as "experts" on their own lives. Perhaps Dr. Bieber remembers the time when white liberals—always with the best intentions—tried to explain to blacks the meaning of their own experience. Perhaps he also remembers the aftermath.

It's good of Dr. Bieber to recommend a "painless" analyst for me. I assume he means the kind that gives gas. I've had several, thanks. A dozen years of inhaling the fumes of "disease theory," "character disorder," *et. al.,* did quite a job on my ability to breathe. Having left the consultation room four years ago, my lungs are now clearing up nicely—in part, I might add, because of a therapist who concentrated on helping me to understand, rather than to berate, myself.

Another of Dr. Bieber's kind offers is still fresh in my memory. When he and I debated the subject of male homosexuality several years ago before an audience of college counselors, he made the same statement I find repeated in his letter: he has never known a "subject" (the choice of words is not unimportant) who "had had a loving, constructive father." An undergraduate took the microphone to say that he was gay and had had just such a father. Clearly used to such "distorted self-evaluations" during his long clinical practice, Bieber offered to give the young man a proper battery of tests if he would present himself at the office. At which point I grabbed the microphone and, in an equally kind spirit, offered to test Bieber for advanced symptoms of homophobia if he would present himself at *my* office (though I could not promise a painless analysis). The doctor seemed startled, which I took to be a considerable advance. The offer still holds.

B.

To The Editor:

I write as an "expert" witness who never got to the stand in the "trial" of Leonard Matlovich.

His attorneys, Hewman and Addlestone, asked me to testify. We developed a line of defense about how sexism is the issue in whether Matlovich should or should not be permitted to retain his job. I was to give testimony about how destructive it is for individuals, for institutions and for the society as a whole when persons are locked into sex roles and are not permitted to leave them. Is not the crux of the crime of Leonard Matlovich that he did not act like a "proper man"? (The armed services apparently still honor men who kill other men, but punish men who love other men.)

I was to illustrate, with examples, how, in recent years, gender stereotyping is being changed in all aspects of our lives. The judge ruled my testimony irrelevant while ruling relevant that of sex experts John Money and Wardell Pomeroy. Actually, it is irrelevant to theorize whether homosexuality is caused by a pregnant mother's reading "The Well of Loneliness," a childhood experience of the individual, or the free choice of an adult.

What is relevant is that as long as women and men have their destinies shaped by their anatomy there will be little liberty, little justice, for any of us—whether gay or straight.

KAREN DE CROW
President, National Organization for Women

C.

To the Editor:
As a social critic and historian Martin Duberman has every right to attack our "traditional sexual formulas" and the "conventional morality used to evaluate them." However, he ventures into an area beyond his expertise and irresponsibly misleads the public when he consigns the most modern psychoanalytic research and findings to the "dump heap", dismissing them as both "homophobic" and "judgmental". He thus disserves the very cause he claims to espouse: that of promoting understanding of the homosexual. He creates despair in homosexuals who wish to change, to say nothing of the untold misery and anguish he produces in their families.

To lessen the damage done by such a travesty of reporting it is vital that his erroneous comments be corrected as a matter of professional responsibility. The public is misled enough by "pro-homosexual" publications; certainly the worldwide community reached by the *New York Times* deserves reliable and up to date scientific information. To do otherwise is to stand silent under this assault as if our profession is divested of all right to use the powers of its mind in its own defense.

This writer was the first psychiatrist in America to ask for the elimination of persecutory laws against the homosexual before a national meeting of physicians (A.M.A. Convention, San Francisco, 1967). A year later in my book *The Overt Homosexual* I introduced the concept that in all obligatory homosexuals (those who must carry out these acts out of inner necessity, in contrast to homosexual acts carried out for deliberate and conscious motivations) there has been an inability to make the psychological progression from the mother-child unity of earliest infancy to individuation (pre-oedipal theory of causation). The significant incidence of homosexuality is due to the necessity for all human beings to undergo the separation-individuation phase of early childhood which is decisive for gender identification. A substantial proportion of children fail to successfully complete this developmental process and, therefore, are unable to form a healthy sexual identity in accordance with their anatomical and biological capacities.

This position has been documented by a substantially large number of cases of obligatory homosexual patients (both my own and those of my colleagues) who have undergone psychoanalysis. This is not an old theory; it is a new one, taught in most of the psychoanalytic and psychiatric institutes throughout America and Europe. My modern, not old, views were recently published in the new edition of the *American Handbook of Psychiatry* (Basic Books, 1975) as the definitive findings on homosexuality, along with other authoritative contributions from the leading psychiatrists in the United States. Hardly Duberman's "dump heap". From 1970 to 1972 I was the Chairman of the Task Force on Homosexuality of the New York County District Branch of the American Psychiatric Association. The conclusions of this Task Force were published in 1974 as representing the combined views of 11 experts representing the major medical centers in New York City and the most advanced knowledge available on this subject. This group unanimously recommended decriminalization of homosexual acts between consenting adults and simultaneously stated: "1. Homosexuality is experientially determined due to a faulty family constellation. (Some few homosexuals come from an institutional background but they present special problems). 2. Homosexuality represents a disorder of sexual development and does not fall within the range of normal sexual behavior. 3. Between one-third to one-half of male homosexuals who seek treatment become exclusively heterosexual as a result of psycho-analytically oriented psychotherapy, including those who had formerly been exclusively homosexual."

It is vital to realize a fundamental point: the diagnosis of homosexuality and its understanding cannot be self-made, imposed by jurists, articulated by clergy, or speculated about by social scientists and historians. Psychoanalysts beginning with Freud have been in the vanguard of those protecting the homosexual against persecution. They believe that as obligatory homosexuality cannot be considered to be a legal issue, so it cannot be viewed as a problem of morality. As with psychosis and neurosis it cannot be regarded as a consequence of sinfulness or a manifestation of evil spirits occupying the body. Only in the consultation room does the homosexual reveal himself and his world. No other data, statistics or statements can be accepted as setting forth the true nature of homosexuality. All other sources, like Duberman's, may be heavily weighted by face saving devices or rationalizations, or if they issue from lay bodies, lack the scientific and medical background to support their views. The best that can be said for the well intentioned but unqualified observer is that he is misguided because he does not have and cannot apply those techniques of psychoanalytic investigation which would make it possible to show the deep underlying clinical disorder and to evaluate the emotional patterns, causative processes all of a psychological nature, an interpersonal events in the life of the true homosexual.

DR. CHARLES W. SOCARIDES, Associate Prof. of Psychiatry, Albert Einstein College of Medicine, New York City

Martin Duberman replies:

Dr. Socarides' letter is such a splendid specimen of his legendary arrogance that I'm tempted to let it speak for itself—especially since he's proven himself impervious to evidence (now approaching flood-tide) that challenges his cherished assumptions. Still, I can't resist responding to a few of his more astonishing statements.

He may consider his own work "the most modern psycho-analytic research and findings," but his colleagues do not agree. The American Psychiatric Association, over Socarides' bitter protest, has removed homosexuality from the category of "illness" to which he has tried to consign it. The APA, it should be noted, consists of those very experts in whose hands Socarides insists we leave all discussion of homosexuality. The whole issue of who qualifies as an "expert" deserves an extended discussion not possible here. But it's worth remembering that it was the "experts" in foreign affairs, with their presumptive monopoly on insight, who got us into Vietnam. And it is the same pervasive deference to "expertise" that causes people to turn over to others the power to run their own lives—to the "qualified" politicians, industrialists, priests, et al.

One can sympathize with Dr. Socarides' anguish at having his views rejected by the only body of peers he will deign to recognize. I happen to sympathize more with those gay men and women whose suffering and mistreatment have been compounded by his characterization of them as incomplete human beings. True, Socarides came out against persecutory laws: He does not believe in needlessly abusing the already crippled. For taking that stand, the man actually seems to think gay people owe him thanks.

The bulk of Socarides' letter is given over to a re-statement of his now discredited views. He remains right about one thing: those views are still repeated in textbooks and taught in medical schools. But, fortunately, in ever-diminishing numbers. I think the majority of behavioral scientists would quite literally laugh at Socarides' characterization of his own work as "the definitive findings on homosexuality." As almost everyone recognizes, the field is in total disarray. Alan P. Bell, Senior Research Psychologist at the Institute for Sex Research, has with commendable honesty entitled his recent survey of the literature, *Research on Homosexuality: Back to the Drawing Board.* Bell points out that the insistence of men like Socarides that "only in the consultation room does the homosexual reveal himself and his world," is precisely why psychoanalytical findings have proven so distorted. The narrow clinical sample has given such work, in Bell's phrase, "a dreamlike quality."

If Dr. Socarides was not so scornful of interdisciplinary effort, of the work of "social scientists and historians," he might long since have understood that the "faulty family constellation" to which he rigidly adheres as the explanation for homosexual development, simply does not test out cross-culturally. (It does not even test out—as the sociologist Evelyn Hooker and her associates demonstrated years ago—as an accurate description of the family backgrounds of those gay people who have never presented themselves for "treatment"— which is to say, the vast majority of gay people). On the bare chance that Dr. Socarides might want to catch up with some of this research, I'd suggest as a starter Wainwright Churchill's *Homosexual Behavior Among Males: A Cross-Cultural and Cross-Species Investigation.*
It's a basic, perhaps over-emphatic text that one would ordinarily hesitate to recommend to an "expert." But in Socarides' case, where cultural deprivation has been so severe, it is wise to begin with elementary remedial work.

D.

Gentlepeople: In his article on the Matlovich hearing, Martin Duberman has gone astray on two counts, in my view.

First, he has built up an elaborate theory of significant change in social and cultural attitudes, based upon the chance choice by Matlovich's lawyers of Dr. John Money as a witness. Dr. Money was chosen (in part at my suggestion), on the basis of a complex group of considerations, of which geography (travel expenses to Hampton) was not the least, and which render badly misplaced the heavy weight given to his views in Duberman's article. There seems to be minimal additional evidence to support the shift in attitude postulated by Duberman, with its more fundamental consequences.

Second, the question of the cause of homosexuality (and of heterosexuality) is totally irrelevant to any of the issues in the Matlovich case (or to anything else of any practical value). Even if homosexuality and heterosexuality were completely free, voluntary, purely intellectual choices, made in adulthood and changeable at will, Matlovich would still have a right, as an American citizen, to serve as a Homosexual, in his Air Force, and the fundamental issues raised by the case would not be changed one iota. (Nor would they be changed were all the arguments alleging the immorality of homosexuality to be granted, since an American citizen has a right to behave immorally by any set of standards, without incurring official disadvantage thereby, and, in fact, is under no legal or other formal obligation even to be cognizant of any standards of morality, even of his own).

The objection of Gays into research into the causation of homosexuality/heterosexuality is not (as misrepresented by Duberman) that such discussion is "unsafe", but that, being utterly irrelevant to solution of the real problem (the cause and cure of homophobia) such research diverts effort, resources and funds in woefully short supply from that problem into useless, non-productive research having only academic value.

DR. FRANKLIN E. KAMENY (an early and prominent gay activist, and, in 1975, President of the Mattachine Society of Washington D.C.)

Martin Duberman replies:

On Dr. Kameny's first point: my view that there has been a shift in our culture towards biological explanations for human behavior and that this shift reflects deep disillusion with the possibility (or even desirability) of social change, predated my coverage of the Matlovich hearings. I based it not on the "chance" appearance of Dr. Money at the trial, but on what I have seen and read over several years; for example, the increased emphasis on congenital factors in the research reported in such journals as *Archives of Sexual Behavior* and *The Journal of Sex Research*. Dr. Money's testimony did exemplify this attitudinal shift and that is why I chose to describe his views at some length. In any case, Dr. Kameny gives no evidence to challenge my theory. He merely says that it's "elaborate." Well yes; is that supposed to be a synonym for "wrong"?

On his second point: the question of the causes of sexual behavior may be "totally irrelevant" to Dr. Kameny's concerns, but that does not automatically make them so for everyone else's. This is not to imply that Kameny's concerns—which I share—are less important. None of us should be issuing papal bulls about the "acceptable" parameters of inquiry or what is or is not a real issue.

E.

Letter from Dr. Willard Dalrymple (head of the Princeton University Health Department) to me, December 31, 1975:

... In general, not only do I agree with your point of view but feel that you had the best of the argument [with Bieber]. Nevertheless there were two points on which I felt you went too far...

First, the matter of family constellation in homosexually oriented men. My own point of view is to be (honestly) agnostic as to how adult human beings develop their sexual preferences; I would guess the process to be multi-factorial, with the pressures of society towards "straightness" being very important. Nevethess, while I too know of homosexuals who seem to have excellent relationships with their fathers, it does seem significant and important to me that an unusually large number of homosexuals did not have, and seem very frank about it. ... Would you not agree that in many lives a poor father-son relationship somehow nudges their owners towards homosexual preference? Not as the sole factor, but as a variably important one.

Second, your phrase, "the tortures of the talking cure" makes me uncomfortable ... my patients seem not to have found it torturing.... Perhaps what you meant is something of the following. "If the therapist takes it as a political or dogmatic stance that homosexuality is by definition sickness and can, indeed must, be cured by talking, while the client (patient, victim) accedes because of pressures of society, etc., then nothing can be accomplished, the process tortures, and the therapist in essence is exploiting the client not only for money but for egotistical defense of his intellectual position." That I would agree with wholeheartedly. I wonder what you think of that....

MY REPLY (January 18, 1976):

You raise two extremely important points—and in the thoughtful, supportive way I wish characterized more such discussions. . . .

As for family constellation, I am, like you, an agnostic. Our personal experience dovetails: of the hundreds of homosexual men I've known, I have the clear impression that the large majority had "poor relationships" with their fathers. Having said that much, I have to add a number of qualifications. My sample (like Bieber's) is largely clinical—meaning, most of my friends (like all of his patients) have have been in therapy, internalized its values, parrotted back the formula response *the therapist* first suggested about the nature of the father/son relationship. This may be yet another generational difference: the younger homosexual men I've known are much less ready to describe their relationships with their fathers as "poor"—in part perhaps for political reasons; in part because they may have a different definition of what a good relationship is; in part because they are confident in their feelings of filial love and support. And there is mounting "scientific" (I always put that is quotes!) evidence to support them—the work of Evelyn Hooker and her colleagues being the most prominent. Besides, even if Bieber is right—that is, even if he has isolated *the* significant variable—what he has done with his findings would remain wholly reprehensible. By which I mean, he has equated difference with disease, assumed that a particular majoritarian configuration can be equated with "health" and suggested that all those who deviate from the statistical norm should be branded as lesser beings and encouraged to conform. Just as other "scientists" have done the same, for generations, in regard to women and blacks. But I needn't harrangue you—it's clear from your letter you agree with me.

As to your second point, I can only say that I wish I'd had your formulation on "the tortures of the talking cure" at hand earlier—it expresses my feelings exactly. I'm well aware that there are therapists (I was briefly and profitably in treatment with one such) who are not imprisoned by the Bieber/Socarides dogma, who do not approach their patients with a heterosexual agenda in mind from the beginning, who do not automatically brand deviance as disability. I'm aware, too, that this number is growing—and rapidly, if my antennae are tuned in. It gives me hope for a more humane society. But I don't think any of us should under-estimate the possibility of sharp reversal. I think here with horror of the fate of the homophile movement in Nazi Germany— the murder of hundreds of thousands of homosexuals in the concentration camps, the total destruction of Magnus Hirschfeld's Institute for Sex Research; all following on a period of changing attitudes in regard to sexual behavior and of increasing "permissiveness"....

My second letter to Dalrymple, later that same day:

I'd no sooner sent off my etter to you, than I realized I'd omitted what may be the most important of all the qualifications to the Bieber theory—namely, the evidence accumulating from primate studies and from anthropology. From what I can gather, recent(i.e. younger, less prejudiced) researchers into animal behavior find homosexuality all but universal; I myself would hesitate to make much of those findings simply because I distrust analogies between chimpanzees and human beings; but at the least, one can't help but wonder if all those gay chimps had "poor relationships" with their fathers. The same doubt enters as soon as one begins reading cross-cultural studies of homosexuality (e.g. Wainwright Churchill, *Homosexual Behavior Among Males*). The majority of "primitive" cultures studied (according to Ford and Beach) in some form and to some degree sanction or overtly encourage homosexuality among males. Yet family patterns are as varied in those cultures as is the degree to which homosexuality is institutionalized. Clearly, therefore, Bieber has not discovered a uniersal ariable—one that would apply to human behavior in other cultural contexts. To the extent that it does apply to our own culture, Bieber may have come up with exactly the wrong reasons. By which I mean: he (and others) have chosen to emphasize "malfunctions" in the father/son relationship as an "explanation" of homosexuality simply because they cannot face Freud's suggestion that we all have a bisexual capacity which society gradually breeds out of us. Not being able to face the implications of the naturalness of same gender sex, the Biebers are forced to explain its appearance as a function of unnaturalness (that is, a pattern of child rearing which does not conform to cultural expectations). Whereas what we perhaps might better be trying to "explain" is how (and why) the dominant pattern of familial relations in our culture manages to destroy the capacity of most children to enjoy sex with members of their own gender. In other words, the "problem" could be re-stated as: how did homophobia become central to our sexual ideology—and how can the majority of parents be taught to stop relating to their children in such a way as to diminish their affectional and sexual expressiveness?

THE ANITA BRYANT BRIGADE

Robert Hillsborough, aged 33, has been killed. A husky, gentle man, he lived in a small apartment in San Francisco's Mission District. As the newspaper accounts have it, he claimed he had only two ambitions in life: to work as a gardener and to live quietly with someone he loved. Two years ago he got a fulltime job as a city playground gardener and called himself "the happiest man in the world." Until recently he'd lived with Jerry Taylor and on the night of June 21 the two had gone out to discuss resuming their relationship. They stopped off at a local Whiz-Burger. In the parking lot a group of teenage toughs baited them with taunts of "Faggots! Faggots!" (initial provocation, if any, unknown; perhaps the two had dared to hold hands, had been seen kissing in their car). To avoid a confrontation, Hillsborough drove off. Four of the teenagers followed, caught him outside his apartment and stabbed him 15 times in the chest and face. He died within minutes.

Two weeks earlier, Anita Bryant won her spectacular victory in Dade County. She had told audience after audience that homosexuals were "an abomination to the Lord. I could tell you stories about these people," she said, "that would turn your stomach." I doubt that Anita Bryant will add the story of Robert Hillsborough to her repertoire.

Simple equations between her inflammatory rhetoric and Hillsborough's murder should be avoided. Homosexuals had been beaten, tortured and burned to death for centuries before Anita Bryant began her crusade. The Christian nations of the West have, perhaps, established the outstanding record for savagery, one that until recently has been suppressed or ignored. Today scholars—gay and otherwise—are beginning to document the sick and sordid tale. Louis Crompton, professor of English at the University of Nebraska, has come away from his research convinced that "genocide"—deliberate, systematic extermination—is not too strong a word to describe the historical record.

After Greco-Roman civilization—in which same gender love and lust had been esteemed and to some extent institutionalized—gave way to Judeo-Christianity, a period of some 1500 years ensued during which homosexual men and women were ostracized, mutilated and killed. "Justification" and penalties varied through time.[1] The sixth century Emperor Justinian blamed homosexuals for the natural disasters of plague and famine; the fourteenth century clergy linked them to sorcerers and "misbelievers"; the eighteenth centruy legal experts—notably Blackstone in his *Commentaries* of 1765-69—cited against them "the voice of nature and reason". The preferred form of punishment also changed; burning at the stake, an early favorite, gave way to stoning and castration. The Swiss, always noted for their intricate ingenuity, liked to cut off one limb at a time over a period of several days—a finger here, a leg there—until the lifeless trunk was eventually ready for the flames. In our own day, Hitler, that exemplar of modern technological impatience, utilized the more direct approach. In his concentration camps some 200,000 gay people (a figure documented by the American scholar, James Steakley and recently corroborated by the Austrian Lutheran Church) were put to death. Himmler, among others, publicly rejoiced in this successful "extermination of degenerates."[2]

And the record of our own country? We came on the scene a bit late to catch the homophobic bug at epidemic height; yet despite this—and limited population resources—the fledgling colonies managed sufficient ferocity to establish a legitimate claim to membership in the commonwealth of nations. As early as 1624, Virginia chalked up the execution of a ship's master, and the New Haven colony served up a notable first in world history when it prescribed the death penalty for lesbianism in 1656. The New England clergy debated "unnatural filthiness" (John Cotton's words) with the nuanced logic that had done so much to establish its theological pre-eminence. In 1642, as Governor William Bradford reports in his *History Of Plymouth Plantation,* three of the colony's most eminent divines carefully considered the question "What sodomitical acts are to be punished with death?" All three agreed that the Bible was final authority and that it ordained the death penalty for "carnal knowledge" between two men. But they were less confident or unanimous on certain fine points of doctrine: whether actual penetration needed to be established, or whether any "voluntary effusion of seed" caused by bodily contact, even without penetration, was itself sufficient grounds for execution. Opinion clustered towards the latter view and New England proceeded to its own series of executions, all the more admired for the conscientious theological exegesis which had preceded.

During this same period in New England, as Jonathan Katz has noted in *Gay American History,* "two heterosexual rapist-child-molesters got off with a fine and whipping; their offense was not found to be a capital one." Katz also notes that by the time of the American Revolution, "Thomas Jefferson and a group of liberal reformers suggested a revision of Virginia law eliminating the death penalty for sodomy—they proposed, instead, castration." So much for those who doubt that history is the story of progress.

Even today the United States may stand in contrast to much of the world in the loathing with which the majority continues to regard same-gender sex as "always wrong," even when between consenting adults in a monogamous, longstanding relationship that is, the kind of relationship which most closely approximates the official model of heterosexual normality). Until the last few years, the "always wrong" majority hovered around 70%—the same percentage that voted against the gay rights bill in Dade County. Recent polls suggest a decided shift in attitude may be in progress—especially among the young. As early as 1973, Daniel Yankelovich found that among noncollege youths between ages 16 and 25, only 47% felt that "relations between consenting homosexuals are morally wrong" (compared with 72% in his survey of 1969). With the onset after 1980 of the twin plagues of AIDS and Reaganism, anti-gay attitudes have taken on renewed vigor; moreover, the relatively enlightened young exert little moral authority and less political power.

Those who do control our public policies usually vary only in the degree to which they're afflicted with homophobia, though sometimes the politicians do seem to be in advance of their constituencies on the issue of gay rights. It was Dade County's elected officials who passed the original ordinance banning discrimination in jobs and housing based on sexual orientation; it was the citizenry, by a vote of more than 2 to 1, who rescinded that ordinance. This is hardly to say that our politicians can be counted on to lead and enlighten the public. During the Dade County struggle, Senator Alan Trask read *Leviticus* aloud in the state Senate, warning that "we must never pass a law that is contrary to the teachings of God." Governor Reuben Askew—he of the "liberal" reputation—went out of his way just before the climactic vote in Dade to announce publicly that he would not want a known homosexual teaching his children and that he has "never viewed the homosexual lifestyle as something that approached a constitutional right."

Sometimes when public officials do climb out on a limb, they rush to slide back down the trunk should their constituents make any move to shake it. In New York City a few years back, passage of a gay rights bill in the city council seemed assured—until pressure from the

Catholic hierarchy (and to a somewhat lesser extent from Orthodox Jewish rabbis) led to the sudden reversal of several critical votes. The church did its bit in Dade as well. A letter from Archbishop Coleman Carroll urging repeal of the ordinance was read aloud in Catholic churches on the Sunday preceding the referendum.

But the Catholic vote alone could not have provided Anita Bryant with her wide margin of victory. She was heavily supported as well by Protestant fundamentalists, the Cuban community, and a coalition of right wing activists who had worked together many times previously to block measures that "threatened the American Way"—busing, ERA, the public school ban on prayers, and liberalized abortion and marijuana laws.

What assumptions and fears bind together these antigay forces? Why would people of such seemingly disparate backgrounds, status and interests—a working class Cuban, say, a Baptist farm wife, a Catholic prelate, a wealthy advertising man—find a transcending commonality in homophobia? Are their stated, public reasons for opposing civil rights legislation for gay people their real reasons? Or are those reasons buried in some tangled web of inarticulate fear and illogic, where they are hidden from everyone—their authors as well as us, their object?

It makes me angry even to formulate such questions. The homophobes have done so little to understand us—and so much to misrepresent and harm us—that to treat their insulting simplicities as legitimate arguments and to dignify their smarmy psyches with a rational probe feels like an exercise in self-hatred—a smiling curtsy to the descending ax. Habits of "rational discourse" die hard.

Not that the stuff needed for such a discourse is even available. The serious research done to date on homophobia is less than piddling—itself an index to social science priorities. Despite vaunting claims to objectivity, most social scientists share the normative values of our culture; which means they've put infinitely more effort into elaborating "explanations" and "cures" for homosexuality than for homophobia. Recently there's been some slight shift in emphasis. The most authoritative work to date [1977] is probably that done by Professor Kenneth Sherrill of Hunter College. He has concluded that those who are against human rights for gay people cluster in the "most-bigoted" category on a wide variety of other issues as well. They are deeply racist and sexist, abhor nonconformity of any kind, fiercely reject all manifestations of the "sexual revolution" (feminism, abortion, pornography, extramarital sex, etc.), are patriotic to the point of xenophobia, and in general show marked fear of all that is "other" or "different." As Sherrill puts it, "it may not matter whether the old order is sexual or political or economic. New ideas may be threatening"—and especially to those middle-aged or older, with a low level of education, living in rural areas and from authoritarian family backgrounds.[3]

Anita Bryant and friends proudly lay claim to most of the values Sherrill describes; they insist, for example, that "women find their greatest fulfillment at home with the family." Yet the public arguments the Bryant-ites have resorted to in opposing civil rights for gay people have largely rested on other grounds. Not only have those arguments struck a deep chord in many Americans, but they seem to vibrate on an emotional frequency not susceptible to information or logic.

The official antigay argument clusters around surprisingly few points. Foremost is the issue of "immorality," the standards of judgment deriving from a literal (fundamentalist) reading of the Bible. One Baptist evangelist, echoing many others, has put the matter succinctly: "We are facing the Devil himself in these homosexuals." A state Senator, Marion Manning of Minnesota, has even managed a bizarre role reversal of victimizer and victim when he declares that gay people are a "threat to my personal rights, a threat to my religious beliefs."

The favorite citation accompanying such pronouncements is *Leviticus 18:22:* "And if a man also lie with mankind as he lieth with a woman, both of them have committed an abomination: they shall surely be put to death; their blood shall be upon them." But fundamentalist Christians seem unable to grasp the fact that interpretations of Holy Writ have, at the hands of mere mortals, undergone almost as many permutations as Supreme Court pronouncements on the Constitution—and in both cases, the most recent "truth" stands in direct contradiction to the official word that immediately preceded. As the Jesuit scholar John McNeill has recently pointed out in his book, *The Church and the Homosexual,* a number of contemporary Biblical scholars have become convinced that the "sin of Sodom" originally connoted "inhospitality," and its current equation with "homosexuality" is the accumulated result of centuries of garbled translations and corrupted texts. The point has been underscored in another recent study, *Human Sexuality: New Directions in American Catholic Thought,* commissioned by the

Catholic Theological Society of America. Its five authors are all eminent Catholics (two are priests, one a nun), yet they conclude that underlying the Catholic tradition that has judged homosexual acts as "against nature and hence gravely sinful, are not only a pre-scientific physiology and unhistorical interpretation of Scripture but also the Stoic conviction that procreation alone justifies the enjoyment and use of sexual pleasure."[4]

Try telling that to the fundamentalist marines. Biblical exegesis is not their strong point, nor scholarly findings among their sources of inspiration. For obvious reasons. To acknowledge recent Biblical scholarship would be tantamount to subverting their basic under-standing of the Universe; Galileo, it will be remembered, was not hailed as a liberator. For people like myself, who don't derive our moral principles from the Bible, theological debate is irrelevant. But for those who do—the vast majority of our countrymen, consciously or otherwise—it's fair to insist they at least be consistent, that they live in a manner comporting with their own literalist interpretation of biblical morality.

Yes, *Leviticus* condemns "sodomy." It also condemns swearing, covetousness, jealousy—and shaving[5]. Adulters, according to the same book, should be stoned to death. Fundamentalists are free to reject the view that ethics, like all spinoffs of the human mind, is subjective and changeable. They are free to insist that moral precepts are static, transcending time and culture, and free to insist that behavior conform to those precepts enunciated 2,000 years ago in the Bible. But they are not free to pick and choose among those precepts as to which ones they will follow. Not, that is, without opening themselves to the charge of hypocrisy. It is fair to expect that if biblical fundamentalists are going to follow the dictates of *Leviticus* to the literal letter, they will show equal nicety in adhering to the rest of the "original" (pre-exegetical) biblical code of behavior. Which means they will no longer break the Sabbath by attending movies or by joining bowling parties. That they will no longer accumulate worldly goods beyond providing for basic needs (one doubts Anita Bryant's $300,000 mansion will qualify). That the men among them will grow luxuriant beards and the women silken hair on their legs. That they will no longer engage in any sexual act other than missionary intercourse—and then only when procreation is the goal. Perhaps on one matter a little hypocrisy should be tolerated; since Kinsey has shown that more than half the male population has extramarital relations, we nonfundamentalists would not demand that adulterers be stoned to death in the streets. We, too, after all, are patriots: we do not wish to see the country decimated.

When not being denounced for offending against Heaven, gay people are excoriated for the baneful influence they exert on Earth. And especially on children. Here the indictment is in two parts: we proselytize subversive ideas and we serve as invidious role models. Anita "Save Our Children" Bryant has taken out full page ads to denounce gay people as recruiters, seducers and molesters of children.

This depiction of us as child molesters has probably been the most potent weapon in the antigay arsenal—and the most impervious to factual refutation. The clinical studies and statistics about the actual nature of the sexual abuse of children have been well publicized and are incontestable. All the studies agree that the vast majority of such cases involve offenses committed by heterosexual men against young girls. Vincent De Francis' *Sexual Abuse of Children* puts the matter beyond cavil. He estimates that of the 100,000 children sexually molested each year, 92% are female and 97% of their victimizers are male—thus making it statistically impossible for more than a minuscule fraction of child molestation cases to involve same-gender assault. But for whatever reason, the Bryantites have been impervious to these truths—perhaps because Americans have grown accustomed to regarding their offspring as mere extensions of themselves, psychological surrogates for their own deepest anxieties, frustrations and repressed desires. (They're no more likely to acknowledge that possibility, of course, than they've been able to absorb the incontrovertible facts about the overwhelmingly heterosexual nature of child molestation).

As for gay people as role models, no one knows why or how a particular sexual orientation develops, nor the extent to which, once developed, it remains fixed. Experts who have spent decades studying these matters—John Money of Johns Hopkins; Wardell Pomeroy, Kinsey's co-author—are far more tentative in their views than the strident advocates on either side of the nature/nurture debate.[6]

Not that the "experts" need be automatically deferred to. The history of scientific thought on matters relating to sexuality is sobering evidence of how the opinion of "experts"—at any given moment in time trumpeted as definitive—has in fact oscillated wildly through time, conforming far more to changing social attitudes than to actual accretions of knowledge. In the late nineteenth century, most sexologists agreed that sexual orientation was biologically determined and not subject to environmental influence, familial or pedagogic. But there was sharp—and in retrospect, quaint—disagreement as to which constitutional factors were significant, with medical men authoritatively advocating alternative theories of "degenerated genes" or "embryonic malformation" or an absence of "optimal spermatozoa"—theories that have since been discredited.

Today we know far too much in some fields (cross-cultural studies, for example) and far too little in others (the barely inaugurated research in endocrinology) to indulge in the confident sophistries of the past. Currently, the nature vs. nurture debate in scientific circles is more polarized and clouded than it has been for decades. Where some of the new findings from hormonal research suggest the possible influence of prenatal factors, the accumulating data from anthropology suggest the contrary conclusion—that the incidence (and kind) of same-gender sexual contact is centrally shaped by social learning. No one with even minimal information (perhaps I mean integrity) would say—as has Mike Thompson, the "brains" behind the Save Our Children campaign in Dade County— "all the evidence indicates that homosexuals aren't born; they're made. They choose." Thompson's prescription for those who cannot or will not "choose" to change their sexual orientation is predictably merciless: They should "suppress their drive."

Perhaps more disheartening than the professional bigots, with their claims on a monopoly of truth and their narrow definitions of the permissible limits of humanness, are those professional intellectuals who disassociate themselves from the crude polemics of an Anita Bryant even as they disseminate in subtler form the basic prejudices that animate her cohorts. Intellectuals are maintaining silence (and silence, as we should have learned from what happened in Nazi Germany, is a political act) or expressing agreement—modulated and selective, to be sure—with the crusade to withhold even minimal civil rights protection from gay people.

Two such examples are George F. Will, the syndicated *Newsweek* columnist and Pulitzer Prize winner, and the political theorist, Michael Novak, heterodox defender of "differentness"—that is, when ethnic not sexual. I single out Will and Novak not because their commentaries on gay rights have been uncommonly intemperate or venomous, but precisely because they have not. Their pained thoughtfulness, their more-in-sorrow-than-in-anger tone better represents the stance thus far taken by well-educated, well-placed heterosexuals than does the outright malice of a John Simon, say, or a William Buckley. And is because of that, dangerous. Nothing persuades like "sweet reasonableness."

George Will entitled one of his *Newsweek* columns "How Far Out of the Closet?" Noting that the American Psychiatric Association had removed homosexuality from its list of mental disorders, Will questioned whether the decision had been wise. Did it not encourage a view already too prevalent that "all notions of moral normality are 'mere' conventions, or utterly idiosyncratic"? Was there not a danger that the notion would gain ground that "no form of sexuality is more natural, more *right* [his italics] than any other ... "? Well yes, I might answer, but isn't that best viewed as a hope, not a danger—the hope that we might become a less hypocritical and conformist, a more comfortably diversified society?

Why does George Will feel otherwise? Because in his mind the prospect looms "of the repudiation of the doctrine of natural right on which Western society rests," a doctrine that allows us to know and encourage "some ways of living that are right because of the nature of man ... more human ways of living ... " The doctrine of natural right? The nature of man? Human ways of living? Large concepts, those. Not easy to grasp or evaluate—expecially since Will provides no specific definitions, does nothing to elucidate the particular meaning he attaches to such grandly vacuous phrases. Instead, he heaps on further abstractions. Not even a liberal society, he tells us, can leave everything to chance. Certain "essential values" must be safeguarded, shored up by law. "Surely healthy sexuality is one: the family, and hence much else, depends on it."

Apparently Will equates "healthy sexuality" with "family". But instead of providing evidence and argument (a formidable task, given all we've learned of late about marital disorder and child abuse), he issues papal pronouncements that do much to clarify the sources of his inspiration but nothing to authenticate them. One example: "surely homosexuality is an injury to healthy functioning, a distortion of personality." Since almost all the recent scientific literature—including the opinion of the American Psychiatric Association which Will himself cites—points to the opposite conclusion about homosexuality, it's not surprising that the sole "evidence" he offers in support of his statement is a tired stereotype: "Homosexuality often reduces sex to the physical ... [it is a] subculture based on brief, barren assignations ... " One might ask George Will—since parody begets parody—if he has ever heard of the notorious "subculture" of traveling heterosexual businessmen, famed for their "brief, barren assignations"? If so, should we assume he would want to deny them access to jobs and housing, too, since they too—by his standards—

threaten society's "essential values"? But then those men *do* have families, no matter the quality of their relationships, no matter the extent of deceit and oppression operative within their households. One comes away from Will's camouflaged sanctimony with a decided preference for the foot-in-mouth rantings of Anita Bryant. Both associate homosexuality with a threat to traditional sex roles and the institutions that embody them and with a "dangerously" elastic view of the permissible range of sexual pleasure. Anita uses the words. George Will, perhaps aiming at the subliminal crowd, moves his lips.

Michael Novak's language is more explicit but his attitudes no less hidebound. In a syndicated column of June 1977, he tried, for openers, to disguise his antique moralism with a few liberal platitudes: "the State should not intrude on the private lives of citizens; in the private sphere, large tolerance ought to be promoted," etc. But, he went quickly on, that does not mean society—as distinct from the state—should cease to make needed "moral discriminations." And guess who needs to be discriminated against? Right— those who follow "the homosexual way of life."

That life, you see, has "two basic deficiencies." The first is "the narcissism of one's own sex." Is Novak here defining narcissism in some special way that would not also force him to deplore deep friendships between people of the same gender? Is he aware that a statement such as his can only be based on the sexist assumption that male and female are polar opposites? We don't know. Like George Will—and most successful moralists—Novak has learned that one garners attention in direct proportion to the firmness, not the subtlety, of one's assertions.

The second deficiency Novak finds in homosexual relationships is that they are transient—"far more so than among married men and women." Perhaps. Given the latest divorce figures and the absence of research on long-standing gay relationships, one can't be sure. But even if Novak is right, he fails to ask any of the questions that could provoke a genuinely searching inquiry into the meaning of "transient." For example: Is it possible serial relationships might provide more optimal conditions for human happiness than lifetime bonding? How many of those lifetime bondings are based on emotional insecurity, lack of options, financial necessity and ingrained cultural imperatives ("the welfare of the children," etc.)—and at what cost in terms of lost affiliation with a larger community, erotic dessication, and the perpetuation of female dependence?

Novak never considers the possibility that sexual fidelity may not be the most significant gauge—let alone the equivalent—of emotional commitment. Many gay people reject the common assumption that a variety of sexual partners is incompatible with a lasting and loving primary relationship. Because gay people are less prone to overinvest in the magical expectation that one other person can fulfill all their needs, the partnerships they do form are often marked by an impressive amount of genuine independence, with both people able to cultivate the joys—so rare in our culture—of important outside relationships.

Novak concludes his article with this appalling statement: "Only a decadent society would grant them [gay people] equal status." Apparently Novak doesn't realize that "decadence" has many definitions and is perhaps most appropriately appended to knee-jerk defenders of the injustices adherent to the status quo, rather than to those outsiders who throughout history have been responsible for initiating social amelioration and change.

The concluding words in George Will's column, comparable to Novak's, makes the point for me: "...people want a few rocks to cling to in the riptide that washes away old moral moorings. Opposition to [Dade County's initial pro-gay] ordinance is a way of saying 'Enough!' And it is eminently defensible."

In short: Right on, Anita! We intellectuals may differ with you on particular points, we may not speak in the same tone, use the same vocabulary or invoke the same authorities—we have, after all, different constituencies and must adjust our voices accordingly. But we *are* united on fundamentals: we view gay people as a threat to the body politic, the enemy outside the gates. They shall not pass.

Robert Hillsborough. Gentle gardener. Stabbed 15 times in the chest and face. Dead in a parking lot, age 33. "Faggot! Faggot!"

Skeptic Nov/Dec 1977

This article was solicited for the "Great Debate Series" of *Skeptic* magazine, to be juxtaposed alongside a piece by Jerry Falwell. Without my consent or knowledge, it appeared with a piece by Mike Thompson instead.

NOTES
1. The most trenchant recent (1980) book on the interpretation of the Bible and the history of Christianity is John Boswell, *Christianity, Social Tolerance, and Homosexuality.* See my review of it on p. 329.

2. Jonathan Ned Katz, *Gay/ Lesbian Almanac* (Harper and Row: 1983)—and his bibliographical citations to the works of Mary McIntosh, James Steakley, Gayle Rubin, Jeffrey Weeks, Lisa Duggan, and Kenneth Plummer.

At the Sex and the State Conference at the University of Toronto in July 1985, Steakley revised his figures considerably downward. For the latest discussion of the whole issue of gays in the concentration camps, see Richard Plant, *The Pink Triangle: The Nazi War Against Homosexuals.* (A New Republic Book/ Henry Holt & Company: 1986), especially chapters four and five. I am grateful to Dr. Lawrence Mass for helping me secure this information.

3. In 1984 the *Journal of Homosexuality* added greatly to the available literature by publishing a special issue devoted to the subject of homophobia (September 1984, vol. 10, no. 1 & 2). The correlates of homophobia may have shifted since the outbreak of AIDS. For additional discussion and bibliography on homophobia see the special double issue of *International Books For Children Bulletin,* vol. 14, no. 3 & 4 (New York: 1983), Leonore Gordon, guest ed.

See also: Alan Bray, *Homosexuality in Renaissance England* (Gay Men's Press: 1982); the essays by John Boswell and George Chauncey in *Salamagundi*'s special Fall '82/ Winter '83 issue, *Homosexuality: Sacrilege, Vision, Politics;* Vern L. Bullough, *Sexual Variance in Society and History,* (Wiley: 1976); Louis Crompton, "Homosexuals and the Death Penalty in Colonial America", *Journal of Homosexuality,* vol. 1, no. 3 (1976); Michel Foucault, *The History of Sexuality: Volume One: An Introduction,* (Pantheon: 1978); Bert Hansen, Joseph Interrante and Robert A. Padgug in *Radical History Review,* (1979); Steven Marcus, *The Other Victorians* (Basic: 1966); and Robert Oakes, "'Things Fearful to Name': Sodomy and Buggery in Seventeenth Century New England", *Journal of Southern History,* vol. 12, no. 2 (1979).

4. These points have since been doubly confirmed by the publication (1980) of John Boswell's, *Christianity, Social Tolerance and Homosexuality.* His important study has revolutionized our historical understanding of Christianity—and has been ignored by fundamentalists. See my review of Boswell's book on p. 329.

5. In a letter to the Editor in *The Native,* (September, 1984), Oren Rachleff enumerates other condemnations in the Bible which would be considered absurd today—those levelled at astrologers, people wearing wool and linen together, a woman in pants, the handicapped, or anyone with a tattoo!

6. For further discussion of their views, see my essay, "Sex and the Military", p 272. See, too, Stephen Jay Gould, *The Mismeasure of Man* (Norton, 1981) and R.C. Lewontin, Steven Rose and Leon J. Kamin, *Not In Our Genes* (Pantheon, 1984).

THE EXPERTS AND HOMOSEXUALITY:
I. MASTERS AND JOHNSON,
II. THE KINSEY INSTITUTE

PART ONE: MASTERS AND JOHNSON

As has been clear for some time now, Masters and Johnson are not noted for their conceptual clarity or sophistication. In their first two books *Human Sexual Response* and *Human Sexual Inadequacy,* their boldly modernist findings on physiology (the multiorgasmic and clitoral nature of female sexuality) were presented in jarring tandem with their highly traditional psychosocial assumptions (monogamous lifetime pair-bonding as the optimal condition for human happiness). Somewhat akin to *sans culottes* clutching Gucci bags. But sympathy for the overall daring of their enterprise disarmed some critics, and their Olympian tone and forbidding technical vocabulary intimidated others. Besides, many hoped that Masters and Johnson's reluctance to speculate signaled the kind of stringent self-denial that might one day result in a carefully constructed theoretical synthesis that would subsume the earlier contradictions in their work.

With the publication of Masters and Johnson's latest work, *Homosexuality in Perspective* (1979), that hope must be foresworn. If anything, the conceptual fog has thickened, the intellectual evasions and simplicities multiplied. One now fears the problem is less presumption than obtuseness, for the most astonishing aspect of Masters and Johnson's altogether astonishing new study is their inability to distinguish the banal from the noteworthy. They overvalue their more obvious findings and negate or misconstrue their most original ones.

They thus announce, with considerable fanfare, the "discovery" that no significant physiological differences exist between homosexuals and heterosexuals in regard to "efficient sexual functioning," or in amenability to treatment for occasional dysfunction. These findings, they predict, will greatly dilute anti-gay prejudice. But why? It has never been widely presumed that gay people are "sexually dysfunctional"; "performance" may be one of the few areas in which they have not been negatively stereotyped. The opposite premise— that gays are too sexual, too active in pursuit of pleasure—has been a far more commonplace assumption in the homophobic culture at large.

Just as Masters and Johnson are overemphatic in declaiming the importance of their most obvious findings, they fail to recognize and underscore their most genuinely startling ones. Though its significance seems to have escaped them, they do offer data of immense importance in helping to advance debate on a number of longstanding (and long-stalemated) issues: Is Freud's suggestion that we are all "innately" bisexual accurate? Is the "gay lifestyle" sufficiently distinctive to warrant designating it a "subculture"? Is sexual fidelity an essential ingredient of emotional commitment? Is monogamous pairbonding the likeliest guarantee of human happiness?

The Masters and Johnson data on bisexuality are found in two sections of their book—those on "ambisexuality" and "fantasy." While recruiting over the years for their various studies, Masters and Johnson occasionally met men and women (ultimately they gathered 12 of them, six of each gender) who reported frequent sexual interaction with members of both sexes, showed "complete neutrality in partner preference" and evinced "no interest in sustained relationships." These last two attitudes convinced Masters and Johnson that these people should be distinguished from bisexuals; and accordingly, they designated them "ambisexuals." Possibly they should be distinguished from the entire human race—if we can believe Masters and Johnson's further findings about them. Ambisexuals, it seems, infrequently fantasize, never feel "performance anxiety," are "confident in their approach to any sexual opportunity", "obviously enjoy" any presented to them, "embody a tremendous sexual appeal [and the] ... freedom to express sexual interest without prejudice or bias that might neutralize the appeal." In short, transcultural, suprahuman beings.

Except we are not quite persuaded they actually exist—not, at any rate, in the pure form Masters and Johnson describe. No one has ever accused Masters and Johnson of exaggerating for theatrical effect (their prose is turgid beyond all reason or belief), but they have often been charged with imprecision. The charge seems applicable to their discussion of "ambisexuality." At one point Masters and Johnson describe the ambisexual's interest in sex as "purely a matter of physical release"; at another, as "primarily for tension release." Which is it—"purely" or "primarily"? The point is not too fine, since "primarily" leaves room for a host of additional possibilities— including an interest in "relating" of which ambisexuals are purportedly devoid. Skepticism increases when we learn that one ambisexual woman has been married. Masters and Johnson try to reassure us: "the marriage was contracted purely for the convenience of her partner; she had no investment in the personal relationship." "Purely" again; Masters and Johnson seem bent on dichotomy.

Suspicions aroused, we read on about these fascinating extra-terrestrials. They have "no histories of trouble with the law or with authority figures; no patterns of poor performance at work, school or in the military ... no difficulty in functioning responsibly in most facets of their lives," no history of "psychologic pathology" and "no physical or metabolic defects." Hmmm. Does the absence of "patterns of poor performance" imply the presence solely of "excellent" ones, or were mediocre performances turned in as well? If ambisexuals function "responsibly in most facets" of life, does that mean they fail to do so in "some"? How is "responsibly" being defined (or for that matter, "authority")? Is it nit-picking to ask whether freedom from so grand a malady as "psychologic pathology" presumes freedom from garden-variety neurosis as well? (Why did that woman marry a man solely for *his* convenience? Isn't apathy of that magnitude tantamount to self-negation—and wouldn't that qualify as "psychologic pathology"?) If Masters and Johnson have persuasive answers for such questions, they withhold them. One would think, if nothing else, they'd feel an obligation to their own reputations to pass on the needed definitions and distinctions.

Instead, they swoop away from the particular into a dizzying spiral of outsized generalizations. Short on answers, they are quick with moralisms. Lest the ambisexual lifestyle strike mere mortals as attractively varied and uninhibited, Masters and Johnson warn that it ends as "an intolerable burden," that "the unceasing parade of new faces and bodies" leads in time to "overwhelming" feelings of "social isolation." How do they know? During interviews, it seems, "the older ambisexuals" told them so. (One of them? Several? It's well to remember that the total study sample consisted of 12 people.) Is their "loneliness" different in degree or kind from what aging people generally feel? One would expect ambisexuals to feel that emotion less—if they are as free of affect and attachment to other people as Masters and Johnson have insisted. Anyway, isn't aloneness an inescapable fact of life, and during every phase of it (regardless of the number and quality of live-in companions)? Isn't recognition of that fact—however un-American—the only plausible definition of ma-turity?

Masters and Johnson will have none of it. They have contended for far too long that a committed relationship is a stay—*the* stay—

against despair, to tolerate any moral ambiguity toward the ambisexual lifestyle. Their agitation and flights of fantasy build apace. Ambisexuality, Masters and Johnson tell us, represents either "a prior point of departure or an anticipated end-point in our psychosocial structuring"—the vestige of an earlier "immature" stage in human development or a grim forerunner of what lies ahead. That covers the two polar bases—pleistocene and lunar—but the air remains a little thin. Without having ever convinced us that ambisexuality is indeed a separate phenomenon of being, Masters and Johnson proceed to endow it with symbolic importance of vast Manichean dimensions. Then—as in all good morality plays—they close on a note of benign reassurance: "The research team is currently more comfortable with the speculation that ambisexuality represents more a prior point of departure than a societal end-point." What a relief! (But did you notice that ambivalent word "more"? Oh for God's sake—be grateful for small imprecisions!)

Moving right along, Masters and Johnson next try to defuse a second storehouse of bisexual explosives: our fantasy lives. They present data on sexual fantasies gathered over a 20-year period and although they try to muffle the material's subversive impact, it still startles, challenging conventional wisdom on several fronts. To give a few samples: homosexuals (according to Masters and Johnson) show "greater psychosexual security" than heterosexuals; all four groups studied—homosexual men and women, heterosexual men and women—express a high level of interest in "forced sexual encounters"; the fantasies of homosexual men contain a greater amount of violence than those of heterosexual men (who envision themselves more frequently as rapees than rapists—as victims of "groups of unidentified women"); lesbian women record the highest incidence of fantasy, and are the only group which includes current partners in their fantasies to any significant degree; the most common fantasy pattern for both heterosexual men and women involves the replacement of their established partners with somebody else.

Masters and Johnson's single most intriguing finding is the high incidence they report in all groups of "cross-preference" fantasies. Among gay men and lesbian women, overt heterosexual interaction was the third highest fantasy; to an only slightly lesser degree, straight men and women fantasized about overt homosexual interaction. That last finding is expecially remarkable, and for two reasons: The heterosexual subjects were overwhelmingly Kinsey 0 (that is, exclusively heterosexual); and during face-to-face discussions and interviews, moreover, they described same gender sex as "revolting" and "unthinkable." Yet the same men and women who vitriolically condemned homosexuality showed in their fantasies "a significant curiosity, a sense of sexual anticipation, or even fears for effectiveness of sexual performance."

If Masters and Johnson fully recognize the explosive nature of these findings, you would never know it from their brief and bland discussion of them. On the high incidence of fantasies involving force, their sole comment is to caution against "necessarily" assuming any desire exists to act on such fantasies in "real life"—a statement that exudes less the air of scientific scrupulosity than personal repugnance. Masters and Johnson have never shown—unlike Alex Comfort, say, or Kinsey—much tolerance or understanding of "perverse" variations on the missionary theme. For them to acknowledge the appeal of "force" would be tantamount to admitting that the household staples (coitus, partner manipulation, fellatio/cunnilingus) do not exhaust the imagination or appetites of even the sexually proficient. It would also mean opening the Pandora's Box of sadomasochism, exploring the rising incidence in our society of sexual scenarios involving domination and submission, retrieving the S/M phenomenon from the "scummy fringe" to which traditional moralists (like Masters and Johnson) have comfortably consigned it.

Their reaction to the "cross-preference" data they present is cut from the same tweedy cloth. They simply warn against assuming that such fantasies indicate "latent or unrealized" attractions. And no more said. Yet it takes no great insight to deduce other plausible readings. It strains neither the evidence nor the imagination to see in the high incidence of cross-preference fantasies confirmation of Freud's hoary suggestion that all human beings are potentially receptive to bisexual stimulation; that even when we have grown up in a homophobic culture and have long since declared ourselves gay or straight, the wish to be both retains a strong subterranean hold.

Masters and Johnson keep to the same adamantly bland posture in the face of their remarkable finding that for both heterosexual men and women, the single most common fantasy is displacement of their established partner. Five years ago in *The Pleasure Bond**, their only book aimed at a popular audience (an aim that required the services of a co-author to translate hieroglyphics into basic English)— Masters and Johnson sternly equated infidelity with immaturity. That same animus, in more muted form, pervades *Homosexuality in Perspective*—indeed pervades all their work. Though enamored of

*For a detailed critique of *The Pleasure Bond*, see my review of the book in *The New Republic*, 1975.

their self-image as "objective scientists" and tireless in referring to their "neutral," "value-free" approach, their books have always been drenched in ideology. In choosing to deny this, they have merely ensured that their own personal values would contaminate their data more, not less; for when the subjective component is not acknowledged, its distorting effect is less easy to measure—and contain.

As far back as 1975, Paul Robinson (in his book *The Modernization of Sex*) succinctly and brilliantly uncovered the ideological assumptions that underlie Masters and Johnson's work. The essential ingredient, he wrote, is an "aversion to all sexual relationships that violate the monogamous heterosexual standard." Their therapeutic concern firmly centers on the *couple*, with the needs of the individual subordinated to those of the marital unit. To maintain or salvage a committed relationship, the individual is expected to sacrifice a certain amount of freedom—especially in pursuing sexual pleasure. Pleasure and union, in this view, are apparently seen as at odds: the sexual drive inherently strong, the marital unit inherently fragile.

What then justifies the heroic effort to curtail the one in the name of saving the other? According to Masters and Johnson the marital unit is the only context in which something called "growth" can thrive. Does that mean "growth" and "pleasure" are discreet, even antagonistic entities? Unlike their Puritan forebears, Masters and Johnson seem never to have posed that question consciously, or thought through an argument for asserting the prior claims of "growth." All that is clear is that on a subliminal level, they associate "growth" with safety—the kind associated with the security of lifetime bonding. But in substituting muddy hints for a reasoned exposition, they prove unconvincing advocates—especially for those who associate "growth" with the ability to remain open and take risks, with a willingness to explore the manifold, hidden recesses of personality.

Given Masters and Johnson's theoretical opacity and evasion, it comes as no surprise to find them in a state of semi-paralysis when confronted with the more subversive implications of their own data. To look at those implications might shake loose some foundation stones in their wobbly value structure. To absorb the fact that heterosexual men and women involved in longstanding relationships frequently—almost obsessively, it seems—fantasize about displacing their established partners, might raise the feared specter that familiarity really does breed contempt (or, minimally, loss of interest). For Masters and Johnson to digest their further finding that among the previously unattached couples they studied, "fewer functional failures" turned up during sex than among committed couples, might lead to speculation that people find excitement in the unfamiliar—that outside "spice" provides respite from the boredom and frustration that commonly assail longterm lovers. Rather than explore such implications, Masters and Johnson simply reiterate their belief in the prime importance of maintaining the marital unit— that "port-in-the-storm," that "retreat from social pressures." Security remains their supreme value, the ultimate benefaction, the essence and sum of human needs. We are in the landscape of the 1950s.

Masters and Johnson's deep distrust of pleasure when pursued outside the context of a committed relationship is of critical importance in understanding the tone and tactics they adopt in discussing gay life. Their earlier studies contained only scattered references to homosexuality; they treated it (in Paul Robinson's words) "from only one perspective: as a factor in the etiology of sexual inadequacy ... as an impediment to successful marital relationships." If a sexually dysfunctional client revealed any history of homosexuality, Masters and Johnson tended to draw a causal link between the two and would bend their (formidable) energy to "restoring" heterosexual functioning and "neutralizing" homosexual impulses. The client was never encouraged to explore the extent of his homosexual drive, to consider whether he might not be happier abandoning heterosexual marriage and committing to a gay partner or lifestyle. In their earlier books Masters and Johnson declined to undertake any extended discussion of the etiology of homosexuality. But they dropped enough incidental remarks to reveal a strong commitment to an environmental (as opposed to biological) explanation for same gender attraction; to view homosexuality as an "organic" predisposition, after all, would have precluded therapeutic intervention.

The same attitudes underlie *Homosexuality in Perspective*, obscured by the mountain of new findings. On the surface Masters and Johnson seem to be presenting data for building the most substantial—and implicitly revolutionary—case for gay chauvinism ever made. Early on, they tell us that their decade-long study comparing heterosexual and homosexual men and women has convinced them that gay people are "more related" and more fully involved in their sexual experiences. Gay people take more time; they make "each step in tension increment something to be appreciated"; they show markedly higher levels of "free-flowing" verbal and non-verbal communication. In contrast, heterosexual couples spend much less time in foreplay, show "greater psychosexual insecurity," and are "far more goal-oriented"—they want "to get the job done." In "only a few instances" did a husband seem "fully aware of his wife's levels of sexual excitation" or try to help her "expand her pleasure"— and these were couples pre-screened for sexual proficiency and freedom from psychological or physical pathology.

But having catalogued the superior sexual and interpersonal skills of gay people, Masters and Johnson swifty proceed to discount their own evidence. That's when the trouble begins—twisted logic, defensive calculations, *ex cathedra* pronouncements. They first stress the advantage gay people have of "intergender empathy." Perhaps—but is empathy a quality that adheres to gender rather than to individuals? Besides, how does intergender empathy, an "advantage" lesbian and gay male couples share, help to explain the very different qualities that mark their relationships? As Masters and Johnson tell us, lesbian women achieve consistently higher levels of sexual excitement and show consistently greater consideration for their partners than gay men do. The latter, after all—a point Masters and Johnson fail to make—are often engaged in traditional male games, emphasizing competition over cooperation, goals over process.

Masters and Johnson assign still greater importance to a second explanation they offer for the "unusually high level of communicative interchange" between homosexual partners. It's the result—hold on to your hats—of necessity. Meaning? Only two "stimulative approaches" (partner manipulation and fellatio/cunnilingus) are "widely popular" among gay people; therefore "these techniques of necessity must be constantly varied and refined to the utmost to avoid the loss of stimulative effectiveness." If we follow this line of reasoning, should we then ascribe the frequent failure of heterosexual couples to reach "optimal" peaks of pleasure during coitus to a *lack* of necessity—to the presumably wider range of stimulative options available? But then why do they also fall short, in comparison with gay people, in the degree of excitement they manage to reach during fellatio/cunnilingus? Are they hoarding skills and pleasure for yet another day? If so, which day? "Partner manipulation"—general body contact, holding, kissing, caressing—is the only other "basic stimulative option" Masters and Johnson recognize, and there, too, heterosexual "accomplishment" is portrayed as comparatively niggardly.

As logic falters, as Masters and Johnson patently fail to explain away the advantages of a gay lifestyle which they themselves have itemized, their own dismay grows palpable. To counteract it, they resort to repeating— in ever more strident tones—that two and only two "basic stimulative techniques" (partner manipulation and fellatio/ cunnilingus) are available to gay people, and that these, furthermore, are fundamentally "my turn-your turn" transactions (one person giving, the other receiving stimulation), unlike the "our turn" character of coitus. They concede that gay people can avail themselves of "the pseudocoital techniques of rectal intercourse and dildo usage, plus occasions of mutual masturbation." But these, according to Masters and Johnson, are theoretical options only. "Only a minority" of their homosexual study group (a grand total of 176 people, 94 men and 82 women) reported using those techniques with any regularity. Ergo: they are not real options for gay people anywhere—and thus require no further discussion. With that sleight-of-hand, Masters and Johnson are able to proclaim that certain "long-range disadvantages" are inherent—that's right: inherent—in even committed homosexual relationships. The tables have been neatly turned: What appeared to be certain advantages in the gay lifestyle have in the nick of time been discovered to be short-term ones only. But at the cost of a characterization of gay sexuality that relies on arbitrary and self-enclosed definitions ("my turn-your turn") and an odious mix of misinformation and ingenuousness.

Such lunatic—and imperious—oscillations scramble the brain, to say nothing of affronting common sense. One would have to be fatuous (or malignant) not to see that every sexual act carries the potential for being a one-sided (my turn-your turn) or mutual (our turn) transaction. *Which* potential will become operative hinges on the consideration the two partners have for each other's needs and their willingness to let their needs be known. On both counts gay people win hands down—by Masters and Johnson's own reckoning. It is they who report that during coitus heterosexual couples only infrequently achieve any shared transaction worthy of the name. It is they—not some polemical gay pamphleteer—who report that a lesbian woman engaged in manipulating or sucking her partner's breasts (ostensibly a my turn-your turn transaction) "frequently reaches" a high level of sexual excitation herself (manages, in other words, simultaneously to receive and give pleasure—the essence of an "our turn" transaction).

It might also be well to remind Masters and Johnson of their own repeated warning in *Homosexuality in Perspective* that their study samples are too small and skewed to be taken as "representative" or to be made the basis for broad generalizations. Would that they had heeded their own warning. Would that—once the temptation to issue resounding pronunciamentos overtook them—they had at least consulted additional source materials to supplement their own limited samples. One would have thought scientific integrity would have dictated as much—or, failing that, an instinct for self-protection. Hubris apparently proved stronger than either.

A substantial library of addition source material *is* available. One recently published book—Karla Jay and Allan Young's *The Gay Report*, an 800-page compendium of lesbian and gay male sexual attitudes and practices—is alone sufficient to embarrass Masters and Johnson's characterizations. Based on 5000 replies to a lengthy and sophisticated questionnaire (yes, 5000-a somewhat larger sample than 176), *The Gay Report* undermines any confidence in Masters and Johnson's description of the "stimulative options" available to gay people; it even contains information suggesting that the range of options employed by gay people may well exceed that used by more timid (not "inherently disadvantaged") heterosexuals.

The Gay Report reveals that anal intercourse—a technique Masters and Johnson disdain as too peripheral to warrant discussion—is a "frequent choice of sexual pleasure for about half of the men" surveyed; a still larger proportion (70 percent) express "positive feelings" toward it. As for analingus—a practice Masters and Johnson never once mention (Dare They Not Speak Its Name?)—it turns out that a majority (54 percent) of gay males engage in it with "some frequency" (though nearly 70 percent of lesbian women have "never engaged in it at all"). *The Gay Report* does confirm Masters and Johnson's statement that dildo usage among lesbians is minimal. However, lesbians feel far more positively about the use of vibrators (again unmentioned by Masters and Johnson)—apparently because (as Pat Califia has suggested in her recent study, "Lesbian Sexuality") vibrators are more effective than dildos in stimulating the clitoris and do not carry the negative associations of male penetration.

With all this as background, we can now approach the single most publicized portion of *Homosexuality in Perspective:* Masters and Johnson's claimed success in "converting" homosexuals. In evaluating that claim, their views on the etiology of same gender attraction is central. Essentially it is the same view expressed in their earlier studies, though now stated more explicitly and in more detail. Reviewing the recent research literature that has tried to identify possible hormonal and biological factors in the formation of a homosexual orientation, Masters and Johnson declare themselves (and I would agree) unimpressed; as yet, they conclude, such research has failed to produce any "secure information." They continue to believe that homosexuality is the product not of genes but of experience. But experience of a particular sort—negative experience. *Homosexuality in Perspective* contains numerous tales of how same gender orientation resulted from prior heterosexual experiences that had been unsatisfactory. One woman "gravitated to homosexuality as a means of sexual release" only after her husband had made it clear that he was "not interested in sex." Another woman, gang-raped at 20 and lacking "psychotherapeutic support," found herself "unable to cope"—which "led to total rejection of the male sex." This etiological perspective, in tandem with Masters and Johnson's longstanding assumption that the *summum bonum* for a happy life is monogamous, heterosexual, lifetime pair-bonding, made it predictable that their prime clinical concern would be to "neutralize" homosexual impulses and "re-establish" heterosexual ones.

Their treatment of "N" serves to illustrate their doctrinal and therapeutic approach. A 37-year old Kinsey 4 (an individual "who has had a significant amount of heterosexual experience but whose sexual outlets have been predominantly homosexual"), N's history included marriage. But after falling in love with a man with whom he then lived for seven years, N shifted entirely to a homosexual orientation, one which (in Masters and Johnson's own words) "completely satisfied" him. That is, until rumors began to circulate at his place of work that he was gay, making him fear exposure—and the destruction of his career. Though it had been many years since he felt any interest in heterosexual contact, N went to the Masters and Johnson Institute in St. Louis determined to "convert" (or, in his case, "revert"). They accepted him into the program. "Strong motivation," they believe, plus the availability of "an understanding opposite-sex partner" during treatment, are the best auguries for "success." They also believe that "the real or implied threat of social rejection or a constant concern for job security" are "good reasons" for an individual to change his sexual orientation. Just as Masters and Johnson have always given priority to the stability of the marital unit over the pleasure-seeking drives of the individual, so they opt for career security over any emotional or expressive needs that might jeopardize it.

During treatment, N's earlier "heterosexual effectiveness" was restored: he was soon able to perform with his female partner. Masters and Johnson then "explained the alternatives" (we are given no details) open to N, and he "evidenced no indecision in making a full heterosexual commitment." Masters and Johnson placed him in their "success" column (as they did with 67 percent of the 54 men and 60 percent of the 13 women in their program)—N, in their view had "achieved" heterosexual behavior. Those percentages are remarkably high in comparison with the 10-20 percent rates claimed by other therapies, and Masters and Johnson allow themselves a little well-mannered crowing: "the current concept among health-care professionals" that the sexual orientation of "dissatisfied" homosexual males or females cannot be changed—a concept which "the homosexual community has also adopted and freely propagandized"—is "simply erroneous."

"Simply," it turns out, is more than a little bald-faced. Masters and Johnson's selection process, first of all, had been so rigorous it is not unfair to call it rigged. Recruitment for the program took place between 1964 and 1968, a period predating the gay liberation movement and the positive changes it has subsequently wrought in self-image and social acceptance, a time when many gay men and women felt desperate—were, in Masters and Johnson's preferred terminology, "highly motivated" to change. Still, some were not thought highly motivated enough: nearly one-fourth of the original applicants were denied admission to the program. Those accepted were atypical in yet another important way. Only five of the 67 men and women finally selected for treatment were Kinsey 6 (exclusively gay). The large majority were Kinsey 3 or 4—"bisexuals," as some prefer to call them. Further, 31 of the men and six of the women were married, and they entered the therapeutic program with their spouses (an additional two men and one woman were currently living in long-term heterosexual relationships).

To call such a sample "skewed" hardly does justice to the matter; the selected subjects were so ripe for change, they would have likely turned yellow at first glance; the real surprise is that more did not. Moreover, Masters and Johnson's longterm "success" rate is almost certainly inflated. It turns out that after treatment ended, 16 men and three women became "unavailable" for follow-up study. It seems logical to assume that unavailability connotes a degree of disenchantment. But not to Masters and Johnson. By indulging in some dubious legerdemain based on "pro-rating," they are able to "estimate" that only four of those lost to follow-up actually returned to their homosexual ways—which further enables them to declare a two-thirds success rate; in truth, it is almost certainly closer to, and possibly below, 50 percent.

The manipulation of evidence at work here is troubling enough, but the underlying ingenuousness is more so. Masters and Johnson are remarkably uninquisitive about the philosophical premises on which their project rests and "innocently" indifferent to its ramifications. This imperturbability reflects enormous self-confidence. Yet given the nature of their enterprise (when closely scrutinized), assurance of that magnitude becomes an indictment, not a virtue.

For although Masters and Johnson will not see it, they are essentially engaged in promoting social conformity—the undertaking made more offensive for being paraded under the banner of liberation. They are bent on helping people pass muster, meet traditional social expectations, "achieve" heterosexual behavior. That this is often done in the name of protecting careers and social status merely compounds the conformism. Masters and Johnson seem never to question whether the emphasis on turning out secure and dutiful citizens is of ultimate advantage either to the individuals or to society (to self-actualization and to democracy); whether in helping their clients achieve a limited mechanical proficiency, they may not have disabled them emotionally, crippled their prospects for finding love; whether gain is best measured by a heightened ability to comply with prescribed sociosexual norms or by a heightened sense of inner integrity (success in living with oneself). Masters and Johnson are expert in creating a well-regimented band—and in muffling the different drummers within.

Recall the case of N, the man who "reverted" to heterosexuality— one of Masters and Johnson's "success" stories. But "success" by what definition, and at what cost? Those who believe that the continuing expansion of options is the best gauge of continuing vitality, will see in N's decision to commit himself exclusively to heterosexuality, not an advance—given the potential he had shown to relate fully to women and men—but a defeat, an artificial truncation wrought by social fear. Masters and Johnson tell us nothing about N's inner life (perhaps they never asked him). But it's possible to wonder whether his "conversion" produced a greater or lesser alignment between his outer behavior and his inner needs. In giving up homosexual activity, did N cease to have homosexual fantasies? A reversal in behavior is not the same as a reversal in desire. One can learn to perform sexually as a heterosexual and still not feel or perceive heterosexually; it is the difference between physiology and psychology—between fucking and loving. A crucial distinction, if one wants to talk responsibly and with precision about "conversion" and "change." It's a distinction Masters and Johnson never draw. One gets the sinking feeling they may be unaware it exists.

The New Republic, June 16, 1979

PART TWO:

THE KINSEY INSTITUTE
STUDY OF *HOMOSEXUALITIES*

The long awaited Kinsey Institute study, in preparation more than ten years, turns out to be every bit as important as advance rumor has had it. The book will produce sharp debate and create perplexing alliances. The strangest of all bedfellows—confirmed homophobes and radical gays—will unite, for antithetical reasons, in challenging its "positive" findings about the mental health, social stability and sheer ordinariness of most gay people.

Homosexualities will also stir controversy unrelated to the issue of sexual orientation. The book's heavy reliance on statistical methodology and its obvious grounding in liberal ideology, will refurbish a long-standing argument over the dominance of those techniques and values in contemporary social science. That argument will be enflamed by a disparity of emphasis in the book: the authors include a prodigal supplement of charts, graphs and "cluster analyses" but only a parsimonious discussion of their own "value set." Anti-statisticians will deplore the multiple print-outs as ostentatious displays of the obvious, while antagonists of liberal ideology will charge that the authors' insufficient attention to their own starting assumptions has seriously contaminated their conclusions.

Under this varied barrage, Bell and Weinberg, the authors, will need what comfort they can get. A fair amount is available. They have unquestionably made good their claim to producing "the most ambitious study of homosexuality ever attempted," one which reveals for the first time the wide diversity of lifestyles within the gay world. Where earlier studies were based on skewed psychoanalytic case histories or on small, unrepresentative segments of the homosexual population, Bell and Weinberg employed an army of specially trained graduate students to conduct lengthy, face-to-face interviews with some 1,500 men and women from divergent backgrounds. The scope of this undertaking, in combination with its generally modest tone and cautious generalizing, should lend maximum credibility to its findings.

Those findings cover so much ground, that only some of the most important can be noted:

Gay people are "significantly more liberal" politically and notable less religious than the general population. Homosexual men have "more good, close friends" than heterosexual men do, tend to like their jobs better (and few are employed in stereotypically "gay" fields, like hairstyling), and have "work histories fully as stable."

A large percentage of gay people—ranging from 64% of white homosexual males to 88% of black homosexual females—have had heterosexual coitus. Gay males place more premium on youthfulness than do lesbian women, and are more sexually active. But even for gay men, the data "fail to confirm the idea" of a "sex-ridden people" (40% of the males look for sex partners as little as once a month, or not at all). The data does confirm that it's "quite uncommon" for gay people to adhere strictly to traditional sex roles; they are also freer than non-gays in engaging in "many different forms of sexual contact" with their partners. Almost all the 1,500 respondents have had long-lasting relationships with a love partner involving "an emotional exchange and commitment similar to the kind that heterosexuals experience."

Only a minority of the respondents expressed any regret about being gay; those who did, usually related it to not having children or to social punition. "It would appear that homosexual adults who have come to terms with their homosexuality ... are no more distressed than are heterosexual men and women." And they are less prone to making "objectionable sexual advances" to others. This is especially true as regards "the seduction of 'innocents'"; there, the most common pattern by far involves "an older, heterosexual male, often a relative, and a pre- or postpubescent female."

Many of these findings will be familiar to those abreast of the recent literature on homosexuality. But since much of that literature has appeared in fragmentary form and in scholarly format, it badly needed the wider dissemination and additional confirmation which *Homosexualities* provides. Besides, Bell and Weinberg are not content merely to list their findings. They make an ambitious attempt at organizing them into a "typology of sexual experience" that divides respondents into five categories (thus the plural title), each said to exemplify a different "type" of gay lifestyle. This is the book's most original contribution, and one sure to prove provocative.

Some will take issue with the typology's focus on gay males. Anticipating that objection, Bell and Weinberg point to the "greater number and visibility" of gay men and to the fact that their "problems and adaptations" were of "greater interest" than those of lesbian women to the study's sponsor, the National Institute of Mental Health. But this "justification" comes uncomfortably close to an apologia for doing what the male dominated social sciences have always done—perpetuate lesbian invisibility by refusing to grapple with possible strategies for overcoming it.

At any rate, for gay males Bell and Weinberg claim to have successfully identified "five major groups." Briefly described, they are: 1. "Close-Coupled" men living in marriage-style monogamy. 2. "Open-Coupled" men involved in a "marital" relationship, but one with a wider variety of sexual contacts and techniques. 3. "Functionals" (together with "close-coupled," more than 1/3 of all respondents): men younger than those in the first two categories, less apt to worry about being publicly "exposed," less afflicted with such "sexual problems" as impotence or "difficulty in finding sexual partners"—in short, something like the swinging singles of the straight world. 4. "Dysfunctionals" (about 1/5 of all respondents): men who scored high in comparison with the other groups on formal education and sexual activity, but also high on the extent of their sexual problems and their regret over being gay. 5. "Asexuals" (about ¼ of all respondents): men with the lowest level of sexual activity, most limited sexual repertoires, least exclusively gay—and most regretful and covert about it.

Despite its deficiencies (which I'll come to), this typology makes two overriding contributions. It challenges future researchers, if only out of disagreement, to further exploration along similar lines— meaning, more emphasis on making facts yield meaning, less on mere fact-gathering. Though later studies will doubtless modify Bell and Weinberg's typology, even as it stands it allows for some important new distinctions about gay life. By separating out "dysfunctionals" and "asexuals" as a distinct minority in the overall gay population, the book refutes previous studies which mistakenly equated a small number of "conflict-ridden social misfits" with the totality of the gay population.

Bell and Weinberg admit that their "five types" don't exhaust "the ways in which homosexual adults can be meaningfully classified." They also candidly report that the typology couldn't encompass fully ¼ of their respondents and that still others "fell on the boundary between two (or more) groups." Faced with these "ambiguous" cases, Bell and Weinberg "decided to invoke theoretical considerations in assigning members to types." Unfortunately, we aren't told what "considerations," and the absence of discussion on this crucial point makes for unease.

Their sampling techniques raise additional questions. All the respondents were volunteers recruited through such devices as public advertising, bar contacts and homophile mailing lists. Though the recruitment effort was prolonged and sophisticated, it could not yield—as Bell and Weinberg themselves affirm—the kind of representative cross-section that a random sample would. They justly add that at present it's impossible to get a random sample from the gay community because fear of exposure is still widespread.

But to this unavoidable distortion in the sample, Bell and Weinberg have built in others, less compulsory. Some derive from their decision to confine the sampling site—after a small pilot study done elsewhere—to the San Francisco Bay Area, a place far in advance of the rest of the country in 1970 (the year they completed gathering data) in its permissive attitude towards same sex relations. It's unlikely that gay people from any other city—and surely not from any rural area—would report (even in 1978) that only a few "have suffered negative social consequences as a result of their homosexuality." Bell and Weinberg do caution that gay people living in less permissive places might report a much higher incidence of such "social difficulties" as blackmail, assault, and job or housing discrimination. Yet having issued the caution, they proceed to suggest, in a generalization not clearly confined to San Francisco, that a homosexual lifestyle is a good deal "less perilous" than usually thought.

There are also problems with the sample in regard to race and class. Bell and Weinberg divide their respondents into only four groups: white or black homosexual males, and white or black homosexual females. But surely we are a nation of more than two races and two colors. Besides, what criteria did they use—merely an unreliable visual one?—in defining "white" or "black," and into which category did they place variously pigmented Latins? The authors also seem unaware of the extent to which their sample is class biased. Whether one defines class in terms of income, occupation, self-image or educational level, it's difficult to credit as remotely "representative" any sample in which the "unskilled and semiskilled" together account for only 18% of the total, and in which 73% of black male respondents report at least some college education.

Another difficulty arises from Bell and Weinberg's reference to their five groups as "mutually exclusive." Do they mean that given individuals through time remain locked into a particular set of behavioral patterns—or that the categories remain constant and individuals shift between them? In not clarifying this point, Bell and Weinberg leave the impression of "once a 'Functional'"—or whatever—"always a 'Functional'." But this is at odds with much of what we know about sexually related behavior. Many human beings—gay or otherwise—dramatically change sexual/emotional patterns (from celibacy to promiscuity, say, or from a closed to an open relationship) at different times in their lives, in response to shifting professional, psychological or physiological changes.

The patterns of a whole culture can shift dramatically, too; sometimes over a short period of time. This has almost surely been true of the past decade in the area of sexual norms. Because Bell and Weinberg's data are eight years old, at least some of the conclusions based on it are already in need of revision. To give one example: it's generally conceded that many more gay males in 1978 than in 1970 eschew the traditional model for primary relationships that equates emotional commitment with sexual fidelity. Or put another way, many now affirm that "sexual variety" (the term "promiscuity" is out of favor) contributes positively to the well-being of the individual and to the partner-relationship in which he or she may be involved.

A similar shift in values has been noted in the non-gay world, though to a lesser degree. And this raises another problem with Bell and Weinberg's typology: that of comparisons. Do the homosexual "groups" differ in kind from what we might expect to find in a study of 1,500 heterosexuals—especially in San Francisco? The language used to define the "five types" is so broad it might easily encompass the new models of sexual behavior emerging in all segments of the population. Except that some of its dimensions have escaped Bell and Weinberg.

This is particularly true of their discussion of "sexual techniques." Whether out of personal squeamishness or from a conscious decision to abide by current definitions of scientific "decorum," they limit that section of their questionnaire to four missionary-like multiple choices: masturbation, fellatio, anal intercourse and body rubbing. Omitted entirely is the whole range of sexual explorations, from armpits to analingus, that many, following the advice of popular prophets like Alex Comfort, have been adding to their sexual repertoires.

Fastidiousness is endemic to "liberal" sexology. Its central figures, Masters and Johnson, have done radically innovative work in physiology but in the area of *values* have continued to champion monogamous lifetime pair bonding and to disapprove of "artificial" stimulants, whether pornography or bondage, which an academic outsider like Alex Comfort recommends for occasional variety. In avoiding impolite areas of inquiry, Bell and Weinberg place themselves in sexology's conventional mainstream.

It's this "value set" which will draw fire from radical gays. The battleground, as often these days, will center on the actual extent of cultural "differences" in America. The very grounds on which the vast majority of gay people will warmly welcome (and homophobes grimly deplore) *Homosexualities*—namely, its overall conclusion that most homosexuals, aside from sexual orientation, do not differ in any essential way from mainstream Americans—will be the same that produce angry rebuttal from the radical gay minority.

The radicals are not indifferent to the struggle for civil rights; nor blind to the fact that *Homosexualities* provides it with essential ammunition; nor unaware(along with growing numbers of non-gays) that the struggle has taken on new urgency now that Anita Bryant's crusade has become a convenient and cynical rallying point for a burgeoning rightwing coalition determined to suppress a wide spectrum of dissent.

Even knowing how much is at stake, radical gays, I'd venture to predict, are going to speak out against *Homosexualities* as a work of "false assimilationism", as an argument for social acceptance premised on discredited liberal "melting pot" theories that underestimate differentness and assume—implicitly even prescribe—conformity to dominant cultural values. They'll do so in the name of the *primary* importance of maintaining the integrity of a gay subculture marked in their view by many profound—and preferable—variations from majoritarian norms of relating and being, variations which hold out whatever slim hope there is for a broad and genuine socio/sexual transformation. They'll see in *Homosexualities* what many blacks saw in the heralded study of slavery, *Time on the Cross:* a sanitized version of their experience offering full membership in the human community on the dubious premise that they are now and have always been devoted adherents to a work-obsessed, sex-negative middle-class culture.

The gay majority, in turn, will likely denounce the radicals in its midst as divisive and dangerous. For as Bell and Weinberg rightly point out, most homosexuals *are* mainstream Americans—centrist in politics, bourgeois in outlook, eager to be "let in". (This is far less true of lesbian feminists, well aware as they are that the Old Boy network of male power and privilege at the heart of our social system must be transformed, not joined).

In repudiating its leftwing, the gay majority has plenty of arguments at its disposal. It can point to disagreements among the radicals as to *which* features of the subculture are most distinctive, most in need of affirmation (exhuberant eroticism? the deliberate blurring of gender roles? the rejection of "stability" as an accurate or desirable way of viewing the shifting personae of Self, and of the Self in relation to others?). The radical fringe is also vulnerable to mockery. Like most radicals in our history, they lurch between disdain for theoretical analysis and protracted debate on doctrinal minutia; they divide between socialists stressing the paramount importance of building strong organizations for collectivist ends, and anarchists insisting on the transcendent claims of "individual expression". They share an impatience characteristic of all radical movements in this country (to some degree of all Americans)—an impatience which can lead to sudden secession from any revolution that annoyingly fails to materialize on schedule.

The gay radicals have some forceful arguments of their own. Like their forebears in other radical movements—from Garrison to Emma Goldman to Huey Newton—they claim experience has amply confirmed certain general principles which subsume their internal differences and which must be adhered to. That you cannot adopt (or pretend to adopt) the dominant values of a culture and at the same time hope to reorder those values. That the token adjustments which the power brokers grant from time to time are insufficient to dilute (and—whether by design or otherwise—in the long run strengthen) our society's instinctive distaste for substantive change, its zeal for homogenization and its entrenched suspicion of the very human diversity it rhetorically defends. That liberals, even when they champion "change", are conditioned to accept as sacrosanct exactly those propositions about human nature (the "maternal instinct", for example, or the equating of erotic adenturing with "fear of intimacy") most in need of scrutiny. That liberals can therefore never be relied upon as allies in any struggle to break through to a genuinely new socio-sexual order. That indeed they may be less reliable than those "true" conservatives who have traditionally resisted submerging individual needs in the Common Good (as defined by the State) and have—conservatives of the aristocratic class, at any rate—traditionally been insouciant about sexual eccentricities.

Cannons to the left of them, cannons to the right, The Kinsey Institute with this study moves massively to occupy the centrist position on a battleground of accelerating fury. One hopes that they—that we all—are not facing in the direction of Balaklava.

The New York Times, November 26, 1978

1980

CHRISTIANITY, SOCIAL TOLERANCE, AND HOMOSEXUALITY:

It is John Boswell's claim in his remarkable book *Christianity, Social Tolerance, and Homosexuality,* that the history of Christianity's attitude toward gay people is not the unrelenting tale of hostility and repression we have long been led to believe. To the contrary,

> most of the attitudes of fanaticism and intolerance which are today thought of as characteristically 'medieval' were in fact common only to the later [12th- 13th centuries] Middle Ages. The early Middle Ages, with few exceptions, had accommodated a great many beliefs and lifestyles with relative ease.

In fact, until roughly 1150 AD, Catholic Europe regarded same-gender love and lust with astonishing equanimity. There were gay marriages and gay saints. Several openly gay men were consecrated as bishops. Much of the popular literature of the day (often written by highly regarded clerics) "dealt positively with gay love." A thriving gay subculture reached its apogee between the years 1050 and 1150; it had a rich body of literature, its own argot and conventions, its demimonde of street prostitutes and brothels catering to a large clientele from all classes and of varied tastes.

Then, during the 200-year period spanning the mid-12th to mid-14th centuries, homosexuality and attitudes toward it underwent a sea change—from "the personal preference of a prosperous minority, satirized and celebrated in popular verse, to a dangerous, antisocial, and severely sinful aberration." What had been morally and legally acceptable in 1100 was by 1300 regarded as an activity subject to the death penalty—often for a single proven act. Why this dramatic transformation in public opinion? We don't know. Boswell offers some tentative explanations: the rise of corporate states with the power and will to regulate the personal aspects of human life, the xenophobia and pressure to conform resulting from the Crusades, as the "sodomitical" Moslems from without and "heretics" from within came to seem an ever greater threat. Boswell is too sophisticated to accept such vague "causes" as sufficient to explain the shift in attitude toward homosexuality from tolerance to hostility. He candidly declares: "it is not possible to analyze the causes of this change satisfactorily"; not yet, not in this rudimentary stage in our revisionist understanding of the medieval period. Yet there is much, even now, that Boswell feels can be stated with confidence about the general subject of homosexuality in medieval Europe. He is entitled to his confidence, for although he is still in his thirties, his labors have been prodigious and his erudition is awesome. For ten years he has analyzed records in a dozen languages, consulted all sources in their original (in the process providing some startling new translations of familiar Greek and Latin texts), and unearthed unknown or obscure materials ranging from Icelandic proverbs to Persian epics to Jewish erotic verse to Hispano-Arabic literature. Most of his conclusions are as startling as they are persuasive.

He finds nothing at all in the writings that eventually became the Christian Bible "which would have categorically precluded homosexual relations among early Christians." Despite misleading translations which have long been thought to imply the contrary, Boswell has discovered "no extant text or manuscript (whether in Hebrew, Greek, Syriac or Aramaic)" that contains the equivalent of the word "homosexual" (or any other word that might correspond to current English usage). Relentlessly tracking down the original context and meaning of those passages in the Bible (the account of Sodom in *Genesis 19,* for example) later used to condemn same-gender attraction, Boswell (and a few lexicographers before him) found that the crucial word or text in question referred instead to such varied matters as temple prostitution, ritual uncleanliness, and masturbation. "At the very most, the effect of Christian Scripture on attitudes toward homosexuality could be described as moot."

Thus when the modern Catholic church speaks as if its doctrines can be traced back in an unbroken line to the patristic fathers and Jesus and the Apostles, it can do so only at the expense of a fundamental misreading of historical facts—at the expense, too, of brushing aside a significant portion of its own heritage: those prominent early theologians (Ausonius, Saint John Samascene, Marbod of Rennes, Saint Aelred of Rievaulx) who expressed positive attitudes toward same-sex eroticism. This, Boswell laconically suggests, may prove "discomforting" to contemporary Christian polemicists against homosexuality. I doubt it, since they have shown no notable embarrassment over the long-known fact that a number of the fathers of the church severely censured such practices as lending money at interest, having sexual intercourse during the menstrual period, shaving, bathing regularly, or wearing jewelry and dyed fabrics. None of these (unlike homosexuality) have become matters of controversy within the Christian community today.

The polemicists prefer to cite Saint Thomas Aquinas's writing, considered both now and in his own day (the 13th century) the apogee and definitive synthesis of Catholic moral theology. They will have more trouble henceforth in doing so, for in a brilliant critique of Saint Thomas, Boswell lays bare not only the internal contradictions in his teachings throughout, but in particular the near hilarious twists and turns he took in order to distinguish "natural" from "unnatural" pleasures. Aquinas emerges from under Boswell's scalpel not as a powerful, ordinal thinker but as a harassed journeyman attempting to accommodate the pressures generated by the shift in popular attitudes toward homosexuality. His writings are best seen not as an accurate, stately summation of the true complexity of preceding Christian tradition, but as a profoundly partial, evasive curtailing of it. A far more truthful summation, Boswell insists, would recognize that moral theology through the 12th century treated homosexuality "as at worst comparable to heterosexual fornication but more often remained silent on the issue."

To characterize this analysis as revolutionary—in its implications for historical studies, for Christianity, for the current debate over sexual mores—is to state the obvious. Boswell's study is indubitably one of the most profound, explosive works of scholarship to appear within recent memory. His book will inaugurate controversies bound to rage for years. As even my partial, cursory summary of its contents makes clear, the issues at stake are large—and the ensuing clamor is bound to match them in magnitude. Points of fact and interpretation will be challenged, debated, disproved, upheld. Experts from dozens of fields will want to put in their oars. But Boswell's erudition is so arcane and his synthesis so encompassing that few, if any, scholars will be able to command the needed range of expertise for an authoritative evaluation. If any such do exist, I am surely not among them. Some graduate school training aside, I am not a specialist in medieval studies. I am no more than an "interested party" (gay, that is, not Christian)—doubtless a disqualification in some eyes. My drawbacks duly noted, I nonetheless want to venture some tentative observations, caveats, doubts.

On a first reading, I found the book overwhelming, on a second merely stunning. That minor declension of enthusiasm is the result of noticing on closer look some occasional vagaries in argument or definition, some possible inconsistencies and overstatements. I had the most trouble with the material in Part I ("Points of Departure") of the book, approximately one-fourth of the whole. In that section Boswell provides an overview. He discusses the problems of historical evidence (and the problem of correcting the errors and falsifications of previous historians), sets forth his themes, provides extensive background discussion of the Greco-Roman precursors of the Christian era, and comments on the variety of contemporary issues embedded in the historical material (the etiology of homosexuality, "boy/man" love, "promiscuity," etc.). I found most of the discussion remarkably careful and compelling. But not all of it. An occasional remark or emphasis suggests that Boswell may be more familiar with historical materials than contemporary ones, and that in certain limited areas (and in terms of subtle overtones only) may harbor a rather conservative set of biases. For example, I think he is simply wrong in asserting "there does not seem to be any evidence that gay people really are more or less sexual than others"; not only could a long bibliography be cited to the contrary, but many gay people (more males than females) now view their heightened sexuality as cause for self-congratulation, not apologetics—they affirm the value of a sex-positive attitude in a sex-negative society. Similarly, I'd question Boswell's view that "much" of the speculation during the 1970s "on the evolutionary significance of homosexuality" has ended in agreement "on the essential likelihood of genetic viability for homosexual feelings through one selection mechanism or another." I'd argue there's been little agreement; Boswell's citation of E.O. Wilson's much controverted *Sociobiology* in support of his opinion will hardly persuade the many research specialists (Masters and Johnson, for example) who find the recent attempt to link genetics and sexual orientation wholly unproven, to say nothing of "politically" suspect.

Boswell's central avowal that "much of the present volume is specifically intended to rebut the common idea that religious belief— Christian or not—has been the cause of intolerance in regard to gay people," will come as particular balm to those gay Christians who have insisted on the compatibility of their sexual orientation with their devotion to institutional religion and who have been working through such organizations as DIGNITY (gay Catholics) and INTEGRITY (gay Episcopalians) to "maintain a dialogue with the Mother Church." But the "balm" strikes me as somewhat suspect.

It is one thing (a monumental thing) to demonstrate that the history of Christianity is not one of monolithic opposition to homosexuality. But it is quite another to expect that today's clerical leaders will welcome and embrace the news, ceasing those punitive campaigns against gay people which in 1980, if not in 1180, are demonstrably the major source for the maintenance and spread of homophobia and intolerance. In reading Boswell, I now and then got the unnerving feeling that at the top of his own set of priorities is the wish to hold gay Christians to their religious allegiance—that he is more eager to defend the viability of church affiliation for gays than to bolster an emerging gay subculture whose left wing is decidedly— in my view, justly—anticlerical. I don't know how else to account for Boswell's curious statement that "It is unlikely that at any other time in Western history have gay people been the victims of more widespread and vehement intolerance than during the first half of the twentieth century." He may be correct in claiming that "the excesses of the Inquisition are often exaggerated," but after all, the death penalty for homosexuality (a rather extreme form of intolerance) had become legal prescription in most of Europe by 1300 AD.

Even if I am only marginally right in thinking Boswell's personal values have in some instances colored his interpretations, I should add that the same can be said of any historian who has ever written— it's a garden variety occupational hazard. More surprising, given Boswell's fierce clarity, are those moments in the book when his terminology turns muddy or his emphasis overcolored.

No one, to be sure, can confidently draw the fine lines needed to determine whether a given set of feelings is best described as affectionate, companionate, or sexual. Boswell himself is fully cognizant of the difficulties. He warns us early in the text that the words the ancient Greeks used to express or describe feelings do not neatly divide into our latter-day categories, but instead ambiguously overlap. He rightly cautions that "one cannot expect and should not demand from historical sources 'proof' of emotional states."

Yet despite his own excellent advice, Boswell now and then makes some overly authoritative pronouncements—statements that seem to go beyond what the fragmentary nature of the evidence warrants; he over-rationalizes, if you like, the evanescent. When discussing, for example, Saint Anselm's "extraordinary emotional relationships" with a succession of his male students, Boswell quotes at length from a letter which he characterizes as "erotic by any standards." Not by mine: I read it as sentimental effusion: "...Sweet to me, sweetest friend are the gifts of your sweetness, but they cannot begin to console my desolate heart for its want of your love ... the anguish of my heart just thinking about this bears witness, as do the tears dimming my eyes and wetting my face and the fingers writing this."

Sometimes it is a contradictory interpretation rather than a muddled definition that leaves us puzzled. At one point, for example, Boswell carefully notes that the exclusivity suggested by the modern terms "homosexual" and "heterosexual" is extremely rare in the literature—and reality—of the ancient world. Yet at another point he tells us that "permanent and exclusive homosexual relationships" regularly appeared in Roman novels addressed to a general public "without any suggestion of oddity."

At other times, Boswell can reopen a debate that has long seemed closed, but then he'll suddenly overreach himself, generalize in a more dogmatic manner than the evidence warrants, leading us to recoil in uncertainty when we had been on the verge of agreement. The best example of this is in his handling of the issue of the age of male lovers in ancient Greece. The matter has long seemed settled: the common view has been that in the classical world gay relationships always involved persons of different ages: older man or woman as lover and guide, young boy or girl as beloved and tutee. But Boswell presents considerable evidence to the contrary. Euripides and Agathon were lovers when Euripides was 72 and Agathon 40; Parmenides and Zenon when the former was 65 and the latter 40. Whereas K.J. Dover, in his recent *Greek Homosexuality*, reports that the idea of continuing an erotic relationship after a youth's beard had begun to grow would have been thought "shocking," Boswell points out that Alcibiades was already full bearded when Socrates fell in love with him, that most Greeks had no doubt that Achilles and Patroclus were sexual lovers, and that in Rome "it seems quite possible" that the distinction between "lover and beloved" was "purely a semantic nicety."

By reopening the debate on the "age" question, Boswell has inevitably reopened a number of other issues related to it: whether same-gender relationships were characteristically carnal or "spiritual," of brief or sustained duration, confined to the aristocracy alone or spread throughout all classes. Boswell (supported here by Dover for the classical period) emphatically affirms the carnal and trans-class nature of gay life and (*contra* Dover) discerns any number of long-term relationships. And he argues his points persuasively. All this is accomplishment enough, especially when one realizes how heavily weighted on the other side of these issues the scholarly literature has been.

But now and then Boswell overreaches. Not satisfied with challenging, often capsizing, earlier "expert" opinions, he goes on to make some generalizations that seem to me too broad and confident for what the available documentation can support. He claims, for example, that it is "manifestly" true that to the Greeks any beautiful man was referred to as a "boy"; surely "manifestly" is too bold a word for describing what remains a murky subject. Similarly, Boswell's statement that it is "unlikely" that "the apparent prevalence of erotic relationships between adults and boys in the past corresponded to reality," though more tentative in tone, still strikes me as not modulated enough to take into account the lacunae in our knowledge. Such evidence as we do have suggests that no one pattern was prevalent.

Even if I am right in feeling Boswell occasionally falls prey to vagueness or overstatement, that is no great source for wonder. What is a source for wonder is how firmly he holds his footing in general. The bulk of his text is characterized by a keen awareness of the ambiguities of evidence and superb control over delicate points of disputation. Care and conscientiousness are the book's hallmarks. If I've dwelt on some few exceptions, it's because of my conviction that Boswell's study is a major achievement likely to have immense scholarly and political influence—and as such deserves and requires the closest possible scrutiny. No doubt, many others better equipped than I in specialized areas of knowledge will carry forward the scrutiny.

Even now it is safe to say that *Christianity, Social Tolerance, and Homosexuality* is that rare item—a truly ground-breaking study. With an abundance of skill and daring, John Boswell has opened up a vast historical terrain for reassessment, some of it never before explored, much of it marked for far too long by barricaded, sealed borders.

The New Republic, October 18, 1980

NOTES
1. See "The Anita Bryant Brigade", p. 297.
2. Ibid.

1982

RACISM IN THE GAY MALE WORLD

It is no news—though the news has not exactly been trumpeted abroad—that racism, along with its kissing cousins, sexism and classism, is rampant in the gay male (I cannot speak for the lesbian) community, albeit not as rampant, I believe, as in the culture at large. Wishful thinking may have fathered that belief—no statistics exist on such matters—but not entirely so. The formation two years ago of Black and White Men Together, an organization devoted to confronting and combating racism in the gay male world, gives some evidence of our subculture's greater awareness of the problem.

Somewhat greater. Until the formation of B&WMT, the subject of racism rarely dared speak its name. Periodically some brave soul has, over the years, openly lamented its existence, been joined in lamentation by half a dozen others—three of whom soon subsided into apathy, three into guilt; neither state conducive to action.

And action is long overdue. In the dozen years since Stonewall, most of the radical goals set by the early liberation movement have been diluted or discarded. As our movement has grown in numbers, its initial values have atrophied. Originally, the gay movement spoke and acted boldly against entrenched privilege based on gender, racial, ethnic and class discrimination. That commitment has been largely displaced by "liberal" goals and strategies which emphasize the need to work within the established system to secure social tolerance and legal redress.

Worthy goals, to be sure. And ones which we have made some notable progress in advancing in recent years. We have gained greater visibility and protection. We are more "acceptable" to the general public. But at no small cost: the cost of making ourselves over better to conform to an acceptable public image, the cost of bending our energies towards adjusting to mainstream mores, to becoming Good Americans, 'jes folks. The inevitable concomitant has been to downplay differences we once proudly affirmed, discard radical social analysis, softpedal our distinctiveness, discourage and deny the very diversity of behavior and lifestyle our conformist society stands most in need of.

This quest for respectability reached an apogee of sorts just two weeks ago when we filled the Grand Ballroom of the Waldorf-

Astoria—1,000 strong and paying $150 a plate—to celebrate the first annual Human Rights dinner. Resplendent in our finery, we gave Walter Mondale, chief speaker of the evening, a standing ovation—roared our enthusiasm for what in fact was a standard (and tedious) anti-Reagan stump speech which never once directly addressed the reason for the occasion: the cause of gay rights. Nor was any resentment apparent when Mondale, the instant he finished his speech, quickly left the platform—missing the subsequent presentations, and resolutely refusing any comment to the crowd of reporters that awaited him at the Waldorf's exit.

It's no coincidence that the dinner crowd which so lustily cheered Mondale's near-shameful performance was composed almost entirely of dinner-jacketed white males (along with a handful of women, and almost no blacks and Hispanics). Surely the nature of Mondale's audience goes far towards accounting for their grateful, even enthusiastic, response to him. A leading member of the ruling patriarchy had—at last!—graced a gay white male event with his actual presence, given it at least token legitimacy. What matter how minimal the gesture. The symbol was what counted. With Mondale appearing at an openly gay affair, surely the time was not distant when the ruling elite would grant full admission to the inner sanctum of white male privilege.

The occasion reminded me of a plaintive question James Baldwin once raised during the height of the black liberation struggle. Cautioning his compatriots about the headlong rush to be integrated into mainstream life, he asked (I'm paraphrasing from memory) whether "we really want to beg to be allowed to rent a room in a house that is burning down. Might it not be better to redirect our energies towards building a new—a better—house?"

His question still resonates. At least for some of us. At least for those black and white men who have banded together to form an organization devoted to confronting, rather than evading, the endemic racism in our community. By doing so they've revived the long-dormant prospect that gay people might yet become the agents of substantive social change we set out to be a decade ago. B&WMT has challenged us to reclaim the radical impulse once characteristic of our movement, to wean ourselves away from the smug and pervasive hedonism now the chief identifying feature of gay male life, to redirect our energies, re-examine our goals.

Will the challenge be met? On the optimistic side one can cite the organization's rapid growth, with chapters now spread across the country. Set against that positive development is the dismaying evidence—in New York City most particularly—of the intractable apoliticism of most gay men and the sterile in-fighting among those few who are politically active. (To say nothing of a conservative national climate and a growing anti-gay backlash which, understandably, is discouraging sustained political commitment—of even the "liberal" kind—among gay men.)

Still, dogmatic—and paralyzing—pessimism is premature. We are a nation—and a subculture—given to sudden shifts of mood, startling, unpredictable changes of course. The ultimate impact B&WMT will make is unforeseeable. What can and should be said about this new organization is that it has punctured the reigning complacency, insisted we face up to serious problems dividing and disfiguring our community, encouraged us to reclaim our radical roots, to rechart our course.

Against a tide of apathy and timidity, they have set us a demanding new agenda and infused new energy to meet it. For all they have already accomplished and for all they bid us to, they deserve congratulations and gratitude.

Presentation speech on awarding a "certificate of merit" to B&WMT at the 7th annual Lambda Legal Defense Fund dinner, October, 1982. B&WMT has changed its name to Men of All Colors Together.

PART THREE:

CODA

THE PAST AS PRESENT:
GAY IN THE FIFTIES

From "Interview: Martin Duberman", *Gay Sunshine,* Spring 1977:

My first sexual experience with a man? About age 20. Well, a few earlier ones. At summer camp in the forties we did something we called "fussing". We had a mattress at the bottom of the closet in our bunk. (The closet no less!) We were pretty well organized. Don't know how old I was—about 12, I think. The code question we'd ask each other was, "You feel like 'fussing'?" If "yes", we'd go into the closet, two at a time. Body-rubbing, essentially. There was a definite hierarchy, too. You know: who got to go into the closet with whom— who did the choosing. Just like a gay bar.

On one level, I knew early on I was gay. At seventeen, for instance, I went on a bike trip—old fashioned "bike"—across the country. Camped out every night, went through the Rockies: all that. At one point we stopped in Calgary, Canada for the big rodeo. I remember going to see a fortune teller. She told me to write on a piece of paper "the question closest to my heart" and to put it under the (literal) crystal ball sitting on the table between us. "Put it under the crystal, close your eyes, concentrate very hard and I will then be able to answer your question". What I wrote on the piece of paper was, "Will I always be a homosexual?"

Fortunately—being rebellious by nature—I didn't follow her instructions to the letter. I peeked. I saw her take the piece of paper out through some opening in the bottom of the table, read it, then put it back. "Open your eyes now," she said. "You're a very troubled young man. I'm getting that very strongly. But your particular trouble can be cured. What you must do is leave your old life and join our gypsy caravan." Even the gypsies were into "cures"!

I was tempted—though I'd seen her trick with the piece of paper. A measure, I guess, of my desperation. "Maybe she *can* cure you," I thought, "maybe you should go with her." I felt terribly torn up, couldn't decide. In the end, I did not show up at dawn with all my worldly goods

The "sickness" model of homosexuality had been drummed into me. That's why I waited so long before I had sex. It wasn't until my first year in graduate school at Harvard in 1953 that I finally got up the courage to go into my first gay bar. Soon after, I met a man—I'll call him "Larry"—and was with him for five years. Our relationship wasn't entirely monogamous, but nearly so for the first few years. I was very close to him. He was different from me in many ways—I'm usually attracted to opposites; not always, but usually. Larry was 19 or 20 when we met (I was 22) working class Irish Catholic, from a small town near Boston. Very attractive physically—to me anyway. He was my romantic ideal, I was his intellectual one. That's one way to put it, I suppose. I was living in the graduate dorm and later, from 1954-57 in Adams House as a resident tutor. Larry lived with his family, but he'd often stay with me. There was no way we could afford to live together on a regular basis. Neither of us had any money. He had a lousy job in a department store, I was trying to get by on my tutor's salary...

You know, sometimes when I think about the Fifties, I think everything has changed—the culture, me, the community. Other times I think very little has changed. A student of mine from when I taught at Princeton (1962-1971) recently came to see me (1977). He's 26 now, but has been "out" only a year. His big breakthrough to date has been meeting a guy in one of the johns at the porno movies he frequents who "actually talked *to me!*" *This is a bright, politically sophisticated guy—active in SDS as an undergraduate. Yet here he is at age 26 not knowing where to go to meet other gay men, except for bathrooms. It made me think things are no easier for gay people now than they ever were. In other moods I know—or hope—that's wrong. But I'm not sure.*

Like take my relationship with Larry. We had a damn good thing. And a support group, a circle of friends. There were bars, too. The life was circumscribed and secretive, of course. And our self-image wasn't so hot. I remember long talks with my gay friends at Harvard about whether we could achieve any *sort of satisfying life, "stunted" as we were. We accepted as given that as homosexuals we could never reach "full adult maturity"—whatever the fuck that means. Then it meant what everybody said it did: marrying, settling down, having a family. We knew we'd never qualify, and despised ourselves for it. But it's too simple to reduce "growing up gay in the Fifties" to a one-dimensional horror story...*

EXCERPTS FROM MY DIARY OF 1956-7—
PLUS MY FEELINGS ON RE-READING THEM IN 1981:

August 28, 1956:

Told Weintraupt today [*the therapist I'd been seeing for about a year*] that I was going to quit. By the time the hour was up, I had, as usual, changed my mind. Mostly because I got him to qualify the ban on homosexual contacts. He now says it's *Larry* I must stay away from [*following Weintraupt's dictate, I'd broken off with Larry a month previously*), not necessarily all contacts—though the greater the abstemiousness, the better. All I needed was an opening: I spent three hours tonight touring the bars, river, common, etc....

August 29:

1:00 a.m.: Just back from the bars. Roger asked me home. He and Paul, it seems, are all finished. Three months ago he was quoted as saying: "I don't think I could live without him." At least not for three months. And so it always seems to go. Is any genuine commitment between homosexuals possible? God knows I miss Larry. How I wish he were here tonight waiting for me in bed, sweet, affectionate . . . and yet I can't really settle down with him. I have no confidence in our building any sort of a life . . .

September 2:

. . . went to the bars. I was in one of my exuberantly vain moods— I looked well, Larry was safely on the Cape [*vacationing*] and couldn't *directly* prick my conscience ("You supposedly gave me up for the analysis, and here you are a month later cruising in the bars")—I had a luxurious three hours to exert my charms on the multitude.

Got quite drunk and came home with a youngish guy who I thought would be a good fuck. But he was lousy in bed— inexperienced physically, inane in every other way: "You're different from any of the others I've met"; "What nationality are you?—part Russian?—they must be a passionate race"; "You're a hairy pest from Budapest."

After two hours of non-erect activity, we finally managed an orgasm. I was afterwards completely repulsed by what I'd done; this absurd compulsive intimacy with an anonymous body—and a disappointing one at that (which is perhaps why I'm so righteously repulsed).

He left early this morning. I've been moping around ever since. Came very close to rushing off to see Larry on the Cape. It's extraordinary how "right" seeing him would make everything. But I've yielded to this too many times before, and always without lasting satisfaction. It's been a full month now since we've seen each other— I've *got* to hold off—I *cannot* form any lasting relationship with him—why, I'm not sure—but this I do know, that it won't work, and I must give him a chance to free himself.

September 3:

The great drought is over—with the usual awful results. Last night Larry called. I was so glad to hear from him, and under almost no pressure, agreed to meet him ... eventually I was talking drunkenly—meaning it all—about giving up the analysis, about missing him terribly, etc. And finally, sex. As miraculous as ever, and followed, as ever, by panic over what I had done and remorse over what I had said. ....

Will it ever be resolved? When I see him I'm lost; and I can't seem to stop myself from seeing him. Yet it's never enough. Could I really give up the analysis and accept my life as it now stands? Also impossible...

September 4:

Nervous about having to tell Weintraupt what happened last night. Half hoping, like a renegade schoolboy, to be "dismissed". But I was unable to goad either him or myself into it.

The confessional did me good. And now, I suppose, the usual drifting till the next crisis. What of all the promises I made to Larry last night? Today I consummate the immorality by not even calling him. What else can I do? If I call, I merely re-establish a lifeline that consists of half-promises that always remain unfulfilled, and yet always remain. If only I could know that after my physical and neurotic needs are spent, there's still something left for us to live on. I sometimes think there is—but Weintraupt has thrown so many of my feelings into doubt and confusion, I can't even be sure of "sometimes". And so I'll continue to drift; trying not to call—hoping he'll call me; continuing to go to Weintraupt—planning imminently to quit.

(1981): Weintraupt was not my first therapist. I had previously gone (been sent, *by my parents) at age 15 to find out why I was so*

monosyllabic and moody. It was enlightened in 1945 to send your kid for therapy. It would have been more so if everyone in the family had gone: I wouldn't have felt that tensions at home were exclusively of my making. The therapist helped further to convince me that they were. I saw him for several months, at the end of which time he announced his "solution": I should embrace my mother and tell her how much I loved her. Yup—swear to God! I paced my bedroom for hours trying to get up the courage; I had trouble talking to my mother, let alone touching her. "Do it!" I yelled at myself, "Do it!!" I went downstairs, grabbed the startled woman, hugged her like a robot out of R.U.R., and said a loud, metallic, "I love you!"—and was promptly showered with tears of joy. "I knew it was going to be all right," she kept repeating, "I knew it would be." Idiot therapist! The thaw at home lasted a couple of days or weeks. Then status quo ante pace.

I never told that therapist about my homosexual feelings— though I was already aware of them. I think I came closest when relating a dream. I was in a glass house masturbating (or was it having sex with a man?), terrified that people were watching from every adjacent apartment house. "What were you terrified of," asked Sigmund Pangloss. "Dunno," I mumbled.

September 7. 1:30 a.m.

Just back from the bars. Larry was there and we mooned around each other—with intermittent snarls—all night. Curse Weintraupt and my bloody fine powers of resistance! I'm so sick of considering consequences, "looking ahead"—to what? To a question mark, to the bare possibility that I may someday be able to marry and have children.

1:45: Larry called a few minutes ago. "Can I borrow your car to get home?" "Sure, I'll meet you at the gate [*of Adams House*] in 2 minutes." And at the gate he looked so beautiful. Then he cried and said he loved me and swore he'd never "bother" me again. How the hell can I resist? I asked him to come upstairs. He hesitated and said he was tired of "taking the blame". We went through this 3 or 4 times. Finally, in a pique at his stubbornness, I walked away—half expecting and more than half hoping to be called back. But no, he let the gate close. So now I'm back in my room. Chastity intact, but virtue assuredly not. So much for self-congratulation—celibacy by necessity this time, not choice.

September 8. 2:00 a.m.

I'm like a stupid child who can't profit from experience. Larry returned the car during the afternoon and I invited him up, although I was playing cards. He slept while we played and then when the others left, I woke him, crawled into bed, caressed him—and that was that. I simply made no effort to resist. Why invite him up in the first place? Why not wake him hurriedly?—"late for dinner"; "let's catch the early show," etc. No, none of those sensible things. Attraction, tenderness, wonderfully passionate sex—and then the usual regret over the destructiveness of my lust, both to Larry and to my analysis.

September 10:

I quit the analysis this morning. After months of indecision, the final action was almost unexpected. I told Weintraupt about Saturday night with Larry—and about a dream in which my "auditing" a course evolved into a symbolic reenactment of my attitude towards the analysis—i.e., an onlooker, an auditor, rather than a participator. From there it was only a step to being told my attitude made the analysis circular and endless; and since in honesty I couldn't swear that I would be able to change it, it was mutually agreed that it would be best to stop. Yet having made the decision, I can't accept it. Accepting it means accepting my life, being satisfied with it. And I can't...

Larry arrived unexpectedly in my room immediately after I got back from Weintraupt. He's just had word that he may have Hodgkin's disease—brought on by his lung ailment.

(1981): Larry had had mysterious growths on his lungs ever since I'd known him. One winter the doctors performed an exploratory operation which did nothing to lessen the mystery but left his torso criss-crossed with ugly scars. His doctors kept shifting their diagnosis—and kept Larry shuttling in and out of hospitals.

I spent the evening with him—the Brockton Fair—and tried to take his mind off the news [*soon after, the diagnosis was retracted*]. His reaction under pressure is (as always) remarkable—his deep upset obvious, but uncomplaining and free of self-pity. He's an extraordinary stoic; I never admire and love him more than when I see his quiet acceptance of unhappiness. I couldn't get myself to tell him about quitting the analysis, because he would expect me now to be propelled into his arms—permanently... What to do? I need more time to think. My first impulse is to resume analysis—but this time making the greatest possible effort to resist all homosexual contact. Have I ever *really* tried before? Or have I assumed incapability and infirmity and comforted myself with the thought that although I continued to act out, I was nevertheless "improving" simply by sticking to the mechanics of treatment. If I go back this time, I must *truly* commit myself to it ...

September 11. 1:30 a.m.

Didn't call Weintraupt. I think I've passed beyond the initial stage of feeling lost and helpless. I'm going to try it this way for a while ... saw Larry for dinner. We had sex later—how great not to follow it with panic and guilt: I told him I'd quit the analysis but that I wouldn't be able to commit myself to a monogamous relationship, that I remain incapable (don't all homosexuals?) of finding satisfaction permanently with one person. He didn't press for further explanation or commitment, since he sensed I wasn't ready or willing. He's extraordinarily perceptive in gauging my moods. And extraordinarily tolerant of them.

(1981): To spell out the obvious: I'd wholly internalized the then standard view of the "homosexual condition"—namely, to be homosexual was to be incapable of commitment to another human being. I'd internalized, too, the sex negativism of the culture: not to be monogamous, to enjoy sex with more than one person was to be "irresponsible". Homosexuality equalled promiscuity, and promiscuity equalled irresponsibility. Put another way, "health" could be recognized by the absence of desire—or at least the need to act on the desire—for more than one person.

Though I now take issue with the perjorative label "promiscuous" being automatically applied to all non-monogamous sexual activity, I do still feel (a residue from the earlier years of psychoanalytic indoctrination?) that some distinction exists and needs to be maintained between compulsive promiscuity and enjoying a variety of sexual experiences. The degree of compulsiveness involved—the driven quality—may be central to that distinction; it's the difference between being open to the pleasures of variety and obsessively needing a multiplicity of sexual experiences (to reinforce a sense of self-worth, or whatever).

As for Larry and me, after being together for three years, I had discovered—as do most people—that after obsession eases, resistance lessens, mutuality increases, the rest of the world comes back into focus—and some of it in shapely form. Again like most people (in the Fifties) I took this deviation from the monogamous ideal as a symptom of incapacity—for commitment, intimacy—even though I deviated more in the realm of fantasy than action.

September 13. New York
    1:00 a.m. Drove down from Boston today for the rehearsal for Don's [*a boyhood friend*] wedding ... so *much* contentment ... wives bearing, husbands beaming ... perhaps I mistake it—and am merely romanticizing ...

September 15. New York
    ... dinner with Kenny [*and old friend; in 1975 he was murdered in New York City by a hustler*] at "East 55". Good meal, but expensive, and my! so elegant. The place filled with babbling queens who, because they can afford to spend $5 on a dinner, feel they are also entitled to talk at the top of their lungs. Oh why criticize—I suppose the sick should stick together!

(1981): Since my homophobia's already well established, the only real surprise in this entry is $5 for dinner being thought "expensive".

Then down to Lennie's [*a gay bar*] in the Village for a night of drinking. Spent most of it talking to a redhead from Toronto named Rick: simple, unassuming, good-natured—and I *thought,* very attractive. As per usual, it took going to bed with him to prove I was wrong. Pudgy, hairy, slight cock, less technique. These disappointments seem to be my stock in trade. Perhaps I purposely single out those to whom I'm only marginally attracted—thus ensuring disappointment. A way of punishing myself? Of preventing any further involvement? Anyway, I swear it—no more nights like tonight. Wholehearted desire or *nothing.*

(1981): A luxurious oath, a function of youth; this demanding American Adam, entitled to uncompromising fulfillment as a birthright. In time, oaths turn to pleas—for that very marginal sex we foreswore as beneath us. The young are marvelously arrogant. Age is grateful for the occasional mercy fuck. Or, if cursed with unrelenting standards of "beauty", learns the importance of money.

September 18:
    Adams House—and Cambridge—full of sound again. It's exciting watching everyone return and bustle about. And being busy. I

love squeezing in my research [*I was working on my doctoral thesis in history*] between appointments, meetings, errands, etc. I exhilerates me to have a crowded daily schedule. Am I afraid of too much free time—empty, unplanned, threatening of the unexpected? Oh in part, yes—but surely not *all* my responses are sick! Being on the threshold of new experiences—buying new books, thinking of a new teaching schedule, directing a new play in the House—it's *fun,* damn it, and I refuse to reduce all my experiences and motives to psychological (neurotic) explanations...

(1981): In these years I was rarely in touch with my anger at being categorized as "sick"—after all, I believed it—and still less often did I let it surface (as in the above entry). Yet a subterranean defiance, however suppressed and deprecated, helped (I now see in retrospect) to sustain and, ultimately to extricate me from reductive psychosocial "explanations" of my being. Yet the rebellion against self-castigation which therapy (society) instilled in me would take a long, long time to consolidate and assert itself with any consistency. Before that could happen, I needed to recognize the importance of culture—of the role social moralizing about same gender love and lust plays in producing disabling self-recrimination. I also needed to understand (and this awaited the gay liberation movement of the late sixties/early seventies) that it isn't individual variations on the norm that require "amelioration" (through "treatment" punishment, guilt) but rather a cultural climate that equates variance with "disturbance".

September 21:
Peculiarly depressed today. No apparent reason. I think I begin to regret leaving the analysis. Every *thing* is in order; all goes well—I am "free", busy, have enough money again, etc. No overt problems— nothing, in other words, on which to focus my anxiety. Nothing is wrong. And yet nothing is right.

September 22:
Big scene with Larry. I told him the plain truth—I don't want to lose him but can't be completely faithful. What a goddamn mess I am. Simply not capable of love. Can anything be worse than a life of promiscuity, of objects not people? That's what I'm faced with and have to accept. Larry put a ban on our having sex. "We've got to try to form a new kind of relationship—friends, since lovers hasn't worked; and occasional sex with each other is merely postponing the adjustment". Sensible, logical. But the unfortunate fact remains that

we *want* to continue going to bed with each other. If exclusive, Larry would consider it ideal; if occasional, I would. But the thought of *never,* frightens me more than Larry. *I* want everything.

(1981): Part of the trouble, probably most of it, was the going social definition of what constituted being a "mess". Homosexuality was sign enough, as the current consensus saw it, but to want to sleep with more *than one man during a lifetime was considered the equivalent of being unable to "love". The One-Person-Now-And-Forever model of "health" was applied in the Fifties almost as rigorously to heterosexuals. That is, officially. As Kinsey had already shown in his books, a large percentage of married* men *paid greater fealty to the ideal of monogamy in their rhetoric than in their behavior. Like most American* women, *I had been trained to believe that interest in anyone other than the Beloved was all at once a definition of emotional immaturity and the equivalent of emotional treachery.*

September 26:
A call from George L. tonight. His trial's been postponed and he needs bail money [*George had been arrested by the state police in Ogunquit, Maine, where our crowd often vacationed. The beach at night was a well-known cruising spot. Police spotlights had caught George just as he was going down on somebody*]. I sent him $50, promising more next week when my salary check arrives . . . I suppose my motive was largely egotistical—"you're a great chap"; "most people wouldn't be bothered," etc. In fact, I feel some but not much sympathy for him; word has long since been out that the beach is dangerous. I sent him money not out of active sympathy but out of the *decision* to be helpful. Maybe that's not so bad. Maybe we could all use more artificiality—the conscious cultivation of our feeble impulses to generosity. Anyway, I did the right act—in which case can the motive ever be wrong?

October 1:
Burning after urination . . . of course I can think of all kinds of reasons for penis pains—guilt over my resumed homosexuality, guilt over my ambivalent treatment of Larry, the desire, by pleading invalidism to *escape* homosexual contact . . .
And so what? Can I *know* which if any of these "causes" is the true one? Is it so impossible for me to have an actual physical symptom—a nice, *healthy* disease? Probably. Weintraupt made me so aware of my hypochondria that I have become a double prisoner of it—as both an

unconscious drive, and a conscious explanation.

October 3:

Started writing today [*doctoral thesis on Charles Francis Adams*]. Very excited in spots. Thought everything put with inexpressible beauty and incisiveness. Then this evening I read the few pages to Larry and it seemed mostly flat and wordy. Now I feel it's all dreadful and I can't possibly continue. I won't try to correct—but will just keep going, otherwise I'll be endlessly polishing. I become absorbed in the writing itself, rather than the content. The *sound* of the sentences and the word patterns interest me more than the material I'm supposedly conveying ... hardly an "historical" approach.

October 4:

Spend the evening with Frank D. He's just failed his Generals [*Ph. D. Orals*] and is badly affected ... a horrible blow to those as self-centered as most homosexuals are. With their intellectual self-respect destroyed, there's nothing much to fall back on, since the "academic queens" at least have been long using it as a compensation—a mask—for what they consider to be their other defects and inadequacies. With the "binder" gone, Frank has quite literally fallen apart.

(1981): Apparently I'd never seen a straight person "fall apart" after failing Generals. Which means I either couldn't see or had a remarkably limited circle of friends.

October 8:

... good luck at the bars. Instead of posing—and waiting—*I* made a move for once, and directly approached someone. Got a pleasant response and left with him but wasn't sure until he actually asked "if I'd like to come up" whether I was going to have to be content with a "nice conversation" ... Probably the best-looking person I've ever been to bed with ... Just graduated from Ohio State—in Boston for a visit—name of Bob E. A marvelous combination of youthfulness (superb skin, lovely body) and yet masculinity. He was shy of certain "practices" [*meaning, if my memory serves, he wouldn't let me fuck him*], yet wonderfully affectionate—even passionate. And I did him without a qualm—in fact with regret when it was over. [*Ordinarily I had such qualms, except with Larry*].

... I spent the night with him at his hotel and was rebuffed when I tried to have sex with him this morning. Nor could I pin him down to another meeting before he goes back to Ohio.

I already have an awful incapacity to remember him in any tangible way ... deep pleasure briefly and then intensified frustration in attempting to re-create it ... anguish at having realized the ideal and having lost it again so soon. I almost wish I hadn't met him. I feel as if I've sleep-walked through the experience ...

October 12:

... continuing discomfort on urinating. Occasionally, seeing a pus-like emission. Called Dr. P. [*urologist*], but he can't see me until Tuesday. In the meantime I sit and fret, imagining—when I do specify the anxiety—cancer of the prostate, the end of sexual activity, etc. Of course P. checked all this last week (but not the prostate) and said I had torn the skin, or some such and there was no disease. Still, this was before I noticed the mucous-like substance and since I've seen him there's been no change whatsoever. What I want, I suppose, is for him to check the prostate, tell me it's fine—reassure me, in other words, as to my "intactness". If I had to bet on it, I would place all odds on the trouble being either a minor one, or wholly imaginary. And yet realizing this does nothing towards relieving my anxiety.

October 14:

Went to a most enjoyable party at Margaret R's—charmed by a cameo-like Radcliffe girl named Ann. But promptly at 10:00—fearing I would turn into a man!—I deserted the party on some pretext and rushed to the bars for a little more self-torture. And I got it. Larry was there, faithfully watching and waiting—compounding thereby my unhappiness. Out of default I left with him and talked "straight"—I hate tormenting him and yet I am incapable now of changing my insane pace of promiscuity. [*As I look back over the diary, I had had sex once in two weeks*]. I said I'm useless to both of us. We agreed not to see each other any more.

October 15:

Went to Dr. P. and this time he *did* find an infection in the urinary tract. I'm relieved that the cause of the pain was such a relatively minor one—and especially that there *was* a cause! ...

Spent a pleasant evening at Ray's [*my closest friend, also a graduate student*] ... lots of drink, talk. Nice people—like them all ... especially David E., who I haven't known before ... warm, sensitive ... not at all an intrusive, "look-at-me" personality. Rare anywhere, but especially in a homosexual. I must stop this business of judging homosexuals as a separate breed (but aren't they?) and being so persistently amazed at the occasional nice ones—there are few enough anywhere and should be admired as such apart from categories—

October 16-17:

...sick the last few days from the acromycin Dr. P. prescribed. It upset me badly—without helping the urinary infection, so today he has switched me to sulphur. No matter how minor the disorder I seem able to cling to it with amazing tenacity!...

October 18:

...Larry called unexpectedly ... The usual happened—talk leading to desire leading to sex ... The desire returns, but not sufficiently to make me want to give up my roaming.

October 19:

3:00 a.m. ... told Larry he could stay over at my place—since he has to go to work in the morning. But passing the river [*Harvard's chief cruising ground*] on our way home, he saw that it was crowded and decided to stop off. That was an hour ago and he hasn't appeared. Obviously he's met someone, and ... I'm upset. But when I dropped him at the river I was actually *relieved.* I didn't want to have sex with him and rushed home to get to "sleep" before he returned... He just arrived. Has only been talking to someone he previously met. He's all affection. What an imbecile I am—I disgust myself at times...

October 20:

...Stayed in tonight ... I feel so much better when I do ... Really a bourgeoisie at heart—early to bed, etc. Feel cleaner and more satisfied with myself.

(1981): Maybe Descartes is where it all went wrong—all the splits and separations, the moralistic dichotomies (staying at home versus the "neurotic" drive to look for sex/companionship, etc.) The hideous overlay of metaphysical categories on garden variety shifts in moods and needs!

October 23:

Larry was here tonight and we had sex ... we simply wanted to and we did. I sometimes think all our "scenes"—eternal farewells, etc.—are indulged in part for pleasure: the stimulation of love forsaken and found again; of playing on the subtler threads of the relationship to test how far we can or cannot drive the other and then how easily we can or cannot recapture him. If we were legally tied to each other—as in marriage—it might soon degenerate into mutual disinterest.

October 24:

...to see O'Neill's "Long Day's Journey Into Night"... O'Neill reminds me of Dreiser—formless, heavy-handed, crudely powerful. Really a mediocre epic poet ... The best lines in the play were Baudelaire's.

November 4:

1:00 a.m. The news from Hungary is shattering. How unimportant our election seems in light of it. Discount political exaggeration, and how much difference does it really make whether Eisenhower or Stevenson wins? A difference between complacent efficiency and at least the possibility of imaginative leadership—but agreement is already established on major questions...

November 5:

1:00 a.m. Heard Stevenson's final campaign speech on TV this evening. It was magnificent. He has extraordinary eloquence ... an imagination equal to the possibilities of our country ... a great man— and one who will never be President.

November 19:

I feel towards this delinquent Diary the way I used to towards Weintraupt—guilt at not keeping it up! ... My routine, in truth, is so busily monotonous, that I'm lulled into a dull sort of contentment... I feel repugnance at merely recording the trivial and the obvious, partly because the thesis writing is proving some sort of catharsis for my energies.

But, we'll try again—

November 20:

One of my tutees, Alex S., a sophomore, came to see me today— appealingly confused, boyishly upset at his sudden lack of interest in history ... He wants to "justify" his work, to find value beyond mere enjoyment (he doesn't seem to realize how rare *that* is among the "professionals") ... I tried to keep my own disillusionment out of it, so as not to confuse him still further . . . I think I did well by him and this pleased me; helped him to see his *own* problems and aims without (miracolo!) obtruding mine. Of course, his extraordinary attractiveness accounted for my special effort . . . we are not indiscriminate in our attentions—no one treats all the world alike . . .

(1981): I do still feel that eroticism is often a component of good teaching. I can be attracted to (care about) qualities of character or mind enough to make a special effort. But if I care about a body too, that much more of myself goes into the contact. And if the body is spectacular enough, the effort will match it—even without qualities of character or mind. I want to matter (become part of?) my somatic ideal. I think the Greeks understood this—even to sanctioning physical contact between older men (teachers, guides) and younger. In our society, the mere recognition that an erotic element is present in teaching—and of course not only male/male—would constitute an enormous advance. Finding a way to acknowledge that element would constitute utopia.

November 26:
     . . . Isabel [*she and I had met at Ogunquit the previous summer*] was here for the weekend—mainly because Don, Joan, *et al* were due from New York for the Yale-Harvard festivities and I felt compelled to produce a date. Isabel means more to me than a convenience . . . yet I was relieved to see her leave early Sunday . . .

(1981): I'm almost sure it was on this visit that Isabel came into my bed one morning (she was sleeping on the sofa bed, in the living room). Sweetly, warmly, she cuddled with me. Tensely, mechanically, I cuddled back, frightened that she wanted to have sex. Either she didn't or she got my message; we never did more than cuddle. And I felt guilty and wretched over my "inadequacy".
     All of which reminds me of my debate at Fordham in April, 1973 with Dr. Irving Bieber. Three out of four male homosexuals he's studied show "fear of female genitalia". Pathology, he says. And the source? A detached, minimizing father. But has anyone studied the degree of fear in male hetero-sexuals? I suspect it might match or exceed that of homosexuals—especially if the sample studied was as skewed (102 patients in treatment) as Bieber's. Besides, Bieber ignores the contribution of social pressure in producing "fear" (whether in gay or straight men). If society didn't insist that the definition of male adultness was an omnipresent desire to fuck females, there wouldn't

be the built-in sense of inadequacy when that desire isn't present, nor the avoidance of closeness with women as a device for avoiding the feeling of inadequacy ... I wonder what it might have been like for Isabel and me if I hadn't gotten into that bed with a destructive set of expectations in my head. I would have enjoyed the cuddle. And maybe more.

... Jim came over ... a new contact [*we met the previous week*], someone I was attracted to and eager to impress. We spent about four hours drinking—and five in bed—which has left me feeling empty and disgusted ... I was interested in Jim—beyond the physical ... the sex partly cooled my ardor (for what? conquest?) and the conversation completed the job. There was something hard about him which came out only by degrees, occasionally blatant egoism, sometimes just (just indeed!) a lack of concern, of tenderness for his partner—in conversation or sex. I suppose I'll see him again, but the disappointment adds to this morning's depression. I keep telling myself I'm looking for something permanent—someone to grow with, to do things for, to bring meaning into routine. Yet when I go to the bars, I consistently look for the most physically appealing person. These pick-up bars don't allow for any other form of contact. Sex is the basis of meeting, and sex is the first, rather than the final expression of the relationship. I tell myself how meaningless this anonymous cycle of body and body is, but I continue to repeat it; partly, no doubt, because of the necessity to keep proving myself, but also because the means of forming a healthier, more complete relationship are slight. With Jim, I thought there was some hope; I really don't now. But my disappointment is real, which makes me hope that my desire for permanence is also real.

(1981): The standard social values and therapeutic vocabulary of the day: sexual pleasure can only be justified in the context of a "meaningful" (i.e. "caring", "permanent") relationship; disconnected lust leads to emptiness and disgust. The self-recriminations that followed my failing to measure up to stereotypic norms were more than a strategy of atonement, expiation for having experienced pleasure not officially sanctioned. They affected the experience itself, diluting and distorting it. As the entry makes clear, what one expects in advance from an encounter is usually what one ends up taking away from it.

December 15:

Up late last night—Adams House Xmas party. Most of today on the bed, reading; due to virus and bad throat. Didn't go to either Margy or Ina's party—not "up to it". Yet miraculously, I found the strength at 10:30 to find my way to the bars. Uneventful. Home with a worse throat.

December 17:

Still feeling sick ... Was going to the bars, but decided to be sensible—that is, to cater to my hypochondriacal rather than my homosexual neurosis!

February 16, 1957:

For some reason I feel like writing an entry today—the first in many weeks. Some impressions I want to get down after a surfeit night of drink and sex. I successfully maneuvered Thom H., one of my heros—at a distance—to bed. Good sex. Though my fantasy of 6'3" of rock-like masculinity progressively flattened as the usual nice, ineffectual mama's boy came out. But still, good, if not ideal. And yet today my guilt, or at least revulsion, is working overtime. All sorts of resolutions, too. Eager for work—never going to waste time bar-hopping again, etc. No satisfaction there anyway. All set for a return to analysis; must have a wife and family, only possible things that matter, etc. These illuminations, of course, are easy to produce after the appetite has been depressed by booze and sex.

(1981): I can't help but smile as I type the above. At the unerring self-dramatization. At the sorrowings of young Werther. At the conviction that everyone else (but especially all heterosexuals) were and would be happier than I. At the effort—age 26—to strike a world-weary elegaic note. And—the smile disappears here—at the air-tight formulas into which I kept squeezing my experience; formulas which accurately parrotted social norms of the day, but almost entirely failed to help me understand what in fact I was living through.

I wish to change ... but parallel with this desire runs the stronger current of neurotic drive and compulsion, thwarting most of my efforts to change. I can neither give up my homosexual activities, nor devote myself guiltlessly to them. Paralyzed on the one side by desire and on the other by knowledge. Is this merely the neurotic or the human condition?

If I could only maintain the strong sense of disgust and renunciation which I felt all day—perhaps then I could make the necessary effort to change the pattern of my life. But I can already feel the resolution draining out of me, and the old empty compulsion taking its place—

(1981): I should have read more anthropology. A Siwan version of the above: When Arah offered me his son last night for anal intercourse—as any thoughtful host would—my pleasure in the boy was compromised by my neurotic equation of sexual satisfaction with heterosexuality. As a result, intercourse seemed little more than mutual masturbation. If I could maintain the strong sense of disgust that I felt all day, perhaps then I could make the necessary effort to change the pattern of my life.

I've sought advice from the Elders. They feel I hold on to my deviance out of defiance—a stubborn refusal to let nature takes its bi-sexual course. Their words make entire sense to me. Yet I can already feel the resolution draining away, and the empty compulsion to sleep only with women taking its place.

June 13::

So much has happened since my last entry [*4 months earlier*] Grandma's death, Lucile's [*sister*] divorce, my Yale appointment, my ulcer, my completed doctorate. Today was graduation. I'm left this evening with nothing much to do and a sense of slight depression, so thought I would start the Diary again. A little something to keep me busy, I suppose—a new project. I can't yet relax from the rush and tension of the last few months. But the sense of incompletion goes deeper. I need work to focus on; these brief pauses, though much anticipated during the preceding months of hard work, are more distressing than the strain of a heavy schedule. I'm already planning ahead for my courses at Yale next year . . . I seem to enjoy myself most when I take occasional hours from a "productive" day rather than indulging in long periods of unplanned, unfilled leisure. Free time—in any large dose—becomes flabby and suffocating.

September 16:

Now that I'm settled in at Yale [*my first full-time teaching job*] I thought I'd try keeping the Diary again . . .

I just got back last night from a quick run up to Boston. Classes begin on Wednesday and after that the chances of my getting away will be less. Spent most of the time alone with Larry . . . Why is it that only on the point of severance do I become most keenly aware of the deep affection ... as if I allow myself the full emotion only when I safely know that it can be indulged in only infrequently.

September 18:

A tough few minutes at the beginning of my first class today. I was literally choked up with nervousness. Arrived ten minutes early, sat in the chair at the front of the room and buried myself in the *N. Y. Times.* As the students poured in (31!) I occasionally mustered enough courage to glance up from the paper. Eventually—after I started to talk (what else?!)—I settled down into mild terror. I must have given a lousy impression—stuffy and stern.

September 20:

Dr. Igen [*therapist*] accepted me as a patient today—3 times a week at $20 per—I don't really want to start the pain and upset of analysis all over again. But I must, if I'm ever to have an identity ...

(1981): Meaning, its perhaps redundant to add, an "acceptable" identity, some placation of my passionate craving to fit in, to "belong".

September 21:

Much depressed—woke up feeling this way. Stomach kicking up, which both helped cause the "pits" and was the result of them. Spent the day reading and doing odds and ends around the apartment [*I was living off campus*] ... evening went to the gay bars, which I had sworn pre-arrival at New Haven, that I would stay out of. Once having started, I'll probably continue; I can't really stay away from it. So I risk my job—but I'm sufficiently depressed not to care. If I could stand still and *understand* the depression (something about teaching and the insecurities it arouses, plus being unsettled and lonesome— but this doesn't get below the surface), I'd no doubt be better off. But homosexuality has been a channel—*the* channel—for so long—that it's easier to keep running.

(1981): Poor bastard. You wanted some companionship and sex, but had "learned" to cover over those human enough needs with a shit- load of self-castigation.

September 24:

Had a good session with Dr. Igen today, but my stomach trouble and depression continue apace. Called Larry this evening for a little long-distance solace. Can't wait till he arrives on Friday. Despite the wild fluctuations in my feeling for him over the last few years, my genuine attachment to him has never been more apparent.

September 29:

Larry just left. We had an awfully good weekend together—didn't really do very much—saw the Yale-Conn. football game yesterday (boring as always) and had dinner at Mory's. Except for that—none of it exactly new and exciting for me—we stayed near the apartment, ran errands, took rides, etc. It all went too fast. If I don't love him, why did I cry so painfully when it came time for him to leave? If I do love him, why has our relationship fluctuated so wildly the last few years. A riddle I long since gave up on. Anyway, it's awful being alone again...

(1981): The riddle's a little less dense these days: it's hard to sustain intimacy if you can't sustain a sense of self-worth. And to have grown up gay in America in the Fifties was to view oneself as emotionally shallow, stunted.

October 2:

Went to the Taft, George and Harry's and Pierelli's [*New Haven's semi-gay bars—that is, bars where gay men were known to appear*] tonight—the works! Nothing happened, but aside from that, I've all but given up the idea of restricting my activity to outside of N. Haven. The hell with it—N.Y. and Boston are too far away and I'm too horny. Anyway I now tell myself that nothing really dire could happen ... if a student reports me to a Dean or some such, what can he really say except that he saw me in a homosexual bar. It's unlikely the Administration would take action on what is only a suspicion.

(1981): My concern was realistic, not paranoid. These were the years when a half dozen male faculty members were hounded from their jobs at Smith when discovered to be in possession of "pornographic" (gay) materials. As I was soon to discover, attitudes at Yale were comparable. In 1958 ('59?) a faculty member and friend of mine—I'll call him "Eli"—was fired, though under somewhat different circumstances than having been seen in a compromising bar. At a drunken student/faculty party, Eli followed up on a student's verbal pass—

groped him in a corner? whispered sweet scatalogical nothings in his ear? I don't know. Whatever, the student freaked, ran shouting (literally) into the night—and ultimately into the Dean's office. The Administration (humanely, some might argue, given the fierce homophobia of the day) hinted that if Eli would deny the incident, it would be overlooked. Eli wouldn't. The Administration then asked for his resignation, offering to help him find work in an administrative capacity (not as a teacher) in some other school. Eli refused that, too.

October 13:

Saturday night, bar-hopping in New York. Met a Bill N. in the Annex [*a gay bar*]. Despite my attraction, shouldn't have gone with him mainly because (a) he had a lover—no future and (b) he was of limited interest to me as a person—also no future. Yet my six weeks in New Haven made me feel as if I "had" to have sex, so off we went and on the whole, it came off rather better than most of my experiences of this nature do. He was sufficiently attractive physically, and technically proficient, to make bearable, even to a degree unnecessary, the lack of emotional attrachment.

October 14:

Feeling lonely most of the day, though a full evening's work has helped dissipate it. The prospect of spending my life alone has become more alive and painful—living off-campus and inaccessible to casual "droppers-in" and having to cook and eat by myself. The prospects of a lasting homosexual relationship are too slim for me to get much comfort from the possibility; and a satisfying heterosexual relationship is still so remote that I can barely even wish for it. But perhaps either luck in the first area or Dr. Igen in the latter will make one or the other come true. In the meantime, I remain skeptical and unhappy.

October 21:

The weekend in Boston started badly, with Larry failing to meet me according to arrangment, or waiting for dinner as I'd asked him to—all the result, though he won't admit it, of my having gone to New York last weekend instead of to Boston. Understandable enough; since we have no "official" ties, his resentment has to come out indirectly. On my side, I was more angered at his studied disinterest than I had a "legal" right to be, clinging as I do to the double standard of my freedom and his devotion ... By Saturday, we had more or less patched things up ... I think.

October 29:

Staying busy, which I need to avoid the very real anguish of
loneliness I've been feeling. I've never been so fully conscious of being
quite literally "apart", "unconnected". My impulse at times like this is
to run—to give up teaching, friends, the future—and devote myself to
find *the* one—that never-never "right" person who'll make everything
sweet and meaningful. Yet when I do search, I invariably end up in
frantic pursuit not of a person but of a mere physical fantasy.

Dr. I. feels that at this point I would be foolish to try to resolve
basic difficulties by any rash decisions—e.g. giving up teaching,
moving to New York, etc. I have to sit tight and try to work the
problems out slowly and deliberately through the analysis. So sit we
will.

*(1981): I still think it makes sense to take time with important
decisions—and to try to avoid making them under the pressure of
momentary panic or impulse. But impulses should be attended to, not
dismissed out of hand; a valuable insight can come swiftly—and
prolonged brooding can dissipate rather than clarify its force.
Besides, some complaints deserve to be taken at face value; they aren't
always a cover, a technique of avoidance. A worker in an automobile
factory who complains about the boredom of the assembly line isn't
necessarily displacing his "status anxiety". The "surface" problems I
brought to therapy—about loneliness, teaching, the life of scholarship, living in New Haven—deserved more serious consideration as
valid issues in themselves; I was never encouraged to regard them as
other than a "blind".*

November 5:

To New York. Ended up going to Everard's two nights in a row.

*(1981): Everard's was a gay bathhouse. It still is, though it closed
briefly a few years back after a disastrous fire—caused by the criminal
negligence of the management in failing, as specified by law, to install
a proper sprinkling system—killed and maimed a dozen men.*

*Everard's was one of the places I frequented during the late
Fifties/early Sixties on my weekend trips to New York. My usual
pattern at the baths was to meet one man and go to a room with him. I
avoided orgiastic scenes, especially the steamroom. If I was going to
be gay, I was going to be gay in a way that was "seemly". In a way that*

approximated how straight people—sensible, adult, healthy straight people—behaved. You find one person and stick with him (her). My sexual repertoire was comparably limited in those days. With Larry I played the stereotypical male (dominant) role: out of bed, made the decisions, in bed did the fucking.

Much reasonably enjoyable sex with moderately attractive people— sufficient to black out any upsetting hesitations and doubts. But lack of sleep (I spent the weekend on Henry's [*a New York friend*] living room floor) soon produced the ripe conditions for reaction. Driving back up here last night filled with thoughts of renunciation, of an acute sense of the "disarray" such wantonness produces in my life. But resolution, like the guilt which prompts it, soon disappears. I can hardly lose sight of the fact that such behavior is destructive, but the compulsion to such activity (the bars being only a lesser version) remains even stronger...

November 7:
 Beginning to pick up the pieces after the upset of my weekend "frolic" in New York; though the degree of upset varies with the type of experience, I'm less prone than in the past to lay my sense of frustration or dissatisfaction at the door of "inadequate" sex (i.e. not the "right" person) ... I begin to see that it's the homosexual act itself which disturbs me—despite the physical pleasure and neurotic gain involved.

(1981): The new therapist—a decent, likeable man—had been helping me to this "clarification". Dr. Igen was less given to ideology than most psychiatrists of the day. Still, he had no doubt that homosexuality was symptomatic of a character disorder. But he never scrutinized—apparently never dreamed there might be a need to scrutinize—any of the assumptions that underlay his diagnoses and prescriptions. He merely accepted (as did most people in the Fifties, therapists and otherwise) the dictum that homosexuality by its nature *was destructive to individual growth; biological law—unspecified, unexamined—not oppressive social norms, produced the disturbing bi-products of same gender love or lust.*

November 10:
 Went to New York last night to meet Tom F., who was in from Texas ... We spent the night together at Henry's (who was away for the weekend). If we could have stopped short of actual sex, the

evening would have been far pleasanter. The preliminaries were deeply satisfying—I felt close and complete—but proceeding beyond, we seemed to draw further apart. I wanted his affection, not his body; being pushed into contact with his body, I gradually lost whatever affection I had felt. Ended up feeling distant and antagonistic and said good bye this morning with feelings of real relief . . .

Dr. Igen left today for his eye operation. Surprised myself by the depth of my upset—surprised and yet pleased at such a sign of significant involvement. He won't be back for at least a month. Rather than "hold the fort", I'll more likely destroy it. Don't see how I can curtail my activity without at least the security and profit of my visits to him. At any rate, a comfortable excuse for future promiscuity.

(1981): Igen, like Dr. Weintraupt before him, had recently made it clear that if I hoped to make further progress in analysis, I had to make a greater effort to control my impulses and show more willingness to face rather than run from my anxiety. I can still hear his litany: "Homosexuality is the channel through which you act out your anxieties. We must close the escape hatch. Only in that way can the anxieties surface, be analyzed and treated." I had explained (implored) that I'd tried that before, with Dr. Weintraupt, and the strain had proved intolerable. He persuaded me that I'd changed since then, that I was now older and wiser, better able to withstand the neurotic pressure to "act out". Besides, as he put it, "the injunction from above now coincides more exactly with what you feel within." Flattered, encouraged, I once more swore to take the veil.

November 22:

Picked the wrong weekend to stay in New Haven. Everything is crawling with Yalies and their dates—the big Yale/Harvard weekend. Stayed here to catch up on work and especially to prepare my next two lectures. Hoped to take in the New Haven bars in the process, but a quick reconnaissance tonight convinced me of the folly of that—too many students wandering into too many strange places. Just not worth the chance. Yet I wish so much that someone was here with me tonight.

(1981): For a moment I thought this might have been the football weekend of my drunken tangle in the small park that fronted fraternity row. But now I remember that was much earlier—when I was an undergraduate at Yale (in 1951 or '52): I followed some

stocky, equally drunk 20 year old out-of-towner into the park and (I think he encouraged me), groped him. He reacted in a rage, swung at me drunkenly, got hold of the collar of my jacket and ripped it down my back as I struggled out of reach and raced down the street. I told my roommates I'd gotten into a fight with "some townie". With my torn jacket as proof, I was treated as a hero. I trembled inside for days.

This was, if my sense of chronology holds, my very first homosexual "contact"—give or take those rubbing sessions as a boy in summer camp; plus one experiment in mutual fellatio with a high school friend (not to orgasm).

But soon after my fraternity row fracas Don, an undergraduate friend, casually mentioned that I should stay away at night from the "Green" (the large park in front of the Old Campus)—"it's a hangout for fairies." I was shocked—and overjoyed; at last a place to meet someone (I was 20 years old). That same night I got drunk, reeled down to the Green and sat on a bench opposite the only other person I could see in the area—a very fat, middle-aged black man. He whistled tantalizingly in my direction. I got up, reeled over and stood boldly in front of him. He started playing with my cock, then took it out of my pants. Wildly excited, I started to fondle him.

"Do you have any place we can go?" I whispered.

"Nope. No place."

Suddenly I heard laughter and noise coming in our direction. I was sure it was some undergraduates—and equally sure we'd been seen. Zipping up my fly, I ran out of the park—ran without stopping, panicked, hysterical, ran for my life back to my dorm room. I stayed in the shower for hours, cleaning, cleaning. I actually washed my mouth out with soap, though I hadn't used my mouth—other than to make a prayerful pact with the Divinity that if He let me off this time, I'd never, never go near the Green again. The panic lasted for days. By the end of the week I was back on the Green, drunk again. I met a dancer. We had sex in his car—that is, I let him blow me.

I can remember only one other experience while an undergraduate: being picked up by an older man cruising the area in his car. I got in, then changed my mind. He begged me to stay, said he'd "do anything I wanted to do." I got out, not unmindful (I now suspect) of the special pleasure fellow victims can derive from tormenting each other. Those are the only undergraduate encounters I can recall, the sum of my "sex life" until age 21. With men, I mean.

I had been through most of the heterosexual rituals. At age 15 (16?), staying with two high school friends at one of their parent's homes in Palm Beach, we went to a whore house one night. (A version of this, with some—and I don't know for certain which—details re-imagined, is in my one-act play, "The Recorder"). I hadn't been able to get an erection. The prostitute kindly put some ointment in the urethral opening of my cock, wrapped it in gauze and snapped on a rubberband. (Can this really have been standard preventive treatment for v.d. in the Forties?). With the outward credentials of having fucked, I could brag about "how great it had been" to my friends (one of whom had no gauze bandage; suspicion deflected to him). I remember the prostitute's effort to comfort me with off-ʰ ᵃnded remarks: "married men often come into the house and can't ᵍᵉt it up either—it's nothing to worry about, kid." I made her promise not to tell my friends that I'd "failed". She agreed; I remember her warm, sympathetic smile.

Still more vivid is the night of the senior prom in high school. I was 17 and had been dating a "wild" girl, Rachel, for a long time. We had promised ourselves—and announced to our friends—that we would "consummate our love" that night. (Some of this is also in "The Recorder"). After the prom our crowd went to Al's family apartment: very fancy, fit setting for the Big Event. Everyone lay around on the living room floor drinking and making out—and waiting for the moment when Rachel and I would go into the back bedroom; the whole group was vicariously losing its virginity through us. In the bedroom, Rachel and I got undressed and lay together on the huge bed. Again, I was impotent—but this time desperate, crazed:

"The doctor warned me that I've been making out too much. He said this would happen if I didn't cut down."

Rachel neither questioned nor accused. "I love you. I love you even if you can't get it up."

Again I lied to my friends. This time the excuse (agreed to by Rachel—I was lucky in my choice of women) was that we hadn't been able to do it because she was having a period. I was celibate till aged 20, when I had those few furtive experiences on the New Haven Green.

During my first year of graduate school at Harvard (1952-3), I made my first timid foray into a gay bar, the Napoleon. I met Ray. We went home that same night and had sex in my dormitory room. For weeks afterwards I avoided him, rushing in the opposite direction whenever I caught sight of him on campus. He finally cornered me one day: "Look—can't we be friends at least?" Caught somewhere between hysteria and relief, I managed to mumble "yes".

It was the beginning of a friendship that's lasted to the present

*day. The beginning, too, of allowing myself to know other gay people
socially, of gradually developing a circle of friends and entering a
subculture that brought me from individual isolation to collective
secrecy—a considerable advance, if one can understand (in a day
when all furtiveness is decried) the quantum jump in happiness from
private to shared anguish.*

*Soon after, I had my first affair—with "Rob" (at the time, as with
most affairs, it seemed a good deal more profound; but then I was
measuring it against the few desperate, anonymous forays of my
undergraduate years, not against the intensity of the relationship with
Larry that was soon to begin). I met Rob on one of my first visits to
the Napoleon. He had been a classmate at Yale, but we had barely
known each other there. Rob had long been "out" sexually, adored
and pursued me, glamorized me with his family estates and
connections. He came from a rich WASP family, long on lineage,
proud of its service in the diplomatic corps.*

*One evening Rob took me to meet his grandmother; something of
a formal presentation. She received us in the library of her
Manhattan triplex (not, I presume, as the prospective in-law her
grandson had in mind—but one can never be sure about the
sophisticated insights of the upper class in these matters). The butler
ushered us into the presence of a seemingly ancient and unquestionably formidable woman. Sitting unmoving in an armchair, dressed in
a full length black gown, a mass of snow-white hair framing a still
beautiful face, she allowed the exchange of a few rigorous plea-
santries. Dazed and intimidated, I neither heard them fully then nor
can recall any part of them now. But I do remember it was that same
night, as Rob and I changed clothes in an upstairs bedroom, that I
told him I probably loved him. For the first time. Tit for tat, he let me
fuck him. I resisted his badgering insistence that I pronounce it the
"best fuck" I had ever had, though I had had precious few. It may
have been my father's peasant stubbornness asserting itself, bristling
at the hint of* droit de seigneur.

*Though we called ourselves "lovers", our lovemaking was sharply
circumscribed. Most of the time I was "trade" for Rob—I would let
him blow me. The boundaries suited us both; they assuaged my guilt,
fed his preferred image as guide to the uninitiated. Within a few
months, our affair ended traumatically. I had to drop out of graduate
school for a series of operations on my back, and while recuperating
at home, wrote a "compromising" letter that my mother intercepted.
She demanded an explanation, tapped a ready reservoir of self-
loathing. I explained that* Rob *was queer, but I, of course, was not; I*

had let him blow me now and then because "my back problem prevented me from seeking the usual sexual outlets"; he had been a convenience. My mother "accepted" the explanation. In gratitude, I broke off with Rob. I've never seen him since. My memories of him are ungenerous, ironic. Even now—my head ostensibly trans-formed—resentment against the man who tried to take me a step beyond furtive anonymity in sex, lies like a stone in my gut, an immutable pleistocene fossil.

December 1:

Disappointing holiday in Boston. Larry and I got along only sporadically. My feelings toward him, as always, fluctuated between deep affection and sudden antagonism. I don't excuse him com-pletely. He did two or three overtly nasty things (suggesting, for example, that we go to the Turkish baths together Saturday night). The weekend ended in a burst of mutual recrimination and sullenness ... Time, I suppose, finally to put an end to the whole torturous business ... But I still feel so tied to him—in some deeply neurotic way—that I can't seriously envision cutting off all contact.

(1981): Why "neurotic"? Because of the fluctuations in feelings? But that's true of all deep attachments. Maybe our arc swung wider and more often than most, but I automatically ascribed that to personal deficiencies, never to the self-distrust engendered in us by a culture insistent that it was wrong ("sinful", "neurotic"—depending on whether the rhetoric was based on the religious or psychiatric model) for two men to be physical lovers, to care "too" much about each other.

December 5:

A lengthy, elegant meal at Jack's [*a gay faculty member I'd recently come to know*] for a group of bachelor fellows. Superb food, beautifully prepared and served; all very "upper-class homosexual". Mozart on the victrola, white Wedgewood plates, much clever banter. Pleasant enough people, I don't deny, but my points of meaningful contact with them are limited and I don't wish to join with an artificial band of "solidarity" what genuine interest and affection cannot cement.

I intend to try to stay put this weekend—not so much because of my workload, but more for the analysis. "Sitting still and suffering for science". (No—I must keep remembering it's for *me*) ... I hope I last through tomorrow night!

December 8:

Depressing weekend. Stayed in New Haven ... ulcer kicking up and generally unhappy.

December 10:

Harry D. [*a graduate student I'd met at a party; we'd been immediately attracted to each other, but he'd let me know his lover was visiting*] called last night at 2:00 a.m.—a surprise to say the least, after 6 weeks of silence. He came over tonight and like last time, I found him very attractive. Still, we went to bed too fast, before he had a chance to become a person to me.

(1981): More of the current cant. Yes, getting to know a person can enhance sex with them. It can also complicate and inhibit sex. No one formula can cover all moods, impulses, needs—and consequences. But an entity called lust does exist, often is evoked and heightened by anonymity and can—quite independent of "emotional commitment"—produce very satisfying sex. All of which is hardly news, but if known in 1957 was rarely acknowledged; and by me, apparently not known.

I didn't really get excited in bed, though physically he didn't disappoint me in the slightest. Too impersonal, I suppose; too routine.

(1981): Nuts. I remember the evening well. Harry had an enormous cock; in these, my reticent years, that got translated—even in the privacy of my own diary—as "physically he didn't disappoint in the slightest". He got instantly and stayed unyieldingly hard—and aggressively insisted his cock belonged up my ass. I demurred (that's the word), secretly thrilled, eager to please yet not in the way he wanted and therefore without confidence I could in any way. The kind of insecurity often present, initially, with someone I'm deeply attracted to. Though "insecurity" may itself be too standard a circumlocution. Realistic fear may be more accurate. Realistic because of the accurate recognition that a stranger is unexpectedly in control of my sense of well-being. Frightened because the transfer of power makes me aware of the fragility of that well-being, aware that primitive urges, a confluence of accidents, can at any moment disrupt my illusion of being in control.

December 17:

Getting lax with this ... nothing vivid enough to make me want to record it. Stayed in New Haven again over the weekend and went to a gay party ... had a long chat with my first two real live "dikes"[*sic*]—both very feminine and talkative. Hope to see them in New York; a safe way of enjoying female company.

(1981): I cringe at this, but have resisted—barely—the temptation to delete it. With the possible exception of the last clause, it could have been written by John Wayne. Which is why I've included it: it serves as a measure of the gulf between gay men and lesbian women (now as well as then, though less so now—I think), as well as graphically demonstrating the usually unacknowledged bond between gay men and straight men. In their behavior and values, gay men are often males first and gays second. The priority has recently begun to shift—at least within limited circles. But many gay men continue to patronize lesbians, dismissing them with the same stereotypic contempt employed by the society at large. And this is the chief (thought not the only) reason gay men and lesbians have had so much trouble working together harmoniously in the "movement". On the other hand, I don't think sexism is as strong among gay men as among straight; some gay men—and in increasing numbers, I believe—are more than rhetorically committed to feminism. But many feminists would dispute that, and others would go no further than wary optimism.

December 17:

I'm writing this to exorcise John D ... At my request, he came to see me about his failing grades ... he told me his whole life revolved around a girl back home; that to him this emotional involvement was far more important than the trivia he was told to absorb in his classes ... I agreed, but argued that love sometimes served as an excuse for blocking off other aspects of available experience that might prove satisfying; that he had in college the opportunity to become interested in those aspects; that it was *natural* for human beings to be curious, alert and involved; that to the degree that he was refusing to be, he was denying part of his nature. But in the process of saying all this, I wondered, and wonder even more now, whether *anything* I said made sense ... I do believe in the function of a University as something above and beyond servicing the social order. I believe education *does* make better human beings, because it raises doubts, instills humility, encourages flexibility. I said all this to John and I think I believe it; but I'm left with a gnawing sense of inadequacy—as

if I said all the "right" things without having said any of the true ones
... I'm so aware of the inadequacy of the "intellectual life" that I
always feel a little absurd in extolling its virtues—especially to one
who already possesses what to me seems infinitely more important
and infinitely more unattainable.

December 20:
   Ever since the bad time with Larry three weeks ago, I've been
rushing around filling the void with the usual pointless activities. The
last two weekends I've had bad experiences. First with a set of lovers
from Jersey—almost panic-stricken with regret after going home
with them.

*(1981): I remember it well. They picked me up in a bar in New York
City, then drove me out to their place in the country. The older of the
two was tall and angular—marginally attractive. The younger was
devastating: a short, powerfully-built farm boy from Maine, with an
enormous cock. We started out to have a threesome, but the older
man soon withdrew and went upstairs to bed. I was surprised and
confused. Did he find me unattractive (as I did him), or had it been
pre-arranged between them—had I been picked up to keep the
younger one happy? I remember how lonesome I felt, after sex, when
Maine withdrew upstairs to sleep with his lover, not inviting me to
join them. I dozed for a few hours on the living room couch, then
woke them early morning and asked to be taken to the bus. Why the
panic? That model in my head again. The contrast between my
aloneness, my "inability to make it with someone on a sustained
basis," and their togetherness.*

   The other bad experience was last weekend in New York ... met a
guy named Lou in the Big Dollar [*a gay bar*] and went home with
him. Rugged Italian type ... one track mind sexually—wanted,
deliriously, to fuck me. His persistence excited me. It brought out all
my passive desires—to be used, possessed, overpowered; which only
occasionally come to the surface and which I act on rarely. I was
tempted to give in this time, but controlled the impulse by telling
myself what I knew was true—that the fantasy of being "taken" was
more exciting than the actuality and that the subsequent psychological upset, plus the worry over disease, would far overbalance the
slight pleasure. I wonder what lies behind the fantasy in the first place.
I present an exterior of manliness, and in much of my actual sex life,
play the dominant role, but there is a parallel and conflicting desire in

me—sometimes very strong—to be passive sexually. In some complicated way I think all my homosexual activity is an attempt (among
other things) to identify with a masculinity I never was sure I had.
Being entered by a man is perhaps the most direct way of
incorporating and absorbing that masculinity. And yet when I do
allow myself to be "browned" [*the going genteel gay euphemism for
"fucked"*] I almost never receive physical pleasure from it; that comes
instead from assuming the opposite role—from browning others. But
the fantasy remains strong: to be possessed by—and thereby to
possess—a real man and his qualities.

*(1981): A "real man" penetrated, dominated, fucked. This kind of
sexual stereotyping—still so prevalent—was an integral aspect of the
medical model of sexuality with which I identified. It managed all at
once to be homophobic and patriarchal: a "real man" was
heterosexual and unyieldingly dominant. All sexual acts intrinsically
denoted "active" or "passive" attributes. There seemed to be no
understanding—certainly none that was transmitted to patients
wavering "dangerously" in their proclivities—that the muscular
contractions of the anus, say, or the vagina, could, by several
definitions, be considered an "active" agent in producing any
cohabitation worthy of the name. The strict division of all sexual
behavior into active or passive categories did serve as a convenient
guide for those terrified of being confused (especially in their own
minds) about the proper role to assume, which acts to perform (or
not) in order to win certification as Male.*

*Though I now get angry at these one-dimensional models—being
"entered" connotes "passivity", connotes "femininity"—that did so
much to shape and constrict my understanding, I have to resist the
urge to be just as categorical in rejecting them, for the latest theories
and vocabularies have no conclusive validation either and will
themselves doubless be subjected in time to yet further reformula-
tions.*

*Besides, the derision with which I view my former values, the
contempt with which I regard my former self, may be designed in part
to keep me from owning (which is harder than owning up to) the
person I was. Yes, I was often callow, fatuous (especially in my
tenacious "self-scrutiny"), grandiose. Yet not taking possession of the
earlier me, amounts to not accepting myself now; for despite my
efforts at disassociation, the two are one, the past is present, has left
some mark; denying it raises the suspicion that the mark may be more
pronounced than I like to admit. Memory is one powerful ingredient*

in forming identity. If I cut off my own legs, that leaves me floating in space. A neat trick, but not one in my non-Eastern bag. It's important to stop talking about "him" and "me"—to accept the totality. "He" may have been simplistic and self-pitying, but so would any mocking disavowal of him be (tempted though I am to indulge it). Not to forgive my earlier self is not to do several things that need doing: to implicate society for the self-sabotage it generated in gay people; to refuse myself an anterior history which, however painful, is an integral part of my being; to deny that I had a place from which I needed to grow...

January 5, 1958:

Back from spending vacation in New York with Larry. Looks like the final split between us. Larry announced it was time to recognize that what was left of our relationship is only a "bad joke", that he felt unwelcome, that I should please not write or contact him at all from now on. I agreed with little reluctance—though I've since had occasional pangs. The simple and absurd truth is that we're basically incompatible and nothing either of us can do will ever change that. Unfortunately, incompatibility is no guarantee against strong attraction and real feeling ... I'm fired up again with the determination to resist all homosexual contact, to change...

(1981): I wish, at this juncture of my life, I'd been encouraged to ask a different set of questions about what did indeed prove to be the final break-up with Larry. They might have produced a different attitude about myself and a different set of expectations for the future. I wish I'd looked more closely at what our "incompatibility" consisted of. I only knew our obvious differences—in background, education, temperament. I doubt if these constituted a significant, let alone sufficient explanation for the problems we had. Our differences often made for some of our happiest times—we knew about different things and saw some things in different ways, and by that much added to each other's lives.

More basic to the split, in retrospect, was our shared assumption (much stronger on my part, though Larry's Catholic upbringing induced guilt enough) that two men could never make it together, that to be homosexual was, by definition, to be incapable of sustained commitment to another human being. Plus the conviction, bred into us by the culture (into heterosexuals, too) that sexual fidelity and an unwavering level of caring were the two crucial indices for evaluating the "success" of a relationship. Any erosion of erotic zest for one's partner was suspect, suggestive of incompatibility as well as immaturity. But the reigning standard of sexual fidelity was applied more stringently to gay men than to straight ones, "adventuring" automatically seen in them as a symptom of character disorder.

Such formulas squeezed my experience into dry moulds that caricatured it. What I needed were terms—ways of thinking—that would have helped me to question those formulas. That's precisely where psychiatry failed me.

I wish I'd been encouraged to ask why *I wanted a lifetime companion, and then—if convinced I did—to recognize that if my choice was to settle down into "matehood", I had better stop thinking of the relationship in the adolescent/romantic terms of perfect accord, unconditional caring, eternal bliss.*

Beyond my relationship with Larry, the standard psychoanalytic formulas (the moral norms of the country, or my corner of it) on which I was weaned in the Fifties, kept me from myself—encouraged me to distrust my feelings, to malign "mere" sexual pleasure, to avoid risk, to associate legitimate social discontent with private neurosis, to doubt my capacity for closeness and to misread and denigrate any evidence to the contrary.

I wish I had spent my time analyzing the tyrannical formulas then current for recognizing a "real" relationship, instead of repetitively exploring the presumed neuroses which I was told (and believed) would forever obstruct its realization. But I learned what was taught. I learned to regard any hope of a loving relationship with another man as the essence of fantasy and to set the goal of monogamous heterosexuality as the essence of reality. What I needed to change during my years with Larry—and for many years thereafter—was my self-centered, perfectionist view of what relationships are—not who they're with.

EPILOGUE

I remained in therapy—with brief time out for bad behavior—for nearly a dozen years, becoming still more intensively involved after I moved to New York City in 1964. At that point I added group therapy to my individual sessions. During those many years I continued to hear the familiar litany about my "sickness", about the need to renounce my ways and devote myself to "getting well". Spasmodically I tried to follow instructions, the effort alternating with intervals of furious rebellion—a cycle already gruesomely familiar from the Fifties. In retrospect, I'm astonished at the tenacity with which I continued to buy into imposed, arbitrary definitions of "normalcy" and self-worth—into a state of self-abdication. Suffice it to say that no one will ever have to explain to me the "mystery" of Jonestown.

By the late Sixties, my entangled cocoon did finally begin to unravel, a process greatly aided by the advent of the modern homophile movement, with its liberating new perspectives and options.

Dispiriting residues remain, sometimes propelling back into my head those once-favorite lines from Matthew Arnold:
"Wandering between two worlds, one dead,
the other powerless to be born..."
Sometimes; but less and less and less.

Salmagundi, Fall 1982—Winter 1983

THE AUTHOR

Martin Bauml Duberman is Distinguished Professor of History at Lehman College, The City University of New York. His nine previous books include *Charles Francis Adams* (awarded The Bancroft Prize); *Black Mountain: An Exploration in Community; James Russell Lowell* (a Finalist for the National Book Award); *In White America* (Winner of the Vernon Rice/Drama Desk Award); *The Uncompleted Past;* and *Male Armor: Selected Plays, 1968-1974.* Duberman is the recipient of a special prize from the National Academy of Arts and Letters for his "contributions to literature". His biography of Paul Robeson—the first work on the man using the Robeson family archives—will be published in 1987.